RACE FOR SUCCESS

ALSO BY GEORGE C. FRASER

Success Runs in Our Race
SuccessGuide: The Networking Guide to Black Resources

RACE FOR SUCCESS

THE TEN BEST BUSINESS OPPORTUNITIES FOR BLACKS IN AMERICA

GEORGE C. FRASER

FOREWORD BY HUGH B. PRICE

WILLIAM MORROW AND COMPANY, INC.

NEW YORK

Grateful acknowledgment is made for permission to quote from the following:
Maulana Karenga. *Selections from the Husia: Sacred Wisdom of Ancient Egypt*.
Los Angeles: The University of Sankore Press, 1982.
Hattie Gossett. *Presenting . . . Sister Noblues*. Ithaca, N.Y.: Firebrand Books.
Copyright © 1988 by Hattie Gossett.

It is the policy of William Morrow and Company, Inc., and its imprints and affiliates,
recognizing the importance of preserving what has been written, to print the books we publish
on acid-free paper, and we exert our best efforts to that end.

Library of Congress Cataloging-in-Publication Data
Fraser, George C.
    Race for success : the ten best business opportunities for Blacks in
America   /   George C. Fraser. — 1st ed.
        p.   cm.
    Includes bibliographical references and index.
    ISBN 0-688-15248-1 (tr)
    1. Afro-American business enterprises—United States.   2. Success in
business—United States.   I. Title.
    HD2344.5.U6F73   1998
    650.1'089'96073—dc21   97-35846
                                                                   CIP

Printed in the United States of America

First Edition

2 3 4 5 6 7 8 9 10

BOOK DESIGN BY JO ANNE METSCH

www.williammorrow.com

*I shall pass through this world
but once. Any good thing I can do,
or any kindness that I can show
any human being, let me do it now
and not defer it. For I shall not
pass this way again.*

DEDICATION

*To those whom I have helped and/or who have helped me . . . my
network*

Todd Abbey
Charlotte Abbott
Eric Abercrumbie
Stan Abston
Pat Acklin
Robert Acquaye
Phyllis Acres
David Adams
Norma Adams-Wade
Selom Adjogah
Na'im Akbar
Lisa Alaimo
James Alexander
Sam Alexander
Renee Allbriton
Bill Allen
Carolyn Allen
Judith Allen
Robert Allen
Theresa Allen
Zuleyka Allenyne
James Amps
Anna Anderson
Claud Anderson
George W. Anderson
Ken Anderson
Sheilah Anderson
Greg Andrews
John Arnold
Martha Artiles
Mel Asbury
Robert Ashley
Nana Ashong
Ken Askew
Pat Atkin
Berneather Atkins

Leslie Atkinson
Angela L. Avant
Lenora Avery
Sonia Babers
Barry Backmon
Cynthia Badie-Rivers
Lee Baer
Clifford A. Bailey
Anna D. Banks
Terry Bankston
John A. Barbee
Thomas Barksdale II
Joy C. Barnes
Ronald Barnett
Ernest Barrens
Lorna Barrett
Alexander Barton
Lyn Battle
Betty Baye
Todd Beamon
Phoebe Beasley
Hal Becker
Al Bell
Gregory Bell
Jacqueline Bell
Janet Cheatham Bell
Jill Gibson Bell
Brandon C. Bellany
David Belton
T. Garrott Benjamin, Jr.
Michael W. Benson
Kenneth Bentley
Paul Besson
Wyoma Best
Jane Best-Simpson
Adam Beyah

JoAnn Blackman
Barry Blackmon
Sylvia Blackmon-Roberts
Judith A. Blackwell
Marcus A. Blackwell
Mel Blackwell
Walter L. Bount, Jr.
Barbara Bolden
Carol Bolden
Alan B. Bond
Norm Bond
Harry Boomer
Louis J. Boson
Kelvin Boston
Wendall Boyce
Joseph L. Boyd
Steven Boyd
Betty Boye
K. David Boyer, Jr.
Peter Boyle
Reginald K. Brack, Jr.
Carolyn C. Bradley
Mike Bradley
Sherman Bradley
Ellie Bragar
Jimmie Brand
Leslie J. Breland
Chuck Bremmer
Judy Brenneman
Ken Bridges
W. Maurice Bridges
Sam Briggery
Bernard Bronner
Glenda Brooks
Jesse Brooks
Jim Brooks

Barbara J. Brouse
Cheryl D. Broussard
Wilbur L. Brower
D. Elaine Brown
Frances Brown
Gloria Brown
J. S. Brown
Lorie Brown
Majid Brown
Michael Brown
Paulette Brown
Renee Cottrell Brown
Rochelle Brown
Ronald Brown
Theresa J. Brown
Paul Brownridge
Tommy Bruno
Marian Bryan
Rodney Buchser
Ruth Buczynski
Jill Patrice Bunton
Charles Burkett
Jesse Burnett II
Janice Burr
Tom Burrell
Barbara A. Burton
Ivan Burwell
Ralph L. Bush
Kamala Bustamante
Darrell Butler
Michael A. Butler
Rita Butler
George J. Byke
David Byrd
Deborah Calhoun
Pam Cammady
Tony Campbell
Cheryl Canady
Joyce Cannady
Paula Caproni
Wendy Carlton
Delmar Carmack
Shirley Bradley Carmack
Ken Carroll
Frank Carson
Bev Carter
Rilous Carter
Julius Cartwright
Danette Casey
Chuck Castine
Audrene Chakmakjian
Eric Chambers
Jocelyn Chang
Kenneth E. Chapman

Mike Chapman
Veronica Chapman
Ken Chenault
Bill Cherry
Faye Childs
John Chinkes
Samuel Chisholm
John Chissell
W. F. Christensen
Rose Christian
Kelly Chunn
Susan Claiborne
Caroline Clark
Richard J. Clark
William Clark
Madelyn Clark-Robinson
Jill Clements
Linda Clemmons
Otis L. Cliatt, Jr.
Harold L. Cochran, Jr.
Don Coleman
Ella Coleman
Linda Coleman
Virgil H. Coleman
William T. Coleman, III
Yvonne Loggins Coleman
Linda Coleman-Willis
Naomi D. Compton
Ed Comwell
Earl Skip Cooper II
Judy Cooper
Mathew G.W. Corbett
Don Corder
Comer J. Cottrell
Shaun Court
Edwin Cowell
Courtnie Crawford
Malcolm D. Crawford
Grover Crayton
Marvin Creel
June Crocker
Michelle Crockett
Franklin U. Cross, Jr.
Andy Crowe
John Crump
Sherry Culpepper
Bob Cunnigham
Francis M. Curd
George Curry
Lavell Dabney
Ron Daniels
Bernetta Daniely
Lawrence J. Dark
Brian Daves

M. Gail Daves
Michael Daves
Sharon David
Pat Fields Davidson
Robert C. Davidson, Jr.
Cherisse Davis
Crystal Davis
Edward Davis
Kelly Davis
Ken Davis
Larry Davis
Robie Davis
Suzette M. Davis
Timothy Davis
Wayne Dawson
Barbara W. DeBaptiste
Normando DeHalle
Stewart Deisher
Jerri DeVard
Theresa Devonshire
Peola Butler Dews
Yvette Dezalia
Jewel Diamond-Taylor
Dierdre Francis Dickerson
Anthony M. DiLauro
Dennis Dillon
Mamalina Diop
Evita Dixon
Jane F. Dixon
John Dixon
Peggy Dodson
Jen Doman
Grace M. Dori
Paula C. Dorich
Linda Dorman
Ivory Dorsey
Tommy Dortch
Rosie N. Doughty
Gregory J. Douglas
Maria Dowd
Dennis Dowdell, Jr.
Norma B. Downs
Dale Draper
Karen I. Duckett
Renee DuJean
Mike Duncan
Leonard G. Dunston
Ed Dwight
Michael Dye
Arlene Dyer
Berthel Eagle
Wayland Easley
Wayne Easterling
Jack Ebert

Ramona Edelin
Henry Edwards
Ron Edwards
William E. Edwards
E. G. Egea
E. David Ellington
Wayne Embry
Rene Etienne
Toby Faber
Nabii Faison
Larry Farmbry
Charles Faulkerson
Toni Fay
Lynn Feaster
Christian Fedor
J. R. Fenwick
Ron Ferebee
Sharolyn Ferebee
Randall Ferguson, Jr.
Chuck Fidler
Reginald Fields
Blake Fischer
Dana Fisher
C. Austin Fitts
Floyd Flake
Thomas Flewellyn
Carl F. Flipper
Kia Fomby
Melvin Foote
Caryl O. Ford
Henry Ford
Renee Ford
Marcelino Ford-Levine
Gerry Foster
Lisa Foster
Marsha Foster
Walter Fountaine
Willa Fox
Evelyn C. France
Mike Frank
Aisha M. Fraser
Bandit Fraser
Monroe S. Frederick II
Leroy Freelon, Jr.
Craig Freeman
Walter H. Fulcher
John Funabiki
Donna Gabriel
Leslie Gaffney
Adrienne Gaines
Earl E. Gales, Jr.
Colleen M. Gallagher
Carlos Garcia

Greg Gates
Anne Gaudinier
Yolonda Gayles
Carole Gellineau
Claire Gengarelly
Marvin Gentry
Oswald J. Gift
Pat Giles
Erick Gilkesson
Sharon Gillum
Norma N. Givens
Kevin D. Glenn, Sr.
Patrice Glenn
Gregory Glore
Maurice V. Goin
Thomas Goins
Bob Gonzalez
Margarete Goodall
Thyonne Gordon
Frank Graham
Keith Graham
Lawrence Otis Graham
Jennifer L. Grant
Willis K. Grant
Jeanette R. Grant-Woodham
Melvin Gravely, Jr.
Paula Graves
Hermenia Grayson
Dorothy Riley Green
Mark Green
Raymond Green
Verna S. Green
Donald Greenwell
Rich Gregory
Nadine Guerrier
Mathis Guice
Dittie F. Guise
Mitchell Guyton
Glenn Guzik
Lou Hairston
Ken Hale
Nathan Hale
Elliott S. Hall
George Hall
Ira D. Hall
Nina A. Hall
Steve Hall
Susan Halligan
Aundrella Hamed
Bill Hamilton
Charlotte Hamilton
Tom Hamilton
Vince Hamilton

Ella Hamlin
Ric Hampton
Kim Hankerson
Noel Hankin
Jan Hanson
John Hanson
Solomon Harge
Steve Harmon
Anthony Harris
Yusef Harris
Shanqua Harrison
Tony Harrison
Reginald Hart
Hermene Hartman
Richard H. Harvey
Roy A. Hastick, Sr.
Andrew Havas
RoNita Hawes-Saunders
Verneda A. Hawkins
Delores Hawthorne
Helen Hayes
Ilene Hayworth
Cheri K. Henderson
Jim Henley
Dennis A. Henry
Marva Herman
Billy Hicks
Michael Hightower
Mike Hilber
Hattie Hill
Solomon Hill
Valerie Hill
Glynese Hilton
Karen Hinckley
Anderson Hitchcock
Ben Hobert
Jerry Hoegner
Leon Hogg
Larry E. Holeman
Victor Holiday
DeLois Holligner
Melvin J. Holliman
Norma Thompson Hollis
Lee Holmes
Michael T. Holmes
Dundee Holt
Donna Hom
Mary Hoover
Noel Hord
Simon L. Horn
Dave House
J. D. Houston
C. Diane Howell

Hamp Howell
Joseph R. Hudson
Mickie Hudson
Charles Huffman
Mary Ellen Hughes
Vera P. Hughes
Sheri Huguely
Leighton Hull
Earl Ofari Hutchison
Sam Hyman
Don Iannone
A. Andrew Ingraham
Andy Ingram
Melody Ivory
Al Jackson
Cassandria Jackson
Charone Jackson
Eugene D. Jackson
Jack Jackson
Jesse Jackson, Jr.
John T. Jackson
Rita Jackson
Warren Jackson
Hanifa Jahi
Reginald B. James, Jr.
Ron Jay
Marcus Jefferson
Al Jenkins
Lorretta Jennings
Byron Johnson
Carolyn Johnson
Chris Johnson
Diane H. Johnson
Felecia L. Johnson
Genita Johnson
Gregory Johnson
Patricia Stephen Johnson
Robert Johnson
Roy Johnson
Shelby Johnson
W. Cedric Johnson
Waymon Johnson
Carmen L. Johnston
Willie Jolly
Amy Hilliard Jones
Bev Everson Jones
Dennis R. Jones
Geneva Jones
George W. Jones, Jr.
Jackie Jones
Kevin Jones
Kevin L. Jones
Liz Jones
Lonnie Jones

Melvin Jones
Paula Jones
Peggy Jones
Percy F. Jones, Jr.
Robert Jones
Roberta L. Jones
Thomas F. Jones
Gale Jones-Jackson
Consuella Jordon
Victor Julien
Newton Kaneham
Maulana Karenga
Charles L. Kelly
Eric Kelly
Kenneth Kelly
Sheila Kelly
N. Joseph Kganakga
Arif Khatib
Barbara King
Bridget King
Bernard W. Kinsey
Jennifer Kit
Gladys Knight
Dennis James Knowles
Glamer Knox
Michelle Kourouma
Fred Koury
Amy Krakow
Jawanza Kunjufu
Aida LaChaux
Gerald B. Lang
Raphael Langford
Aleyne Larner
Jenny Laster
Brenda J. Lauderback
Abina Law
Magdalena Lawson
Charmaine Leary
Katherine Leary
A. Tsepo Lebona
JoAnn Lee
McKinley Lee
Richard Lee
Sonja Lee
Steve Lee
Verna Lee
Ronald A. LeGrand
Bret Leonard
Tony Lesesne
Liz Leslie
Wanda F. Lester
Jeffrey A. Levey
Ed Lewis
Jerry Lewis

Lucius Lewis
Barbara Lindsey
Lorenzo Littles
Thelma Liverpool
Philip A. Lockhart
Yvonne Loggins-Coleman
Saundra Lohr
Elena Looper
Ross Love
Jay Lovinger
Chris Lowery
Kay Lucas
Jory Luster
Maxine Lynch
Jay Lynn
Traci Lynn
Mary M. Mabaso
Felicia Mabuza-Suttle
William E. MacDonald III
John Mack
Ramon Maddox
Midel E. Mahoney
Ricky R. Majette
Richard H. Mallory
Merrick Malone
Antoinette Malveaux
Roy L. Manley, Sr.
Marc X
Leroy Marius
Gregory Markham
Debra Mars-Marshall
Brian Akil Marshall
Pluria W. Marshall
Clarence T. Martin
Larry Martin
Mary S. Martin
Quinta A. Martin
Jose Martinez
Marilyn Mason
Reginald Maynor
Leslie Mays
Charles F. McAfee
Jewell Jackson McCabe
Anthon McCall
Robert C. McCall
Alex McCamey
Debra R. McClain
Nancy McClaran
Patricia Russell McCloud
D'Joane H. McCorkel
Bill McCreary
Cynthia McDaniels
Mark McDiarmid
Monica McDonell

Barbara McEachern
Maria McFarlane
Angela McGlowan
Deborah McHamm
Mel McHenry
Jimmy McJamerson
Therman McKenzie
Patrice McKinley
Lois McKinney
Angela McLowan
Jerry L. McMillan
Darryl McMillon
Hope McNish
Thomas McPherson, Jr.
Kweisi Mfume
Bennie Miles
Avis Miller
Donald L. Miller
George Miller
Howard F. Mills
Frank Miranda
Deborah J. Mitchell
Clarence Mixson
Michael A. Mobley
Sybil Mobley
Linda Mokeme
Eloise J. Molock
Alvino Monk
Valerie Montague
Cynthia Moore
Gail A. Moore
James F. Moore
Jeff Moore
Parasada Moore
Allen Morgan
Andrew Morgan
Henley Morgan
Jerry Morgan
Sheila Morgan
Deborah Morris
Eugene Morris
Chuck Morrison
Ruth J. Morrison
Avis Mosby II
Joe Moscheo
Joseph Mouzon
Yvette Jackson Moyo
Marvin Muhammad
Miriam Muley
Laura Mullens
Murlan J. Murphy, Jr.
Joe Muse
Glenda Myhand
Mike Nash

Muhamed Nassarden
Jeff Nathenson
Gaston Ndyajunwoha
Carol Neal
Kathy Neal
Cathy Nedd
Carl Nelson
Donald P. Nelson
Michael L. Nelson
Mickey Nelson
Ed Nesfield
Lisa Neu
Jim Iredelle Nixon
Jeffrey Noble
Liz Nolley
Larry Norton
Leroy D. Nunery
Donald K. O'Bryant
Lea O'Neal
Patricia O'Neal-Williams
Cyrus Oates
Ernie Oden
Mary Oldham
Vickie Oldham
Kenneth N. Oliver
Patrick Oliver
Jeff Olson
Charlotte Ottley
Lisa Overton
Lynn E. Owens
Lloyd J. Oxford
Charles Panky
Al Parham
John Parham
Amelia Parker
Debra Parker
Gene Parker
Don Parks
Kathee Parks
Richard Parnell
Joan Parrott-Fonseca
Alice Patterson
Carol Lynn Patterson
Lisa Patterson
Sylvia Patterson
Bill Patton
William E. Pauli
Suzanne Payne
Fred Peacock
Yvonne Pearson
Gerald Peart
Heddy Pena
Jeff Perry
Charlotte Peters-Hamilton

Coleman Peterson
Donald E. Philips
Diane Pillow
Denise Pines
Mark Pinn
Mary Pitt
Darryl Pittman
Doris Polite
Greg Polvere
Marcus Poole
Tom Pope
Earl John Powell
Inez Powell
Margaret Powell
Mamon Powers
Pam Pratt
Hugh Price
Tawana Price
Kamala Prince
Karen Proctor
Kimberley S. Pryor
Catherine Pugh
Lisa Queen
Tina Rahman
Willie Ramoshaba
Marya Randolph
Ralph Ransom
Marty Raphael
Talut Rasul
Harry K. Ratiff
Sandra Rattley-Lewis
Dori Ray
Joyce Raynor
Charles Reaves
Darryl Reed
Dewayne H. Reed
Marc Reede
Noel Reede
Herman Reese
Ilinda M.J. Reese
Frank X. Renner
Rodney Reynolds
John Ribbins
Mark Ribbins
Larry Richards
Bill Richardson
Denise Richardson
Hank Richardson
Kenneth O. Richardson
Rhona Richardson
Michelle Riley
Douglas Ritter
John Rivera
Don Rivers

Mike Rivers
Susan RoAne
Martha Roberts
Mike Roberts
Roland Roberts
Craig J. Robinson
Deirdre G. Robinson
Elaine Robinson
J. Terry Robinson
Ken Robinson
Romona Robinson
Shauna A. Robinson
Stacia Robinson
Tom Robinson
Emma Rodgers
Max Rodriquez
Lynne Joy Rogers
Mikki Rogers
Don M. Rose
Glenn Skip Ross
Michele Ross
Rose Ross
Sharon Roth
Michelle A. Rousseau
Philip Rowell
Anita Royal
Victor Rubell
Cecil Rucker, Jr.
James R. Ruff
Ben Ruffin
Judith Ruggie
H. Jerome Russell
Janet Saboor
Anika Sala
Mario F. Sanabria
Clarence Sanders
Desiree Sanders
Ben Sanford
George W. Sanker
Clarence Saunders
Ingrid Saunders-Jones
Eric L. Sawyer
Pauline A. Schneider
Brenda B. Schofield
Bonnie Schollianos
Douglas Scott
Lynne Scott
Winifred Scott
Steven B. Seaton
Jan Sebastian
Jean Sebastian
Adib Shakir
Carolyn Shaw
Julia Shaw

Angela Shelton
Lawrence Shorter
Betty Shorts
Sondra Sibley
Andrew E. Silver
Alan Silverman
Dee Simmons-Edelstein
Joseph A. Simms
Jane B. Simpson
William I. Sims
Joe Sinegal
Becky Singleton
Renee Singleton
Maceo K. Sloan
David Slutzky
Wayne P. Smalls
Barbara Smith
Dean Smith
Donna Rae Smith
Joshua Smith
Kevin Smith
Marlon Smith
Rosie Smith
Sharon Ann Smith
Wayman F. Smith, III
Willie Smith
Thomas A. Sobeck
Roland Somerville
Mark Spain
Ricky Spain
Romeo O. Spaulding
Don Spears
A. Jonathan Speed
Jocelyn Spencer-Hilaire
Lynne L. Spiller
Pamala Springs
David R. Squires
Renee Squires
Hilbert Stanley
Suzanne Stanley
Everett Staten
Ollie Stevenson
Gary V. Stewart
Marie Stewart
Pam Stewart
Joseph Stills
John T. Story
A. S. Strane
Emery Streeter
Denise Stroder
Lisa Stuart
Edward J. Stuck
Henry Stuckey
Thelma Sullivan

James C. Sutton
Pepi Sutton
Percy Sutton
Cathy Swartz
Isaac Taggart
Beth Tassinari
H. Lebaron Taylor
Jerome Taylor
Sonia Ellis Taylor
Buddy Teaster
Barbara Ann Teer
Donald M. Temple
Oney Temple
Sabria Terry
Sabrina Terry
Linda Thigpen
Tony Thomas
Craig Thompson
Emerson R. Thompson, Jr.
Geraldine Thompson
Jim Thompson
John Thompson
Lora M. Thompson
Andre Thornton
Denise Thurman
June Tims
Jaime Tineo
George Tinsley
Pat Tobin
Barbara Tomczyk
Rafael Toro
Dean H. Townsend
Nathan Townsend
Brenda Townsend-Milton
Brian Tracy
Wilhelmina L. Tribble
Glendora Troy
Ramona Truss
Jerry Tubbs
C. Delores Tucker
Janee Gee Tucker
Sheryl Hilliard Tucker
Irie L. Turner
Lana Turner
Melvin Turner
Melvin L. Turner, Sr.
Debra Tyler
Tracy Underwood
Ben B. Ussery, Jr.
Nate Valentine
Laura K. Van-Brockle
Ron Van-Johnson
Roger Vann
Cedric Varner

David L. Vaughn
Martin V. Vaughn
Vanessa Vaughn
Lorraine Vega
Tony Vidal
Claire Villarosa
Linda Villarosa
Robert J. Wade
Anthony Wainwright
Adele Walker
Carol Walker
Juliette Walker
Michael C. Walker
Seturah Walker
Woodson D. Walker
Robert L. Wallace
Joseph B. Walton
Cecil M. Ward
Reginald D. Ware
Shawn Warner
Angela Washington
Harry Washington
Jan Washington
Marlene Washington
Merien Washington
Simone Washington
Steve Washington
Valerie E. Washington
William H. Washington
Albert Wasserman
Elizabeth A. Waters
Paul Watkins
Dennis Watson
Geoffrey Watson

Al Way
Frank C. Weaver
Sonya Webb
Cassandra H. Webster
Tina Weed
Al Wellington
Delores West
Douglas West
Pat Weston
Al White
Colleen White
Gregory White
Leonard E. White
Monifa White
Esjaye A. Whiters
Deborah Whitt
Nathaniel Wilkes
Yvonne Wilkes
Alonda S. Williams
Carolyn Ruth A. Williams
Dick Williams
Faye Williams
Gail Williams
George K. Williams
Gregory Williams II
Johnnie B. Williams
Jon Williams
Juan Williams
Keith Williams
LeAndrea Williams
Myrna Williams
Otis Williams
Richard Williams
S. L. Williams

Samuel Williams
Sharon O. Williams
Suzanne Williams
Venlue Williams
Vernona H. Williams
Eleanor Williams-Curry
Desi Williamson
Ramon Williamson
Gerald Wilson
Josleen Wilson
Valerie F. Wilson
Yvonne Wiltz
Paula Winn
Charles Winston
Jocelyn Winston
Sherma Wise
Jill Wittner
Wona Wossen
Cecelia Wooten
Bill Wright
Cheryl Wright
Janice Wright
Sanford Wright
William W. Wright, Jr.
Leon Wynter
Malika Yamini
Kym Yancey
Bill Young
Leola Young
Leonard Young
Nicholas M. Young
Ricky Young
Calvin Zanders
Craig Zellner

. . . To be continued

FOREWORD

by Hugh B. Price
President, The National Urban League

LAST SPRING WHEN I was in Indianapolis for the National Urban League, I had an opportunity to talk with George Fraser. In the course of our conversation it became apparent that our views—on the future of African Americans—converge. We in the Urban League Movement believe that the next civil rights challenge for African Americans is achieving economic self-reliance. To emphasize this, we chose "Economic Power: The Next Civil Rights Frontier" as the theme of our 1997 annual conference. George Fraser, too, understands the need for economic self-sufficiency and parity for Black people. He also understands that, in spite of the negative images in the newspapers or on television, we are an enterprising people of great intelligence and spiritual fortitude. The very fact that we have not merely survived, but prevailed against tremendous odds, attests to this.

Motivated by his understanding of African Americans, Fraser researched the success stories of individuals, both well known and unknown. He sought to uncover the key to their success and extrapolated a set of principles shared by each person who'd achieved his or her goals. With this book, Race for Success—The Ten Best Business Opportunities for Blacks in America, Fraser is sharing what he has learned. "Sharing," in fact, is one of the key principles he uncovered during his research.

The very concept of sharing is integral to a sense of community. While it is the responsibility of each individual to make the most of his or her life, it is the responsibility of the larger community to provide the conditions that encourage success—a healthy, stable environment and opportunities for educational and economic achievement.

We have a credo at the Urban League, "Our Children—Our Destiny." We know that if a society wants productive adults, it must first bring up healthy, well-educated children. For many of the people chronicled in *Race for Success* the difference between success and failure can be traced to an adult who took an active interest in them when they were children.

Economic self-reliance ultimately helps the community to help the children. Young people, in turn, grow up to be contributing members of society. As welfare reform chips away at the meager resources available to the nation's poor, there is a pressing need to overcome poverty among our people. Even if racism were expunged tomorrow, urban poverty would persist unless low-income children are prepared academically and attitudinally to operate in this competitive economy.

To reverse the blight of poverty among African Americans, the Urban League mission entails the following: ensuring the academic preparation and social development of children, fostering economic self-sufficiency for their parents through gainful employment, entrepreneurship, and home ownership; and promoting racial harmony and inclusion so that the opportunities inherent in the structure of American society are open to all.

We, as a movement, can work with business and government to accomplish our mission. Fraser's book, on the other hand has the power to reach individuals in the privacy of their homes or the quiet of a public library. The lives he bears witness to in this volume and the information he shares are indeed inspirational and of value. He shows us that the course of our lives, ultimately, is up to each person individually and collectively. We can succumb to the defeats we meet along the way or learn and transform them into victories.

The worst enemy of African Americans is the myth that many of us must live out a life sentence of economic insecurity and the ill health it breeds. That myth is not, nor has it ever been, true. If you don't believe me, read Fraser's book. It is a blueprint for success.

ACKNOWLEDGMENTS

THANK YOU, GOD, for the vision, words, and discipline to write this book. A warm thanks goes to the hundreds of friends and associates who so freely shared with me their insights, words, and wisdom. They are responsible for this collection of knowledge. I am the sum of them, and through me you hear their voices. I have dedicated this book to them: my network.

I have saved this part of the book to acknowledge those who in some extraordinary way helped me to grow and thrive. First, there is my mother, Ida Mae, my father, Walter Frederick, and my foster parents, Ariah and Francis Morse. Then there is my family—Jean, Kyle, and Scott. Together, they are the solid foundation from which my life as a Black man has been built.

In each person's life there are those friends who are special. They are always there, through the peaks and valleys of life. They love you because you are you. I count among those in my lifetime only a few who fit this category. They include Corky Williams, Greg Williams, Edward Fraser, and Sherry Winston, the incredible sister who helped to start me down the path as an author. Enough cannot be said for the gift of loving family and friends. It is upon this rock that whatever I have achieved rests.

Most people are inspired by the ideas of others. You can count me among those who continually need inspiration to do the hard work of creative thinking, writing, and traveling. For this book the work of two authors had a significant impact on the content and messages contained within. They are the late Reverend Howard Thurman's extensive writing on spirituality and Dr. Claud Anderson's insightful book *Black Labor, White Wealth.* Additionally, the inspirational words and writings of Jesus Christ, Joseph Campbell, Cornell West, Toni Morrison, Frederick Douglass, Langston Hughes, bell hooks, Molefi Asante, Maulana Karenga, Les Brown, David Whitaker, Susan Taylor, Dennis Kimbro, Tony Brown, Clarence Page, and Bob Law continue to provide me sustenance from which to draw.

A book of this size requires teamwork, from beginning to end. My agents, Barbara Lowenstein and Madeleine Morel of Lowenstein-Morel Associates, diligently worked to make the right deal with the right publisher. To that end, they once again turned in a stellar performance. Paul Bresnick, my senior editor at William Morrow and Company, gave me the space and flexibility to write a book that was close to my heart and at the same time fulfilled his mission. His trust, encouragement, and savvy have added significantly to the final product. No single person brought more to the table than Josleen Wilson, who helped to shape my ideas, thoughts, themes, and voluminous manuscript into a cohesive whole. Josleen's experience, skill, and knowledge are greatly responsible for the end product you are about to read.

Everyone's job was made easier by the work of an outstanding team of researchers and reporters, headed by the dedicated work of Inge Hanson and including contributions from Judy Andraski, Philip Dray, Jeffrey Felshman, Molly Murray, Bernard Rittersporn, Lynne Rogers, and Lee Williams.

A special thanks to Hugh Price for taking time from his busy schedule as president of The National Urban League to add his insightful thoughts in the foreword.

Then there are those who gave of their time to allow me to interview them for the various chapters of this book. They include Leon Hogg, Mary S. Martin, Wayne Embry, RoNita Hawes-Saunders, Cheryl Broussard, E. David Ellington, Rodney Reynolds, Shirley Carmack, Carole Gellineau, Cecilia Wooten, Eugene Jackson, and Iris Randall. For this I am most grateful.

Special thanks also to the following people who generously shared their personal and professional experience: Naomi Gans, Hans Hageman, Dominick Stanzione, Elizabeth Martin, Tom Perkins, Clarence Wooten, Jr., Monica Harris, Tara Watts, Charles F. Whitaker, Cheryl Todmann, Bobby Clay, Victoria Beerman, Linda Burchette, Jennifer

Shirley, Liz Pettiford Pfeiffer, Ron Pfeiffer, Barbara Taylor-Young, LaShae Anthony, Herman Martin, Eric J. Barkley, Karole Dill, Charles Butler, Walter Zacharius, and Georgette Bieber.

Writing a book requires a few skills I do not possess, one of which is typing. My heartfelt gratitude goes to Millicent Fraser (my sister-in-law) for the long hours she put in typing and retyping my manuscript.

In my travels, my ideas have been supported by a loyal group of Black bookstore owners and a brilliant group of Black media person-alities. They include Mike Roberts, Pat Lottier, and Bernard Bronner in Atlanta, Ken Ferguson, the Bustamante family, Charles Huffman, Tom Greer, Mack Clemmons, Harry Boomer, Wayne Dawson, and Leon Bibb in Cleveland, Tom Pope and John Ray in Kernersville, North Carolina, and Bob Law, Susan Taylor, Gary Byrd, Earl and Butch Graves in New York.

I have been fortunate over the years to earn the friendship of some wonderful people. Each has contributed time and resources to help me realize my many dreams. They are Gee Tucker and Preston Edwards in New Orleans, Stacia Robinson in Montgomery, Alabama, Hermene Hartman in Chicago, Frances Wright in Columbus, Ohio, Pat Roper Saunders in Dallas, Texas, Ricky Young, Bret Leonard, and Toni Fay in New York, Owen Montegue, Rebecca Franklin, and Cynthia Jones in Atlanta, Rev. Walter Fauntroy and Jim Moore in Washington, DC, Jerald Tillman and Christine Spencer in Cincinnati, Cathy Nedd, Bill Pickard, Helen Love, and Marilyn French Hubbard in Detroit, Carole Hoover, Norman Thomas, John Schambach, Hubert Payne, Henry Creel, Bob Donaldson, and Judith Allen in Cleveland, and William Byers, Barbara Lindsey and Pat Tobin in Los Angeles.

Finally, there are those who hosted, introduced, and taught me the ways of their country. They include Dr. Henley Morgan, Magdalena Lawson, and Jackie Jones in Jamaica, West Indies, Rose and Oliver Christian and Joyce Spencer-Hillaire in St. Thomas, Virgin Islands, and Willie Ramoshaba, Sam Alexander, and Newton Kanehama in Johannesburg, South Africa.

I started this section by thanking God for His blessings. I would like to end by thanking God for the many people who have influenced me and helped me to grow. I am grateful that He has given me so much of your love to enrich my life.

CONTENTS

INTRODUCTION

Please, Stop Here First . . .

YES, I'M BLACK, in case you were not entirely sure. In fact, that is the beauty of our race: We come in all shapes, sizes, skin tones, and hair textures. There are lots of options. Now that I've got that straight, it has been nearly four years since the release of my first book, *Success Runs in Our Race*. God is good. He granted me the words to write your thoughts and thus a bestseller emerged. Thank you for the opportunity to serve and share with you. But make no mistake, your sharing with me has illuminated my thinking and my life. I've always known that the ocean of love and excellence among Blacks in America was deep, but it was not until I stepped out in faith to test the waters that I realized how warm and broad it is as well.

I promised you that someday I would follow up my first book with the answers to your questions regarding your personal concerns. I also promised to help you find opportunities to use the principles, strategies, and tactics contained in *Success Runs in Our Race*. To that end, I included an "answer back" questionnaire in the book and I invited you to call me. Over two thousand people have responded, and I'm still receiving calls and letters every day.

Because of you, I've become a very popular keynote speaker, addressing some two hundred colleges, organizations, and corporations per year in over 125 different cities. This was an unplanned career move, but this too has been enriching, and I mean "enriching," thank you again. Speaking as often as I do has added to my industrial-strength Soul-O-Dex/Rolodex and has enabled me to ask many of you questions and to be asked literally thousands of questions; many I had the answers to and many I did not. I have since done my homework and among other things have included the answers to most of your questions in this book.

I love it all because over the last three years, traveling and speaking has given me a unique vantage point from which to view the progress of Blacks and analyze our challenges and opportunities. What I've learned would fill up five volumes, too many to easily digest and use, so I have tried to synthesize this information to fit between the covers of one book. I hope it will encourage you and enable you to attain your goals.

What you are about to read is not written by a social scientist or futurist, but by a Black man who has committed his life to listening and sharing what he has seen, heard, read, and experienced. I'm not oblivious to the harrowing statistics we are all reminded of so regularly by the media. I know that nationally nearly 30 percent of Black families with children live below the poverty line, an increase from 20 percent in 1969. I know that while the number of Blacks moving into the middle class has increased, the proportion of Blacks has not. I also know that the root cause of much of our poverty is the alienation of Black males in the workforce, as well as the increased incarceration of Black males. More than 40 percent of Black males are not part of the U.S. labor force and one third of all Black males between twenty and twenty-nine are either in prison or on parole. As a result, the Black male image is the most vilified in America, which contributes to the Black male being the most unused and unwanted person in America's labor force. I know that a more compassionate set of new public policies would help, but that alone is not the answer. As individuals, as a people, Blacks will make it using their own resources and effectively networking with others.

My intentions are to remove you from the comfort or perhaps the discomfort of your current world and to introduce you to the new economic and intellectual boom in Black America, with all of its exciting areas of growth and opportunity. Whatever your age, you'll be encouraged to follow your dreams, seize new opportunities, and pursue your aspirations. You'll be guided on this journey by dozens of top achievers who share the secrets of their success.

I am aware that saying "follow your dreams" is not enough. We need to know what the important categories of opportunities are—the opportunities that will help us to strategically marshal our resources and to succeed in an increasingly amoral America. That's what this book is about: opportunity. It is broad in scope but rich in detail.

My goal is to bring you the key business opportunities based on our needs, as I've analyzed them. I've identified opportunities in education, health care, and neighborhood redevelopment as those that address some of our greatest long-term needs. Opportunities in technology and global commerce address our need to capitalize on areas that provide great potential. Opportunities in sports, entertainment, and publishing fulfill the need to build on our greatest strengths. You'll also learn about opportunities in small business development and finance and banking, because our community needs more than anything to focus clearly on shifting Black America's agenda toward strengthening our financial resources. Finally, you'll learn the building blocks for economic success.

But please remember that this book is steeped in my opinion—it is, in a sense, the gospel according to George—and there are many opportunities I didn't have the space to cover. The ones that are covered are in my opinion the critical ones for building bridges between those that have the least and most among us. I've supplemented my opinions with information based on extensive research. I scoured the bookstores and libraries for helpful books to recommend, in addition to the 150 or so I read each year. I've looked hard to find role models beyond the ones I've met. To that end I've rummaged through ten years of *Black Enterprise, Essence,* and *Ebony*—the official chroniclers of success in Black America. I've clipped and saved over 2,500 magazine and newspaper articles. I've surfed the Internet and searched for expert advice in my 100,000-name Black professional database, which is used annually for the various versions of *SuccessGuide.* And finally, I have dug deep into my own life to share with you the challenges I've faced and the answers and solutions I have found.

Race for Success is for those who are starting down new career paths, are restarting their careers, or are not fulfilled by their current careers. This book is also for those who are looking for a sense of purpose and some new moral and spiritual guideposts. It focuses on the critical categories of opportunity Blacks need to pursue to help move our race and America into the twenty-first century and proposes that all of us have the ability to do well while doing good, to make a profit *and* make a difference.

What I've learned through observation is that so many of us just need some guidance, some advice or counseling regarding the many opportunities that quietly present themselves without fanfare all the time. It reminds me of the old adage about the tree falling in the forest. Worded somewhat differently, if an opportunity exists but no one knows it's there, does it really exist at all?

There are unlimited opportunities for wealth creation for Blacks in America in spite of the inherent obstacles, but you must be able to see the trends and apply the principles that are the building blocks for success. Only then will the opportunities come into focus and be within your reach. As an optimist I see hope and promise everywhere, but while looking I have also seen the darkness and the weaknesses and despair that can be so crippling. These things do not frighten me, however; they only inspire me to do more. That's because the most important and beautiful thing my research did for me was to illuminate the common threads that tie us all together and have kept us sane and productive for nearly four hundred years. Can I say all of this in one book? Judge for yourself. Read on or just thumb through the chapters. I believe once you've digested a small sampling, you will want the whole. In fact, I'm counting on it. Our potential, you see, is more magnificent than even I had dared imagine, but we must . . .

Stay the Course

The ship of life sails at Sea in search of life

As captains of our fate, we must steer the course confident our inner compass will always be true

The Seas will be stormy, but
  stay the course

Your scope will view danger, but
  stay the course

You will be tempted to change direction, but
  stay the course

Your crew may threaten mutiny, but
  stay the course

Stay the course, and you will land on an island where
no one else has landed

It is there you will build your paradise.

—George C. Fraser

RACE FOR SUCCESS

1

TEN TRENDS MOVING BLACK AMERICA FORWARD

Trends, like horses, are easier to ride in the direction they are already going.

— JOHN NAISBITT

We move when the spirit moves us. Anything outside is God's business.

— ANDREW YOUNG

IN A CAPITALISTIC society, if you want to make a difference, you first need to make a profit. I believe that economic power through business ownership, workplace excellence, and wealth creation strategies is the next major movement in Black America.

For each one of us, wealth creation is now our foremost moral responsibility, because as the individual grows stronger, the community grows stronger; the stronger our community, the stronger the nation. I realize that one person alone cannot solve all of our economic ills, but if each of us succeeds personally, together I believe we can change society.

Where do "trends" come in?

A trend is a prevailing tendency moving society in a general direction. The economic trends I see evolving will lead to Blacks and whites building powerful new partnerships to win in culturally diverse workplaces and globally competitive marketplaces. Economic parity will improve race relations and create new jobs and wealth for African

Americans because in the eyes of those who control America's wealth we will be seen as equals at the table of capitalism.

The matter of race and color has always been about conserving wealth and power. Today, with greater access to education, technology, and opportunity, we can finally address the only color that determines real power in America: green.

Over the past three years, in my quest to find out what people are doing to solve some of our most complex economic and social problems, I have traveled over a half million miles to over a hundred different cities. I have given more than five hundred speeches—to audiences as small as twenty-five and as large as three thousand people, in churches, clubs, boardrooms, halls, and conference centers. Along the way I have met hundreds of business and community leaders from all walks of life.

From these experiences, as well as reading and studying the extensive works of today's top economic and social analysts, I have come to perceive what I consider to be the top ten trends moving Black Americans forward.

TREND 1: FROM CIVIL RIGHTS
TO ECONOMIC POWER

THE FIRST WAVE of Black empowerment in the nineteenth century was dedicated to obtaining our physical freedom. The second wave, in the mid-twentieth century, targeted civil and human rights and created affirmative action. Now the third wave is squarely focused on freeing ourselves from economic enslavement and achieving economic power in the twenty-first century.

Educational opportunity, civil rights, and affirmative action have enabled many African Americans to become gainfully employed and to become business owners and key players in the national economy. Economic activism will be the new springboard for political power, job creation, and wealth accumulation. The elimination of personal debt and overuse of credit will also contribute to the creation of wealth in Black America. A new Black consciousness is being driven by economic literacy programs and multiple options.

Over a five-year period (1987–1992) Black business start-ups rose by 46 percent and job creation was at an all-time high. With a 1996 Black American economy of nearly $400 billion a year, our population growing at about 3 percent each year, and our income growing approximately 5.1 percent each year, within one more generation our economy will exceed $1.5 trillion, a financial force to reckon with.

In the interest of community development, church associations and coalitions are getting together to start more banks and member-owned credit unions. Several groups are setting up rotating credit associations, which allow participants to contribute to a single fund. When the fund reaches a preestablished goal, it is given in part to an individual contributor. Then the fund starts building up all over again. The same principle will be used to pool resources among member organizations, which would allow institutions to lend each other large sums of money.

Real estate acquisition is a crucial piece of the economic development puzzle, and one that has been extraordinarily difficult for Blacks to work out in the past. In the near future, more community-based home-purchasing programs will become available through nonprofit organizations and churches; these lenders will be more amenable to giving mortgages to those with inadequate credit or collateral. Cleveland, Oakland, Detroit, and other large urban centers already have "No Money Down" and "Low Down Payment" programs in place. And if you are willing to live in the inner city, you may be able to obtain a mortgage and also money to rehabilitate the property. For those able to work as a group, the potential for real estate acquisitions will be magnified.

Small business start-ups will continue to multiply; the number of Black-owned businesses today stands at 620,165, representing a 46 percent increase from 1987 to 1992. The traditional mindset of "Get a good education and then get a good job" is shifting to "Get a good education and then create a good job" by starting your own business or being more entrepreneurial in the workplace. What is abundantly clear is that Black folks are focused on getting a larger share of the economic pie.

TREND 2: THE GROWTH OF TRIBALISM

WE ARE BECOMING a nation of strong tribes in which each group looks to its own heart for validation and its own traditions and resources for upward mobility. Common ethnicity, language, culture, interests, and spiritual beliefs empower these groups. As they gain confidence and power, I believe they will reach out to other groups to network for economic development and creative problem-solving.

For many in an enlightened society this trend represents a throwback to the basest kind of clannishness, usually identified with the excesses of Islamic fundamentalism, the present chaos within the former Soviet bloc, or the tribal strife in many African nations, such as Somalia and the Congo (formerly Zaire). Increased emphasis on religion and ethnic culture promotes the likelihood of humanity breaking itself into narrow, exclusive, and often hostile groups.

Yet I believe that beyond such visions lies another kind of tribalism, one forged by globally dispersed ethnic groups. Operating from the strength of their traditions, these global tribes and their worldwide business and cultural networks will increasingly shape the economic destiny of mankind, so long as we all can manage to balance our tribalism with a willingness to learn from and accept others. Supporting each other and building from within is a common theme in Black history and will play a vital role in the progress of the community in years to come. Said another way, the stronger Blacks become, the stronger America is, just as other ethnic and racial groups have demonstrated. No one wants to be the weak link in this great multicultural chain called America.

TREND 3: NETWORKING

I KNOW, I KNOW . . . that word conjures up disturbing images of buppies and yuppies standing around drinking white wine spritzers and exchanging business cards, but believe me, that is where much of our future promise lies.

Today there is a significant effort among Blacks from all socioeconomic classes to use networking for community empowerment. More and more Black professionals are organizing networks for mutual support and are sharing information and resources, because, as the writer James Atlas has observed, "A shared pool of knowledge is as important as a common language." Memberships are growing in most Black business organizations. At the 1996 National Black MBA Conference in New Orleans, over six thousand people were in attendance, a record for the annual event.

Networking opens doors and creates opportunities, and one idea leads to another in a community chain reaction that will benefit widening circles of African Americans. Individualism, the "me-ism" of the 1970s and 1980s, is out, and aspiring Blacks are recognizing that no one achieves success in a vacuum. Indeed, many other ethnic groups in America have demonstrated that mutual assistance can go a long way toward creating wealth and opportunity.

Said another way, all entrepreneurism, job searches, and upward mobility are inherently networking initiatives. It is one's ability to "shape the scope" of his or her search for human resources and then bring those resources to bear on each challenge and/or opportunity that will ultimately determine the degree of success a person will have throughout their life. Blacks have finally internalized this concept and are creatively acting on it in greater numbers. Exposure and access to a broader range of opportunities through a wider web of contacts and relationships is the new challenge for the twenty-first century.

TREND 4: FROM A GOOD EDUCATION TO EXCELLENCE

FOR ME, ONE of the most exciting "new" developments is the deepening respect and appreciation for excellence in education on the part of Blacks, who are effectively competing to get into the best schools. In addition, millions of dollars are being poured into private schools and other Black educational institutions. And what I find particularly encouraging is that many of our young people are focusing on business and science. According to a recent report:

- For the first time in history, the number of Blacks graduating from high schools or receiving GEDs in 1995 was almost identical to the number of whites graduating (86.5 percent and 87.4 percent, respectively).
- Between 1990 and 1995, the number of college degrees awarded to Black Americans rose from 11.3 percent to 15 percent of the total.
- Approximately 2,800 Blacks graduate from MBA programs every year.
- Between 1990 and 1995, business schools experienced a 42 percent increase in the number of minority students entering their Ph.D. programs.

Certainly the most reassuring part of this trend is that the educational performance of our children—measured by the National Assessment of Educational Progress—is beginning to improve.

A century ago, W. E. B. DuBois wrote: "The Negro race, like all races, is going to be saved by its exceptional men. The problem of education . . . is the problem of developing the Best of this race that they may guide the mass away from the contamination and death of the Worst, in their own and other races."

Today, we have attained a critical mass well beyond DuBois's expectation, and in the process we have kicked down many closed doors. Our gifted college grads are no longer relegated to civil service jobs in the post office. Indeed, the opportunities and models for building excellence are all around us. From the late Ron Brown, Reginald Lewis, and Barbara Jordan, to Colin Powell and Ann Fudge, excellence is on display. Two African Americans, George Washington Carver and Percy Julian, were recently inducted into the Inventors Hall of Fame in Akron, Ohio. Two others, Madame C. J. Walker and John H. Johnson, were selected to the Fortune Magazine Business Hall of Fame. But lasting change, based on education and career-building, takes time. For at least another generation, public and corporate policy must continue to be committed to affirmative action by lowering the barriers but never the standards.

TREND 5: THE ADVENT
OF MULTICULTURALISM

AS A NATION we are getting away from the "America as melting pot" concept, which since the great tide of immigration to our shores began in the late nineteenth century has meant an emphasis on assimilation—the merging of separate, distinct cultures into one. Groups are no longer interested in suppressing their individuality just to fit in. To include new groups and to understand the unique differences of those groups but place no real value on those differences is not multiculturalism. The goal is to change organizational structures to accommodate differences. Equal opportunity and greater productivity are the desired result of multiculturalism.

Multiculturalism is taking us to a different place altogether. It seeks to acknowledge and celebrate unique ethnic traditions, fostering individual pride while at the same time adding to the cultural sensibilities of all Americans. The idea is not that we isolate ourselves within our cultural groups, but that everyone learns more about many different cultures, with the goal of valuing our diversity and creating tolerance, respect, and communication among all people.

Multiculturalism makes it possible for Blacks to recognize and recapture the historical contributions made by their African ancestors, while paving the way for African-centered traditions to become the basis for new programs and new businesses.

The economy generated from the goods and services purchased for Kwanzaa celebrations and African Rites of Passage programs and from sales of Afrocentric cards, art, clothing, gifts, books, and memorabilia is estimated to be more than one billion dollars annually, with much of the money moving through the hands of small Black-owned businesses. Meanwhile, large corporations like Avon, Spiegel, Kraft, General Foods, Coca-Cola, and Procter & Gamble are also using the trendsetting power of urban young people and their culture to sell their products. Keith Clinkscales, publisher of *Vibe* magazine says, "Black culture has overwhelmed American industries from music to fashion to sports and entertainment."

Multiculturalism has also opened the doors for numerous mainstream movies and books about Black history and lifestyle, which draw large audiences. And Black and Latino music continue as dominant influences on the mainstream music scene. Today, multiculturalism is seen as one of America's greatest strengths as we tool up to compete in a global marketplace.

TREND 6: BUILDING COMMUNITY LEADERSHIP THROUGH VOLUNTEERISM

MANY WELL-EDUCATED Black professionals in their late forties and early fifties are leaving their jobs, either voluntarily or involuntarily, and bringing back to the community their talent, knowledge, experience, contacts, and financial resources. They are organizing wars against Black-on-Black crime, teen pregnancy, and drug usage and trafficking. Many are starting new businesses, employing members of their families and communities.

They have discovered that the divide between "us" and "them" is slim to nonexistent if your heart has made the leap. A 1995 survey conducted by *Black Enterprise* found that 90.1 percent of Blacks said they felt a moral obligation to help others who were educationally and economically disadvantaged.

Community groups are taking over urban schools and rebuilding neighborhoods, uniting power bases on the front lines. Many are ordinary people doing extraordinary things—ministers, local politicians, executives, professionals, and skilled workers.

In a 1995 press poll of 1300 Black readers, 46 percent said they were dues-paying members of civil rights organizations; 34 percent said they took up social and political issues through their fraternities, clubs, and professional groups. With and without federal assistance, folks are stepping up to the plate. More than three hundred Black national social, professional, and civic organizations are developing scholarships and mentoring programs for Black youth.

In some instances, old programs are being redefined and reprogrammed. For example, the FreedomFest Coalition now offers an alternative to Atlanta's annual Freaknik celebration, a weekend-long, spring-break party of Black college students that is known for lewd and violent behavior. By contrast, FreedomFest promotes African unity and open dialogue between young men and women on a variety of issues confronting them today.

The Washington, DC, chapter of Concerned Black Men (CBM) is reaching out to about a thousand young people each year with various events and mentoring programs, among them an African Son-Rise Rites of Passage, a derivative of the ancient African tradition in which men formally usher boys into adulthood. And while CBM focuses on the positive obligations and joys of Black manhood, it isn't blind to dangers that often await young men. Volunteers take boys to observe the trauma center at Prince George's Hospital Center in Maryland to give them a firsthand look at the fruits of violence: gunshot wounds, drug overdose victims, bloodied bodies from drunk-driving accidents.

These are only a few examples of the tens of thousands of African Americans who are personally leading our community in new, more empowering directions.

TREND 7: A GROWING BLACK WORKFORCE

IN THE 1970s, most major companies and many smaller ones began adopting formal policies to recruit minorities. Since then the number of Blacks in the workforce has risen by about 50 percent, and numerous

Black families have moved into the middle class. However, nearly 97 percent of senior executives in the biggest U.S. companies are still white, and for every one hundred dollars a white person earns, a Black person earns sixty-three dollars.

Despite these discrepancies, there's no denying that affirmative action, diversity initiatives, and access to higher education have made an impact on the private and public sector workplace.

Black Americans have risen to the top as scientists, educators, aviators, politicians, artists, lawyers, judges, and athletes. Black executives who are considered potential Fortune 500 CEOs include

Ann Fudge, president, Maxwell House Coffee
Ken Chenault, president and chief operating officer, American Express
A. Barry Rand, president, U.S. Marketing Group, Xerox
Richard D. Nanula, president, Disney Stores Worldwide
Lloyd Ward, president, Central Division, Frito-Lay
Richard Parsons, president, Time Warner

I am proud to say that I fervently believe we'll see the growing Black workforce and Black executives become less and less a "minority" voice in business leadership as we enter the twenty-first century. Instead of the occasional and unique phenomenon of a Black person rising to the top, I expect to see a whole generation of African Americans, better trained and educated, assume countless roles as corporate captains and business owners.

TREND 8: FROM WELFARE TO WORKFARE

SEVERAL LARGE-SCALE polls over the past few years revealed the growing frustration among Blacks with a welfare system that has been perpetuated by disincentives to work and incentives to have more children. As a result, welfare recipients became locked in a cycle of poverty that eroded their self-esteem and group progress and produced a stereotype of poor work ethic, laziness, and promiscuity.

African Americans have grown tired of it. The congressional welfare reform bill passed in 1996, while not perfect, is a beginning, but the danger is that beneficial programs will be thrown out with the bad ones. For example, in 1995 the illegitimacy rate in America dropped for the first time in twenty years, and the number of babies born to teenagers also declined for the fourth year in a row. The improvement was due in large part to government-sponsored contraceptive programs and family-planning services, which means that continuing to fund these services will be a smart investment.

Several states are trying to adopt plans that eliminate welfare but also make a commitment to quality child care. A study by Marcia Meyers of the Columbia University School of Social Work showed that reliable, quality child care is the key factor in whether a mother can perform well on the job and stick with it. "Quality" is the operative word. Several studies have shown that when children are understimulated for long stretches of time or moved among ever-changing caregivers, their cognitive abilities fail to develop optimally. Although day care is expensive in the short term, it is hugely cost-effective in the long term.

Many corporations and organizations are working to help welfare recipients make the transition from welfare to workfare. Access to health care and day care and to training programs that teach skills to adults will be crucial to the success of such programs. Transportation systems used for "reverse commuting" will also help get trained inner-city workers to suburban jobs. It is a lucrative business waiting to happen.

Another innovation will be a move toward more scattered-site public housing. Segregating people in large housing projects breeds hostility and crime, reinforcing poverty and unemployability. By contrast, scattered-site housing, which mainstreams poor people in middle-class communities, removes the weight of constant negative reinforcement and brings people closer to job opportunities. As more companies relocate to the suburbs, scattered-site housing can help overcome the spatial mismatch between employees and potential workplaces. It also brings many African-American children into better school districts. Busing, although a valiant effort, has never been able to prevent a child's sense of being an outsider, and I believe in years to come we will see that the answer is for Black and white Americans not only to work together and go to school together but also to live together.

TREND 9: EXPANDING OUR INFORMATION BASE THROUGH TECHNOLOGY

BECAUSE TECHNOLOGY IS color-blind, computer literacy has the potential to democratize this nation as no other force ever has. The information superhighway can provide new economic, political, and educational power bases for Blacks in America.

We will see an exponential increase in content that speaks directly to the Black experience. On-line services like America Online and Prodigy already have created content areas specifically for Black users, and scores of sites on the World Wide Web now target Black audiences, such as the Nation of Islam, Congressional Black Caucus, AfriNet, the Blacklist for minority business owners, gay and lesbian Blacks, and the National Society of Black Engineers, to name a few.

We are living through a revolution that is changing our world to a greater extent than either the agricultural revolution ten thousand years ago or the industrial revolution three hundred years ago. Channels of distribution to our marketplaces are on the Internet, within direct reach of our churches, organizations, clubs, and professional associations. For the first time in our history we will participate fully in leading-edge technology. We will move from the African oral tradition to a cyberdrum in the digital world, reaching millions with new information and new ideas, and the barriers to entry that once limited our upward mobility will collapse with a loud thud.

TREND 10: REPOSITIONING BLACK IMAGES

OVER THE LAST forty years the media have played the biggest role in perpetuating negative racial stereotypes. Except for athletes and entertainers, Blacks are still largely depicted as criminals, drug addicts, welfare cheats, and objects of pity.

Less than 7 percent of our population is driving the image of all of us. But new influences on the media are beginning to redefine the Black image and display the diversity of our excellence. Television, advertising, and other media are beginning to offer opportunities to those who can create programming and ads that draw Black viewers and marketers. Director Spike Lee has recently founded a new advertising agency, called Spike DDB, in partnership with DDB Needham Worldwide, one of the largest, most influential agencies in the world. "My whole thing is this," Lee told Lynn Hirschberg in an interview for *The New York Times Magazine*, "I know African Americans spent $360 billion last year—$360 billion! So I don't have to come hat in hand or come bowing or shuffling as an African-American commercial director." His work, along with the good work of a core of solid Black-owned ad agencies and media properties, will contribute significantly to improving our image.

Control of our own media helps redefine and improve African-American images by presenting new heroes and heroines and accurately portraying our excellence, culture, and lifestyles. New access to capital will increase our media ownership, and as a result our public image will improve significantly. Magazines such as *Essence, Ebony, Black Enterprise, Upscale, Emerge,* and *Heart and Soul* are now reaching audiences with new heroes and heroines and new standards of beauty.

New surveys and market research support the importance of "inclusion" and "positive reinforcement" as key strategies to attract the $400-billion Black economy. One study, by Paul Sladkus International in New York, found that more than 70 percent of Blacks agreed they were more likely to buy a product if its ads showed people of their race. Similar studies show that Black women are more likely to purchase a product if the pitch comes from someone who looks like them. It's so obvious it makes you want to holler!

Surveys indicate that marketers who want to attract African-American dollars are positively depicting our images in all forms of advertising and that this trend will continue. At the same time, the number of books written each year by Black authors is greater than the sum total written during the entire period of the Harlem Renaissance. Surely this is having a positive impact on Black images and perceptions.

On a recent trip to Baltimore, I picked up *Baltimore City* magazine because I was intrigued by a cover blurb: "The Ten Most Intelligent Men in Baltimore." On the cover was a photo of Dr. Ben Carson, the famous Black neurosurgeon. It was the first time I had ever seen a Black person honored on a cover of a mainstream popular magazine for something other than sports or entertainment. Finally, images of Black people as three-dimensional human beings with families, intellect, and dreams are beginning to be seen.

THESE ARE THE trends in the making. But let's not just sit back and say, "Well, that's great, it's good things are finally changing." No, the idea is to get involved. The fact that you are reading this book shows that you're one step ahead of the crowd already—you're curious, you want to be a player, someone who at the end of the day has made a difference for yourself and your community.

I think that's great! There are major changes coming for Blacks in business and all professional walks of life that you will want to be part of. I sincerely believe that within the next generation Blacks will

- Help set new standards for "values-based" business development in America
- Elect a president of the United States, as a result of strategic alliances with other key minority groups
- Rebuild the inner cities with new low, moderate, and upscale housing that will attract middle-class Blacks
- Improve the quality of education for inner-city children, which will further fuel the return to urban America by Blacks
- Increase our investments in savings accounts, stocks, bonds, mutual funds, and property to match the best models among America's cultural groups
- Increase small business ownership to three million plus, employing nearly four million Black people
- Become an important creative force on the information superhighway
- Triple Black household computer ownership, vastly expanding our powers to network and share information
- Become major employers and employees in the health-care, sports, education, entertainment, and financial industries
- Participate in the ownership of at least ten major league sports franchises
- Run or own at least three major mainstream media, entertainment, or publishing companies
- Become CEOs of at least ten Fortune 1000 companies
- Become important investors and developers in sub-Saharan Africa, the Pacific Rim, the Caribbean, and Latin America

Maybe you will become part of one of these predictions! So what are we waiting for? Let's look ahead and see how we can best realize our dreams.

I know what you're saying—"Sure, George, you make everything sound rosy, but where do I start? Which career path makes the most sense for me?"

When the goal is economic power, it makes sense to concentrate on jobs and businesses in which our best talent and most money are already invested. Which area you choose—and how you choose to work within it—depends on your personal strengths and interests. Let me suggest what I believe are some of the most promising areas of opportunities for Black Americans today.

Education

THIS IS AN industry that needs more Black teachers and vendors. It also needs new and better schools, as well as more pre-school and after-school programs. These are businesses waiting to explode. All of this will develop significantly in the next twenty to thirty years to make our schools more competitive with each other and more responsive to students. In Milwaukee, Chicago, and Detroit nearly one hundred charter and private schools have been started by Blacks for Black children. These schools employ hundreds of Black teachers and support staff in addition to providing urban kids with a better education. Everybody wins!

Finance and Banking

JOHN ROGERS, OWNER of Ariel Capital Management, a two-billion-dollar Black-owned fund management firm in Chicago, is helping Blacks invest and multiply their money through selling mutual funds and other stock portfolios. Investment banker Eric Small recently created a mutual fund product of successful Black businesses traded on the stock exchange. Other Black bankers, financial advisors, insurance brokers, and stockbrokers are employing similar methods to help Blacks more wisely invest, shed debt, and multiply their money.

Small Business Development

AT $469 BILLION in 1997, according to an economic forecast study from the University of Georgia, Black buying power in America ranks among the world's richest economies, larger than the economy of the entire continent of Africa; yet less than 5 percent of this wealth recycles in our own communities. A recent survey of 125th Street in Harlem showed 95 percent of all businesses were owned by other cultural groups, but we're still the customers. There is tremendous opportunity, as well as a great need, to start and own our neighborhood business, both urban and suburban, both retail and manufacturing. It's right there in our faces.

Technology

THE INFORMATION SUPERHIGHWAY and digital technology are providing a new economic and creative outlet for African Americans. This is a perfect arena in which to expand our tremendous creativity by developing new software and moving into positions where we can influence and control the content of the Internet and World Wide Web. "NetNoir," "MelaNet," and many other Afrocentric Web sites and on-line services are examples.

Publishing/Media

ONLY IN THE last four or five years has publishing discovered the financial power of Black writers and reading audiences. Before that, Black writers, particularly those who wrote nonfiction, were rarely published, based on three myths: Black people don't read books, Black people don't buy books, and white people don't buy books by Black writers about Black life.

After *Emerge* and *Heart and Soul* magazines were successfully launched and books like *Waiting to Exhale, Jazz,* and *Possessing the Secret of Joy* hit the top ten on the *New York Times* bestseller list, the industry woke up. Today there are huge new opportunities in all publishing and media endeavors.

Urban Redevelopment

REAL ESTATE AND HOUSING are prime business opportunities for African Americans. Land is limited, and survey after survey shows that proximity to downtown America is becoming desirable again for both housing and business. Technology and home-based businesses will increase the value of real estate. According to the Washington, DC–based Hamilton Securities Group, $2.6 trillion in multifamily and commercial real estate equity and debt will change hands over the next decade. Retromigration back to the city is in. These are our neighborhoods, and we should be the prime developers and contractors of the regentrification of decaying urban America.

There are political and financial challenges to overcome in getting the business, but Black builders in Cleveland, Detroit, New York, and Chicago are putting it all together to do well while doing good.

Health Care

THIS VERY BROAD category is expected to increase twice as fast as the rest of the economy. An aging population, as well as medical advancements, is driving the need for health related occupations. As long as insurance companies and hospitals mandate shorter hospital stays for patients, the increased demand for health-care services and those who can provide them in innovative ways will continue. Once more, African Americans are ideally suited to meet these needs. All trends in health care point toward prevention, wellness, and holistic therapies that integrate mental, physical, and emotional wellbeing—the hallmarks of our healing traditions. Just as important, Black doctors, dentists, scientists, researchers, and technologists will be in huge demand. The needs are great, the opportunities abounding.

Sports

BY ANY ECONOMIC standard, Black sports stars are earning top money, yet it's obvious we all can't be Michael Jordan. The opportunities in sports are not all "in the paint." Former NBA star Isiah Thomas has for years been the only basketball player to invest his money in a team (the Toronto Raptors). That's just the beginning of a change, as a few big-money players are getting together in ways that can really pay off. Football legend Walter Payton, for example, is leading an investment group to purchase majority ownership in an expansion NFL franchise. With these new ventures you can expect the front office staff to become more inclusive of Blacks, women, and other races and cultures; the possibilities all the way down the ladder are enormous.

Entertainment

LIKE THE SPORTS industry, show business is another place where we have a high profile and also spend a lot of time and money. But when it comes to controlling the product, we're just beginning to get our feet wet. Certain segments (and their offshoots) of the entertainment industry—specifically, film, television, and music—are rapidly becoming arenas of spectacular growth for African Americans looking to get involved behind the scenes in the many divisions and departments within this multibillion dollar industry.

Global Commerce

SOUTH AFRICA, HERE we come. Michael Giles and his wife left Xerox, got an eleven-million-dollar loan from the World Bank, then began opening 110 laundromats in Johannesburg. Sound impossible? Opportunities will be opening up all over Africa and Southeast Asia, Latin America and the Caribbean.

ALL OF THESE business opportunities require focus and hard work. No one is going to just hand you an opportunity. You can earn opportunities, however, by performing the smallest jobs to the best of your ability. Remember, those who are watching you, including teachers and even competitors, are the very people who can make all the difference in accelerating your career path. So look to your network and your community. You cannot do anything out there totally on your own. All the trends agree: First, draw on the strength and unity of the Black community, then leverage it to expand and include others as you seek to attain your personal goals. Please remember, all entrepreneurship, job searches, and upward mobility are inherently networking initiatives. Life is a contact sport; start building your network today.

ONE FINAL THOUGHT: A NEW MORAL ASSIGNMENT

MICHAEL NOVAK WRITES in his insightful book, *Business as a Calling: Work and the Examined Life*, "business is about creating goods and services, jobs and benefits and new wealth that didn't exist before. The moral nature of business is creative and can transform the conditions of human life for the better or the worse." Many practicing it often see business as a way of giving back to society. Business has a special role to play in bringing hope and economic progress to the poor. Business is the best real hope of the poor, and that is one of the noblest callings inherent in all business activities: to raise up the poor. If the huge numbers of poor Blacks are ever to lift themselves out of poverty, they need those of us with ideas and capital to invest in creating the industries, jobs, and wealth that will give them a base from which to build. To that end, it could be summarized, to engage in business and create new wealth, morally, is every Black person's moral assignment and imperative in the twenty-first century. In a democratic capitalist society that is a sure road to freedom and equality.

2

OUR EDGE:
INNER POWER—
Seven Moral and Spiritual
Principles for Success

The night is beautiful,
So the faces of my people.
The stars are beautiful,
So the eyes of my people.
Beautiful, also, is the sun.
Beautiful, also, are the souls of my people.
— LANGSTON HUGHES, "MY PEOPLE"

One of the ways by which men measure their own significance
is to be found in the amount of power and energy other men
must use in order to crush them or hold them back . . . The
persecution becomes a vote of confidence, which becomes, in
turn, a source of inspiration, power and validation.
—HOWARD THURMAN

ONE DAY, NOT too long ago, Susan Taylor was an unemployed single
mother searching for help in Harlem. Today she is the high-profile
editor-in-chief of *Essence* magazine.

For years, Kweisi Mfume was a Baltimore street thug and a unmar-
ried father. Today he is president and CEO of the NAACP and former
Democratic congressman from Maryland's 7th District.

Les Brown was born on a dirt floor in Liberty City, Florida, abandoned by his parents and labeled retarded by his teachers. Today he is a world-renowned motivational speaker.

The most remarkable aspect of these remarkable stories is that each person had a unique spiritual experience that changed his or her life, and yet each story is not an isolated event. In the Black community, stories like these are part of everyday life.

My business partner, Greg Williams, for example, is a successful entrepreneur, even though he lost his mother when he was twelve years old and has never seen his alcoholic father. My own mother was institutionalized when I was five years old and my five siblings and I were split up, lived in a shelter, then placed in foster homes, where we remained until we became young adults

What has made so many Blacks succeed beyond anyone's wildest predictions and against the worst possible odds? What, besides the color of our skin, do we have in common? I believe the answer is a moral and spiritual inner power that has manifested itself in every generation of Blacks since the Middle Passage. It is the same inner power to succeed that fueled Frederick Douglass, Harriet Tubman, Booker T. Washington, and Sojourner Truth, and it is at work today.

Often when people try to describe this power, they call it dogged faith, or perseverance, or indomitability. But a single word or phrase cannot adequately define it. This is a force that springs from our ancestral memories and is fired by our cultural experiences. It is rooted in African legacies, genetic endowments, American history, religious beliefs, family upbringing, and cultural values. It is inherently spiritual—the distilled essence of the teachings of ancient and modern African shamans, of Muhammad, and of Jesus Christ.

A cursory inspection of the ancient Nile Valley civilization of Kemet (Egypt) should inspire all people of African descent to respect their history and to hold themselves in high esteem. Among the most ancient hieroglyphic writings is this passage from *The Husia*, translated by Maulana Karenga, the father of Kwanzaa:

Do not terrorize people for if you do, God will punish you accordingly. If anyone lives by such means God will take bread from his mouth. If one says I shall be rich by such means, he will eventually have to say my means entrapped me.

If one says I will rob another, he will end up being robbed himself. The plans of men and women do not always come to pass for in the end it is the will of God which prevails.

As African Americans go, every person of African descent in the world goes. I believe that part of our task is to use our inner power to help America fulfill the promises implicit in the Declaration of Independence and the Constitution, and those of Wall Street, too. How else can you explain our extraordinary ability to constantly succeed against the odds and make a way out of no way?

Like all African Americans I am fascinated by our success stories. We find our own way by listening to the stories of brothers and sisters who have overcome in magnificent ways. In my case, success stories are also my business. I publish *SuccessGuides*, a series of regional networking directories in print and on the World Wide Web (www.frasernet.com).

They include the names of thousands of successful Black professionals, business owners, and community leaders. Each of these achievers knows all about the tremendous obstacles that can impede success. And yet they found hope and opportunity all around them. They are those among us who are living joyful, productive lives, shaking things up and making things happen right now. They are people we admire— Quincy Jones, Maxine Waters, Oceola McCartey, Percy Sutton, Rachel Robinson, Colin Powell, and Marian Wright Edelman.

They stand out because their success is imbued with grace and dignity. Their minds, bodies, and spirits are in harmony with a greater power, and they have integrated their dreams with whatever opportunities they found around them, no matter how small. They are able to answer the hard questions with candor, commonsense, and mother wit. They know exactly who they are, and they have a purpose for living. Other people like and admire them, want to do business with them, hire and promote them, and cast their votes for them. They have tapped the inner power. How did they do it?

Some years ago I embarked on a mission to unravel the components of that power source. My purpose was to define a set of principles, to create a sort of moral and spiritual road map, so that finding and drawing from the power would be less a matter of intuitive chance and more a conscious act.

I began to examine my own life on a deeper level. Above all, I drew on the experiences of the thousands of successful African Americans I knew. I read and explored the writings and teachings of the most famous among us from the past and present.

What emerged from my thinking and research was a handful of principles held in common by successful African Americans—from corporate executives to entrepreneurs, schoolteachers to movie stars, political activists to plumbers. These are people who continue to make a way out of no way. Whenever and wherever I meet African Americans in the process of achieving and also of contributing to their communities, I find these principles in place and actively engaged. Each principle explores a special corner in the souls of Black folks.

Principle 1: Seek Spiritual Growth
Principle 2: Give First, Share Always
Principle 3: Discover Your Unique Purpose
Principle 4: Find Inspiration in Your Suffering
Principle 5: Support Your Race and Culture First
Principle 6: Maintain Ties to the Extended Family
Principle 7: Achieve Success with Dignity

These seven principles embody our greatest strengths and meet our greatest needs. Individually, each is strong, resilient, and full of hope. Combined, they are a force much greater than the sum of its parts, a force powerful enough to move mountains, and Lord knows we have.

PRINCIPLE 1: SEEK SPIRITUAL GROWTH

Unless you call out, who will open the door?
—ETHIOPIAN PROVERB

People see God every day; they just don't recognize Him.
—PEARL BAILEY

THE AFRICAN SPIRITUAL value system views life in a circular, holistic fashion. Our ancestors passed on to us the belief that we are not merely human beings having a spiritual experience, but spiritual beings having a human experience.

This deep spirituality was burnished by our experiences during nearly four centuries of oppression. Africans traded to North America encountered a slave master who worked them hard for their lifetimes, with no chance for freedom or education. To justify their unchristian acts, slave owners reinterpreted biblical passages to prove that God created certain groups to be enslaved by others. The Africans rejected this manufactured evidence, while responding fully to the familiar bib-lical stories of redemption which had taken place on their own conti-nent. For two thousand years or more, the escape of the Hebrew people from Egypt, Daniel walking unscathed from the lion's den, and the resurrection of Jesus of Nazareth had been told around African rituals and spiritualism.

Despite efforts to deny Africans any form of education, some taught themselves to read the Bible. Sunday morning service in makeshift plantation churches became the bright center of each week, the one place where Africans could share their beliefs and dreams that some day their suffering would be relieved and they would be free.

Their faith was justified. But in the terrifying excitement following the Emancipation—clothed in rags, without shelter or even shoes on their feet, most unable to read or write—African Americans had to find a new way to survive. Church became more important than ever. Since that time, church networks have been the constant and central help of our community. In our churches, we educated ourselves, de-veloped leaders, and organized. Like the phoenix, we began to rise like no other displaced people in the world.

Such a passionate commitment to life is more than mere ambi-tion—it has a decidedly spiritual element. Many successful African Americans believe, in fact, that the spirit of God is not "out there," but inside of them. Our dreams of success become immediately more viable when we fire up our spiritual center.

Seeking spiritual growth promotes social tolerance and helps provide a moral road map for your day-to-day actions. It puts you in touch with your deeper side and adds a powerful, more meaningful joy to life and work.

Spirituality also has direct, practical benefits. Growing up in Brook-lyn, I attended a predominantly white Catholic church because my foster mother was Catholic. I never felt moved by that church. In fact, I was always a little afraid of it. When I was seventeen, I moved back with my father, whose habit was to attend different neighborhood churches as the spirit moved him. He encouraged me to do the same. I started experimenting, going to different services, looking for some-thing, although I couldn't say exactly what.

At the time, I had a job working in my brother's printing plant, but things weren't going so good for me. The neighborhood we lived in was literally going to pot. Drugs and crime were everywhere. I decided to leave Brooklyn in search of a new life. I chose Cleveland because my married sister, Myra, lived there. My first job there was working in the laundry room of the Cleveland Clinic; then I moved on to a part-time job wrapping Christmas gifts in Halle Bros. department store; then I got a job selling encyclopedias. Feeling lonely and rudderless, I resumed my practice of attending different churches.

A friend recommended Mt. Zion Congregational Church. On my first Sunday morning there I found everything I had been searching for. The rapturous gospel music moved me, the pastor preached a word that eased my fears and stirred my hopes, and all around I saw people who looked like me.

In that church I did my first networking with God and his disciples. I met my best friend, Corky, found my first serious girlfriend, Leslie Blackman, and met the Jones family in whose home I would later be married. I sold my first sets of encyclopedias. Churchgoing was as much a social and business boom as it was a religious awakening. It was like being in heaven.

Cleveland had its problems, but moving there proved serendipitous for me. I later found out it was part of God's plan to help deliver me from my deteriorating circumstances and provide a new vantage point from which to meet what was in store for me in the succeeding thirty years.

Our greatest leaders have always believed that faith, hard work, perseverance, and belief in a higher power will pull us through the darkest hours. This belief is so pivotal to our success that it is uniquely Black to go public with these deeply felt beliefs in our moments of triumph. I wonder what white people think when we "give God the glory."

A. G. Gaston, the millionaire Black businessman who bailed out Martin Luther King, Jr., from a Birmingham, Alabama, jail in 1963, said, "God first, others second, me third."

Paula Cholmondeley, corporate vice president of Owens Corning, when asked her secret to success, proudly said, "My religious beliefs first."

Myron Bell, all-star strong safety for the Pittsburgh Steelers, after knocking down a Hail Mary pass to secure a spot in the 1996 Super Bowl, said, "It's always in the hands of God. It went our way today."

Sandra Galloway, president of the Galloway Braintrust Groups, says she puts a call in to heaven every day. "I thank Him, then we talk about what we're going to get done that day."

Academy Award–winner Cuba Gooding, Jr., has said publicly that everything he does is a "direct stem" from God's plan: "I'm a sinner and I fall to some of the enticing sins of the world," he says. "But my relationship with God has guided me."

Whitney Houston remembers a turning point in her life when she was fourteen. "I got to know the Lord," she says. "I remember being in church—I had gone all my life, but it's nothing till you experience it yourself and accept it in your life, till you know what He's all about and what He wants from you, which is basic respect, love and consideration."

When Evander Holyfield won the world boxing championship from Mike Tyson, he gave the "glory to God" in the same way that Muhammad Ali always did. Holyfield went one step further a couple of weeks later when he took out a full-page ad in *USA Today*, thanking his family, friends, and fans for their prayers and the role those prayers played in his victory. The ad closed with this biblical reference: "I can do all things through Christ which strengtheneth me" (Philippians 4:13).

Basketball's finest center, Hakeem Olajuwon of the Houston Rockets, calls the game of basketball "an act of worship."

Kweisi Mfume says that he felt a cold shiver up his spine one night while hanging out with the fellas on the corner. (Mfume swears it was delivered by the spirit of his beloved mother who had died seven years earlier.) He left the corner, walked to his house, got down on his knees, and prayed that if he could just get beyond this low period in his life, he'd never go back to the street. God answered his prayer and Mfume is fulfilling his promise.

Seeking spiritual growth and guidance brings out the best in all people. It teaches us humility, gratefulness, and generosity and steels us against envy, greed, and materialism. It helps us to understand that high personal achievement comes from using the unique gifts possessed by each of us. As we grow spiritually, we see the bigger picture; as we acknowledge a deeper source of power, we begin to see opportunities all around us. And we believe that perhaps we were not brought here but *sent* here, by a higher power to help America get back to its moral and spiritual center. Why don't you take a few minutes to think about that?

PRINCIPLE 2: GIVE FIRST,
SHARE ALWAYS

When you clench your fist, no one can put anything in your hand,
nor can your hand pick anything up.

—ALEX HALEY

A sure way for one to lift himself up is by helping to lift
someone else up.

—BOOKER T. WASHINGTON

MANY PEOPLE WHO want to succeed in life set a goal, then proceed
to make what they think is a straight drive toward attaining it. Giving
back will have to wait, they say. This is a backward system. Because,
let me tell you, the best way to get what you want is to find a way to
give it.

If you want love, you must give love; if you want joy, you must give
joy; if you want affluence, you must help others attain affluence; if
you want business, you must give service. You will always get back
more than you give. This is the law of increasing return: For every
single thing you give, you will get ten things in return. Maybe not
when, how, or where you expect it, but it will come. I can attest,
without doubt, that every significant thing that has ever happened to
me began with me giving first.

Many people have asked me how I got on the cover of *Black Enterprise* magazine. I promise you it was not because I was cute or lucky,
or because Earl Graves felt an urgent need to do me a favor. My
relationship with the Graves family started more than ten years ago.
Black Enterprise was sponsoring Networking Forums in major cities,
and Cleveland was one of the stops. The event planners needed a
volunteer to help organize and draw local audiences.

Two of Cleveland's Black business leaders, Carole Hoover (president
of the Growth Association) and John Bustamante (publisher of the
Call & Post) recommended me. I agreed to chair the event, and our
group worked diligently for three months to help make the forum a
success. I remember the first time I met Earl, on the day of the event.
He was gracious, charismatic, friendly. And well dressed. When I said
I liked his tie, he took it off and gave it to me! He was a role model
for many of us then, as he still is today.

Our relationship grew over the succeeding years. I shared my database of Black professionals with *Black Enterprise*, and I invited Butch Graves to come to speak at my monthly SuccessNet programs, which were modeled on *Black Enterprise's* Networking Forums. Some six years later, in 1993, I sent a copy of the manuscript for *Success Runs in Our Race* to Earl and his former editor, Sheryl Hilliard Tucker, asking for their opinion. I felt the content was consistent with Earl's powerful vision and mission for Black folks. They both liked it very much, plus it didn't hurt that I had a good relationship with both people. The editorial staff at *Black Enterprise* collectively decided to excerpt the book and feature me on the cover. From that day forward, book sales soared, and my life changed significantly. All because of a simple act of giving first some eight years earlier, not ever knowing where it would lead.

There is a direct correlation between serving and being served, between giving and getting. You cannot take anything out of a bank that you have not first put in. You don't have to take my word for it. Just go down to a bank and ask them to give you five hundred dollars. Likewise, you cannot take anything out of life that you have not already put in. Let me put it simply: "If you ain't givin', you ain't gettin'."

It's no different in business. You want to get ahead on the job? Offer to help someone else—without being asked. Expect nothing in return. An enormously wealthy owner of a communications company got her first job working as a clerk in an accounting firm. Whenever she had a lull in her own work, she looked around to see who in the office was most frantic and offered to help that person. It didn't matter if that person was another filing clerk or an executive.

We must give even when it hurts and continue giving until it feels good. We must reach past what is easy for us. I used to try to avoid speaking at inner-city high schools. I had my reasons. It had been hard to move out of the New York tenements and bootstrap my own life. It hurt to look back, and I felt I had to keep moving forward. Plus it took time—and what was I going to say, anyhow?

But the requests kept coming. Eventually, I forced myself to show up. Here's the kicker: Over time, it began to feel good. In fact, every time I looked into inspired eyes and heard eager questions, I felt great. Ostensibly I was there to role-model for them, but after one hour of talking to young people, I felt good all day. My reward is becoming the person they see in me—not someone with power and wealth, but someone with love and service.

Often, significant business opportunities have come out of simply giving courtesy. Not long ago I secured nearly fifteen thousand dollars in speaking engagements from someone I hardly knew. When I thanked her, she said, "You're welcome. I like you." I asked her why she liked me so soon. "You gave me respect," she said. "I felt what I was saying was important to you. I liked that." After that, I felt like proposing marriage.

Deborah and Michael Waller of Solon, Ohio, give thousands of dollars every year to their church and deserving Black charities. Deborah has a thriving public relations firm, and Michael has a multimillion-dollar telecommunications business. As a result of an open hand and heart, they both have been blessed with even more abundance.

After Bill Cosby and Oprah Winfrey gave millions to Black colleges, Oprah signed the richest TV contract ever, and Cosby got another hit TV show. Both operate from an abundance mentality.

Dr. Doris Evans, one of Cleveland's most successful pediatricians, gives as a way of achieving justice. "I'm opposed to charity," she says. "Charity occurs when rich people decide to give based on how much is left over. I'm joyful in my duty to share what God has so generously given me."

What we give is not gone, it's invested. At some point in time, we all receive returns on our investments. The farmer understands this concept. The Creator has designed it that way.

PRINCIPLE 3: DISCOVER YOUR UNIQUE PURPOSE

Every man is born into the world to do something unique and something distinctive, and if he or she does not do it, it will never be done.

—BENJAMIN MAYS

The opportunity that God sends does not wake up him who is asleep.

—SENEGALESE PROVERB

PEOPLE IN TOUCH with their purpose or calling in life perform with a creativity and energy that outstrips the competition. They are often people of vision who can make others see and act on their ideas. These are the people who can't wait to get up in the morning and get started. As soon as they enter any situation, other people immediately feel better. This kind of charisma comes from going about the business of doing what you are meant to do. They have asked the difficult questions: Who am I? Why do I exist? Am I all that I am capable of being? They have searched long and hard for the answers.

Finding one's purpose or calling in the business world can be defined as doing daily that which gives you the greatest pleasure, and what at the end of your life gives you the greatest satisfaction. Theologian Michael Novak says, "Each calling is unique to each individual. Answering the call requires talent and a great love for what you do, to include the drudgery it involves." There must be enjoyment and a sense of renewed energies each time one engages in his or her calling. Finding your calling is not easy and following many wrong paths may be necessary before you land at just the right place.

Frank Mathews was an eighteen-year-old gang member serving time in an Alabama state prison. Frank got lucky: While in jail he found God. After his release, he decided to devote himself to saving his homeboys from gangs and jail time. Frank was street-savvy, creative, and determined. But what was the best way to achieve his goal? Become a social worker? A schoolteacher? Maybe a cop? Frank tried something else.

Within two years, he was hosting his own television show, a raw, plain-talking interview program called *In Your Face*. Frank takes his cameras onto the streets of Birmingham and talks to all kinds of people in every walk of life. Whenever dignitaries come to town, Frank is right there "in their face," asking tough questions. No one turns him down. Frank produces the show himself, selling advertising to local stores. His crew is composed of former gang members.

When Frank was a boy, no one could have envisioned him succeeding at what he's doing now. Yet he feels completely at home in his new role.

The great religions teach us that human beings are here to make the world a better place, a heaven on earth. Successful African Americans, wherever we are working and in whatever capacity, share an additional purpose: to better the lives of all people of color. How you go about it is up to you.

Creation's great mystery is that, like snowflakes and fingerprints, no two people are alike. Each one of us is an original. To succeed in any endeavor requires commitment and limitless energy, which come only from hooking into your power base—your core strengths. If you have the core strengths essential for a given job, you can always go about acquiring the necessary training for the job.

Begin by asking yourself, What special gifts did God give me? Frank Mathews's core strengths had been near at hand throughout his life. He had always been persuasive. As a boy he had been a great talker; he was curious about people and always asked lots of questions. Persistence came naturally to him. In fact, he nagged grown-ups until they told him what he wanted to know or gave him what he wanted to have. Although persuasiveness and doggedness seemingly have nothing to do with producing a television show, in fact both traits are at the heart of his success today.

Like Frank's, your core strengths are likely to be traits you displayed in childhood—things that you were naturally good at without even trying. When you add your acquired skills into your mix of special interests and core God-given strengths, you begin to focus in on your unique purpose.

Many people who appear to be successful feel empty and unfulfilled on the inside because they are not doing what they were meant to be doing. Dr. Howard Thurman said, "There is something in every one of you that waits and listens for the sound of the genuine in yourself. It is the only true guide you will ever have. And if you cannot hear it, you will all of your life spend your days on the ends of strings that somebody else pulls." I will tell you, "Leap, and the net will appear." And the great mythologist Joseph Campbell will tell you that if you leap, "there will be a thousand unseen hands waiting to help you."

PRINCIPLE 4: FIND INSPIRATION IN YOUR SUFFERING

Openings are made in a life by suffering that are not made in any other way.

—HOWARD THURMAN

To live is to suffer; to survive is to find some meaning in the suffering.

—ROBERTA FLACK

MANY BLACKS IDENTIFY strongly with the example of Jesus of Nazareth, who suffered betrayal, denial by his friends, humiliation, beatings, torture, and crucifixion. Only after this suffering did the resurrection come. I believe the message of this story is that if you pay the price, you too will be resurrected. The idea is not to suffer only—but to make something from your suffering.

Of course, Jesus was perfect; but *we* all make mistakes. You must first be willing to do something badly before you will ever be able to do it well. Therefore, there is a direct correlation between purpose and pain. All great achievers understand this.

Spiritual people believe that everything happens for a reason. This belief is older than the Old Testament. Even though we may not clearly see the reason for our suffering, we have faith that we can turn it toward a good purpose. You can't erase the past, but you can keep moving forward, even when it's hard and even when you feel bad.

All of life is about hills and valleys, twists and turns. There is no straight road for anyone. There is an African proverb that goes "Beyond the mountains, more mountains." You cannot achieve anything significant in life without paying a price. If you're not making any mistakes, then you're not taking any risks. Without risk of failure, there is no advancement. We'd all just be tramping in place.

One day, when we look back over our lives, all of the fateful twists and turns will fit together like a puzzle. Brothers and sisters, we are writing our stories right now, and they will become our legacies. We want to write passionate stories that we can hold up to the Creator with pride and say, "Here, God. I've done what you have asked."

An ability to recover from setbacks and get started again is essential to long-term success. If you are taking risks and really trying to achieve something in your life, you will always have some failure and some problems. The only people who don't have problems are dead. Could it be that the more problems you have, the more alive you are? I can testify to the peaks and valleys of life, both on and off the job.

It was one of those business days when every sales call resulted in a resounding "no!" Then my accountant, Henry Creel, called with even worse news. A long series of risky business decisions to fund my publication *SuccessGuide* had finally caught up with me. Trying to personally fund this venture meant that it was really perpetually underfunded— yes, I had champagne ideas but beer pockets; I wanted to grow my business fast, an affliction common among new entrepreneurs. I had also insisted on taking the hard road and had refused to accept cigarette, liquor, beer, or wine advertising.

Henry informed me that several of my creditors were filing suits and levies for their money. I had no choice but to file for bankruptcy. It was one of the most traumatic experiences of my life.

I lost everything I had worked for and believed in all of my life. I was most concerned about my family, whose security was now in jeopardy, and my friends, whose investments would also be lost. I had no place to hide, no way to preserve my reputation or my dignity.

There are disadvantages to being a high profile "doer" in Black America—everybody knows or wants to know your business, especially if it's bad.

Shortly after I filed for bankruptcy, a reporter from the Cleveland *Plain Dealer* asked for an interview about my "tragedy." I was reluctant, but he was so affirming and friendly (and he was going to write the story anyway) that I finally agreed. Little did I know that my story would end up the following Monday on the front page, under the bold headline "Meteoric Career Reaches Bottom." I freaked out.

However, after the opening negative paragraphs, the story focused in on persistence, values, and the peaks and valleys of business life. In short, it was a fair story. I received a flood of sympathetic phone calls and letters from people who had read the story and felt inspired by it. My pain and suffering had served as a lesson not only for me, but for many others as well.

It all turned out to be a new beginning, an opportunity to move forward in wiser and better ways. Most of my good friends have forgiven me for the loss of their investment (they will be blessed tenfold for it), and my creditors are ready to do business with me again. Businesswise, I've been to the highest mountain and the lowest valley and I'm better because of it. I wish I had learned earlier, but that was not in the Creator's plan; I obviously needed that lesson as I traveled down my success path.

Setbacks happen in business and in life, sometimes because of mistakes you make and sometimes just because of circumstances genuinely beyond your control. Even when you're working your hardest, doing your very best, stuff happens. You have to have the resiliency to bounce back and move forward. Circumstances may knock you down, but they can't knock you out unless you give in or give up. Never give up—tomorrow is just around the corner.

PRINCIPLE 5: SUPPORT YOUR RACE
AND CULTURE FIRST

We are Africans not because we are born in Africa, but because
Africa is born in us. Look around you and behold us in our great-
ness. Greatness is an African possibility: you can make it yours.
—CHESTER HIGGINS, JR.

BEFORE I START each speech, I always pause for a second, stare at the
audience, and then say, "Yes, I'm Black." They usually burst out laughing. Why? Because I'm light, bright, and look almost white, with "good
hair." I add, "That's the beauty of our race and culture. We come in
all shapes, sizes, skin tones, and hair textures. Lots of options out
there, no need to stray." They laugh even louder. (Of course, anyone
who's been Black long enough can look at my large nose and lips and
not be fooled.)

Yes, I'm a race man, someone who believes in celebrating my race
and culture first, not to suggest that I'm better than anyone else, but
that I'm just as good and just as worthy. I'm a reawakened race man.
Because of my crossover appearance, I've always been able to open
closed doors. I've used this to my advantage in the past, although I
never felt quite comfortable with it. My days in corporate America
were productive, but I wasted a lot of time proving that negative racial stereotypes didn't apply to me. Occasionally I found myself thinking I was the exception, a clear sign that I, too, had bought into
stereotyping.

Over time, as I read more and got more involved in my own community, I became increasingly more uneasy with my pseudo-whiteness.
I wasn't one of them; I was Black, and proud of it. I had God-given
strengths, good skills, and the desire to succeed. I needed to use these
gifts to better my community, as well as myself, because I was inex-
tricably tied to its demise or success. Not surprisingly, the more I re-
invested my financial and intellectual resources back into my own
community, the more successful I became. Putting race and culture
first improved me as a human being, brought needed skills back to the
community, and put me on the road to success.

Historically, African Americans have always supported their own.
The fewer opportunities we had, the more we learned to rely on each
other. During the 1960s, however, new civil rights laws provided greater

access to public venues. We were able to move into new neighbor-hoods, attend new colleges, and find work in the private and public sectors. Many of our most gifted put their energies into building other people's businesses. Even as they gained significant opportunities, they lost much of their sense of community.

The new Afrocentricity thinks of race and culture first—without espousing separatism or Black nationalism. For hundreds of years history has been written from a European perspective, meaning that many of the contributions of other ethnic groups, particularly Afri-can Americans, have either been distorted, undervalued, or com-pletely left out.

African-centered history makes a positive contribution to world his-tory and to Black self-esteem by pointing out many of these things. If we guard against the extremes, if we are balanced and scholarly in our approach to history and culture, our efforts will not be divisive but will build up the whole body of world knowledge. Developing processes and programs to raise Black self-esteem is an important goal.

Maulana Karenga committed his life to researching, writing about, and promoting the seven principles of Kwanzaa, now recognized and celebrated by over fifteen million Blacks worldwide. African-centered values are being taught to thousands of young people through Rites of Passage programs, implemented by community-based organizations in major American cities. And African-centered values are being taught by Black educators and professors in schools, colleges, and community centers.

People like John Henrik Clark, professor emeritus of Hunter College in New York, teach us that one is African-centered when "any effort on the part of a person of African descent is made to reclaim what slavery, oppression and colonialism took away. It took away your land and the minerals contained within, and it took away your birthright to images of greatness."

Frederick Douglass said that we must use our "specialness" to assist in the healing of America's deep racial wounds, "first by admitting and solving our own problems, then by challenging the problems that plague us all." This requires coming to the economic table as equals.

We must all work toward a "kinder and gentler" nation on one hand, and on the other hand go within ourselves to do everything we can to strengthen our skills, our businesses, and our minds first.

Shelley Anthony, a forty-four-year-old restaurateur in Atlanta, Geor-gia, has built an eight-restaurant chain featuring drive-through chitlins.

Generating over one million dollars per year and employing more than thirty people, this plainspoken man has done remarkably well thinking race and culture first.

J. R. Fenwick received a three-thousand-dollar bonus check from his job as a pharmaceutical representative. He then purchased some basic recording equipment, set up shop in the basement of his home, and started Digital Dialogue. His fast-growing company focuses on recording books on tape by Black authors who self-publish—a great and profitable idea.

Chu profitably produces and markets an American flag in traditional African colors. Maria Nhambu Bergh successfully sells her professionally produced exercise videos, filmed in South Africa, and Afrocentric body wear, marketed as Aerobics with Soul. Shababa manufactures Conscious Wear, a well-designed array of high-quality caps, T-shirts, and polo shirts, each with a positive Black message.

Bruce Adams, president of W. B. Adams in Landale, Pennsylvania, is a puzzle designer and small manufacturer. His beautifully designed Black history puzzles and Kwanzaa puzzles have been featured in *Ebony*. They sell briskly in toy and gift stores, but he has experienced his greatest sales from Black-owned bookstores and direct mail.

Support your race and culture first is about unity of purpose. It's about creating jobs, not just finding jobs. About spending your money first with Black businesses that offer quality, value, and service.

PRINCIPLE 6: MAINTAIN TIES TO THE EXTENDED FAMILY

For I am my mother's daughter, and the drums
of Africa still beat in my heart. They will not let
me rest while there is a single Negro boy or girl
without a chance to prove his worth.
—MARY MCLEOD BETHUNE

ONE THING THAT has made African-American culture unique among all others is its ability to preserve the structure of the extended family unit across all socioeconomic lines. When we attend church, there are people in the pews from all walks of life. When we're just hanging out, there is no telling whom we might run into. I was walking through the

Atlanta airport not long ago when I saw three Black men standing at the Delta ticket counter, talking and slapping high fives. One was dressed in a suit and tie and carried a briefcase, one was a ticket agent dressed in airline blues, and one was a baggage handler dressed in fatigues with knee guards.

On the plane, the corporate brother told me that they were all old schoolmates and they still hung out socially. "We are family," he said.

This closeness is partly due to social restrictions that forced us to live our adult lives in the same neighborhoods where we grew up. But it is also related to our cultural mores and values. In recent years, better educational and professional opportunities have made mobility in all directions more common. As a consequence, the extended family is losing some of its cohesiveness. This is a tragic loss to a race for whom unity has always been strength.

Those who have lost touch with this family, no matter how successful they appear to be, are on a road to nowhere. Four thousand years ago, Ptah Hotep of Egypt wrote, "Poor is he who shuns his kin."

Maintaining these ties not only supports the race and culture, but it keeps *you* reality-based. Blacks who are succeeding in mainstream America, particularly those in powerful positions of leadership, all say they go back home to their families on a regular basis. One assembly member told me, "There is a lot of stress out there, people are always trying to knock you down. When I need to get my batteries recharged, I go home."

Others recognize the dangers inherent in success. "It's easy to start thinking you're something special," one Fortune 500 executive told me. "The downside is that when trouble comes—and everyone runs into trouble sometime—you feel demolished. You have to keep your balance, through thick and thin, and the best way to do that is by staying connected to your extended family." My dad taught me to ask each day, "Is the community well?" Because as the community goes so go I. For those who have forgotten, I submit a poem I have written:

Black Apology

I'm sorry that I ignored your cry for help. I
left the neighborhood, traveling down the
road to success in a limousine by myself
when there was room for many more.

I got caught up in the champagne and
caviar, and soft leather seats and all that
room as I stretched my weary legs . . .

not realizing that when I reached my
destination I was still Black but now alone!

I don't want to be alone anymore 'cause
having my family just feels more right.

Is there anything I can do now to make your
journey easier? Of course there is . . .
please, take my hand . . . hold on tight . . .
'cause together we can soar!

PRINCIPLE 7: ACHIEVE SUCCESS WITH DIGNITY

You will see that from the start we tried to dignify our race. If I
am to be condemned for that I am satisfied.
                                        —MARCUS GARVEY

Human dignity is more precious than prestige.
                                        —CLAUDE MCKAY

AT THE AGE of sixty-seven, C. Delores Tucker, founder and chairman
of the Black Women's Political Action Committee, is still a tough
woman. She is religious, aggressive, and never takes no for an answer.
Together with former Secretary of Education William Bennett, Ms.
Tucker brought the wrath of God down on Time Warner because they
were one of the main corporate forces behind gangsta rap.

Time Warner claimed that gangsta rap was free speech and a valid
form of art. C. Delores Tucker disagreed. She stood up at a Time Warner board meeting and asked HBO president Michael Fuchs and Time
Warner chairman Gerald Levin to read aloud the lyrics of a Snoop
Doggy Dogg rap. Neither man could get the words out of his mouth.

Ms. Tucker drove home her point. "If the words are too disgusting
for you to read aloud behind closed doors, among your own people,"
she asked, "why do you broadcast them everywhere in our commu-

nity?" Two months later, Time Warner got out of the gangsta rap business.

Dignity is that quality of high self-esteem and personal ethics that can drive individuals to succeed and groups to change history. Dignity has a moral and spiritual center. More than anything else, Rosa Parks was having a dignity fit when she refused to give up her bus seat and changed history.

Dignity helps you perform with excellence under extreme pressure. Jackie Robinson withstood cruel public abuse and became the most explosive and exciting ballplayer of his time, without ever losing his dignity.

Snoop Doggy Dogg has earned millions of dollars writing and recording gangsta rap, but has he succeeded with dignity? Judge for yourself, but consider this: How much dignity can a man have saying what he does about Black women? I believe such "artistic expression" takes one more chip out of our moral foundation and makes urban pathology even worse. At the same time, rap groups like Arrested Development, the Fugees, the Roots, and Poor Righteous Teachers use the same art form to tell a story of both oppression and opportunity. And now Snoop has made a turn for the better.

When I think of success with dignity, I think of people like Ernesta Procope, a New York insurance broker, Bob Holland, former CEO of Ben & Jerry's Ice Cream, Ron Brown, and Arthur Ashe. I also think of my dad, Walter Frederick Fraser, Sr., a proud West Indian who drove a cab in Brooklyn for forty years while trying to keep his wife, who was desperately ill and confined to a mental institution, connected to all of her children, all living in foster homes. Somehow my dad managed to do that, to the benefit of all of us. His was a hard road indeed. But he knew the right thing, and he did it.

We all know men and women of dignity, people whose self-worth has nothing to do with material goods or the opinion of others. Rich or poor, they know that success in life is never a one-step deal. It is a journey of many steps. Take pride in each step, the person of dignity tells us, for this is what life's about. The destination is secondary.

3

KEY BUILDING BLOCKS FOR ECONOMIC SUCCESS

"Blacks use wealth for pleasure, Whites use wealth for power. Power lasts longer than pleasure."

—Raymond St. Jacques

"No finance, no romance!"

—Traditional saying

I HAVE TALKED about the special power each of us has within that propels us toward success. But I'm not blind. I know the problems and liabilities that ravage Black America. I've been there, seen them, lived through them, and, like all African Americans, I continue to struggle with some of them.

The kinds of liabilities I'm talking about are the same concerns that everyone in our community talks about all the time: lack of money, racism, crime, poverty, mediocrity, inadequate training, backbiting, envy, lack of trust, and poor products and services.

If you flip the complaints over, however, you can turn them into a series of building blocks for economic success. None requires a national imperative, only a personal commitment to change.

BUILDING BLOCK 1: RACIAL RECONCILIATION

IN A 1997 Gallup poll the majority of 1,289 Blacks and 1,680 whites surveyed agreed on one thing: Race relations will always be a problem in America. Why? I believe because at the core of our being and culture we are both tribal and narcissistic. We love ourselves and are most comfortable with those who look like us and share our values and traditions. It's human nature to favor your own. We see this played out in our entertainment, sports, and socializing choices. Of course, this is no reason to hate someone outside of your culture or to believe you are better than others. It's also no reason to place a superior value on your own cultural identity. We know that kind of thinking is the foundation of racism and supremacy ideology.

Most major polls also show that while admittedly still a problem, race relations and tolerance are improving in America. But isolated acts of racism continue to be magnified under the intense scrutiny of mass media. People are fascinated by extremes and sensationalism sells. Over all, I don't think racism is increasing in America but is only more intensely reported, which in itself seems to generate fear and loathing. I believe history demonstrates that Blacks—because of our moral and spiritual grounding—are uniquely suited to take the lead in improving race relations. But African Americans may rightly ask, "Why should we always have to go the extra mile?" We could debate that question endlessly on a moral plane, but when it comes to business, the answer is clear: Because it's to our benefit to do so. No one can afford racism—not Blacks, whites, Latinos/as, Asians, East Indians, or Native Americans. The simple fact is that racism is morally wrong and bad for business.

The job we need to do in America requires a marketplace bigger than our own community, which means that we must work with and through other people. We do not control the capital markets, the job market, the political/judicial system, communications, science, technology, or the educational system. To be fairly represented in these institutions, we need cooperation from others.

Yet some of us believe that all white people are racists, even those who have stood up all their lives for civil rights and liberal agendas. I disagree. In my experience, many white people are willing and able to judge individuals on the content of their character. Insisting that these folks must be racists underneath, despite any evidence to the contrary, is insulting to them and detrimental to us.

I've also met many white people, as well as people of other races, who would like to improve their relationship with us but are hampered by their own stereotypical thinking and simply do not know what to do. We can reach out to these people, and it's important that we do so. Alliances among people of good will are the only way to overcome the actions of that small group of intractable racists whose goal is to oppress or eradicate people of color.

The most successful African Americans I know balance racial pride and solidarity with doing everything they can to heal racial hatred and prejudice.

We have everything we need to produce racial harmony in America, including the greatest political and judicial system in the world and the greatest opportunity for collaborative economics. All we need for racial reconciliation is a *personal* model that is shared by all. We can begin by forgiving each other (I didn't say forget the past), before we destroy ourselves with hate, envy, and mistrust. That means we have to forgive white people as a whole and begin to judge each by the content of his or her character, just as we wish to be judged.

I believe that committed and close personal friendships are foremost on the road to racial understanding. Everyone, of every age and every social and educational background, can achieve this. If you are Black and do not have a close white friend, go out and get yourself one. If you are white and do not have a close Black friend, do the same. Yes, I know, we can't pluck our friends off street corners. But each of us should go out of our way to meet people from different cultures and races at work, in the neighborhood, and where we shop. We have to reach out and take the risk of talking to people. Forget about what your friends say. Because of my light, bright skin color, I've had racial epithets directed at me from both sides. I've been called "Oreo" by Blacks and "nigger-lover" by whites. Who cares?

Here's my formula for making friends across the color aisle:

Invite someone to dinner in your home.
If you are white, visit a Black church several times a year. If you are
    Black, do the reverse.

Keep your hand on the plow. New friendships like these require extended effort because they can easily break down over misunderstandings, disappointment, and sometimes defensiveness. Like marriages, friendships are not honeymoons. But it's worth hanging in there, because the rewards are great. Be sincere, open, and honest with the people you meet. Spend time together, doing and talking about things both related and unrelated to issues of race. Be a little forgiving about inadvertent comments stemming from ignorance. Take the time to listen and truly understand both sides.

If you are white, open yourself up a little more to our reality. We know a lot more about you than you know about us. You can read our literature (as you're doing right now) and join our organizations. (Yes, you are welcome to join the NAACP, the Urban League, National Minority Supplier Council, and others.) Share what you learn with your family and friends, especially when someone says something out of line. The Gallup poll mentioned above reported that 75 percent of whites surveyed said they had at least one close Black friend and 59 percent of Blacks said they had at least one close white friend.

The most successful Black people I know in America have close personal friendships with all kinds of people. Ron Brown and Reginald Lewis knew this. John H. Johnson, Bob Johnson, Vernon Jordan, and Dorothy Height know it as well. Yes, some of my best friends are white, Latino/a, Asian, and Jewish. Some of my kids' best friends are too. Are yours?

BUILDING BLOCK 2: EXCELLENCE

SPEAKING OF MY sons, on a few occasions Kyle and Scott laid "discrimination" on me as a reason for failing in school or getting low grades. After careful and respectful investigation of each complaint, I found no basis for their claim, other than their lack of personal commitment to do what was required.

When I questioned them further about such claims, it turned out to be outside influences and the frequent and reckless public use of such a diatribe that prompted them to test its effectiveness on me as an excuse. When "the dog ate my homework" didn't work, they tried something that was close to home. It didn't work for them, and sooner rather than later, it won't work for us in spite of its persistence.

We cannot have the lowest SAT scores, regardless of family income, or the lowest GPAs, or have over half of our primary and secondary schoolteachers failing the annual state competency examinations and still talk about excellence to America. (Even if in some states such exams have been skewed against them, they still have to do better than everyone else.) Our parents and grandparents told us we had to be better prepared. They were right then and they're still right; if you are Black and mediocre in America you had better leave, because you will be marginalized and ultimately destroyed. Those with Third World skills will earn Third World wages in the twenty-first century.

We know the number-one obsession in America is the hype of racism, but the number-one issue is profit through excellence. In most cases excellence inevitably wins. When racism is legitimately "ruling," everybody loses. Ask Texaco, Denny's, and numerous others who have been caught in the act. Therefore, focus on excellence through preparedness, and most of the time you will prevail.

BUILDING BLOCK 3: SUPERIOR PERFORMANCE STARTS WITH HELP

IF YOU'RE BLACK and you want to succeed in America, there is no room for mediocrity. You have to be twice as good as the competition even to be considered equal. It's a hard fact. Yet we know that many of us do turn in mediocre performances on SATs and in our jobs. Many of our businesses leave something to be desired as well.

One woman wrote to me complaining about her business problems. Here is her letter, verbatim.

Dear Mr. Frasier:

I meet you in person at a seminar at Avon Corp. on June 26, 1995. I was very impress with your speech about networking in the African-American community, so I send my $6.00 and got the New York networking boo. I wrote and call about two dozen prospect form that book and I personally want you to know not one have answer my eltter or return my phone call. I strongly believe in networking and helping one another. I am a personal image consultant and must of my client are thou networking.
Sincerely Yoursm
XXXX, Consultant

And her business was as an image consultant!
I called her. I thanked her for coming to the event, congratulated her on her business, and expressed my appreciation that she took the

time to write. Then I asked for her permission to give her a little constructive criticism of the letter itself.

"Oh, yes, please," she said.

I was straightforward. "The grammar isn't what it should be. In fact, there are twelve typos in the letter. If the letters you sent to the two dozen prospects you mentioned were like this one, I'm not surprised that you didn't get a positive response. Your words and your writing are part of your image, and you are in the business of personal image building."

We then read the letter together over the telephone. Part of her problem was carelessness—she had not proofread the letter nor asked anyone else to read it before sending it—and part was lack of skills. She was embarrassed. We laughed a little and went on from there.

Finding someone who will take the time to critique our efforts in a positive way is an important step toward superior performance. Listening to their suggestions and acting on their advice is the next step.

BUILDING BLOCK 4: THE POWER OF FORGIVENESS

DESPITE THE WORST kind of oppression, most African Americans have always managed to forgive their oppressors and move on.

Everyone runs into life's buzz saws at one time or another. Those who are able to forgive go the farthest in life because they use their energy to move forward. Those unable to forgive, those who continuously see themselves as victimized, become paralyzed. They turn rage inward. All of their energy becomes dissipated. They see a future with no hope.

When we talk about forgiveness, we're talking about forgiving all kinds of sins committed against us—from ordinary hurt feelings all the way to robbery and racism.

Forgiveness benefits the one who forgives by releasing fear and anger and making it possible to move forward. The principle applies, regardless of the circumstances. Nelson Mandela's ability to forgive white South Africans for two hundred years of Black oppression and thirty years of inhumane imprisonment is a remarkable example of forgiveness.

Forgiveness is not easy. It means giving up all claims on the one who has hurt us and letting go of the emotional consequences of that hurt. It means being able to wipe the slate clean, to release others from a debt, and to personally accept reconciliation. Only then are we in a position to create meaningful, successful lives.

BUILDING BLOCK 5: TRUST BUILDS YOUR EMOTIONAL INTELLIGENCE

SOME PEOPLE SAY it's smart to trust no one, especially in business. I believe the opposite is true. The most successful among us trust people first and continue to trust them until they demonstrate absolutely that they cannot be trusted. By following this principle, you will be burned occasionally, but not often. The vast majority of people will go out of their way to live up to the trust you put in them.

You must learn how to listen, persuade, exercise patience and restraint, offer sympathy, feel empathy, ask questions, be polite, and recover from the emotional assaults common to daily life. Today, people call this "emotional intelligence" and it's every bit as important as IQ.

Many African Americans need remedial help in this area. Many Black folks are easily offended. We are sensitive to the slightest igging (being ignored, being disrespected, being discounted). We take everything personally. We do it with each other, and we do it with white folks. Being constantly on the alert for insults and second-guessing other people's motives uses up valuable energy and can be a drag on momentum toward success.

To advance in life, you must solicit help from others. There are no exceptions to this rule. And to get help you must trust others and be trustworthy yourself. Trust is the basis for building meaningful and productive relationships across the board.

BUILDING BLOCK 6: GIVE PRAISE AND AFFIRMATION TO ALL

I RECENTLY MET a young brother who shines shoes at a large hotel in Dallas, Texas. He caught me going to my room one evening with the following rap:

"Hey, my man, that's a beautiful suit you got on there."

"Thanks," I snapped back, flashing a broad smile.

"Why don't you let me give you a shine to match that beautiful suit and bright smile? It'll only take a minute."

His conversation for the next five minutes included a series of short, pointed questions:

"What do you do for a living, sir?"

"I'm a speaker and author."

"Sounds interesting, I bet you're great at it, too."

When I got up from his chair I was infected by his enthusiasm and his affirming questions and remarks. Was he a great salesman? Sure he was, but what mattered was how he made me feel and the quality of service he provided.

I gave him a two-dollar tip on a three-dollar shoe shine. I complimented him on his work. He replied, "Give God the glory." The brother made my day.

African Americans who go out of their way to affirm others have a jump start on success. The truth is, we often do not get much praise from sources outside our community. If we fail to emphasize the positive in one another, who else will do it?

One way to give affirmation is to stop petty, destructive criticism of each other. The most violent weapon we carry is our mouth. The Hebrew Bible says that talking trash and spreading rumors is akin to murdering someone. It's true. My father always said, "The words you speak today are waiting for you tomorrow." Once spoken, words never go away. For better or for worse, they roll around our minds forever and ever.

We should all concentrate on making our words "for the better." This is especially important in our community. Professor James D. Johnson has studied the effects of negative information on Black high school and college students. The study showed that young African Americans are able to dismiss racist messages from whites. But the same messages, when repeated by a Black individual, will sink in.

In a very practical way, bad talk will come back to haunt you and has the potential to hurt your business and all of your efforts toward building success. Conversely, positive talk can always help you. Experienced sellers use it as a strategy.

Affirmation can change your thinking, your attitude, and, most important, your heart. Affirmation is merely a positive declaration of something you believe to be true.

How many times have you bragged to people about the results of an idea you are either planning or dreaming, before you actually completed it? You're affirming your ideas. I try to use this method with my friends and family every chance I get. Words are powerful.

The criticism or praise we heap on each other is a reflection of our attitude toward life and how we feel about ourselves. We must look for ways to uplift every person that comes into our lives.

- Tell people when they are doing a good job or making a sincere effort.
- Be nice, be congenial, smile, laugh—you'll get more done.
- Use your sense of humor.
- Stop always looking for the things that are wrong.
- Hug somebody each day. Find a reason to put your arms around someone and say something positive.
- Stop criticizing. If deep down you get the slightest bit of pleasure when making a criticism, don't do it, but if it hurts you as much as it will the person you've targeted, then it's okay. Always be sensitive about what you say; you can hurt people for life. However, that doesn't mean we can never speak out about behaviors and practices we believe to be wrong. When it comes to issues such as gangsta rap, urban pathology, and so on, by all means, speak up. Write letters. Let your opinion be known.
- Pay attention to people. Listening is the ultimate compliment and "act of connection." Listen for the "meaning" between the words.
- Share information and knowledge freely.
- Roll with the punches. Everybody makes mistakes. It's okay if it doesn't kill you. Work on compassionate solutions.

Attitude is everything. I am convinced that life is 10 percent what happens to me and 90 percent how I react to it.

Finally, enthusiasm is infectious. I've seen more great things done on sheer enthusiasm than on any other source. It is said that your "music" (enthusiasm and energy) is more powerful than your words.

BUILDING BLOCK 7: EDUCATE YOURSELF AND BECOME A SOURCE OF KNOWLEDGE

ELIJAH MUHAMMAD HAS said, "We must educate ourselves and our children to the rich power of knowledge which has elevated every people who have sought and used it."

African Americans who are succeeding are those who have made a lifelong commitment to learning and bettering themselves each day.

I RECEIVED AN invitation from my good friend Dr. David Whitaker, to take part in an "African Reincorporation Ceremony." As it turned out, I was formally being asked, as a part of traditional African practice, to share with my neighborhood sisters and brothers what I had learned during my extensive travels away from home.

David had invited fifty of my closest family and friends to this ceremony in his Afrocentric gift shop in a large, specially designed room resembling an African village. On the night of the ceremony, David gave me a beautiful African robe to wear. African drums played softly in the background, and I sat on a replica of a king's throne. For the first time in my life, I felt quite regal indeed. David had provided several people in the audience with special ritualistic words to repeat to start the ceremony.

I told of my impressions of Black America beyond Cleveland and my experiences while writing and promoting *Success Runs in Our Race*. After an hour or so, African music was performed, I signed books, and we talked together and ate delicious snacks. It was more than a book signing. It was a ritual, a revived African oral practice of sharing important knowledge and information with our extended family.

I believe that wherever two or more African Americans gather together, we should share and tell each other all that we know about the world and its opportunities. To do this, each of us must become a source of knowledge and information for others. This requires shifting to an archival as well as an oral culture. It means writing down our thoughts, knowledge, experiences, learned skills, recipes, poetry, and words of wisdom. This is important because we would not want this valuable knowledge to be lost or stolen.

So many of us die with our best stuff inside of us. Les Brown tells us, "The graveyard is full of good ideas and knowledge that no one shared." The two greatest gifts we could pass on to our children would be our diaries and journals and our books. Could you imagine how incredible you would feel if you could open up a journal or diary written by your great-great-grandparents?

If we are truly to become sources of information and knowledge for each other, quite frankly we must turn off the damn television and read. It is not possible to be intelligent in America and not read. In spite of a massive literary output (over forty thousand books are published each year) and the existence of huge bookstores and libraries where you get to take the books home for free, Americans still don't read enough. The average American reads only one book per year. If African Americans read just one book per month, in five years we would each have read sixty books—and the average American would have read only five. Who's going to be smarter or better prepared?

The busiest retail stores in our communities ought to be bookstores, but instead they are either the bars or the video stores. Recently a Barnes & Noble superstore and a Blockbuster Video store opened in a new strip mall in Shaker Heights, a racially mixed, affluent community in Cleveland. Within a year, the bookstore closed while the video store thrived. The only way to get our children hooked on books is to read ourselves. We cannot tell our children to read if we're watching TV four hours a day.

The future for all of us will be about skills security, not job security. A commitment to lifelong learning and personal growth and development will contribute significantly to inherent strengths.

OUR GREATEST STRENGTHS

WE ARE MORALLY grounded and spiritually rooted. Instinctively we have faith and hope in a brighter day.

WE ARE CREATIVE, as reflected in our high level of skills and achievements in the creative and performance arts.

WE PERSEVERE, fueled by common sense, street smarts, mother wit, and a strong sense of survival. We are focused and flexible in our quest for freedom and equality.

WE ARE COMMUNAL and loyal to those who sincerely reach out to us.

WE ARE FORGIVING of those who have hurt us the most.

OUR ADMITTED WEAKNESSES

WE TEND TO distrust each other, due to a long history of tactics used to divide and conquer us.

As a whole, we tend to have low self-esteem and race-esteem, due to hundreds of years of negative reinforcement.

We shy away from risk, choosing instead to safely conserve and protect the material resources we worked hard to acquire.

* * *

CONTINUING TO ACCEPT our weaknesses by blaming them on historical oppression, conspiracies, plots, and racism gets us nowhere. Somebody else may have forced us into this corner, but we are the only ones who can get us out. All anyone can control is his or her own attitudes and action. The issue is no longer what "they" are doing or not doing; the issue is what we are doing, and who's doing it!

In 1996, in an effort to understand Black men's employment problems, Philip Moss of the University of Massachusetts at Lowell and Chris Tilly of the Russell Sage Foundation in New York interviewed fifty-six employers. Their findings, reported in *The Wall Street Journal*, revealed that businesses ranked Black men poorly in terms of their "soft skills"—personality, behavior, and attitude—rather than formal or technical knowledge. "It's partly stereotype, partly cultural gap, and partly an accurate perception of the skills that many less-educated Black men bring to the labor market," they said. "It's inevitably subjective."

Nonetheless, we know that attitude is as important as, if not more important than, technical skills. Give me someone with a good attitude and I can teach them almost anything.

While changing an attitude can be very hard, it can also be very simple. The only action required takes place in your own heart and mind, places to which you have ready access.

TEN IMPORTANT CHANGES

TAKEN IN CONTEXT, these are the ten most important changes that must be deeply internalized and acted upon if we are to compete successfully with other cultural groups.

1. We must see hard work in all things not as a necessary evil but as a way to escape poverty and as a wish of God.

2. We must have an attitude toward all work that insists on precision and attention to detail. In other words, high personal achievement is the goal.

3. We must see high educational achievement as something that is greatly valued; therefore we must push ourselves and our children.

4. We must be committed to lifelong learning and see learning from others as a way to build cooperation and partnerships.

5. We must now focus on wealth and job creation by leveraging our God-given strengths to overcome our weaknesses.

6. We must see saving and investing as a commitment to future generational prosperity.

7. We must mobilize and share the intellectual resources of all Black people in service of our race.

8. We must have a bottom-up (community-based) approach to problem-solving, instead of a top-down approach.

9. Each must take personal responsibility and have a positive attitude toward solving our problems to facilitate change.

10. We must hold to the moral path and refuse to participate in the generalized decay in values in business, family, and community.

SAVING FOR AND INVESTING IN OUR FUTURE

SEVERAL YEARS AGO, at the ripe old age of fifty, I decided to simplify my lifestyle and downsize my cost of living. For years, I had lived above my means: a big home in Pepper Pike (the richest community in Cleveland), fancy foreign cars, expensive Caribbean vacations, and at least eight credit cards stuffed in my wallet, all maxed out to the limit. I was living the American dream but was a slave to creditors, a four-thousand-dollar monthly house note, and a money-hungry, underfunded new business. I was spending over forty thousand dollars in annual interest payments and, as you might imagine, my savings were nil. I was scheduled for a rude awakening and my dream dissolved into a nightmare when I ran out of money.

From that pain came a new vision, a new purpose, and a network of supportive friends that set me on my feet. Although my annual income tripled in the coming years, I decided to live substantially below my means and to invest in the future. Like me, too many of us are either living above or barely within our means by spending every dime we earn. Few of us restrict our spending to necessities and invest the rest. But if we don't save, we are flirting with financial disaster and making it that much harder to create wealth within our families and within our race.

Cheryl Broussard writes, "African Americans are among the nation's richest consumers, but they're not saving for the future." She bases this statement on figures showing that on average Black Americans save about 2 percent of their earnings, as compared to the general population, which saves about 4 percent. Among certain ethnic groups, savings are even higher, with Asian Americans averaging a 15 to 25 percent savings rate. The problem is that we haven't been taught how to save and budget properly. As relative newcomers to the credit card market, African Americans are easily swayed by billions of dollars in advertising that tells us to spend, spend, spend. We look for instant gratification without implementing strategies to release ourselves from what can become shackles of debt.

The key to wealth creation and economic success is debt reduction and smart financial planning. If beginning at the age of twenty-one, you earned $33,000 per year and began investing $250 per month (the cost of three packs of cigarettes a day) in blue-chip stocks, by the time you turned sixty-five you would be a millionaire. My good friend Henry just retired from General Motors after thirty years of service as a computer specialist and ended up with a $987-per-month retirement check and a gold watch. His millionaire status will have to wait because his investment strategy was similar to my own. He is still young enough and smart enough to change course and he has.

When carefully analyzed, a significant part of Black wealth is going into thirty-year home mortgages, interest payments on multiple credit cards, and a "designer, name brand" lifestyle. Blacks are the most aggressive consumers in the country and our spending sprees are the target of heavy advertising that encourages us to spend more and more and more! If this spending doesn't stop, most of us will have to work beyond the age of sixty-five and will not have the resources to invest in our own businesses or to leave anything to our children. Here's what I've done to put a small dent in this problem; I hope it encourages you to trim the fat in your budget.

I've reduced my business expenses by 50 percent—my office is smaller, I hire fewer people, and I try to pay as I go. I've downsized my taste in cars and drive a well-maintained Honda LX that's great on gas and low on maintenance. I've moved to a smaller house, which has reduced my house note and other associated expenses by more than 50 percent. I cut up all but one credit card and never charge more than I'm budgeted to "pay in full," which has allowed me to save and invest at least 5 percent of my income each month. Most important, I established a detailed monthly business and household budget, which I have stuck to. I've also found a way to commit to paying off my new thirty-year mortgage in one third the time, which will turn me into a millionaire. (I explain this "secret" method on page 52.)

HOW A THIRTY-YEAR MORTGAGE CAN TURN YOU INTO A MILLIONAIRE*

It's simple to do. Just pay your mortgage every two weeks instead of monthly (that alone takes off about seven years of payments), but with each payment double the "principal" portion. (You must remember to flag this incremental principal payment "apply to principal only.")

Since the first several years of your mortgage is mostly interest, the increase in your principal will be small at first; but as the interest goes down, the principal goes up. Using this method, you will pay off your mortgage in about ten years, saving you tens of thousands of dollars in interest.

Then, for the next twenty years (the balance of time left on your old mortgage), take the money you were formerly paying and invest it in the capital markets. Here's how the numbers compute for an average mortgage of $100,000:

Old Method (30 years)
$100,000 @ 7.625% Interest

BEGINNING BALANCE	AVG. MONTHLY PAYMENT	TOTAL PAYMENTS	TOTAL INTEREST
$100,000	$708	$280,004	$180,004

New Method (10 Years)
$100,000 @ 7.625% Interest

BEGINNING BALANCE	AVG. MONTHLY PAYMENT	TOTAL PAYMENTS	TOTAL INTEREST
$100,000	$1,194	$149,586	$49,586

INTEREST SAVINGS: $130,418

240 Monthly Investments of $1,194 each
20th year return at:

4.0%:	$ 439,389
8.0%:	707,979
12.0%:	1,192,983

It is said that those who don't understand interest pay it, and that those who *do* understand interest collect it! Get with the plan!

*Based on computations from the Financial Fitness Centers. Average monthly payments do not equal totals because of the fluctuating ratios between principal and interest payments over the life of the mortgage. The totals are accurate.

STRATEGIES TO CREATE WEALTH

MANAGING PERSONAL AND household expenses better isn't the whole story, not by far. We need to begin betting on the "white man's race-track"—investing in the capital markets instead of the Lotto and doing business with investment banks instead of the cash exchange on the corner. Our goal should be one million Black millionaires within the next generation, which would mean one trillion dollars in accumulated wealth to solve our own problems. The majority of our millionaires (which I estimate at eight to ten thousand) are physicians, athletes, and entertainers. But you don't have to have talent to get rich, just common sense, patience, and a disciplined work ethic that will lead to fulfillment of our individual and collective financial goals. Can we accomplish this? Of course we can, one person, one family, and one day at a time, starting right now!

Hey! Why should our wealth be deposited or invested exclusively in mainstream institutions? Asians and Latinos/as have invested billions of dollars in banks they own and control. In south Florida, Blacks own one bank, while Latinos/as own thirty banks. In less than a generation Latino banks in that area have generated assets of over eight hundred million dollars and earned not just interest but respect and admiration from the outside world. We must support Black financial institutions that have consistently demonstrated business excellence under the most difficult and competitive circumstances. From my vantage point, here are a few things each of us can do that will enhance our personal, institutional, and community wealth.

What Blacks Can Do

- Make more deposits in Black-owned financial institutions where available, i.e., paychecks, small business accounts, etc.
- Open savings accounts and save more (at least 5 percent of monthly income). Pay yourself first!
- Take out more "qualified" loans, i.e., real estate, collateral-based small business loans, etc., with Black-owned financial institutions.
- Improve your credit and regularly balance your checkbook.
- Invest in well-managed financial instruments, i.e., mutual funds, bonds, CDs; start or join investment clubs.
- Buy stock in healthy Black-owned institutions (*Black Enterprise* now publishes a list of publicly traded Black-owned companies).

- If you are a financial professional with solid educational credentials and experience, make your services available to a Black institution in need of topflight talent. Our best and brightest are often making downtown banks and investment houses wealthier.
- Use respected and financially healthy Black banks, brokers, and investment houses for professional, small business, and Black church financial dealings.
- Invest in long-term instruments like mutual funds, CDs, or stocks issued by Black institutions. These products are protected by the same laws and standards that apply to mainstream investments and are generally priced very competitively.

What Black Financial Institutions Must Do

- Focus on urban customers by expanding retail services, i.e.,
    open more branches
  provide more ATMs in our neighborhoods
  issue secured credit cards and debit cards to help us establish
    credit
  offer credit-management courses
  provide low-cost check cashing
- Establish strategic alliances with Black churches, i.e.,
    support church-based Community Development Corporations
    (CDCs)
  put ATMs in the church for electronic tithing, deposits, and withdrawals
  provide technical support to help with church finances
  provide "pledge loans" for church expansion projects
- Provide "collateral-based" small business loans.
- Establish nonprofit affiliates to help with community restoration, wealth creation, debt reduction, and small business development workshops.
- Hire Black suppliers and technical support services, i.e., lawyers, accountants, insurance agents, etc.
- Offer educational loans.
- Consolidate where "proximity" to another Black bank is diluting market share.
- Focus on the new low- to moderate-income housing that is now

being supported, subsidized, and/or guaranteed by government
agencies.
- Network and build relationships with foreign investors,
  i.e., Africa, Caribbean, China, and Latin America.
- Open new banks in first- and second-tier cities where the Black
  population exceeds 20 percent.
- Recruit, hire, and pay competitive wages to the best and brightest
  Black financial talent.
- Start a Black-owned property/casualty insurance firm on both east
  and west coasts.
- Increase the marketing and promotion of church-based credit un
  ions, and expand the services to more effectively compete with
  banks. Consolidate or merge assets where possible.

Few of the preceding suggestions are new. They all cost money and
time. Few financial institutions can accomplish every objective, but
each idea represents a significant opportunity to expand our wealth by
supporting financial institutions that provide jobs, training, and upward mobility for many of our professionals. More important, it sends
a profound message that we are serious about our business.

BUSINESS ETHICS AND BLACKS
OR
Don't Do "Anything" for Profit

BALZAC ONCE SAID, "Behind every great fortune is a crime." It's still
true that too many individuals and organizations will do anything for
profit. In a series of national surveys over the last fifteen years people
were asked "Does business balance profit and public interest?" In
1968, 70 percent of the respondents said yes. In 1994, only 26 percent said yes.

Unethical treatment of Blacks in the workplace and ethical deterior-
ation in business have been historical problems in democratic capitalism. A democratic society has inherent weaknesses, and maintaining
high moral ideals in its business institutions is one of them. It is said
that when you mix two incompatible substances (money and ethics)
you get a suspension. And no matter how you stir them you'll never
arrive at a solution. Too often businesses, large and small, pander to

and exploit humanity's natural impulses toward sexuality, violence, aggression, and greed, all in the name of "giving the public what it wants." Ethicist Michael Novak calls this "a form of prostitution." He is right; we must limit Black participation in these negative business behaviors and continue to find creative ways to make a profit and make a difference.

The examples are egregious. Fortunately, there are examples on the other side as well, companies and people driven by values rather than profit alone. Companies such as The Body Shop and Ben & Jerry's prove that you can do good while doing well. So do people like athlete Hakeem Olajuwan of the Houston Rockets, who demands that sneakers marketed with his name on them do not sell for more than thirty-five dollars, and people like Oprah and Cosby, who reinvest millions in Black colleges.

I believe that in the future more Americans will be impacted by social entrepreneurism and will aggressively support businesses and individuals who have a vision and mission dictated by values that create products and services that fulfill real human needs.

Someone once said that any formula for success is better than no formula. Here's my four-part formula for a successful ethically based business: First, start with clarity. What do you stand for and believe in? In a study of disadvantaged youth, Dr. Sandra Taylor, professor at Atlanta University, asked, "Would you rather be rich and not so smart? Or smart and not so rich?" Ninety-three percent of the children answered, "Smart."

Then she asked, "What major contribution would you like to be remembered for?" Seventy-four percent answered, "Helping others"; 22 percent said, "Excel in career"; and 4 percent answered, "Being myself." At an early age, kids have clarity. They know what's important.

Second, competence. The great motivational speaker Brian Tracy asks, "What is your competitive advantage in life, in business? What could or should it be?" What one skill or ability if you became excellent at it would make the most difference in your life and in the lives of others?

The third part is creativity. Are you creative enough to create new wealth and new job opportunities, as well as provide real value, quality, and service at a competitive but fair price? This is a lot easier said than done; too many people look for shortcuts and an easy way out on this part. Don't let that happen to you. Be creative, but honest.

One final thought about Black economic success. In spite of the numerous opportunities you are going to read about, greater success will not come to Blacks until more are horizontally and vertically networking: reaching down and lifting up, reaching back and pulling forward those who are less fortunate. For many Blacks of significant means, this new consciousness has become a cause célèbre, and as a result, their rewards have been significant and deeply satisfying. For those who have acted alone and ignored the need to give, share, and serve, thus eroding the foundation for future generations, the price must be social isolation and ostracism. The new Black status will be your caring, not your car. Your money will simply be a measurement of your capacity to give and serve. Bragging rights and recognition will go only to those who reinvest their high personal achievement into the community to improve the human condition.

The fourth part of my formula is courage. Winston Churchill once said, "Courage is the foremost of all virtues, because upon it all others depend." Do you have the courage to take risks, do the right thing when no one's looking, and walk your talk?

I know you do.

4

EDUCATION AND TRAINING: KNOWLEDGE IS POWER

Without education there is no leisure,
without leisure there is no thought,
without thought, there is no freedom.
— HOWARD THURMAN

All of our Mercedes Benzes and Halston frocks
will not hide our essential failure as a
generation of Black "haves" who did not
protect the Black future during our watch.
— MARIAN WRIGHT EDELMAN

MARY S. MARTIN
FOUNDER AND PRESIDENT
S. R. MARTIN COLLEGE PREPARATORY
  SCHOOL
SAN FRANCISCO, CALIFORNIA

Mary Martin, the youngest of ten children, was the only one in her family to finish college. Her dad was self-employed, while her mom ran the household. Mary's older sisters worked so that Mary could go to Xavier University, a historically Black college where she was educated by committed teachers who had high expectations for their students. Mary was to become a teacher determined to give Black students the chance to learn with the same support and care she had been given. She knew from personal experience how damaging a teacher's low expectations could be. A white professor once told Mary that she would never make it in college. Today she has a master's degree in education and has established a college prep school for Black children, called S. R. Martin College Preparatory School (SRMCPS) in memory of her late husband Shedrick R. Martin. The success of SRMCPS speaks for itself: Since the school's opening in 1990, all of the graduates have been accepted into colleges or universities.

Success did not come easily. Mary stresses that to start a school, "Understanding business is just as important as understanding education." She advises taking business courses and becoming an experienced school administrator to run a school the right way— like a business. For Mary, profit is important but not the key reason she is in this business. "I do it because I have the sincere desire to raise the intellect of Black children even if I have to stand alone in this quest." SRMCPS started with thirteen students, and now has forty-nine.

Mary Martin loves what she is doing because she is doing what she loves. She sees a future for Black children because she *is* the future for Black children. "We will need thousands more committed Black educators in years to come, to help take on a holistic approach to basic education." During graduation ceremonies, Mary Martin reads to her students the following farewell:

> As you accept your diploma, severing your relations with high school, you step into new relationships with parents, friends, and the world. The "apron strings" that have been lengthened as you grew up must now be cut. You have earned more than freedom from high school. You have proven yourself trustworthy, dependable, and ma- ture enough to try your own wings, but we will be "on call" through- out your life.
>
> Your are fully accountable to God, your heavenly Father, who loves you far more than we can; who has riches in store beyond your comprehension, but who expects much more of someone as talented and capable as you.
>
> We commit you to His care as the fire of the world tests the gold

of your character and we will be in prayer as you face the challenge of tomorrow.

FAVORITE BIBLICAL PASSAGE:

The Lord is my light and my salvation;
whom shall I fear?
the Lord is the strength of my life;
of whom shall I be afraid?

—Psalm 27:1

ON THE FIRST day of school, Jean Thompson told her students, "Boys and girls, I love you all the same." But teachers sometimes lie, and Teddy Stollard was a boy that Jean Thompson did not like. He slouched, didn't pay attention, wore rumpled clothes, and smelled. Teddy's school records traced his steady decline. First Grade: "Shows promise in his work and has a good attitude, but a poor home situation." Second Grade: "He does what he is told, but too serious. Mother is terminally ill." Third Grade: "Falling behind in his work; he needs help. His mother died this year; father shows no interest." Fourth Grade: "In deep waters; withdrawn; in need of psychiatric counseling."

Jean Thompson tried to hide her dislike by not paying much attention to him. Christmas came, and the boys and girls brought their brightly wrapped presents and piled them on Jean Thompson's desk. Teddy's gift was wrapped in brown paper and held together with Scotch tape. When Ms. Thompson opened the package, a rhinestone bracelet, missing most of the stones, and a nearly empty bottle of perfume fell onto her desk.

The boys and girls began to giggle, but Ms. Thompson dabbed some of the perfume on her wrist and put on the bracelet. Taking their cue from their teacher, the children stopped laughing and switched their attention to the next gift.

At the end of the day, after the other children had left, Teddy lingered at her desk. "Ms. Thompson, all day long you smelled just like my mother. And her bracelet looks good on you, too." Teddy flushed and ran out of the room while Jean Thompson squeezed back tears and asked God to forgive her.

She began to tutor Teddy after school, and by the end of the year he had caught up with many of his classmates and even pulled ahead of some. He graduated from elementary school on schedule and continued to excel.

Several years later, Jean Thompson received this note:

Dear Ms. Thompson,

I'm graduating second in my high school class. I wanted you to be the first to know.

Love, Teddy

Four years later, she received another note:

Dear Ms. Thompson:

The university has not been easy, but I like it. I wanted you to be the first to know.

Love, Teddy

Four years later, another one:

Dear Ms. Thompson:

As of today, I am Theodore J. Stollard, M.D. How about that? I wanted you to be the first to know. I'm going to be married in July, and hope you will come and sit where my mother would have sat. You are the only family I have.

Love, Teddy

Jean Thompson went to Teddy's wedding and she sat where Teddy's mother would have sat, and no one had a better right to be there.

THIS IS ONE of my favorite true stories about the impact a teacher can have on a student and the rewards that come with the profession. I heard Marian Wright Edelman talk about Teddy and his teacher in one of her speeches, and I often use his story myself to encourage young people to pursue a teaching career. If you feel you have a bit of Jean Thompson in you, teaching could be your niche in a profession where African Americans are desperately needed.

Many of our children are not receiving the quality education necessary to prepare them for the increasingly complex world all of us are struggling to understand. The statistics are daunting: Four million young people are currently enrolled in inner-city schools where guards and metal detectors are commonplace. Many inner-city (read minority) students are failing—they can't read or write at grade level or pass state competency exams. Minority children make up 85 percent of the students enrolled in special education classes for kids with learning or development problems. Instead of demanding high academic standards, educators graduate students who cannot read or write.

As a parent, I am pained by the picture these numbers paint. We want the best for our kids and may go to extreme measures to provide what they need. Frustration over lack of quality teaching led one thirty-six-year-old Black mother to falsify her downtown address so that her five-year-old son could enroll in a suburban school district. She was sentenced to ninety days in jail for her crime, and when the judge asked why she had lied, she wept: "Because I wanted him to have a better life and a better education. I know I did wrong."

The example is extreme but for me crystallizes the deep concern we feel about our children's educational futures. We are right to deplore the poor state of their education, but we can't simply wring our hands and do nothing. We can and should take part in the educational lives of our children. We have in the past and we can in the future.

OUR EDUCATIONAL HERITAGE

WE HAVE A long educational tradition, dating as far back as the late 1700s when Black activists were establishing schools for African-American children. Forty-five years after Emancipation, 259 schools had been established in the South, often founded by Blacks with the assistance of white missionary teachers from the Northeast. In his moving memoir *The Substance of Things Hoped For*, the late Dr. Samuel Proctor, one of the foremost educators of the modern era, writes of his grandmother's experience as a young student attending the Hampton Institute of Virginia, a school founded for Indians and freed Blacks by Union Army General Samuel Armstrong.

"She was not afraid of being brainwashed or made 'White' by her teachers," Dr. Proctor writes. "She stood hopefully and willingly at the portals of her fuller emancipation, the freedom of the mind. Most impressive of all was the lofty expectation of these White New England teachers and the Black teachers they trained."

"Lofty expectations" is the key—you've heard it from Mary S. Martin and from Samuel Proctor. We need teachers who are committed to encouraging students—students like Teddy who are unwilling, unresponsive, and, on the surface, downright unpleasant. Studies show that African-American educators bring to the classroom a unique philosophy needed to wake up our little brothers and sisters. Our presence in the schools says, "I made it, so can you."

As African Americans, we share a common experience and cultural heritage. When I speak in schools, I always let the kids know I'm Black and that "I love them." And they always challenge me: "Are you really Black, Mr. Fraser? Do you really love us?" They are asking if I really care. And I tell them yes, yes, and yes.

But the sad news is that from 1971 to 1986, the number of African-American teachers declined dramatically. By 1992, only 6 percent of the teaching population in the United States was Black, and it is estimated that the number will drop to 5 percent by the year 2000.

1954: A STEP FORWARD OR BACKWARD?

IRONICALLY, THE 1954 Supreme Court decision that put an end to legalized school segregation contributed to the disappearance of Black teachers from the classroom. Certain states instituted hurdles, such as periodic competency testing skewed toward a white model, that made it difficult for Blacks to attain or renew teaching certificates. From 1954 to 1972, more than thirty-nine thousand African-American teachers lost their jobs, were demoted or forced to seek early retirement, or left teaching voluntarily to take advantage of careers opening up in business, government, and other industries. There are fewer African-American teachers today than in the early 1970s. Consequently, many African-American students graduate from high school and college without being taught by someone who shares their racial and cultural identity.

The opportunities are out there for us to join the ranks in an industry that, at a rate of 28 percent, is growing faster than nearly any other profession. Population growth, particularly in many western states, has forced school systems to increase staffing at all levels, and it is expected that 2.5 million teachers will be needed by the year 2000.

Educators are aggressively seeking African Americans, and particularly African-American men, to fill teaching positions and serve as role models for young Blacks who may lack positive adult influences in their lives. Bo Dailey, a graduate in aeronautical engineering at the University of Illinois, became a math teacher in rural North Carolina, although he could be making more money in some large corporation. Dailey told *Black Collegian* that he feels richly rewarded: "Beyond affecting the lives and skills of my students on a purely academic level through strong and dedicated teaching, as an African American male in a rural [community], I am able to be a unique, stable role model for all of my students."

The education industry offers a wide range of opportunities in virtually every imaginable setting, from private learning and reading centers and small charter schools that nurture a handful of private students to giant corporations looking to train personnel in highly specialized skills. We need to take up the challenge to educate our children.

The education industry divides roughly into five broad segments:

• Teachers and other professionals
• Executive, administrative, and managerial
• Administrative support
• Services
• Corporate trainers

Let's take a closer look at each.

TEACHERS

WE ALL HAVE stories of special people who have had a profound impact on our lives. You guessed it, many of these individuals were teachers. What makes certain teachers so memorable, and what qualities make them stand out in our minds?

To me, the essential quality of a good teacher is love—love of students, love of learning, and love of good, old-fashioned hard work. And when I say love, I mean love in action, not just words. Jean Thompson showed Teddy her love with the special tutoring and attention that pushed him toward medical school instead of the streets. All teachers, but particularly those in schools serving disadvantaged neighborhoods, must be patient, disciplined, and focused. Schools in poor communities are often overcrowded and understaffed without adequate supplies or equipment. You must love your work and feel a strong sense of commitment to the job or you risk suffering burnout.

Demands on teachers' time outside the classroom can be substantial and include supervising extracurricular activities, attending community meetings and parent-teacher conferences, and spending time after school hours preparing for class or reviewing student work. If you plan to teach at the college and university level, be prepared to spend time researching, writing articles and books, and pursuing advanced degrees. And teachers often take summer jobs to supplement their earnings during the two- to three-month summer vacation.

To keep going, you can't be watching the clock. Like all good teachers, you have to be in it for the work, not the money. One of my friends teaches tenth grade in an East Harlem high school where he spends several hours after class coaching the basketball team. A tall, lanky ex-Marine who played college ball, he loves shooting hoops with the guys and even coaches a summer league when school lets out. "I know a lot of these kids don't have positive male role models in their lives, and I come from the streets so I know where they're at," he says, explaining why he spends so much of his free time with students he already sees every day. "I like to show these guys that you can get respect without hanging out on street corners playing the fool." This teacher loves what he does, and he's teaching kids a lot more than just addition and subtraction. And I know he feels rewarded by his work. The question is, would you?

Preschool Teachers

OUT OF THE mouths of babes! I sometimes feel that I learn more from the preschool crowd than from professionals with enough degrees to wallpaper an office. Their curiosity, resilience, and sense of wonder over the simplest things refreshes and inspires me. If you feel drawn to our baby brothers and sisters, consider teaching the preschool and nursery school set. The rise in two-income families and the increase in the number of boomer babies (children born to baby boomers) is expected to continue, which means a lot of parents will be looking for quality pre-schooling for their youngsters.

About half of all three- to five-year-olds nationwide are enrolled in preschool programs, including Head Start, school-based pre-kindergarten programs, nursery schools, and private child care, and, according to the 1995 supplemental census, 3.4 million of these youngsters are African Americans. These kids need our special brand of tender, loving care. Study after study demonstrates the importance of the preschool stage to a child's development. Recent statistics show that inner-city children exposed to early education programs are less likely to be held back or placed in special education classes, or to drop out of school.

My own experience with Dorothy Johnson, a wonderful educator and friend, made me a firm believer in the value of providing young children with a positive, structured learning environment. Every morning at 6:30 A.M., my wife and I would arrive with our son Kyle at Dorothy's meticulously appointed Shaker Heights home. Although she was not related to us by blood, we called her Grandma Johnson. A big woman with a warm smile and a huge embrace, she loved taking care of children for young Black professional families like ours.

She would feed and play with Kyle and his "classmates," letting them pounce around her carpeted living room and amuse themselves with educational toys, activities, and television shows. Grandma's kids were nurtured, loved, and encouraged to explore and be creative. She had the patience of Job, which anyone who has cared for young children can appreciate. Grandma Johnson was a godsend for us and our Black neighbors. When Kyle turned three, he was fully prepared for preschool, thanks to Grandma Johnson's TLC.

Sad to say, many Black children are not as lucky as Kyle and don't get the early nurturing care that our son received. If you like young children, please consider joining the preschool ranks by teaching or by starting your own program. These are professional and business opportunities that need you and are waiting to explode.

The skills and training required to open or teach at the preschool/ after school level vary from state to state. Requirements can range from a high school diploma to a college degree in child development and early childhood education. The trend today is for all teachers to go on to earn advanced degrees. In fact, in school systems with high academic standards, a master's degree may be required to teach at this level.

Primary and Secondary School Teachers

FROM KINDERGARTEN TO high school graduation, these educators cover every subject area from algebra to zoology. Elementary, junior high, and high school teachers are in demand, with the greatest need for specialists in math, science, and bilingual education.

Elementary school teachers teach the fundamental skills and study habits that support the students' educational future. The best teachers also encourage students to explore their creativity. One of my son's grade school teachers captivated the class by asking each student to prepare a dish of rice from a particular country and teach the class a little about the geography and culture. The kids had so much fun cooking and eating the various rice dishes, they forgot they were learning at the same time.

Junior high and high school teachers build on the basics by delving more deeply into subjects like chemistry, physics, foreign languages, and calculus. Good high school teachers not only instruct but also guide adolescents toward adulthood, lending an ear to their academic and personal problems and helping prepare them for colleges and careers.

Steady growth is predicted, with 2.2 million jobs forecast for the next decade. Because African Americans will likely fill only 5 percent of these positions, educators are scrambling to attract qualified candidates. These teaching jobs are available if you have the credentials and the desire. You'll need a bachelor's degree in education from an approved teacher-training program, plus state certification.

Requirements for certification vary from state to state and may also depend on the particular school system or district. Usually states allow teachers to teach pending the completion of any course work necessary for certification. Regardless of the requirements, many teachers with BAs take extra courses or earn higher degrees to sharpen their skills, meet the competition, and increase their salaries.

College and University Teachers

THE NEED FOR Black role models is especially acute in our colleges and universities; however, competition for faculty positions, especially for full-time contracts, is keen. Funding reductions at government and private levels have forced many colleges and universities to lower costs by hiring part-time or adjunct professors, a trend that is likely to continue through the next several decades.

Teaching at the college and university level can be a heady experience if you enjoy academia and the excitement of working with young adults. Living in a college town, with all the lectures, theater, art, and music, isn't bad, either. Responsibilities include giving lectures, leading seminars, supervising laboratories, advising students—any variety of teaching duties, depending on the professorship. Professors also conduct their own research and publish articles and books. "Hot" fields are medicine, business, health care, and technology.

Generally, you will need a doctorate degree (Ph.D.) in your area of specialty to teach at a college or university, although assistant professors and instructors may teach with only a master's degree while working toward their Ph.D. Requirements vary from institution to institution and depend on the school's size and academic standing. A Howard University professor will command a higher salary than an adjunct professor at a local community college.

Special Education Teachers

WALK INTO A special education class and you are likely to find a classroom filled with minority students. African Americans committed to working with youngsters who are physically or emotionally disabled, mentally challenged, or learning disabled are in high demand and there are more teachers hired each year in special education than any other teaching field. Part of this demand is a response to recent legislation mandating programs for disabled students.

An African-American presence is particularly important for students of color who must overcome not only cultural barriers but the alienation of being physically, mentally, or emotionally "different" from their classmates. If you think you've got what it takes to teach these special students, you'll need a bachelor's degree from an approved teacher-training program in addition to a state license. Some states require licensing in a specific area, e.g., learning disabled.

Because of the urgent need for special education teachers, states are instituting emergency licenses, which permit applicants to teach while accumulating the education and experience necessary for licensure or certification. Requirements for licensure beyond a BA depend on the state issuing the license.

Adult Education/Vocational Training Teachers   Adult education or vocational training programs are growing at faster than average rates, which means that African-American vocational teachers are in high demand. Growth here results from the demand for skilled workers in jobs that do not require a college degree. Within our communities, 85 percent lack college degrees and over 75 percent do not attend college at all, so vo-tech training has great importance for this segment of the population.

Vo-tech and adult education teachers work with students who lack basic reading, writing, and mathematics skills, do not speak English, or need to brush up on their skills before moving on to college. These teachers may help teenagers and adults prepare for the General Educational Development (GED) Examination, which offers the equivalent of a high school diploma, and help older adults prepare for college entrance exams. Continuing education teachers focus on subjects like cooking, photography, and exercise.

Corporate downsizing and welfare-to-work programs have created a need for vocational training that teaches useful skills leading to highly paid jobs. A skilled plumber can earn as much as or more than many management executives. Without marketable skills, however, young Blacks will be locked out of well-paid jobs and relegated to flipping burgers for a living.

To attract African Americans into careers and to compensate for outdated training programs, some businesses are going into the education business themselves. This creates a winning situation for students and teachers alike. Not only is Joe Louis Dudley an entrepreneurial success—he built a forty-million-dollar company out of a door-to-door sales job—but he has invested his substantial resources in the future of Black youths by founding Dudley Cosmetology University, which offers young people without college degrees an opportunity to build a career or business in cosmetology.

Joe Dudley's extraordinary success grew out of a ten-dollar investment in a training course and a sales kit, which set him on the road selling Fuller products door to door. He started his most lucrative venture by selling door-to-door products that he and his family created at night. By age forty, Joe Dudley had become president of Fuller Products, earned a million dollars, and laid plans for the cosmetology university that he founded ten years later. With schools in North Carolina, Washington, DC, and Chicago, the university has launched over three thousand people into careers and businesses that buy his products in truckloads. "Everybody wins," explains this modern-day Booker T. Washington.

To teach adult education or become a vocational trainer, you will need a bachelor's degree, teacher certification, and specific experience in the field you teach.

TEACHERS' SALARIES

LET'S FACE IT: Joe Louis Dudley aside, you don't become a teacher to make your first million by age forty. Teachers can make a comfort-

Average earnings for elementary, secondary, and special education teachers:*

To start	$20,000–$25,000
With experience and added training	$36,900–$70,000

Average earnings for college and university teachers:*

Professors	$63,500
Associate professor	$47,500
Assistant professor	$39,100
Lecturer	$32,600
Instructor	$29,700

Average earnings for adult/vocational education teachers:*

$27,600–$50,000

*Occupational Outlook Handbook, 1996–97 Edition

able living and supplement their incomes by as much as 50 percent with after-school, consulting, and/or summer jobs. Teaching salaries vary considerably from state to state, with the highest salaries paid to teachers in Alaska, Connecticut, and New York. Advanced training, degrees earned, and years of experience can also make an enormous difference in pay. The highest earners are college and university professors in specialties such as medicine, law, business, and engineering.

COUNSELING PROFESSIONALS: SCHOOL COUNSELORS, PSYCHOLOGISTS, AND SOCIAL WORKERS

AFRICAN AMERICANS ARE uniquely qualified to address our students' dual struggle to cope with school and to understand what our color and culture mean to them. At the elementary level, counselors generally focus on students' social and personal concerns. In high school they address vocational and academic concerns, including college choices and preparation. All school counselors must address the myriad of problems that children and teenagers bring to the classroom and the school yard, for example, developing programs on substance abuse, teenage sexuality, domestic violence, and conflict resolution.

On-site counseling and social work services also remove the stigma that many Black and Latino families attach to psychological counseling by eliminating the families' need to seek outside help for their children. Parents may be more willing to allow their children to receive counseling if they feel that these services are not targeted at their child but are part of an overall school curriculum.

The demand for school counselors, psychologists, and social workers is expected to increase as schools become more involved in their students' lives. The continued emphasis on integrating disabled children into mainstream classrooms, now mandated under federal law, will increase the demand for this segment.

Counselors, psychologists, and social workers normally have a master's degree and some work experience, in addition to the appropriate state license and certification.

LIBRARIANS

INCREASINGLY, LIBRARIES ARE more than just book repositories; they are multimedia and computer centers. Librarians must be able to understand and teach use of computer systems and various types of software. Since most inner-city families do not own computers, the library may be a child's only link to the digital revolution.

Although cutbacks in educational budgets have reduced resources and staffing, innovative librarians can become adept at raising funds to build book collections and purchase state-of-the-art computer equipment.

Naomi Gans, an experienced librarian and teacher who works in an East Harlem school in New York City, created the library that serves four schools in her building complex by raising money to install a computerized database, purchase thousands of books, and set up a computer center that students use for research and educational games.

School librarians must have a master's degree in library science and teacher certification with a specialty in library science.

INDEPENDENT AND PRIVATE SCHOOLS

IF YOU LOVE teaching but balk at working within the public school system, consider an independent school—or even start one of your own. Jaceta McCladdie, who runs the Kumon Math and Reading Center franchise at Severance Town Center in Cleveland, believes such small private classrooms diminish behavior problems and excessive stress among children. "We are one on one and we don't have any discipline problems because there is no reason for it," she recently told the *Plain Dealer*.

Independent schools are alternatives for children who may be given short shrift in the public school system. At last count, approximately three hundred and fifty Black-owned and -operated day schools are teaching more than fifty-two thousand of our children, while Black boarding schools are educating an additional one thousand students. These schools are multiplying, as parents seek out safe environments with rigorous academic courses, including Black history, culture, and arts.

Hans Hageman, founder of Exodus House, a private school in East Harlem, New York, starts his week by clearing the sidewalk in front of the school of empty beer and soda cans, crumpled bags of junk food, and occasional glassine envelopes and crack vials. He often orders drug dealers away from the school's barred gates and carries a licensed pistol underneath his shirt. After sweeping up, Hans unlocks the steel grating, goes down into the school kitchen, and prepares to meet the half-dozen boys and girls assigned to make breakfast for the entire student body of sixty.

After a breakfast of oatmeal and orange juice (a menu Hans initiated when he realized that many kids woke up to a candy bar and a Coke), students line up in the school courtyard to prepare their minds and bodies with a series of exercises based on Tai Chi Chuan. Then they gather into a circle to discuss problems, raise grievances, admit and apologize for misbehavior, and affirm and acknowledge acts for which they are grateful.

Classes begin. These kids are reading Shakespeare and Toni Morrison; they are learning about contributions made by Africans and Americans to their own African-American culture. They study science and math, compete in judo tournaments, learn how to make films. And they are doing well. Most of the graduates go on to high-quality private boarding schools and top-rated magnet schools within the public school system.

Hans's dream of creating a positive learning environment for ignored and forgotten students is succeeding. Instead of taking his Columbia Law School degree to Wall Street, where he could be earning a six-figure salary, he came back to the community that raised him to make it better. If Exodus House makes a difference in one child's life, Hans will have done more than most of us.

Hans told me, "I realized that even with all my degrees, I couldn't do enough in Washington or on Wall Street to help kids in East Harlem. Our community needs grassroots efforts that create role models for our children. If we don't do it, nobody will."

Almost all independent schools like Exodus House are state-accredited with class sizes of fifteen students or less and an average tuition of $2,000 to $4,500. For those unable to pay, costs are often underwritten by foundation, corporate, or individual grants. An estimated 64 percent of the students at Black independent schools score above the national average on standardized reading tests and 62 percent score higher in math.

Teachers are drawn to these schools because they can design courses and extracurricular activities that would drown in the bureaucracy of the public school system. This freedom compensates for low pay scales and overcrowded offices.

EXECUTIVES, ADMINISTRATORS, AND MANAGERS

SCHOOL ADMINISTRATORS ARE like ship captains steering their schools through stormy seas. Without strong administrators, schools can literally sink to the bottom.

Education administrators establish educational policies and develop academic programs. They train and motivate teachers and staff, administer record-keeping, prepare budgets, and handle relations with parents, students, and employees.

If it takes a village to raise a child, these individuals are the chiefs. They must be politically savvy and socially adept, develop strong ties with local politicians and school board members, create relationships with potential funders, and establish bonds with every segment of the community.

Within our community, elementary and secondary school principals are currently launching activities targeted at the special needs or interests of their students, such as "Rites of Passage" programs based on African rituals that lead adolescents into adulthood. To counteract violence, many administrators are implementing conflict resolution and mediation workshops. In short, school administrators today must be men and women "for all seasons."

Average earnings for administrators:*

Primary school administrators $38,000–$50,000

Secondary school administrators $50,000–$86,000

Occupational Outlook Handbook, 1996–97 Edition

Eric Holmes, a principal of a thousand-student middle school, manages over eighty staff members who fill the ranks of teachers, administrators, and support staff. Holmes emphasizes teacher, student, and parent empowerment through shared decision-making. A strong believer in student-centered learning, he has instituted curriculum changes that promote critical thinking skills.

His credo? "Draw strength and guidance from your family. Surround yourself with people who share your dreams, have high expectations for themselves, and are motivated to succeed," he told *Black Collegian*. "The debt that you owe those who led the struggle before you will never be repaid until you give back to the community."

Administrators, principals, and assistant principals may work the entire year, and frequently spend afternoons and evenings in meetings and conferences with faculty, parents, politicians, fund-raisers, and other policy-makers. This is not a job for the nine-to-fiver.

Principals and assistant principals start as teachers with a master's or doctoral degree in education administration or educational supervision.

School administrators at all levels generally earn higher salaries than their teacher counterparts. The higher the grade level, the higher the pay. Pay scales also vary according to geographic location and the nature of the institution; private schools pay their administrators more than public schools.

ADMINISTRATIVE SUPPORT STAFF

ADMINISTRATIVE SUPPORT POSITIONS offer opportunities without requiring advanced degrees or experience. These jobs include teacher and library aides and secretarial and clerical workers. My sister Emma, who is a top administrator within a suburban New York school system, started her career thirty years ago as a school secretary. Employees usually work part-time throughout the school year, their hours following the normal school day.

Parents are ideal candidates for these jobs, since they can work at the school their children attend while learning valuable skills. Cesar Vasquez, now a special education counselor, turned a support staff job into an opportunity to get ahead. He spent every afternoon at the school "just lending a hand," and his ability to maintain order among students attracted the attention of the school principal, who offered him a part-time job as an aide. Cesar accepted and eventually became responsible for developing an after-school program that serves hundreds of children.

Impressed with Cesar's dedication and his results, the principal arranged for him to attend night school where he completed a college degree and earned credits toward a master's in education. Cesar is becoming a certified full-time teacher and plans to launch an independent school of his own. I have every belief that he will.

Angela Bowman became a teacher's aide after volunteering as a "parent mentor" at her daughter's school. Angela's hard work paid off—she was hired to assist teachers in overcrowded classes where many children were suffering from behavioral and emotional problems. Angela ultimately became responsible for the after-school program on a full-time basis. She is proof that dedication can turn volunteer work into a job.

Responsibilities assigned to teacher's aides vary widely. In some school systems, aides provide supplementary instruction for students, in addition to organizing after-school projects and programs and field trips. Other duties may be secretarial or clerical. Educational requirements range from a high school diploma to some college training. Becoming an aide is a good way to get a taste of teaching before jumping into the profession.

Library aides and technicians support the school librarian by performing a variety of duties, including teaching students to use the school library/media center, checking out and receiving library materials, collecting overdue-book fines, and shelving materials. These positions can be ideal for student workers, although the wages are generally low.

Training requirements for aides range from a high school diploma to a two-year associate of arts degree in library technology for technicians.

Average earnings:*

For teacher's aides assisting in actual teaching	$8.77/hour
For teacher's aides performing non-teaching tasks	$8.29/hour
For library aides	$18,800/year
	$10/hour

*Occupational Outlook Handbook, 1996–97 Edition

SERVICE JOBS

SERVICE WORKERS MAKE up 12 percent of the total workforce in the education industry and range from low-paid janitors to multimillion-dollar food and beverage contractors. (For a detailed description of these positions, see *Jobs Almanac 1997*, Adams Media Corporation, and/or the 1996–97 edition of the *Occupational Outlook Handbook*, U.S. Department of Labor, Bulletin 2470.)

For entrepreneurial African Americans, the service segment offers the chance to launch or expand a successful business. For example, Sylvia's Restaurant, the famous Harlem eatery, recently negotiated to supply the Columbia University cafeteria with Southern cooking.

The money is there to be made. As an example, 31 percent of the Atlanta school system's four-hundred-million-dollar budget is allocated to minority businesses. To get a piece of the action, we must start small; network, build friendships, trust, and credibility; and provide the best possible service at the lowest possible price. Again, remember the old networking adage: People do things for people they know, respect, and like. Find out what the school systems are looking for and give them the best of what you've got.

CORPORATE TRAINERS

NEWCOMERS TO THE education industry are corporate trainers, who design and present customized seminars and courses which may be tailored for young professionals or captains of industry. The range is enormous. Trainers are either in-house corporate employees or independent consultants with diverse backgrounds and areas of expertise.

Having just established her own business, Iris Randall marched con-

PRIME GROWTH AREAS FOR
CORPORATE TRAINING PROGRAMS

Based on my research, prime areas of growth in this field will be:

- Managing diversity
- Customer services
- Total quality management
- Welfare-to-work skills
- Telemarketing
- Computer literacy
- Small business development (Black America's next big movement)
- Home-care aides and professionals

fidently into a room crowded with IBM vice presidents to pitch her idea for implementing an entry-level training program. Iris was energetic, pleasant, and to the point. Her approach reflected the depth of experience she had acquired during her years as Avon Products' training director.

When Iris completed her presentation and asked for the order, the executives politely explained that they had just implemented a similar program. Embarrassed, but poised, Iris learned a valuable Lesson: Find out the customer's needs first. Your needs come second.

Despite this initial setback, Iris pulled herself up and wrote a popular book. A radio interview landed her a lucrative consulting job at Avon, which mushroomed into several major corporate assignments that built on Iris's expanding areas of expertise: cultural diversity, sales, team-building, and leadership.

Corporate trainers must have skill or expertise in one or more technical or professional areas. They must also have excellent speaking, presentation, and people skills. Most have college and advanced degrees in their area of specialty. Experienced trainers may head up corporate training departments or launch their own businesses. Corporate trainers who teach advanced courses in SEC regulations would probably look for clients on Wall Street, while trainers who teach conflict resolution skills could find work in any area of the country.

Earnings for corporate trainers tend to top average earnings for the rest of the education industry. Income depends on whether the trainer is a salaried employee or an independent contractor, the type of consulting performed, and years of experience.

EDUCATING THROUGH PUBLIC SPEAKING

I CONFIDENTLY WALKED onto the platform, smiled, greeted the attentive audience with an energetic "Good evening," then launched into my opening—a joke that I had practiced for a few brief moments before the speech. After I completed the joke, no one laughed. In fact, they looked puzzled. I reflected for a moment, now also perspiring, then realized I'd forgotten to tell the punch line. Things went downhill from there. It was one of my first public speeches, in a church, among friends. They were kind.

It is said the number one fear we have is public speaking, the number two fear is dying, and the number three fear is speaking and dying in front of a audience. I did all three at once. You want to know how to go to heaven? You have to die first! I died, but I learned. That was fifteen years ago; I've been speaking ever since.

You learn public speaking by doing it. Those who learn how to verbally communicate with impact will experience the greatest success at work, at home, and in the community and make the biggest contribution to humankind. It is education at its most glamorous. My office phone regularly rings with people who want to pursue public speaking as a profession. Many Blacks have joined the ranks, but many more are needed in America's schools, colleges, and organizations to present the pertinent topics of the day.

Topics in big demand in the seventy-five-billion-dollar a year meetings industry include: dealing with change, customer service, global marketplace opportunities, future strategies, total quality, new technologies, productivity and performance, diversity, legal issues, health and fitness, and racial healing. On all of these there is a bounty of expertise within the Black professional ranks.

If you want to join this lucrative field of education, here are a few tips:

Have a well-defined personal vision and philosophy in your area of
expertise. Be willing to be open and sharing. People want to know

your story, to find out how human and/or regular you are. They are not looking for perfection.

Write a book. Be an expert on something. My speaking engagements increased tenfold after my first book was released.

Practice, practice, practice. Hone your speaking skills by reading books, listening to tapes of other speakers, and speaking for free if you have to. I gave over one hundred free speeches during the early years of my development in places like churches, clubs and organizations, schools, and Rotary Club meetings—anywhere that gave me a chance to gain poise, test my ideas, and build confidence and relationships. The relationships are important because for the most part the engagements will come through recommendations by people who have heard you and were inspired by your message and vision.

Join professional organizations. Networking is the best way to learn new techniques, get business, and meet people in the industry.

Join Toastmasters International and the National Speakers Association (see Resources).

Create your own style and niche. My style is friendly and open and my look is corporate. My niche is networking valuing diversity, racial healing, and economic development.

You cannot be all things to all people. You can only speak about what you know deeply and are passionate about, what you have experienced, and what you have spent your life learning up to that point. I once sat through an award-winning eighteen-year-old speaker's presentation. The speech was well written with great quotes and platitudes. He spoke with a great vocal range, full of energy. His gestures were well rehearsed. The two hundred adults in the audience were courteous but not moved. Why? He did not speak from his experiences, his knowledge or insights. His speech was textbook in content and theatrical in presentation. He was without credibility; the emperor had no clothes. Had he given the same impassioned speech from his eighteen years of life experiences, he would have been believable and a hit.

Speak to the world. My advice is to develop a series of speeches that address the needs of all people in your chosen area of expertise, then develop a series of speeches on the same topic that focus specifically on the unique cultural nuances of African Americans. For example, we are spiritual people; therefore a few selected Bible quotes or verses peppering your text will help reach Blacks at a spiritual level and bring the point home. In the resource section of this book you will find a list of some of Black America's brightest young speaking stars. They would be more than happy to provide additional insight and guidance for your speaking career. They are also for hire.

Public speaking can be a rewarding part-time or full-time profession. Megastar speakers like Les Brown can earn as much as $30,000 per speech, not to mention the money made from selling books and tapes at the engagement. Beginning speakers may start at $100 per speech; however, fees can increase rapidly for those who persist, write and publish, and become known in their field. On average, seasoned speakers earn from $1,500 to $5,000 per speech, and many make much more.

A FINAL WORD

EVEN IF YOU never enter the education industry, there are ways that you can take part in our young people's educational lives and positively influence their accomplishments. Here are some of my suggestions on how you can participate in our future.

If you are a Black professional, business owner, or community leader or you have a craft or skill, become a role model. Visit a local inner-city school once a month and talk to a classroom of kids—just call the principal and request a time. National organizations like 100 Black Men, Concerned Black Men, and Alphas and Omegas send in hundreds of professionals each month. Join them.

Be creative, do something. Frank and Faye Clark, both retired corporate executives living in Cincinnati, Ohio, were appalled by the lack of basic supplies in some nearby Southern schools. They used their network of contacts (me included) to round up furniture, school equipment, books, and calculators from wealthy Midwestern school districts and major corporations. They shipped this care package to ten of the poorest school systems in Alabama and Mississippi. Using their own money, Frank and Faye founded "Educate the Children Foundation," which is committed to improving the lives of poor children by bettering their schools.

Lobby for neighborhood schools and advisory boards who participate in the democratic governance of schools. Efforts are under way in cities with large urban populations, including New York, Cleveland, Detroit, and Houston.

Support bureaucrats who sincerely focus on education as their top priority.

Lobby for implementation of African-centered standards of discipline, respect, and manners in predominantly Black schools.

Help bring dignity, respect, and esteem back to teaching. Recognize outstanding teachers in community events. Local Urban Leagues do a good job at this, but more Black organizations must include teacher recognition programs as part of their annual awards agendas.

Encourage more young people to go into the teaching profession. Convince your company and your business associates to create a special scholarship fund for students with a demonstrated interest in pursuing education as a career. Contact your local chapter of the National Association of Black School Educators to find out how.

Support church-based, private, and independent schools. Use your business expertise to develop their income sources.

Become a tutor—devote a few hours a week or month to tutoring young people. Contact your local school board or district to find out how to start.

Encourage your company to become part of a corporate mentoring program to bring students into your company once or twice a month. Contact One-to-One New York at (212)339-0141 or the local chapter of Big Brothers/Big Sisters to find out how to get set up.

5

FINANCE AND BANKING:
THE MANIFESTATION OF POWER

The issue is no longer whether you can sit on the bus
or whether you can drive it: it's whether you can
develop the capital to own the bus company.
> —WILLIAM GRAY

Without money, one becomes dependent on other people,
who are likely to be—even in their kindness—erratic in
their support and despotic in their expectations of returns.
> —ALICE WALKER

CHERYL D. BROUSSARD
CEO
BROUSSARD & DOUGLAS, INC.
PALO ALTO, CALIFORNIA

A native of Phoenix, Arizona, Cheryl
Broussard understands heat. And
as a Dean Witter stockbroker for
seven years, if she didn't produce
she felt another kind of "heat"—she
didn't get paid. As a commission-
only professional in the competitive
world of money management and

investment counseling, she earned her stripes the hard way.

Cheryl Broussard's path as a financial advisor started more than twenty years ago when she was hired as the first and only Black at Dean Witter. She performed so well that she left to start her own firm, then went on to write a bestselling book, *Black Women's Guide to Financial Independence*, followed by a second book called *Sister CEO*. The rest, as they say, is history.

Cheryl credits her mom, who was a postal employee for forty-one years, for instilling the proper values and work ethic in her at an early age. Her rigorous training at Loyola College, she says, taught her the importance of "discipline, research, and reading." The greatest obstacle Cheryl had to overcome was the racism that existed in the male-dominated world of white establishment finance. Today, she feels that to continue to succeed in this elite world she still must overcome stereotypical thinking but, just as important, she must have a deep understanding of the complicated world of investment.

"The baby boomers want to take charge of their own finances," she observes. "They are no longer trusting the responsibility of money management exclusively to the expert. Therefore, to compete and to earn their trust you must be exceptional. Good is not enough, especially if you're Black and female."

The types of people who make it in her business, she says, "are those who are self-starters, good networkers and marketers, and truly enjoy meeting and serving people."

Although there is still a reluctance for whites to take financial advice from Blacks, Cheryl feels that attitude is slowly changing. In the meantime, most of her business is focused on helping Black women achieve financial success at work, at home, and in the community.

For those wanting to enter the financial realm, Cheryl advises, "Follow your dreams, don't ever give up, and if you stumble and fall, get up, dust yourself off and move on, girlfriend." Cheryl Broussard is the best example of how her own advice can bring successful results.

FAVORITE BIBLICAL PASSAGE:

For I consider the suffering of the present time is not worthy to be compared with the glory which shall be revealed in us.

—Romans 8:18

"BLACK POWER" WAS the rallying cry of the civil rights movement in the late 1960s. Today, we are demanding "Economic Power." Andrew Young summed up the current battle in a speech to the National Association of Securities Professionals, whose members include some of our smartest and wealthiest young executives. "You are [today's] Civil Rights Movement," he said. "Now we're trying to integrate the money. You're at the forefront of the movement for equality."

Black America has the means to wield tremendous economic clout—but we have yet to do more than spend our wealth. We are 33.5 million strong and control nearly $400 billion in annual income, which makes ours the tenth-richest economy in the world. But as a group we spend most of our money on new homes and fancy cars, designer clothes and "keeping up with the Joneses." On average, we earn $29,259 versus $43,133 earned by the average white household, yet our median net worth is $8,300 compared to the median net worth of $56,000 of a white family.

Those figures demonstrate that even though we earn less than whites, we are spending more, while they are saving and investing.

I believe this disparity illuminates the misdirection of Black spending, poor financial planning, and the attitude that we can "buy now and pay later." In other words too many of us suffer from a compulsive spending disorder. I hope that our days of being enslaved to credit cards are ending. Today we are looking for effective ways to reduce debt and invest our substantial income in starting new businesses, planning for our children's education, and having more income to retire on and pass on to the next generation.

To achieve economic equality, we need to invest at the personal as well as the institutional level. Many brothers and sisters have made inroads into the fast-paced world of banking and finance. We need to take advantage of the investment advice they can provide especially to those of us who still have a hard time balancing our monthly checking accounts. Our community of Wall Street financiers can also help the rest of us learn to save and invest instead of spend and consume.

THE WAY WE WERE

IN THE EARLY 1960s, a century after the Emancipation Proclamation, we were just taking our first baby steps on Wall Street. In 1961, there were only six or seven Blacks in the securities trade; in 1970, John L.

Searles III became the first Black floor member of the New York Stock Exchange (NYSE); and in 1971, Daniels & Bell Inc. became the first Black-owned firm to buy a seat on the NYSE.

Getting a seat at the table doesn't mean much unless you also have the means to dish some business onto your plate. At first, Black financiers had a hard time finding customers and working deals on the Street owned by the white establishment. Undaunted, the late Travers Bell, Jr., one of the founders of Daniels & Bell, created a niche market in public finance by convincing Black politicians to hire Black brokers to underwrite state and local projects. Maynard Jackson, mayor of Atlanta, and Carl Stokes, mayor of Cleveland, made it clear that they preferred to do business with securities firms that included Black professionals. As a result, white firms going after the bond issues business began to recruit employees from the African-American community. In this way, municipal financing became an entryway onto the Street for pioneering Black firms and individuals.

The initiatives begun by Daniels and Bell continue to grow. Herman Martin, a young vice president at Salomon Brothers, was inspired to pursue a career on the Street by the example set by Bell and his former partner, Willie Daniels. "I had been told that I would have a hard time getting a job in trading since I was Black and had graduated from an all-Black college [Florida A&M], but I knew that was incorrect because Willie Daniels had already been there," Martin told me.

The walls keep tumbling down. Independent firms such as First Harlem Securities Inc., Doley Securities, and W. R. Lazard & Co., have joined the small number of Black independent securities firms. In 1981, BET Holdings Inc. (Black Entertainment Television) became the first Black-owned company traded on the NYSE. In 1987, the late Reginald F. Lewis, then president of TLC Group Inc., instituted the largest off-shore leveraged buyout in business history with his $985-million acquisition of Beatrice International Foods. These groundbreaking efforts have made African Americans players in the financial industry.

Although municipal financing continues to be important for us, the collapse of the bond market in 1994, coupled with the disappearance of numerous Black politicians from the political scene, forced enterprising African Americans to find new ways to make money. John W. Rogers, Jr., who founded Ariel Capital Management Inc. in 1983, had the wisdom to investigate mutual funds. Other Black-owned firms have pursued global financing, federal government business, and alliances with other firms. Utendahl Capital Partners L.P., which established a niche in the taxable fixed-income securities area, was launched with Merrill Lynch's support; Blaylock and Partners L.P., the first minority-owned firm to exclusively manage a corporate bond sale, has Bear Stearns as an investor.

Black bankers have found opportunities by serving minority communities and by snapping up banks that went belly-up during the savings and loan crisis. On the insurance side, Black brokers have built businesses by providing minority communities with an array of policies. Black churches are also playing an important role in building and empowering their communities with loan services and housing development programs.

If you're interested in working in the financial services industry, your timing is right. Based on several predictors—growth of new products and markets, deregulation of banking laws (which has expanded the kinds of services banks can offer), and the globalization of the securities and commodities markets—jobs are expected to increase at the faster-than-average pace of 26 percent over the next five years.

To get ahead in this industry takes plenty of guts, persistence, and self-confidence. Perhaps more than most businesses, financial investments are based on personal trust. "There's an additional question mark when [white] clients talk to someone they're not familiar with," says one Wall Street trader. "We're still more accepted on the basketball court than on the trading floor."

But the challenges and the earnings can make the job worth the hard work. Herman Martin of Salomon Brothers, told me, "The fact that I've been in the business for ten years means that I must like what I do. I love the risk, the element of uncertainty, and the excitement. This is the closest to entrepreneurship that I can get while working within a large corporation."

Eric J. Barkley, the first Black institutional salesperson on the equity side at Bear Stearns, agrees: "Finance is one of the most lucrative fields where the rewards can come early in your career. But you have to be extremely focused to compete in this complex and competitive environment."

Both Herman and Eric are living well, saving for the future, and creating a financial base for their families and their clients. I hope that some of you will be inspired to follow their lead.

I have roughly divided the financial services industry into three segments:

- Wall Street securities and investment firms
- Banks
- Insurance companies

The lines between these segments are increasingly blurred these days, primarily because government deregulation now permits companies within these industries to compete for customers. For example, investment banks now offer services previously offered by commercial banks, while commercial banks also offer investment advice and can engage in limited brokerage activities.

WALL STREET SECURITIES AND INVESTMENT FIRMS

THE ECONOMY IS booming and Wall Street firms are eager to recruit young African Americans with college degrees, especially MBAs. But because the jobs are extremely well paying, competition is tough. "You only get the job if you're overqualified," says Eric Barkley, who recruits from his alma mater, Morehouse. "I'm probably harder on Morehouse students than on anyone else because we want to establish that Morehouse graduates exhibit strong abilities, so that, eventually, people will feel the same about us as they do about Ivy League grads."

You want to work on Wall Street, but aren't sure how to get there? Here's a rough road map that can help get your trip organized.

Wall Street institutions are financial intermediaries that make their money by accumulating and distributing capital. These firms assist companies and municipalities to raise cash to build businesses or public works. Firms may also act as retail brokers, buying and selling stocks, bonds, commodity futures, and other financial products. Some also provide cash management and basic banking services. And some provide specific kinds of investment advice or financial analysis.

A basic mechanism for raising money is selling stocks or bonds, either to the public, via a stock exchange, or to groups of private investors. Investors buy shares of a company, hoping to capitalize on the increased value of the company's future profits. Bonds are loan notes issued by a company or by the government to the lender, who makes money from the interest paid on the note. More complicated deals involve selling other types of financial products, such as derivatives, to generate cash.

Stocks are sold to the public through exchanges which are central meeting places for member firms to trade stocks of approved companies. In addition to meeting basic standards of size and profits, companies whose shares are traded on a stock exchange must also agree to regularly publish financial information about their operations and financing.

Exchanges such as the New York Stock Exchange (NYSE), the American Stock Exchange (AMEX), and regional exchanges (the Midwest Stock Exchange and the Pacific Stock Exchange) monitor stock transactions and enforce a variety of rules and regulations designed to maintain fair and orderly markets. Brokers who trade on the exchanges must purchase a "seat" and must also pass a battery of examinations.

Large firms, like Bear Stearns, Merrill Lynch, and Salomon Brothers, are Wall Street's financial department stores, offering a full range of financial services to individual and corporate clients. It's called "one-stop shopping." For example, they may work with an individual to create a stock portfolio, which will depend on the amount of money the person has to invest and the risk he or she is willing to take. These firms also sell stocks to institutional clients, such as banks and pension or mutual funds.

Some firms also help companies and the government raise capital for growth or, in the case of federal or state municipalities, to build public works, like dams or bridges, or fund deficits.

Financial firms may either fully or partially guarantee the sale of a block of the company's stock to raise the necessary cash. For example, if Company A wants to raise $10 million, it might put together a deal where a bank makes a $5 million loan secured by collateral such as the company's buildings, equipment, and accounts receivables. To generate the remaining $5 million, the company may hire a brokerage firm to arrange the financing by issuing shares of stock to the public or to a private group of investors.

Sales to the public must be registered with the Securities and Exchange Commission (SEC), a government agency which was created to supervise the securities industry after the market crashed in 1929. If the facts submitted by the company appear misleading or incomplete, the SEC can prohibit the sale.

Sales of unregistered stock to private investors, and other private financing deals, are outside the SEC's supervision. Companies may prefer such deals because public disclosure about their finances might make them a takeover target or cost them an opportunity to acquire another firm. Private placements are also appealing to new companies that need cash but have not been operating long enough to meet all the SEC qualifications to trade to the public.

Smaller "boutique" firms also abound on Wall Street. These companies generally handle particular types of transactions, such as municipal financing, private offerings, or deals for issuers with below-investment-grade credit ("junk bond") ratings. Some specialize in raising capital within a specific industry, such as telecommunications, high technology, or new media.

Money can also be made in the commodities market, which is Wall Street's high-stress scene. Here individuals and companies trade futures contracts—agreements to buy or sell such commodities as soybeans, pork bellies, silver, gold, and other product staples in the future at the current price. Commodities exchanges, including the Chicago Board of Trade and the Chicago Mercantile Exchange, are similar to stock exchanges. Trading in commodities originated to protect farmers against declines in grain or livestock prices across the planting and harvesting seasons. Today, these trades are sophisticated "hedges" against rises or falls in global market prices.

Within these industries, a broad range of exciting careers thrives.

Securities Brokers

BROKERS (ALSO CALLED registered representatives, sales representatives, or account executives) make up the single largest occupation within the industry. Brokers represent brokerage firms and create orders to buy and sell securities and commodities.

At the retail level, brokers sell to individuals like you and me. They find clients by networking and by flogging the phones with "cold calls" to sell products and services to potential buyers and to develop long-term relationships. Retail brokers must know their product cold and be able to advise clients on the history and potential growth of the stock they are selling.

Institutional brokers specialize in handling large corporate accounts, such as banks, insurance companies, mutual funds, and state and/or corporate pensions. Their clients are sophisticated money managers interested in getting the highest return possible on their investment. Generally, brokers act as investment advisors, providing their accounts

BASIC TERMS

Stocks: certificates representing share(s) of corporate ownership in a company.

Bond: an interest-bearing certificate, or IOU, issued by the government or a business representing a unit of debt.

Securities: stocks, bonds, and other financial products.

Mutual Fund: a pool of money invested into a variety of stocks. These funds are not insured by the government. Funds may specialize in particular kinds of industries, featuring low, medium, or high risk.

Brokerage house: a firm that sells securities; often engages in a variety of other financial services aimed to fill clients' every financial need.

Stock exchange: a place where stocks and bonds are bought and sold. The most famous U.S. exchanges are the New York Stock Exchange (NYSE), the American Stock Exchange (AMEX), and regional exchanges such as the Midwest Stock Exchange and the Pacific Stock Exchange.

SEC (Securities Exchange Commission): a federal agency created under the 1934 Securities Exchange Act to supervise securities trading.

National Association of Securities Dealers (NASD): created under amendments to the 1934 Securities Exchange Act, the NASD was organized as a self-regulatory body responsible for monitoring the securities market.

Public offering: the sale of securities to the general public; must comply with SEC regulations.

Private offering: the sale of securities to private investors; not registered with the SEC. Private financing is also subject to government regulation, although disclosure requirements are less than those for a public offering.

Initial public offering (IPO): a company's initial sale of securities to the public.

Municipal financing: deals that generally provide public infrastructure financing for city, state, and county governments to underwrite, for example, the cost of building public highways, bridges, dams, airports, etc.

Commodities: products such as agricultural produce and livestock (wheat, soybeans, cotton, coffee, sugar, pork bellies, cattle) and other products such as gold, copper, silver, plywood, and various energy sources.

Commodity futures: agreements to buy or sell commodities at a future date based on prices immediately available.

Commodity exchanges: membership organizations regulated by the federal Commodity Futures Trading Commission; provide facilities and equipment for commodity futures trading.

with advice tailored to meet their specific needs. They may also specialize in particular types of transactions, such as bond issues or public financing.

Traders

TRADERS EXECUTE THE buy or sell order and provide up-to-the-minute advice on the order to brokers and their clients. Traders must be prepared to answer questions on the technical aspects of the stock transaction and be informed on economic conditions at the moment the trade is made.

Financial Analysts

FINANCIAL ANALYSTS HELP brokers and investors determine which securities are hot and which to stay away from. Analysts generally choose to follow stocks within a particular industry—from high technology to sporting goods—and spend their day studying and analyzing the financial performance of the companies within their portfolio. They must be up to date on the company's day-to-day financial performance and examine new and planned product releases, competitive activity, and events that might impact on the stock's market value. For example, an analyst may determine that poor performance of a high touted laptop computer will negatively affect the manufacturer's stock value. Analysts share the results of their research with everyone in the shop—from traders to retail and institutional salespeople to top management.

Investment Bankers

INVESTMENT BANKERS ADVISE sophisticated professional investors. Within the industry, the term generally refers to those individuals at a brokerage house who raise the capital necessary to underwrite a particular deal.

GETTING STARTED ON WALL STREET

THE SKILLS AND training you'll need to get into this challenging industry depend on the job you have targeted for yourself, although the higher your educational level, the more opportunities will be available. In general, to get a Wall Street career moving you need an undergraduate degree in accounting, finance, or economics; while you're at it, an MBA is a good idea, too. "Although an MBA is not necessary for a job in sales or in trading," Herman Martin says, "the degree is worthwhile because without extra qualifications, getting the first job is more difficult, if not impossible."

Increasingly, knowing how to access the newest computer-based information sources is essential, and Wall Street veterans stress the importance of summer internships. Some colleges and universities offer ready-made intern connections. (See an advisor and ask about a direct link to a firm.) If your school isn't visited by company recruiters, try using the Internet to inquire about intern programs and to list your availability.

Starting out at a large brokerage house like Merrill Lynch, which offers excellent on-the-job training, makes you an appealing employee to other firms. Sales traders may get their foot in the door by starting as runners or administrative assistants who literally "run" paper on which the trade is recorded from the trading floor to the office where the order is processed.

Most positions in securities trading are located near one of the big trading centers—Chicago or New York—although regional offices are located throughout the country. Financial services specialists and stockbrokers can work just about anywhere.

Anyone who deals with the public in the securities industry must pass a battery of tests known as the Series 7 exam and must also undergo a training period and continuous supervision. Institutional salespeople must also pass a series of exams which demonstrate that they have a firm grasp of the legalities of a transaction and of who they can and can't sell to.

In an industry where a 60 percent drop-out rate is typical for first-year retail traders, you'll need to love what you're doing to have the dedication and energy necessary to make the cut. Eric Barkley's advice: Research the market, determine what areas appeal to you, and make your goals color-blind.

"If I had limited myself to jobs offered to African Americans, I wouldn't be in institutional sales," Eric said. "You have to determine your interests and your strengths. Don't go down a path just because African Americans have traditionally taken that route. Society steered us wrong for generations."

In sum, think about what might be most rewarding for you, and begin there. Both Eric and Herman discovered what their dream job looked like through internships they took while still in college. Eric found his internship by thumbing through the yellow pages and making cold calls to retail brokers. He offered his services for free, in exchange for a chance to learn the business. That approach landed him a position with a retail brokerage firm where he learned enough to realize that retail sales didn't appeal to him; at the same time, he became familiar with the institutional market, which he found fascinating.

"The internship taught me what I didn't want to do," he explained, "so when I went into a job interview, I could be extremely focused about where I did want to be."

At that time, most of the firms recruiting at Morehouse were offering jobs in municipal finance or backroom positions. Eric persisted: "I would tell the recruiter that I was really interested in sales and trading, and would ask them to pass along my resume to the appropriate person at the firm." The result: Eric got a job in institutional sales straight out of college, which is rare in a field where most candidates wield an MBA.

Herman applied what he calls the "stone soup" approach to learning about the industry. "Start off with a rock—meaning yourself—and go around to different people and tell them that you're building a career. As you make the rounds, everyone will add to your portfolio of information, until you get the information and, ultimately, the job you need. Nineteen out of twenty people may hang up on you, but the twentieth person will give you what you're looking for. Networking is the key."

Herman developed his contact list by culling names from publications like *Black Enterprise*, adding the names of alumni from his alma mater, and talking to people. "Above all," he says, "be persistent and confident about your goals. Don't settle for anything less."

THE ROAD UP

ONCE YOU'VE GOT the job, it's pretty much up to you to chart your own course. Finding a Black mentor may be difficult since our history on the Street is relatively short. "Morehouse has a strong network of alums on Wall Street who I can call if I have a question or need support," says Eric, whose network of mentors is multiracial.

However, Wall Street is no different from any other professional setting: You are in charge of your own destiny. "You're only as good as your last trade," Herman says, "which makes the job exciting. Even if yesterday was bad, you can have a great tomorrow. People respect production and you'll only be visible if you are one of the 20 percent who produce 80 percent of the work."

You'll need to do what it takes to stand out, even if it means pulling all-nighters and begging for the chance to do more. If you're working until 11:00 P.M. there's probably someone else who is working until 2:00 A.M. You also need to build in time for keeping up with the business by reading all domestic and international financial publications. Continuing education through advanced courses and industry conferences is another part of maintaining your edge.

Networking should be part of your everyday life. When I asked Herman what he had planned for an upcoming vacation, he responded enthusiastically that he and his wife, Elizabeth Martin (the real estate entrepreneur who is featured in Chapter Six), were attending the Black Enterprise annual networking conference, which in 1997 was held in Florida.

No matter how many hours you put in, the chances of getting to the top are slim. Only 2 percent of top management jobs are held by Blacks. Herman concludes that most who succeed are "crazy like a fox, because they know—before their friends, their family, and enemies know—that they are going to make it. But it can be lonely until the rest of the world finds out." Sure, Herman acknowledges, there are glass ceilings, but "a glass ceiling is being broken every day by those crazy people."

Once Eric got the position he wanted, he realized that the only color his clients really cared about was green. "As an institutional salesperson, I deal with professional money managers who are responsible for getting their companies the highest return. They'll use me if they like my ideas, and they'll use someone else if they like his or her ideas better. At my level, the only color that makes any difference is the color of money."

With their approach, you have my guarantee that Herman and Eric will be breaking glass ceilings of their own pretty soon.

THE INDEPENDENTS

FOR SOME PEOPLE, shattering corporate glass ceilings is not the goal. They prefer to use their energy and experience to forge their own businesses, either as independents or by forming alliances with existing institutions. John Utendahl formed Utendahl Capital Partners in 1992, and soon the firm was co-managing a Federal Home Loan Mortgage Corporation deal, the first Black-owned brokerage firm ever to do so. Utendahl got his experience as a corporate bond trader at Salomon Brothers and Merrill Lynch, then allied himself with Merrill Lynch to form his own company.

After cutting his teeth as a trader at PaineWebber, followed by a brief stint with Utendahl Capital Partners, Ronald E. Blaylock struck out on his own with Bear Stearns as his limited partner. Utendahl and Blaylock both got backing from white firms, but J. Carl Sneed did quite well building a small real estate and mortgage brokerage business on his own. He edged out bigger players on his home turf in the Bronx by giving potential customers free computer software that contained information on a mortgage-interest savings plan. Many mortgage brokers charge customers for the same information, but J. Carl Sneed used

TRENDS OF THE BLACK INVESTOR

Ariel Mutual Funds has just released the first national survey of African-American investors.* This group has approximately thirty-six billion dollars in disposable income. The Ariel study reveals that:

- African Americans rely on conservative investment vehicles and risk-averse strategies, look for higher returns in a shorter time span, and are more likely to seek the advice of a financial planner.
- African Americans favor diversely managed investment firms and those with track records of socially responsible investments and community involvement.
- African-American women are more likely to make household financial decisions related to investments and savings.
- African Americans who invest, like others, invest 11 to 12 percent of their income, but achieve less on investment because they use more conservative vehicles, such as savings accounts.
- African Americans have shorter investment horizons, with six years being the longest they are willing to invest money, compared to 7.3 years on average among non-Blacks. They also want bigger payoffs, looking for average annual returns of 14.6 percent compared to 11.2 percent for non-Blacks.

*N'Digo magazine, May 7, 1997

the African-American way of spreading the news. The way he does business, everybody wins.

Another person I admire is John Bryant, a young man who was inspired to found Operation HOPE, America's first nonprofit investment banking organization. Bryant told *Black Enterprise* that Operation HOPE was his "guilt-ridden response" to witnessing the riots in South Central Los Angeles after the Rodney King verdict.

"Here I was, a Black man who had left his community and become successful, thinking discrimination didn't exist. [After watching] the buildings burn the night after the verdict . . . I wanted to—I *had* to do something."

Bryant convinced his colleagues in the Los Angeles area that they could make money and do good at the same time by investing in the communities ruined by the rioting. Since 1992, Operation HOPE has

MONEY MARKET

The following sets out average income levels in an industry where market fluctuations, the number of your clients, and the deals they make can make your income soar or plummet.

Sales traders: Traders can expect to earn six and seven figures in a relatively short period of time, with starting salaries beginning at about $50,000.

Retail/Institutional salespersons: In 1994, the average income for stock-brokers selling to individuals was $117,037 per year, while institutional sales representatives earned an average of $217,000. Remember that most firms offer bonuses based on commissions, which can far outstrip the base salary.

Financial analysts: Financial analysts begin at about $50,000 and top out at $150,000 to $200,000.

arranged for over $7 million worth of loans to minority businesses located primarily in South LA, and Bryant hopes to raise that figure to $50 million in the next five years. Although few of us can follow his path, John Bryant is an inspiration to all of us.

So, the hours are long and the challenges are many. What can you expect to earn? In this business, the sky is the limit for those smart enough and tough enough.

BANKS

IN 1993, MARK Winston Griffith and Errol T. Louis founded the Central Brooklyn Federal Credit Union to support business development in Bedford-Stuyvesant and Crown Heights, predominantly Black New York neighborhoods that had traditionally been bypassed for economic development by mainstream banking and lending institutions. The credit union is the fastest growing financial institution in New York City, with a membership of over five thousand. It has loaned over $3.5 million to individuals and organizations and has $5.2 million in assets. Services to members include savings and checking accounts, check cashing, utility bill payments, financial management workshops, and personal and small business loans.

Black-owned credit unions like Central Brooklyn fill a tremendous need in our communities. Many of us are uncomfortable putting our money in the hands of elite banking institutions, which traditionally have been reluctant to serve minority customers. A long time ago we learned to hoard our cash in the mattress or to spend our whole paycheck during the first week of the month. As a result, we tend to lack credit histories and access to the financing necessary to launch small businesses or make other long-term investments. That scenario is changing, thanks in part to the pioneering efforts of credit unions like Central Brooklyn and banks like the United Bank of Philadelphia, financial institutions specifically founded to serve the needs of communities that larger banking establishments refused to acknowledge.

Other changes are also driving this trend. Technology, economic indicators, and changes in government banking regulations have reshaped the banking industry. Banks are now butting heads with insurance companies and brokerage houses in a scramble to provide an increasing range of services to corporate and individual consumers.

This scenario arose amidst the savings and loan banking crisis of the 1980s, which left a thousand banking institutions in the dust and many thousands of people without jobs. On Wall Street, the rip-snorting bull market turned bearish and crashed in October of 1987. Partly as a result of these economic earthquakes, banks were subjected to a tight regulatory net that restricted their lending policies and increased the minimum cash reserves they must maintain against potential loss.

At the same time, certain regulatory barriers that had prevented banks from selling investment products were removed. Now, bankers can enjoy profits that once tumbled automatically into the pockets of investors and securities dealers.

Another development was a number of mergers and consolidations that created megabanks. For example, Chase absorbed Chemical Bank which had already merged with Manufacturers Hanover, leaving one bank standing instead of three.

These changes left smaller, community-centered banks shuddering and forced them to find new ways to market their services or perish. Most Black-owned banks simply refocused their efforts on marketing their services to the Black communities. Carver Federal Savings Bank in Harlem took a different approach by becoming the first African-American bank to raise capital by going public. Other banks turned the S&L crisis to their advantage by acquiring failed institutions that had been liquidated by the government.

Emma Chappell's thirty-five-year trek from bank clerk to founder of United Bank of Philadelphia is among the most celebrated examples of entrepreneurial success in banking. Emma took her first banking job at the suggestion of her pastor, civil rights activist Leon H. Sullivan of Zion Baptist Church in Philadelphia, who helped her secure an entry-level position at Continental Bank. Realizing that she would need a college degree if she were to advance, Emma attended night school for five years, at the same time taking every opportunity within Continental to learn various jobs. After graduating, she entered a training program which sent her through each of the bank's departments. In 1977, she became Continental's first Black and first female vice president.

While she worked hard at the bank to advance, Emma also made time to engage in community activities, including work as the vice president of Jesse Jackson's National Rainbow Coalition and treasurer for his presidential campaign. By this time, Emma's accomplishments, which would fill the rest of this chapter, made her the logical person for Black business owners and investment bankers to approach with the idea of founding her own bank. She had the experience, the community connections, and the drive to accomplish what seemed to many a formidable undertaking.

Emma spent five years drumming up the financing necessary to open United's doors in 1992, with over 50 percent of the capital raised at the grassroots level in church congregations and community groups. Community banking had indeed become a reality.

After two years, the bank had turned a profit and, in a stunning deal engineered by Emma, went on to acquire several failed S&Ls. This expanded United's earnings and its outreach. Today, United stands as an unqualified success and an inspiration to entrepreneurs hoping to forge their own path in the financial marketplace. United has helped minorities buy homes, establish businesses, and build the credit histories necessary to acquire loans and credit ratings.

Not all of us can become the next Emma Chappell, but climbing the corporate ladder may be easier in this industry than in others. According to the Equal Employment Opportunity Commission, 12.4 percent of bank executives were minority as compared to 11 percent in all U.S. industries.

Hot jobs in the field include commercial lending, private banking and client services, marketing, and sales. However, though banking is the largest sector in the financial industry, overall employment opportunities are predicted to grow at a slower-than-average rate over the next decade. Support staff positions, such as bank tellers, are disappearing. Limited growth in jobs stems from the ongoing trend toward consolidation, new technology which is replacing workers, and rising competition from non-banking sources.

Yet banking remains an important career opportunity for African Americans who are motivated and committed to building our communities. Community and regional banks are likely to thrive, since Black bankers know our local market and our business and personal needs.

There are four main types of institutions to consider:

1. Commercial banks form the largest sector of the banking industry; they are owned by stockholders and provide a full range of services to individual and corporate customers, including checking and savings accounts, loans, and trust and estate services. Loans made by commercial banks to individuals and to small and large businesses total hundreds of billions of dollars each year.

2. Savings and loans associations are owned by depositors and are the traditional source of home mortgages.

3. Federal reserve banks are quasi-government-owned and -managed institutions that regulate and control the U.S. money supply.

4. Credit unions are formed by people with a common bond, often members of the same company, union, or church, who pool their savings for greater financial clout and services.

Starting salaries vary with the size and location of the bank. Large megabanks pay better than small, community-based independents. Applicants with college degrees can expect to earn from the low to the upper thirties, and senior vice presidents can pull in six figures.

Above the rank of tellers or clerks, most bankers have a college degree, with a focus on personal finance and economics. Banks generally offer training programs to help employees broaden their skills in specialized fields, which might include accounting, budget and corporate cash management, financial analysis, international banking, and data-processing procedures.

In banking, too, an internship and/or membership in a professional organization can be a big help. The more you know about what you want, the better prepared you'll be to find mentors who can help you get your dream job.

INSURANCE COMPANIES

OVERALL, JOBS WITHIN the insurance industry are expected to grow at an average rate of 23 percent. Insurance is a hot industry for minority applicants because insurance corporations are realizing they've missed out on a huge customer base. It used to be that so-called "debit" companies sent agents around door to door to collect from Black customers who paid a few dollars a month on their burial policies. That was the only insurance we had. But today, African Americans buy insurance to help prepare for retirement and investing, too.

Linda Burchette, an agent for State Farm insurance, who opened one of the first national insurance company branch offices in Harlem, has been working around the clock to fill the insurance needs of a neighborhood other insurers had been loath to enter.

Health insurance companies like Cigna and Oxford Health Plans are also taking advantage of changes in the health-care laws that now permit them to solicit Medicaid and Medicare patients for business. By joining with community-based organizations (CBOs), these companies employ a variety of techniques to inform potential customers of their services. They sponsor Little League baseball teams, hold community health fairs, and engage in any number of programs designed to get the word out. Job applicants who can relate to potential customers are in demand with these organizations.

If you like flexible hours and want the chance to build your own business, becoming an insurance broker might suit you. Insurance brokers (also called agents) work on commission and create their own client base by signing up customers. They may sell a range of policies, such as life insurance, property-casualty insurance, and accident and health insurance. In addition to writing policies, some brokers also manage retirement and pension funds.

Brokers make up about 15 percent of the industry. Other careers available include underwriters, who evaluate applications to determine whether to accept or reject them; claims adjusters, who decide whether a claim is covered by the policy and the amount payable on the claim; claims examiners, who determine whether claims have been appropriately settled under the company's policies; and actuaries, who study the probability of an insured loss and determine premium rates. Actuaries are one of the highest-paid segments of the industry. One of the hottest careers in insurance is in computer programming and analysis; computer science majors are being recruited almost as fast as they get their degrees.

Earnings depend on the nature of the job—the more agents sell, the more they make.

Insurance companies usually locate their regional offices near larger urban centers, although agents, who deal directly with the public, are scattered throughout the country. Hours for agents can be irregular, since they often work their schedules around their clients' hours, making visits in the evening or on the weekends when people are available to discuss their insurance needs.

Most insurance companies seek out candidates with college degrees for sales, managerial, and professional positions. A degree in business administration with an accounting background is a plus. Actuaries must generally have degrees in actuarial science, math, or statistics, and candidates must also pass a series of examinations to become fully qualified. All insurance agents and brokers must obtain licenses in the states where they plan to sell insurance.

MY FRIEND KEVIN L. Jones, a founder of the Obsidian, a Cleveland investment club, echoed Andrew Young's speech to the National Association of Securities Professionals when he recently told the Cleveland *Plain Dealer*, "What we're doing now is no different than what was done in the '60s . . . Our leaders paved the way for us politically. It's now time for us to pave the way economically for our children." Kevin means you, me, all of us together.

6

SMALL BUSINESSES LEAD
TO BIG BUSINESSES

Do you ask what we can do? Unite and build a store of your own ... do you ask where is the money? We have spent more than enough for nonsense.

— MARIE STEWARD C. 1872

Wherever you spend your money is where you create a job. If you live in Harlem, and spend your money in Chicago, you create jobs for people in Chicago. If you are Black and the businesses are run by people who are not Black, then those people come in at 9 A.M.; leave at 5:00 P.M. and take wealth to the communities in which they live.

— TONY BROWN

Successful businesses are founded on need.

— A. G. GASTON

CAROLE GELLINEAU
CAROLE JOY CREATIONS
DANBURY, CONNECTICUT

Carole Gellineau credits three important things for preparing her to start her million-dollar greeting card business, Carole Joy Creations. As a young girl she attended the Ophelia DeVore School of Charm in New York City, which gave her strong self-esteem and the confidence to present herself in a professional manner. Second, her older sister and her father exposed her to music, dance, and the arts, from which she learned to appreciate that hard work is necessary to succeed. And finally, as a young adult she worked for several years as a real estate agent, which provided her with "sales skills and the ability to handle rejection gracefully."

Armed with this background, she started her now-thriving card business at home, part-time. Married to a corporate husband and raising three children, she pressed on by herself, but soon her husband Victor left the safe haven of Kraft Foods, where he was a marketing executive, and joined the family business. "It was then the business really began to grow," Carole remembers.

Things are still tough in a business dominated by powerful competitors, but the Gellineaus wouldn't have it any other way. They contributed greatly to expanding the Black greeting card niche and are reaping the benefits of years of hard work. Carole attended Queens College but got most of her training on the job. Today she says, "You need a degree in business with a minor in fine arts to go into the greeting card business specifically, but the bottom line for anyone considering getting into a small business is to do good research on the industry you are considering getting into, then define your niche, identify a gap in the market, and fill it.

"Don't be afraid to get some help" is her advice to would-be entrepreneurs. "There's no replacement for the hard work necessary to succeed, therefore love what you're doing, because you'll be doing it seven days a week. Make sure you leave something good behind every time you deliver a product or service. Try to make a difference in whatever you do."

FAVORITE BIBLICAL PASSAGE:

Teaching them to observe all things whatsoever
I have commanded you; and, lo, I am with you always,
even until the end of the world.

—Matthew 28:20

MY PLANE TOUCHED down at the Kingston airport on another of those hot, humid Jamaican days. I had flown to Kingston at the invitation of the Jamaican Management Institute (JMI) to be the keynote speaker at a dinner, but I was so tired from the flight that I winced when the Institute's greeters led me to a private airport lounge for a press interview. Smiling was an effort, but I pressed on.

As we settled into the lounge, the young reporter confessed that he had always wanted to be self-employed and would someday take the plunge. "Yeah?" I chuckled. "Well, be careful what you ask for, you just might get it." He laughed, then threw me his first question. He seemed to want the answer more for himself than for his readers.

"What is the greatest obstacle that Black people must overcome to become self-employed, and what is the greatest deterrent to our entrepreneurial success?"

I took a minute to search deeply through a well of experiences, my own and those of the thousands of people I'd talked to over the years. Determined not to be trite or superficial, I thought hard and answered with two words: "Fear and commitment."

The reporter started scribbling.

"Too many are unwilling to enter the cave and slay the dragon," I began. "We fear failure and the unknown. We fear losing ground— our status and hard-won material gains. We operate more from a desire for instant gratification than a passion to shape our dreams into reality. We have in the past and even today sought social acceptance by whites, working for them instead of developing our own Black business enterprises. We have long feared losing their acceptance, yet what are we trying to penetrate? A society where wealth and capital are controlled by whites."

I took a breath and continued. "The greatest deterrent to long-term entrepreneurial success is lack of commitment. How have we lost this characteristic, which our ancestors breathed in their struggle for freedom? . . . So many lose faith, fast, when they are threatened by obstacles. Only with the commitment to persevere over the long haul, to work through the problems and the pain, will people overcome their fears and succeed in business."

"You can't put a dollar figure on these two qualities." I stood up, telling the reporter about John H. Johnson, A. G. Gaston, and Madame C. J. Walker, Black business heroes who'd found the strength and resources to see their visions through.

I paused and glanced down at him. "Will we be able to say the same thing about you?"

The young man swallowed, smiled, and stared at his pad without answering.

THAT YOUNG MAN'S silence has often disturbed me as I wonder whether we, as African Americans, have the courage to overcome our fears and the commitment to meet the daily challenges we must confront to create and sustain our businesses.

Black America's vision for economic and business development must be driven by values first and profits second. Easy street is at the other end of a long, hard road. If we focus solely on trying to get rich quick, we won't have the staying power necessary to succeed—real profits come slowly.

Entrepreneurism is like a good sweet potato pie; you must start with the best ingredients. Meet some of our best bakers—Madame C. J. Walker, John H. Johnson, and other Black entrepreneurs turned pennies into millions, spurred by necessity, vision, and courage. Orphaned at age six, a wife at fourteen, and widowed at twenty, Madame C. J. Walker became a laundress to support herself and her family. In addressing her own hair-care needs, she developed a straightening comb that also met the needs of millions of other women. The "Walker System" of styling led to her becoming a millionaire cosmetics manufacturer.

John H. Johnson, multimillionaire entrepreneur, convinced his mother in 1942 to let him borrow five hundred dollars against her furniture so he could publish the *Negro Digest* and show, in print, a positive side of Black America never seen before. His three-hundred-million-dollar company now publishes *Jet*, *Ebony*, *Ebony Man*, and owns *Fashion Fair Cosmetics*, in addition to owning pieces of other businesses.

I started SuccessSource from the extra bedroom of our house with my Soul-O-Dex/Rolodex, and Greg Williams, a good friend and partner. My new business suffered all of the travails most minority enterprises encounter, principally lack of capital. Greg and I worked virtually without pay for several years, and more than once I had to go to friends for cash or counsel. Surprisingly, although my family's entire financial future and quality of life was at risk, I never felt stressed. I was much more comfortable being an entrepreneur than getting into a corporate mold.

As it turned out, my Soul-O-Dex was the key to my company's eventual success. I had saved the names of hundreds of people I had met over the years with whom I had developed trusting business and personal relationships. These contacts proved vital to my small business enterprises. Networking is key for all successful entrepreneurs—including you.

Countless others are making their mark. I wonder if the young man I met in the Kingston airport, and you, are willing to join their ranks?

THE STATE OF OUR BUSINESS

THE NUMBER OF Black-owned businesses is skyrocketing, according to a recent U.S. Commerce Department survey. The survey says the number of Black-owned businesses grew from 424,165 in 1987 to 620,165 in 1992, a 46 percent increase, which far surpassed the growth rate of 26 percent for businesses overall.

There may be strength in numbers but money talks, and in 1992 Black businesses had about $32.2 billion in revenue to shout about. That sounds like a lot until you consider that total business revenues were $3.32 trillion during the same year. The total revenues of all one hundred of *Black Enterprise*'s top-rated industrial and service companies didn't add up to the revenue of one Fortune 100 company.

Black-owned firms lag far behind their white counterparts in the race to bring in the bucks. In 1991, for example, average revenues for individual Black-owned businesses were a paltry $51,000, compared to the $192,000 streaming into small businesses generally.

The good news is we're growing, and this growth appears to be stim-

WHERE ARE WE?

Top Three Locations for Black-Owned Businesses

STATE	# OF BUSINESSES	REVENUES
California	68,968	$5.5 billion
New York	51,312	$2.2 billion
Texas	50,008	$2.3 billion

ulated by a larger, more confident Black middle class that wants the satisfaction that comes from being your own boss. According to Timothy Bates, a professor at the New School for Social Research in New York City, the new crop of Black entrepreneurs is better educated and builds larger companies than previous generations. "[They are] less likely to locate in inner-city neighborhoods, and are more likely to sell to racially diverse customers," he adds. This spells jobs for African Americans, who are more likely to be hired by this expanding army of Black business owners and managers.

The new entrepreneurs generally have a college and business school degree hanging on their walls, and fifteen years of experience under their belts. This profile fits my career progression. I was educated during the 1960s, spent nearly eighteen years in private-sector positions at Procter & Gamble, United Way, and Ford Motor Company, then launched my own business, SuccessSource Inc., in 1987 when I was forty-two years old. I've been moving up and encouraging others to do the same ever since.

TRENDS

BEFORE YOU CHOOSE your dream business, take a look at what's hot and make sure the market wants what you've got. Knowing how to make the best typewriter won't get you far these days (unless you can turn it into a computer). Here are some businesses to look out for, and businesses for which you'd better watch out!

According to *Black Enterprise*, the fastest-growing fields over the next ten years will range from day care to homes for the elderly. Demand will also rise for job-training companies. Credit-reporting businesses will surge, as will firms that lease various types of equipment. Medical and dental laboratories will be hot spots. Architectural firms,

THE TOP TEN*

A recent overview of small business opportunities highlights ten top areas for entrepreneurs to consider:

1. Export
2. Education and training
3. Information/technology
4. Subcontracting to big business and the government
5. Cost-cutting and financial management
6. Convenience and time-saving products and services
7. Products and services for children and seniors
8. Health care
9. Personal safety
10. Financial security

*Black Enterprise, June 1995, based on survey prepared by Kessler Exchange

as well as engineering companies, will have about 30 percent more jobs to fill.

Computers, telecommunications, the Internet, and the support industries growing up around them are fast-track businesses where fortunes are being made and lost with the daily stock report (mostly made). But anyone without technical savvy and a hard head for business is going to get lost on this track. As Pedro Alfonso, president and CEO of Washington Dynamic Concepts Inc., said in a published interview, "Minorities will be excluded if they don't understand, appreciate and accept new technologies."

However, the number one business opportunity as we enter the twenty-first century is projected to be in export. The government offers several programs to encourage minority businesses to expand their sights beyond U.S. borders. Contact the Department of Commerce's International Trade Administration for help with understanding details of an exciting, and possibly very lucrative, business. (To learn more about Global Commerce, see Chapter 13.)

Watch out for businesses within the traditional areas of retail, construction, and manufacturing, which are subject to fluctuations. Entrepreneurs who tap into less traditional areas, such as transportation and finance, can take advantage of the potential for steady growth these industries reflect.

CAPITAL—WHERE TO FIND IT

WHETHER YOU ARE planning a baby-sitting service or a multinational software development company, you'll need money to get your business up and running. Don't forget that you and your family will need a roof over your heads and food on the table, so make sure you budget your personal finances into the picture as well.

Now the bad news—or the challenge, as I like to say, since in my experience, if you have faith and persist, you can wring something good out of a problem almost every time. Financial institutions may show you the money, but that doesn't mean they're going to lend it to you. Time and again, Black and other small business owners complain that capital necessary to start up, run, and expand a business is the scarcest resource.

It's true, but irrelevant. No one should try to start a small business by borrowing money. The first thing lenders or investors will ask you is, "How much money are *you* investing?" The money you scrape together yourself is your only sure capital.

Despite a heritage of building a multitude of businesses mostly on a shoestring, Black women face special hurdles in acquiring capitalization. Yet their numbers are growing. Of nearly eight million female-owned businesses, an estimated 250,000 are piloted by Black women, and these figures have been called an underestimation.

The lack of precise figures on entrepreneurial Black women suggests what many feel—that they are not taken seriously. In a published interview in *Black Enterprise*, Sharon Hadary, the executive director of the National Foundation of Women Business Owners, confirms that "being taken seriously is still one of the biggest challenges women entrepreneurs face, whether they are bankers, vendors or customers, many people continue to question whether a business run by a woman can deliver." Lack of recognition makes overcoming obstacles all entrepreneurs face, such as lack of capital, particularly difficult for female business-owners.

Man or woman, without money your dream will be no more than a sweet potato pie in the sky. But entrepreneurs without a credit history or collateral often find it difficult to secure a bank loan. So where does the money come from?

Often from personal savings accounts or loans from family or friends. (Nice folks, if you've got them.) Many thriving enterprises were started with personal bankrolls. A *USA Today* survey showed that 70 percent of all business start-ups are funded by personal savings. Lurita Brown took fifty thousand dollars she had stashed away to set up an art gallery specializing in fine Afrocentric artwork.

Likewise, fifty thousand dollars in savings was what ten Morehouse grads had when they started Delights of the Garden, a raw food vegetarian restaurant. The group had trouble securing financing, and as one of the young partners pointed out, "It's a Catch-22. If you can make the criteria, you don't need the loan."

Even if your enterprise is off the ground, financing may not get much easier. Laverne Morrow, president of Emprise Designs Inc., has been in business for ten years, has revenues of $3.5 million annually, and still has trouble securing financing. She turns to private investors to raise the cash necessary to fertilize her ever-expanding business. Awarded a hefty government contract, Morrow was turned down by two commercial banks for the four hundred thousand dollars she needed to open additional offices to complete her end of the bargain. She finally convinced several investors to lend her the money.

These experiences are not unique. Commercial banks have been stingy about lending to small minority-owned businesses, especially to start-ups. Timothy Bates found that "Blacks starting businesses received 37 percent less in bank financing than their White counterparts did for each dollar of equity invested in their companies."

This despite laws on the books that require bankers to lend to small businesses located in the communities they serve. These laws, grouped under the Community Reinvestment Act (CRA), have not been vigorously pursued or enforced. Make it a point to get information about the CRA from your local bank to find out whether your business falls within the scope of their lending.

If the bank won't give you a loan, try the government. Loan programs and assistance are available for minority small business owners through the "Black-friendly" agencies: the Minority Business Development Agency (MBDA), which is part of the Commerce Department, and the Small Business Administration (SBA), which operates as an independent government agency. Though their missions are different, both offer a range of assistance programs and services. Anybody who's paid taxes has worked part of their time for the government and these programs give the government a chance to work for us.

The centerpiece of the MBDA is its Minority Business Development Centers, which provide valuable information on starting and growing a business. If you need financing, they can put you in touch with venture capitalists. If you want to know what the competition is doing, they've got current estimates on pricing and bidding. For import/export businesses, they can help you navigate through a sea of laws of many nations. And if you're looking for customers, they can hook you up to the biggest customer in the known universe—the United States government and its local and state agencies.

The SBA oversees and assists the entire small business community with several programs of particular importance to small minority-owned businesses. The Section 8 (a) program requires federal agencies to designate a percentage of their contracts for economically disadvantaged small businesses. (Section 8 (a) has been teetering on the brink of extinction from efforts to completely sack the program.) Other credit programs overseen by the SBA include the 7 (a) Guaranteed Business Loan Program, which will back a loan of up to $750,000 to small businesses that are good credit risks but can't get a loan. Small businesses can also apply for "micro-loans" from small community lenders under the SBA's "micro-loan and prequalification program." The SBA will vouch that you prequalify for a 7 (a) loan before you approach a bank or commercial lender.

Some small businesses have "joint-ventured" with large, cash-rich companies that have the money, credit, and business savvy to get the budding company on its feet. Frito-Lay, Inc., helped to create a minority-owned packaging supplier by acting as a corporate match-maker. Frito-Lay suggested to Bob Johnson (an African American experienced in the packaging business) that he joint-venture with a white-owned company. The deal made everyone a winner.

Companies like Prin Vest Corp of Memphis, Tennessee, and Law-renceville, New Jersey, are actively seeking minority suppliers and have established favorable policies and rates to attract Black-owned and -managed businesses.

Large institutional investors have also seen the green in Black-owned firms. They've set aside over five hundred million dollars to invest in minority businesses, and for good reason. These businesses are growing, and growing fast. BET Holdings Inc., Envirotest Systems Corporation, and United American Healthcare Inc. are some of the major Black-owned corporations that secured financing from venture capitalists looking to invest in the African-American market.

GETTING OFF THE GROUND

MONEY ISN'T EVERYTHING, although it may sometimes seem that it's the only thing. But even if you are lucky enough to have your financing in place, you need a lot more than cash to hatch a successful business. A group of organizations known as "business incubators" can help your baby company fly.

Incubators offer a range of services to start-ups that are similar to those offered by the government agencies but that also include sales and marketing and help with financing and contracts with the private sector. They may also provide a "nest," a suite of offices where fledgling businesses are charged minimum rates for office space, administrative services, and equipment and with access to a cadre of consultants—lawyers, accountants, management experts—who work pro bono or at reduced rates.

Owners who lease incubator space can grow their businesses, network, and learn their trade within the incubator's nurturing environment until they are ready to fly the coop and strike out on their own. Of the 530-some business incubators in North America, thirty are targeted at minority- and women-owned businesses. In general, incubators cater to small businesses with serious potential for growth rather than one-man shops that have no plans to expand. If this fits within your future, an incubator could be the answer to helping your business lay that golden egg.

These and many more resources are out there that are too lengthy to list in this book. So how will you find them? My suggestion—networking. (How did you guess?) You just can't do enough of it. Networking is the heart and soul of a small business. People do business with people they know, trust, and like. You can forge valuable relationships that will open doors to a wealth of business opportunities by joining forces with other small business owners whom you'll meet by joining trade organizations, advocacy groups, and networking organizations. Tap into the Internet where networkers are making connections by surfing sites like NetNoir, AfroNet, and MelaNet and see for yourself.

Several excellent networking organizations deserve special attention. The National Minority Supplier Development Council (NMSDC) is a private nonprofit organization that expands business opportunities for minority-owned businesses. Chartered in 1972, the NMSDC encourages mutually beneficial economic links between minority suppliers and the public and private sectors to support and promote minority business development.

Specifically, the NMSDC network, which includes forty-three affiliated regional councils, matches more than fifteen thousand certified minority businesses with its more than three thousand five hundred corporate members (including most Fortune 500 companies) that want to purchase minority-produced goods and services. In 1994, NMSDC member corporations' purchases from minority-owned businesses exceeded $27.3 billion. Harriett R. Michel, longtime president of NMSDC and networker par excellence, has helped to grow corporate purchasing from eighty-six million dollars in 1972 to its current level. As a small business owner herself, she has been its greatest advocate inside the walls of corporate purchasing.

Harry Alford, chairman and CEO of the popular National Black Chamber of Commerce (NBCC), and Jesse Jackson's Operation PUSH have functioned as small business watchdogs, challenging both white business and government to play fair with minority businesses. NMSDC, NBCC, and Operation PUSH alone help to secure billions of dollars worth of new business each year for Blacks.

We have come a long way, but there is more to do. New Black businesses must be launched and nurtured, while existing companies need cash infusions to increase revenue and profits. With our support, the number of Black businesses will increase, and the increased competition will improve their quality. There is strength in numbers.

MY ADVICE IN A NUTSHELL

- Buy your goods and services from minority-owned firms whenever possible—we're in this together.
- Form "strategic alliances" with CEOs from large corporations—why re-create the wheel?
- Prepare yourself—know your business backward and forward before you take the plunge.
- Enter a new field with growth potential—the competition is less established.
- Be realistic about money—everyone wants it and supplies are scarce, especially when you need it most.
- Increase your visibility—let people know you exist.
- Consider joint ventures with existing enterprises—you'll not only get

support, you'll learn valuable lessons from someone who's been there, done that.

- Join an advocacy group—you'll learn what's going on at local and national levels and forge business relationships.
- Be creative when looking for clients—sift through minority trade and business periodicals and local news for new leads.
- Join or contact a minority business organization—NMSDC is a good example. Link yourself to any group that can help your business. Chambers of Commerce, Rotary Clubs, and industry groups are good organizations to consider. Contact the National Black Chamber of Commerce, the SBA, and the MSBA.
- Check out local universities and colleges to find out if they offer free or low-cost business consulting. (Examples include the Minority Business Consulting Program at Duke University's Fuqua School of Business in Durham, North Carolina, and the Urban Business Assistance Corporation at New York University's Stern School of Business in New York City.)
- Read, read, read—scour the business sections of your local bookstores for books targeted at minority business people.
- Get a subscription to *Black Enterprise* (800-727-7777), *Minority Business News* (214-606-3986), and your local Black Pages.

DO WHAT YOU LOVE

PASSION AND PURPOSE, not profits, are the fuel that drives the small business engine forward. If you don't love your work, you won't like what you have to do to keep your business going, and, believe me, you'll soon lose the commitment to carry on. I like this definition of commitment I once heard from a pundit: "Commitment is doing the things you said you would do, long after the mood has left you." If you do what you love and know, if you give consumers an excellent product or service they need, and if you invest in your idea and secure the financing, you're off to the races.

The first two questions to ask yourself before you even begin thinking about drafting a business plan is who you are and where you want to go. You say, "I know that! Just get me on my way." But you'd be surprised how much more you can learn about your unique skills and values by taking a few days, weeks, or even months to delve into your imagination, your memories, and your heart. Uncover the strengths, values, interests, and goals that will energize your spirits and motivate you to keep on keepin' on when the going gets rough (and believe me, it will).

Try this: Think about and write down memories—call them stories—that had an impact on you for whatever reason. Study your stories and you'll begin to see patterns that reveal interests and activities that hold a special meaning for you. Do any of these translate into a business you could start? Remember that you'll be spending almost every waking hour nurturing your company. You'd better love what you're doing so that when times get rough, you'll have reason to stick it out.

Joyce Hunt's love for her son Mitchie forced her to leave her job as a senior systems analyst at a bank. Mitchie had been paralyzed in a car crash and needed his mother's loving care. Part of his rehabilitation involved using his hands, so Hunt encouraged him to draw. She was surprised to see that Mitchie sketched only white people and discovered that he had never seen any pictures by Black artists.

Inspired to introduce Mitchie to the vast heritage of Black art, Hunt began collecting African and African-American art, which she displayed throughout her home.

Soon Mitchie was not the only one admiring the works. Hunt's friends began asking where she had purchased the pieces and even offered to buy her collection. Hunt sold pieces from her living room but the demand went further; she started a mail-order business that turned monthly profits of $1,700. From there, Hunt rented a storefront and named it Mitchie's Fine Black Art in honor of her son.

Today Hunt operates out of a huge building she renovated, where she leases space to several other African-American small businesses. Called African Village, it is an African-centered incubator. She provides advertising, accounting, and loan information services to her tenants. As Hunt says, "By helping others grow, we also increase our traffic flow."

Last time I checked, *Black Enterprise* reported that Hunt had dozens of contracts in hand and was approaching the one-million-dollar mark in sales. What's love got to do with it? Everything.

Five years ago, Elizabeth Martin was negotiating leases and real estate deals for Fortune 500 companies from the plush offices of Julien J. Studley, Inc., a high-powered commercial real estate firm. Despite a promising career path, she kissed corporate America good-bye and headed off on her own to launch E. L. Martin & Co., a commercial real estate brokerage that handles an A list of clients, including music impresario Sean "Puffy" Combs (Bad Boy Entertainment), Earl G. Graves, Ltd. (*Black Enterprise* magazine), North General Hospital in Harlem, the YMCA, and Soul Cafe 42.

With a BA from Yale and a graduate degree from New York University, Martin had also spent several years at Prudential learning the ropes of the real estate trade. She had the smarts and the experience to know what she was in for by going solo, but like every successful entrepreneur she thoroughly prepared. Her first order of business was targeting a gap in the marketplace that she could fill, and she already had one in mind.

"Real estate is an industry where African Americans, and particularly African-American women, are so underrepresented. I saw that I could fill a niche by targeting [my real estate services] at entrepreneurs, especially African-American and women-owned businesses," she explains, adding that existing real estate companies were not focusing on this unique segment of the market.

She approached her employer with the idea and he encouraged her to "go for it." She did, using forty thousand dollars in personal savings to kick off her venture. To keep initial costs low, Elizabeth negotiated a deal with her boss to rent office space at reduced rates; this gave her a chance to get her feet on the ground before completely cutting loose. Four years later, she runs a six-person office on Park Avenue with the value of her annual transactions at the five-million-dollar mark.

As far as being a Black woman in a business that is predominantly white and male, Elizabeth says that people are "surprised to see me doing what I'm doing," but extremely supportive. To succeed, her advice is "persevere." "The road is rocky but you can make it if you fundamentally believe in what you are trying to accomplish. A passionate belief in what you are doing will push you forward."

Margie Lewis translated her fascination with science fiction into a multimillion-dollar environmental management company with offices in five states. She became a nuclear engineer and spent fifteen years advising nuclear plants on safety as an inspector with the Nuclear Regulatory Agency.

Tired of working for someone else, Lewis decided that she could provide better service than the larger corporations she felt were "more concerned with just the bottom line." With ten thousand dollars in personal savings, she launched Parallax and quickly secured a two-million-dollar contract with the Department of Energy. Her business has boomed. She expected 1997 revenues to hit fifty million dollars in what she described as "a very lucrative industry." What an understatement!

If you have a hobby you enjoy, think about whether you can get paid for doing what you would spend time on for nothing. Todd Alexander did. He started with a love for Italy and a passion for its wines. After graduating from Cornell University's School of Hotel Administration, Alexander found work with a stateside distributor. He then traveled to Italy to research a book on wines he was planning to write.

Alexander's research uncovered a lot of dissatisfaction with American distributors among Italian wine manufacturers. Learning this gave him an idea. He started his wine-importing business, Vendemmia, with a fifty-thousand-dollar loan from his family and low-cost space in a family-owned building. After a year, Vendemmia is profitable and moving toward Alexander's personal goal of four-million-dollars in sales. He keeps his perspective. That goal "would be a very good size and still very manageable. After that it becomes a whole other thing, and I wouldn't be having fun anymore," he told *Black Enterprise*.

This from a young Black man whose ambition was to "go to Italy a lot, drink good wine, eat good food, and get paid." Who wouldn't want that? And Alexander is making some money doing it. Think hard. Maybe your hobby can do the same for you.

Even if you lack work experience, the skills that you learn as a parent or a homemaker can be tremendous assets in the workplace. Don't give up on your dreams because you have never held an office job or run a business. Take a careful look at your life, and distill the talents and skills you employ on a daily basis to handle what you may consider mundane tasks. Then roll up your sleeves and get ready for the future.

WHAT DO PEOPLE WANT?

JUST FIGURING OUT what you want to do isn't enough. Make sure that people need the goods and services you plan to provide, or you'll end up hawking your wares to deaf ears. Mitchie's Fine Black Arts, Parallax, Vendemmia, and E. L. Martin & Co. filled needs—what niche does your business dream fill? Don't get started until you research. Remember—educate yourself before you do anything.

Small business expert Geoffrey Kessler, president of Kessler

FIRST THINGS FIRST

Ask yourself:

Does this line of business fit with my purpose in life?
Am I passionate about this line of work?
Have I researched the risks involved?
Have I looked into the competition?
Have I discussed this idea with experts?
Do I have the financing necessary to start the business and to support
    myself and/or my family for one year?
Who needs my business?
Will they need it more in a few years?
Is this the best choice for me based on my background and experience?
Do my family and friends say, "Go for it!"?

Exchange, a small business research firm in Northridge, California, cautions, "Small business owners need to constantly reassess every aspect of their business and their industries to come up with products and services nobody else can offer, in ways that are increasingly efficient. They have to make their business indispensable."

LOW-COST START-UPS

Putting the Cart Before the Store

HERE'S AN INNOVATIVE idea that gets entrepreneurs without much capital into the swim with less chance of drowning in a sea of expenses: pushcarts and kiosks. If you've ever been to a mall, you know what I'm talking about. Pushcarts dot the indoor landscape of America's shopping centers, train stations, and airports. Carts loaded with everything from fashion jewelry to bagels stand ready to tempt you to fork over your cash.

Underground Atlanta Mall is a center for thriving pushcart vendors who hawk their wares beneath the city's bustling avenues. With start-up costs averaging three thousand to eight thousand dollars and monthly rents of approximately one thousand dollars, you can be well on your way to becoming an entrepreneur without sinking tens or even hundreds of thousands of dollars into your idea.

Adeena Smith exemplifies the pushcart route to success. She sold mixed nuts in Atlanta's underground complex, then dumped the nuts and sold customized caps. As *Black Enterprise* reports, her cart took in between two thousand and seven thousand dollars in weekly gross sales. After five years with the cart, Smith moved into her own store called Hats Under Atlanta, which grossed nearly two hundred thousand dollars in its first year.

Running a pushcart is still a business venture despite its small proportions. Successful businesses flourish only if you follow the principles that we've already discussed. Can you deal with long hours and slow days on your feet, every day? Can you deal with the public? Have you researched what products sell best on pushcarts? Have you checked out locations? (Location can make or break many businesses, but especially retail.)

Take a look at the *Mall St. Journal,* which has listings of wholesale catalogues and manufacturers. The National Retail Federation (202-723-2849) offers educational seminars and puts out a directory of services, and Sales Dynamic (609-482-7600) sponsors seminars and trade expositions throughout the year.

Home Cookin'

IF YOU ARE ready to give up all the glory and benefits of corporate life to do your own thing, your home might be a good place to start. I started SuccessSource Inc. on a table in my living room some ten years ago and relocated to offices after two years. For businesses like event-planning and consulting, working out of the home is a low-cost natural.

Computers have driven an explosion in home businesses, but Michael Howie found an unusual route. Howie ran a computer repair service that grew so popular, it had to leave home. His store, Second Byte's, repairs and sells rebuilt computers, software, and parts. Howie found that a large group of consumers want to ride the information highway but don't have the cash for a souped-up hot rod. There is such a demand for Second Byte's' services that Howie is contemplating franchises. That's proof that you can find diamonds in the rough if you look hard enough.

NETWORK MARKETING

ANOTHER HOME-BASED BUSINESS is network marketing, also called Multi-Level Marketing (or MLM). People often associate network marketing with the ring of the doorbell and the chirpy greeting "Avon calling," but don't discount the wealth potential within this market. Network marketing is reported to be a sixty-billion-dollar international industry with a number of MLMs consistently hitting the Fortune 500 and New York Stock Exchange (NYSE) lists. Several network marketers have consistently outsold their "highbrow" competitors: Mary Kay is bigger than Johnson & Johnson, Amway is bigger than Revlon, and Avon is bigger than Estée Lauder. Even traditional sales companies like Colgate-Palmolive, Gillette, and Rexall Drug have network marketing subsidiaries that market their products door to door.

Network marketing groups have pioneered entire industries—such as the businesses of selling natural vitamin supplements, nutrition and diet drinks, and concentrated and environmentally friendly household cleaners. A network marketer almost single-handedly created the home water filtration business.

What powers these organizations? Network marketers pay a fee to sell the company's product on commission. In return for the fee, which some MLMs call a "franchise fee," the company provides its goods or services and training in how to sell them. Commissions rise with sales to regular customers, but they really take off when the network marketer brings in another salesperson. The person who brings in that salesperson gets a small percentage of everything that person sells.

Raymond S. King, Jr., was so impressed with the concept of network marketing that he started Black Heritage Products, one of a few Black-owned network marketing organizations in America. The fifty-plus products in his line address African Americans' special health, cleaning, and personal care needs.

King is also unique in that he uses his products to teach customers a little bit about their own history. Each product label features a photo and brief history of a famous African American. Much of the sales material emphasizes the need to recycle Black dollars and support Black businesses, a philosophy that has made King financially secure. Ken Bridges and Al Wellington, founders of the Matah Network, in Oaklyn, New Jersey, have given up their lucrative businesses to start their own MLM organization. It too is targeted to "self-help"-conscious Blacks. Using the African-centered spirit of "community" and "race first" they are using the powerful networking tools of cyberspace (computers and the World Wide Web) to launch an innovative approach to distributing and selling computers and a group of frequently used products, many of which are produced by Black-owned businesses.

Bridges, Wellington, and King are prime examples of entrepreneurs who have targeted and filled a niche market while committing themselves to promoting the grassroots notion of Blacks helping Blacks. We'd all be in better shape if more people followed their lead. Many blacks have used mainstream MLM companies to build large, predominantly black organizations; Shirley and Delmar Carmack are good examples of this approach.

Shirley Carmack has always been a caring person, someone actively concerned with others' well-being, and in her job as a registered nurse she came to appreciate the importance of a healthy diet and the need to counterbalance our poor eating habits with vitamins and nutrients.

A Philadelphia native, Shirley was also always something of a go-getter, drawing inspiration from self-help books, motivational tapes, and the autobiographies of people she admired. She liked the challenge of setting goals and working to achieve them and enjoyed the approval and respect that came with success.

In the early 1970s, after several years as an RN specializing in anesthesiology, she embarked upon her ambition to enter the business world and spread the gospel of wellness. For the next dozen years she worked as a marketer for a number of struggling health food and vitamin concerns, before landing in 1985 with Diamite, now Golden Neo-life Diamite. She thought their product line of vitamins and nutrients was one of the best in the business, felt comfortable with her colleagues, and respected the leadership of the company. Shirley believed she had found her place and purpose in life: At Diamite, she could make a profit and make a difference.

"It was not an easy road," she remembers. "Good health was not the hot topic it is today. And network marketing had a bad reputation. Getting people to believe it was a viable industry was difficult." Shirley persisted. She knew her products were backed by science instead of hype, so with the support of her husband Delmar, a former painting contractor, she hung in, determined to make it work. It took them ten years to build their predominantly Black nationwide organization and become millionaires in the process.

Shirley and Delmar's advice for those wanting to enter the business of network marketing: "Believe in your product, believe in yourself, be willing to pay the price, and be adaptable, because you will meet all kinds of people in this work and you will need to be able to get along with and inspire them all."

I've had several good experiences with MLMs that I can pass on to you. At the suggestion of my good friends Les Brown and Gladys Knight, I recently joined The People's Network (TPN), an organization that markets personal growth and development products (books, tapes, TV programming) via satellite television. Because the company's mission fits perfectly with my own values and personal goals, I got several of my close friends involved. Kym Yancey owned an advertising agency, but he was so impressed he began selling the materials himself. He ultimately became vice president of marketing for TPN Corporation, a multimillion-dollar enterprise where he got me on faculty as a TPN speaker. What can I say? But that's networking, folks.

If you like what you've read, here's how to get involved in MLM. Corey Augenstein, consultant, industry watchdog, and publisher of the popular quarterly *MLM Insider Magazine*, is an expert on the ins and outs of network marketing. Here are some of his suggestions for questions to ask:

When did the company start?
In what states is the company registered to do business?
Are the products totally unique to the company?
Are the products competitively priced?
What is the compensation plan?
Does the company offer high-quality videos, audiotapes, and literature
   covering the products and the company?
What should you look for in a sponsor?
What will your sponsor look for in you?

The rationale for these questions and many more are provided in Corey Augenstein's low-cost quarterly magazine, as well his guide to understanding compensation plans, which he sells for $9.95. (See the resource section at the end of this book.)

FRANCHISING

MORE THAN A dozen new franchises open every business day. Franchising is appealing because the businesses tend to be well defined and ready to operate. Franchising operations offer varying degrees of support to their franchisees, so you must carefully review the franchise agreement to fully understand what help to expect and the requirements for your performance.

A successful franchise can be highly lucrative. Revenues generated by more than six hundred thousand franchises in the U.S. reach eight billion dollars annually, according to *Black Enterprise*'s annual franchise guide. Profits at the individual level vary, of course, and start-up costs can be hefty, ranging from the one thousand dollars it takes to get a janitorial service up and running to the five hundred thousand dollars you'll need to get a McDonald's cooking. On average, you'll need about $147,000 to get going.

Sidney Warren, thirty-two, and Chuck Baker, twenty-eight, joined up with Joey Nugent, a white friend and neighbor, to find a way out of corporate America to do their own thing. They left "good" full-time corporate jobs to pursue their dreams, bringing a special strength to the partnership. Sidney's was in sales, Chuck's was brand management (with Procter & Gamble), and Joey brought food and beverage experience. They settled on opening a joint franchise with TCBY Treats and Mrs. Fields cookies, which was available at the Atlanta airport.

With a thirty-three thousand-dollar down payment from personal savings on the two hundred thousand-dollar start-up loan from Host Marriott Corporation, they recovered their initial investment in the first forty-five days of business. Soon the trio was grossing $1.2 million in sales. Based on this successful launch, they opened a second store in downtown Cincinnati. Franchising has paid off for their twelve- to fourteen-hour days. As young entrepreneurs, well educated, willing to work hard and risk their savings, they selected the right new business strategies for them and increased their odds of success by leveraging a proven and profitable business concept under a known and respected name.

Experts claim that a strong franchise will outperform a business start-up most of the time, but only if you choose an operation with a good track record. Look for franchises with a proven business plan, thorough training, and quality products with a top-notch reputation. Hundreds of choices are available. Drive past any shopping mall and you're bound to see a few—McDonald's, Burger King, and KFC are franchises (and each of these have a great number of African-American franchisees at the helm).

All of the principles for starting your own company apply to franchises. Franchises, however, have track records that you can research before taking the plunge yourself.

Calvin B. Haskell, Jr., president of Franchise Solutions, Inc., suggests asking current franchise owners these key questions:

Is the company always available to answer your questions and help you?

What kind of ongoing training and development do you receive?

What kind of marketing assistance?

Is your business generating profits?

How long did it take to show a profit?

How do you spend most of your time?

Which of your expectations has ownership of this franchise failed to meet?

Would you buy this franchise again?

Another suggestion: Try to work at a franchise you are interested in replicating to see if you really like the environment. You can save yourself a small fortune and many wasted hours by learning early on whether the franchise feels right for you.

OWNING THE STREETS, AND MORE

MANY HAVE ENCOURAGED Blacks with education and training to play a larger role in improving the inner cities' crumbling infrastructure by starting more businesses in urban locations and by training and hiring their impoverished Black brothers and sisters. I do too. Though a higher calling, this mandate does not require self-sacrifice. James McQueen's remarkable success in Cleveland is just one example of how small business owners can make a fortune while providing homes and jobs in urban communities.

James McQueen was born in Mississippi in 1929, the oldest of nine children and the son of a successful farmer. At the age of eighteen, McQueen headed to Cleveland, Ohio, with nothing except an intense desire to be successful. He started down his road to success by getting some free training and discipline in the army—one of the few promising career options available for poor Blacks in those days. He left the army twenty-one years later as a first sergeant and returned to Cleveland to pursue his lifelong dream of building a business for himself and his family.

In 1971, with nine children under his roof and some money in the bank, McQueen opened a Sohio service station on a busy street in a deteriorating Cleveland neighborhood. With his family helping at the pumps and the cash register, McQueen's business expanded so rapidly that he moved to a larger space in the 'hood. McQueen purchased a tow truck to bring more business into his station and soon bought another to meet growing demand for his services. More hands were needed to get the work done, so McQueen put out the word that he was hiring, making a point to offer the jobs to neighborhood residents. Soon outgrowing his second location, he purchased a much larger site, again an inner-city lot that he used to launch a new business in salvage.

As his business expanded, James took heed of his father's advice to "always own a piece of the land." He bought and renovated several buildings, which he rented to Black tenants at reasonable prices. With thirty-three rental units, McQueen had the capital to start another, larger enterprise: He started a bus company.

Ten years later Erie Shores Bus Lines Inc. owns and operates ten luxury buses and twelve minivans that shuttle elderly and disabled folks from the block to health-care facilities and take inner-city workers to their suburban jobs. McQueen has made millions by providing good housing to the urban poor, employing people from the neighborhood while raising twelve children, most of whom work in the three family businesses.

I hold James McQueen out as a model of the contributions a single individual can make to urban renewal—contributions that translate into jobs, opportunity, and stability.

You won't read about James McQueen in *The Wall Street Journal*, but there are thousands like him and his wife, Wilma, who are quietly and systematically making a difference in urban communities all across America by building small businesses and creating jobs for people desperate to earn a working wage.

Several government programs are aimed at stimulating job creation and small business development within America's inner cities. Empowerment zones established in urban areas provide seed money for small business development, while tax incentives encourage larger corporations to expand into underserved neighborhoods.

These incentives would be meaningless if the inner-city environment could not foster economic development within its borders, but studies provide powerful evidence that urban communities are fertile ground for business profits. A major report by Michael Porter of Harvard University, which was published in the 1995 *Harvard Business Review*, clearly spelled out the advantages of relocating businesses to American's inner cities.

Inner cities are strategically located in what can be economically valuable areas—near high-rent neighborhoods, major business centers, and heavily traveled highways and streets. Close proximity to downtown Cleveland and its highway system was one reason Fred Findley chose to purchase a storage facility in a depressed neighborhood. Truckers could easily access his facility. The building was also in plain view of traffic crowding the interstate, which inspired Findley to raise three towering billboards advertising his services. The billboards worked, and he added more employees to his staff. Overall, the inner-city site has boosted Findley's annual revenues to $2.5 million. He has thirty-six full-time employees.

Contrary to popular belief, people in low-rent neighborhoods do have jobs and money to spend. But where are the stores? Retailing and financial and personal services are scarce and sorely needed.

Take bookstores as an example. The market for African-American literature is booming, but try finding a good bookstore in the inner city. For the past twenty years, Marcus Bookstores of San Francisco has made a profit by feeding inner-city Blacks' craving for literature in a market the major chains have largely neglected. The Marcus chain has succeeded by positioning its stores as cool places where readers and authors hang out, discuss literature, and buy books. Its success can be duplicated in any number of industries—so let's bring that cash back into our communities.

INTEGRATION WITH REGIONAL CLUSTERS

REGIONAL CLUSTERS ARE companies operating in close proximity that have developed symbiotic relationships in which each feeds the other's unique needs for goods and services.

For example, Cleveland Clinic draws professionals and patients from around the world. It is also near a depressed neighborhood. Several travel agencies just "downstream" from the clinic promote travel and accommodation packages for the families of long-term patients.

Businesses that provide supplies and support services to "cluster" companies can take advantage of the inner city's customer base. Gwendolyn Johnson, a twenty-nine-year veteran of Cleveland's inner-city schools, was frustrated with the home care her sickly grandmother was receiving. Instead of just complaining, she retired from teaching and recruited her son (a successful corporate salesperson) to help her survey the Cleveland health services market. Her research disclosed a significant gap for geriatric patient care, which Gwendolyn decided to fill herself.

With the help of professional business managers and a Black-managed venture capital company, Gwendolyn launched Geric Home Health Care, Inc., in 1995. She located her new company in an inner-city office complex to take advantage of low cost and its proximity to the elderly poor who formed her client base, as well as to the hospitals and other health-care organizations that provided her with referrals. In less than two years her business is thriving and profitable.

CARPE DIEM

CIVIL RIGHTS, VOTING rights, set-asides, affirmative action, Section 8(a) contracts, community reinvestment acts, empowerment zones, and subsidized loans. Black colleges, Black banks, the Million Man March, a four hundred-billion-dollar economy, Black elected officials, and hundreds of thousand of successful business role models! Can you think of something else we may need to promote economic and business development in Black America? I sure can, and it's YOU.

7

TECHNOLOGY: CASHING IN ON THE DIGITAL REVOLUTION

People get ready, there's a train a-coming,
You don't need no ticket, just get on board.
— CURTIS MAYFIELD

It's better to waste time doing almost anything on a computer
than to sit passively watching TV.
— ESTHER DYSON

E. DAVID ELLINGTON
FOUNDER/PUBLISHER
NETNOIR
SAN FRANCISCO, CALIFORNIA

David Ellington is a Renaissance man, a Howard grad with a law degree from Georgetown University and a certificate in Japanese from Cornell. He is also something of a visionary, having created the first major on-line service for Blacks worldwide, NetNoir.

"Attending a predominantly all-white high school in Stamford, Connecticut, sensitized me to race," he says. "Before that, I believed I was just your average American boy. That experience helped me to understand I needed to do something with my Blackness that would enable me to do well while doing good. I felt education was the key and technology was the vessel."

Today, helping other African Americans get over technophobia is David's mission, as he provides useful content on the World Wide Web. His ultimate goal is to create an interactive community using chat rooms, games, and real-time surveys and questionnaires. He is well on his way. His award-winning Web site on America Online has helped to set the standard for culturally specific on-line content and creativity.

It has not been easy or cheap. Millions of dollars have gone into his venture, and thousands of hours of analysis and market research have been expended to keep up with the ever-changing needs and interests of his lively customer base. Being a techno-information junkie has driven his passion for the business. And being a workaholic hasn't hurt.

"The real financial benefits of on-line entrepreneurism will become evident after the year 2000," David predicts. "Today you can use the Web as a marketing and/or public relations tool. For those who are addicted to it, as I am, the short-term money is in finding productive business applications and selling them to the big corporate customers. But whatever you do, once you've decided to pursue this path, don't stop. Be flexible and well read and be prepared to change gears immediately. What to me seems very clear is that technology will evolve and be central to man's experience for the rest of time."

FAVORITE BIBLICAL PASSAGE:

When I was a child, I spoke as a child,
I understood as a child, I thought as a child:
but when I became a man, I put away childish things.

—I Corinthians 13:11

PEOPLE OFTEN DREAM of traveling to a land of opportunity where streets are paved in gold. Wake up! That land may well exist in the electronic "Oz" called cyberspace.

My fifteen-year-old son, Scott, thinks nothing of scooting onto the

Internet to research homework, combat virtual monsters, and communicate with friends living thousands of miles away. He spends as much time on his computer as he does on the phone with his girlfriend.

In 1989, I published the first version of *SuccessGuide* by using a labor-intensive pasteup process on old-fashioned layout boards. Within two years, I delivered *SuccessGuide*, its database, graphics, color photos, and text to the printer on two high-density computer disks produced on Macintosh computers.

With technology, each one of us is living through a revolution that is changing our world to an extent greater than the agricultural or the industrial revolutions. The most exciting revolution of all is the learning revolution, being driven today by computers, satellite television, wireless communications, the Internet, and the World Wide Web.

The Internet was actually born during the 1960s as part of a defense research project accessible to a select group of scientists and researchers who used boat-sized computers to navigate the data networks we now call the Net. In 1977, Apple Computer smashed the barriers locking consumers out of this huge information base by introducing the first personal computer designed for home use. The desktop revolution had begun, changing our personal and business lives forever.

Today, twenty million users from businesses, schools, government agencies, and homes are riding the Internet's more than thirty-two thousand specialized data networks to exchange information on any subject, ranging from soul food restaurants to procurement contracts. The number of businesses hooking up to the Internet grows by 10 percent each month. The revenues generated through electronic commerce on the Internet shot to five hundred million dollars in 1996 and are expected to mushroom to five billion-plus dollars at the dawn of the millennium.

So what does this say to African Americans? It says: Don't let this train pass you by.

The World Wide Web is the segment of the Internet consisting of "Web sites," electronic pages of text, graphics, and sound that are accessed by traveling the Net. By dialing into an on-line service provider like America Online (AOL) or Prodigy, computer users can find a Web page on virtually any topic they want.

My own Web site, Frasernet, connects visitors to new people, key contacts, free advice, and timely information that is free and easy to use and open to everyone. I invite you to visit our Web site and become part of an extended cyberfamily that focuses on traditional values of sharing and caring.

Web pages are not only excellent information sources but powerful marketing and networking tools. Entrepreneurs may construct as many Web pages as they wish by setting up their own Web server (computer, software, and telephone services) or by renting space on another company's existing server.

Take Welcome to the Future, an interactive TV company started by two brothers in Maryland. They had great ideas but no corporate identity. Enter Metamorphosis Studios, headed by two young cyberpreneurs who created a high-tech professional corporate look for the one-office company by developing a logo, electronic brochure, and computer-animated Web site. The virtual makeover made a difference. About four to six months later, Welcome to the Future was awarded a three-million-dollar contract, largely due to the reimaging.

Although Internet technology is already developing at warp-speed rates, the estimated growth in related high-tech industries, such as telecommunications and computer communications, is mind-boggling. The high-tech sector accounts for $420 billion in consumer and business spending.

With all the hoopla surrounding the Internet, what opportunities are particularly suited to African Americans? Which roadblocks and potholes on the information highway stand in our way?

To excel and lead in the information age, African American–owned companies must stay on top of the game. First, we must become proficient with the ever-changing technology. Unfortunately, although we are the nation's most aggressive shoppers, only 12 percent of African-American households own computers (compared to 29 percent within white communities). Even more shocking, only 3 percent of Net travelers are African American or Latino.

Second, we must ensure that communities of color are not excluded from the revolution in information technology. There is already reason to fear that the less privileged (of all colors) will be victims of the latest form of segregation, called "electronic redlining." Without computer skills and in-home access to the information available electronically, they will not be competitive in the new digital world.

Besides the lack of access to computers, there is a dearth of sites that appeal to minority users. Tony Brown, executive producer and host of the Public Broadcasting series *Tony Brown's Journal*, warns of a future in which people are divided not by race but by technology.

The "haves" will have the tools to learn about and take part in the information revolution, while the "have-nots" will be excluded.

I've personally chosen to commit my life to working within four areas that are intricately tied into the digital world, and I hope you will join with me:

- Facilitate the networking process among Blacks worldwide by taking advantage of the new tools the digital revolution offers to connect people and ideas.
- Share information among Blacks and whites as a basis for racial healing and valuing diversity. On the Internet, we can all be colorblind.
- Enhance learning among African Americans through the use of new technologies.
- Showcase the breadth and depth of Black excellence, using new technologies.

A 1996 study found that Black and white households in similar income groups are likely to have similar PC ownership patterns. This is contrary to the perception that Blacks are uninterested in the benefits of technology.

Hundreds of ambitious Black technological wizards are applying their creativity to this new arena. According to a 1996 study, 51 percent of Black Internet users are women, 51 percent are younger than thirty-five years old, and 45 percent are single. All of these numbers are well above the national averages.

We are taking steps to help disadvantaged communities become computer-literate and we can do more. This is a top priority being addressed by organizations such as Plugged In, which uses government and private funding sources to provide computer and Internet access to low-income minority populations. Playing to Win (ptwinc @iqc.apc.worg) is a Harlem-based nonprofit that provides computer access information to inner-city youth and adults. We have to help our communities get on the entrance ramp for the information highway.

How can we make our voices heard? Generating Black-oriented content and services on Web sites will encourage others to get involved on the Net and will also create a more positive image of who we really are and what we stand for.

Sites like NetNoir, African American Haven, Meanderings, and The Black Cinema Network, among dozens of others, are up and running with a smorgasbord of information aimed at Black Net surfers. But there's plenty of room for more of these sites. Lots more.

More and more companies of all sizes, ranging from Fortune 500 giants to mom-and-pop new-wave hair salons, are relying on temporary workers and outside consulting firms to address their high-tech needs, which means there are plenty of lucrative opportunities out there for cyberspace entrepreneurs. Black-owned consulting firms have an opportunity to come to the rescue in an industry that is growing at the rate of forty thousand new jobs annually. Future prospects in the high-tech communications field are not just bright—they're blinding.

Although the industry is volatile because of uncertainty about consumer preferences in the face of countless new technologies, economists and business forecasters alike predict that high-tech opportunities will continue to multiply, especially for those who produce and market multimedia services, like CD-ROMs. Project managers who can help to create custom systems and develop on-line information services are also in demand.

The award-winning NOLA Computer Services of New Orleans, for example, provides systems engineering services, one of the hottest areas in the industry. Smart Technology Inc. of Alexandria, Virginia, also has made its mark by providing training, computer-aided design, and digital engineering services.

Any one of these reasons should encourage you to take part in the digital revolution! In the following sections, I will guide you through the hottest trends in the industry.

THE CONSULTANTS

THE DESPERATE NEED of many companies to find the ideal computer solution and implement it now, if not yesterday, has spawned a huge boom in consulting firms versed in digital language. These computer and telecommunications consultants are becoming rich by helping businesses and individuals tap into the vast supply of information available in the high-tech age. According to a top executive at Peat Marwick, one of the world's major accounting firms, management consulting is growing at a rate of 40 percent a year.

Take the example of a New Hampshire company that made trailer hitches and snowplows. The owners were sinking in piles of paper without the ability to cross-reference or quickly access data about their

TEN REASONS WHY I BELIEVE TECHNOLOGY IS A DRIVING FORCE IN BLACK ECONOMIC AND BUSINESS DEVELOPMENT

1. To participate successfully in today's business environments, African Americans must be technologically literate.

2. Technological literacy provides greater job security in work environments where computers are used for virtually every imaginable task.

3. Technology provides a low-cost means of marketing and distributing product throughout the national and global marketplaces.

4. Technology provides instant access to information, which can improve the quality of life at home, at work, and in the community.

5. Technology enables us to make better and more informed decisions.

6. Technology enables us to compete and deliver a service or product more cost-effectively.

7. Knowledge increases value, which is facilitated by technological advances.

8. Technology enables us to predict what's coming next.

9. Technology permits us to control, manage, and distribute Afrocentric products on a far broader scale, across the boundaries of nations.

10. Technology gives small, nimble, entrepreneurial companies opportunities to compete.

stock. Having grown their business to a twenty-employee company, with annual revenues of five million dollars, they couldn't identify how much inventory was in stock or ready for shipment. Their customer base was eroding because they were getting lost on their own paper trail. Talk about mistakes!

With the help of a consultant and a ten-thousand-dollar investment in computers and training, they learned how to use accounting software that was custom-made to track hitches and plows, thus regaining control over their wayward inventory and their dollars.

A consulting firm may be a large conglomerate or a one-person operation. Consultants must have technological expertise and a head for business. They must understand the nature of the industries they serve. Systems suitable for a bank, for example, will be very different from those that are right for a literary agency or a law firm.

Computer consultants should be familiar with the most up-to-date programming languages, as well as with networking and database management systems. For those who want to go into consulting or advance up the management ladder, a master's degree in computer sciences and business administration may give you the extra edge to succeed.

Systems Analysts

SYSTEMS ANALYSTS ARE best described as "professional problem solvers," although they often seem more like electronic spirit guides capable of leading us out of offices stuffed with file cabinets and stacks of mail into efficient, computerized operations where clutter is compressed and organized on high-tech systems.

We contracted with a systems analyst and paid the young brother one thousand dollars for a day's work to network all five of our computers so they could talk to each other (share software). He also set us up on a high-speed modem so we could call the printing and production plant to download the latest data and layouts for the various versions of *SuccessGuide*. We calculated he saved us over twenty thousand dollars per year in software and production costs.

A systems analyst will study the data-processing problems of a business and find a solution, either by developing an entirely new computer system or by transferring manual operating into the firm's existing database systems. (Systems integrators are specialized systems analysts who design and install networks that bring existing computers together into a single system. They do for computers what I do for people—bring them together to capitalize on the combined strength of their resources.)

Businesspeople rely on consultants not only to recommend the appropriate technology but to set up and maintain the computer systems they purchase. And that job may require programming well into the night and over weekends to get a job done quickly.

According to the Department of Labor, systems analysis will be one of the fastest-growing occupations through the year 2005. Moreover, tens of thousands of job openings will accrue annually as employed analysts move into managerial positions and related occupations or leave the workforce altogether.

Systems analysts usually have undergraduate degrees in computer science, information science, computer information systems, engineering, or data processing. Additional courses in business and communications help them understand the business needs of a variety of clients. A systems analyst who wants to work for scientific organizations should also have a background in the physical sciences, applied mathematics, or engineering.

Systems analysts typically begin their careers as programmers in banks or as contract workers for consulting firms. Assuming supervisory responsibilities, as well as taking on bigger chunks of a consulting project, leads to the top.

This is the path that Tom Perkins, founder of Perkins Financial Associates, took. Initially he provided computer-assisted accounting services, but he swept into consulting when he realized that most of the clients were clueless about the technology best suited to their needs. The result? In 1994, Perkins was named the New Hampshire Minority Small Business Person of the Year for building a firm that posted annual revenues of two hundred thousand dollars.

Tom, a consummate entrepreneur, has since launched The Legal Maintenance Group Corporation, a company that creates networks between lawyers and potential clients. Tom says that his system gives working-class Americans the chance to get legal services, with the added benefit of developing a client portfolio for his computer consulting services. His lawyers can hook up to Tom's network, which he is more than happy to install. The result? He gets two jobs with one sale. Lawyers get clients, clients get low-cost legal services, and Perkins gets business. It all adds up to success.

Tom got where he is because he had a good education. "You can lose everything," he says, "but no one can take away your education. You can always get back on your feet."

Tom also stresses the importance of thinking logically, which he believes is key to becoming a good systems analyst. Systems analysts must also have good communication skills and a genuine interest in people. Since analysts often work in teams, the ability to get along with others is also critical.

Design Consultants

POWERFUL MARKETING AND presentation tools inspire customer confidence and enhance the bottom line for many Black companies. Media studios design on-line and off-line digital showcases, including interactive presentations, diskette brochures, and Web sites that position a firm to reach the seventy-five million (and growing) companies and households that own computers.

Metamorphosis Studio, the company that contributed so much to the success of Welcome to the Future, was founded by two twenty-something hotshots, Clarence Wooten, Jr., and Andre L. Forde. This is one African American–owned company that is not afraid to run with the future. Masterminds of a full-service interactive multimedia design firm specializing in interactive consulting and marketing services, this digital duo also produces CD-ROM products. Visit their Web site at htt://www.mstudios.com to see what they've done and what they are planning. In the works is a networking search engine they've named 2MPower, which is targeted at African-American tastes and interests. I plan to be one of their first visitors and hope to see you at www.2MPower.com.

Relying on a network of freelancers to keep overhead low, Metamorphosis has developed products for such companies as Procter & Gamble, the Marriott hotel chain, Alfred Angelo (the country's largest manufacturer of bridal gowns), and Woolrich (a well-established designer and manufacturer of wool clothing). The pair estimates that within five years their gross income will be twelve million dollars. Not bad for two guys who were in grade school when the first Macintosh appeared on the market.

Wooten got his start as a computer animator; Forde's background was in computer graphics. While thoroughly learning his trade by earning degrees in computer animation and finance, Wooten used his free time to develop an award-winning computer-animated video that landed him his first client. His advice to African Americans who are interested in launching computer design companies? "Go for it."

Wooten stresses that, although there is no clear road map for starting your own company, "You must be persistent, get as much technical training and equipment as you can, and surround yourself with people who can help."

Webmasters

ENERGIZED AND CREATIVE African Americans, step right up. The digital revolution has resulted in a new specialty—the Webmaster. Webmasters combine creativity with technical savvy to develop and maintain Web sites. Many Webmasters start as part-time technical writers and become full-time Webmasters by spending hours trouble-shooting and working on the Web.

Male Webmasters outnumber females by a ratio of five to one; however, communications experts predict that by the year 2000, nearly 50 percent of the on-line community will be women. So to women of color, I say, "You go, girls!"

You don't have to be a programmer to become a Webmaster, but familiarity with multimedia applications and a thorough knowledge of the latest communications software are musts. Understanding design applications such as Photoshop or Java scripting is also a big plus. You can acquire these skills by taking specialized courses or through on-the-job training.

Of course, editorial and management experience always makes a candidate for Webmaster attractive to potential employers.

Technical Trainers

EVEN THE BEST and most advanced computer system or design package is worthless if the employees of the company for which it was developed can't use it. Consequently, technical training has become an essential and lucrative consulting business. Technical trainers may work for a consulting firm or for a corporate human resource department.

In 1995, Stephen Jackson, principal owner of an employee-leasing firm, Jackson & Jackson Management Plus, Inc., got his first inkling of what the Net had to offer when he and his staff began E-mailing information to each other. Seeing the potential for saving on overhead, Jackson designed an electronic database that zapped information to clients.

Realizing that most companies are "electronically challenged," Jackson began offering courses in Internet training, marketing, and Web page development. The response was eye-opening. He ultimately closed the employee-leasing segment of his company to focus on Net training, which generated more than six hundred thousand dollars in revenues during its first eight months.

Jackson practices what he teaches; his own Web site (at http:/www.tnp.cm/~joker) provides information about his company and step-by-step instructions on registering for courses. For him the information highway is literally paved with gold, but he did not take his first step without researching and preparing for success.

Technical trainers must have specialized knowledge of the areas they teach and the ability to translate complex technical language into terms understandable to people with little or no computer experience. Excellent communication skills and patience are also prerequisites.

THE PROGRAMMERS

PROGRAMMERS USE COMPUTER languages to write lines of code that tell the computer what to do. Programmers write the instructions that connect you to your computer and to the technology it accesses.

There are programs for games, for calculating payrolls, and for launching missiles. A large proportion of the programming done in the 1990s has been for packaged software, which remains one of the most rapidly growing segments of the computer industry. Applications like Quicken or Microsoft Word contain millions of lines of code and employ teams of nearly a hundred programmers and developers.

The instructions involved in updating inventory are different from those required to duplicate conditions on board an aircraft. Simple programs may be written in a few hours; complex mathematical formulas can involve more than a year of work. In major corporations, several programmers work as a team under a senior programmer's supervision.

Programmers often work with an expert from a particular industry to customize existing software to that trade's specifications—developing estimating systems for home remodelers, for example, or billing systems for physicians.

Programmers are classified into two groups: applications programmers and systems programmers. Applications programmers write codes to accomplish a specific task, like instituting a stockroom checklist or guiding an infrared sensitive weapon to its preselected target. Applications programmers usually have fairly extensive knowledge of the area in which they work, whether it is banking, insurance, engineering, or science.

Typically, a systems programmer generates and revises programs that direct the central processing unit (CPU) of an entire computer system. Because of his or her knowledge of the "big picture" of a corporation's entire computer network, a systems programmer will assign tasks to applications programmers and provide them with help when needed.

Multimedia Programmers/Specialists

DEVELOPING MULTIMEDIA PRODUCTS and technology is one of the hottest specialties in computer programming and one particularly suited to cyberpreneurs with the personal and financial resources to compete against the heavy hitters like Microsoft, Sega, and Nintendo. Multimedia is just that: a combination of graphics, text, and sound on a single compact disc, the CD-ROM.

In multimedia applications, African Americans can use their creativity to design and produce software that specifically addresses Black interests and needs. This is one good way for entrepreneurs to step onto the information highway. But be forewarned: Research, development, and marketing expenses—and competition—are relatively high, while initial revenues are low.

Despite the obstacles, several start-up companies launched by young, enterprising African Americans have created a niche by using innovative strategies to develop and market their multimedia software and consulting services. Let's take another look at Metamorphosis Studios.

In addition to their design services, these digital whiz kids developed "multicultural edutainment" for Bingwa, a Black-owned Atlanta-based software publisher, and are producing CD-ROM titles based on books written by Judi Craig, a nationally syndicated clinical psychologist.

Afro-link Software, founded by Kamal Al-Mansour, produces software that specializes in Black American and African culture, history, health, education, and politics. Al-Mansour has successfully targeted his titles to schools, medical centers, and companies who want to learn about the African diaspora. Afro-link Software is proof that Afrocentric interactive software fills an educational void. *Black Enterprise* reported that in 1996, the company generated one million dollars with its seminal products including *Who We Are*, a CD-ROM program featuring more than five hundred questions and answers about Black American and African history, and *Imhotep*, which is used by such clients as Meharry Medical College and Howard University Hospital to educate people about diseases that disproportionately afflict Black people. Its most recent product is *Pride and Purpose*, which teaches self-esteem.

Interactive Games Programmers

INTERACTIVE MEDIA IS growing steadily, particularly in the rapidly expanding market for Internet games. Net addicts can hook up to game sites and compete against friends living thousands of miles away.

Microsoft boasts of becoming the "biggest name in on-line games" with its revamped Internet Gaming Zone. America Online is publicizing its upcoming Games Channel, a three-dimensional site where AOL's eight million members will be able to play games between chats. In the works at MCI Communications is a service where players can access their favorite CD-ROM games on the MCI network.

Because the big boys are involved, entry into this new market will be difficult. Research and development takes years, and sky-high costs make it tough for small enterprises to turn either a quick or an easy profit. However, developers can create games and then license them to big corporations that have pockets deep enough to create and place products on the Web. This focus on gaming will open new job opportunities for programmers within the Internet landscape.

THERE IS NO set career route for computer programmers since the businesses served are so varied. Programming is taught in grade school through high school, and on through advanced education. Most programmers have a four-year degree and have studied computer programming as well as accounting, inventory control, and database management. Many have degrees in mathematics, engineering, and the physical sciences. Programmers interested in designing systems generally have degrees in computer science and in-depth knowledge of such operating systems as UNIX or DOS. But even if you majored in liberal arts, you can become a programmer by taking training courses in the evenings. Most corporations will expect beginning programmers to attend training classes and continue to update their skills by participating in additional workshops and seminars. The trick is to learn a computer language for which there is a high demand or a projected high need. Find the void and fill it, before everyone else jumps on board.

Above all, programmers must be able to think logically, pay close attention to detail, and keep a cool head. Programmers also should be able to work well with others, since teams are often required to design and write increasingly complex programs.

Skilled programmers have a good chance at advancement and may be promoted to supervisory or lead programming positions. They also can become top consultants and executives. Remember, Bill Gates, the CEO of Microsoft, is first and foremost a programmer.

THE WRITERS

WRITERS ARE CRITICAL to digital commerce and fulfill a number of different roles, such as translating technospeak into prose accessible to the general public and writing detailed technical instructions for commercial hardware and software packages. Writers also produce stories, articles, and text for the vast complex of Internet publications and communication sites, including Web sites, electronic games, books, magazines, and newsletters.

Technical Writers

COMPUTERS AND SOFTWARE may be getting more user-friendly, but they are also becoming more powerful and complex every day. For most users, scrolling page-by-page through help screens isn't nearly as useful as flipping through a clearly written manual. If you are able to write a manual for African American–created software, like a historical game for children, get thee to the marketers, Jack!

Technical writing runs from detailed documentation of standards and procedures for international financial institutions to transcriptions of technical concepts into books for computer dummies. Often, a technical writer backs up the programming team—writers often discover bugs in the system when writing manuals for new games or other software packages.

If you find it deeply satisfying to solve a problem logically, and if you have the patience to work in the increments needed to take a job to the finish line, this may be the career for you. You don't have to be good-looking or socially adept.

I once worked with an extremely pleasant technical writer/programmer who had the misfortune to hit the scales at three hundred pounds and most of the time didn't realize he was covered with bits of the potato chips he had for lunch. But that didn't matter at all. What did matter is that he worked all night to fix my computerized phone-answering system so that by morning incoming callers requesting mailers got their information sent out that day.

Optimally, a technical writer should have a degree related to the field he or she is "documenting," be it engineering, computer programming, business, or one of the sciences. However, the greater need is to have the ability to absorb information and concepts quickly. An in-depth knowledge of computers and technology is important. Above all, technical writers must have good writing skills and the ability to translate technobabble into fluent, concise prose. Theoretically, employers prefer writers with college educations, but they are generally most interested in hiring people with a proven ability to produce good pieces of technical writing.

On-line Content Developers

ON-LINE CONTENT DEVELOPERS are writers of a certain type. In addition to text, they also write visuals and sound effects. Content developers supervise writers and researchers to create new stories or reformat print articles onto the Web. Developers also may work as cyberspace talk show hosts and tour guides. So, if you're a writer with personality, this may be the job for you.

On-line content developers are hired by companies such as America Online and CompuServe. For example, NetNoir provides me with space for my SuccessGuide Web site, which is written and produced by Web Marketing Services. NetNoir's on-line developers are knowledgeable about subjects that appeal to African-American audiences. Hosted by America Online, NetNoir has set the standard of excellence for Black-oriented Internet sites. These sites can be located through The Universal Black Pages, which provides linkages to African-American resources on the Internet.

On-line content developers should have a bachelor's degree with an emphasis on communications. Some experience in publishing is also useful. Employers favor people with backgrounds in media production, graphic design, writing, and programming. However, the field is so new, and the need so great, that talented and motivated men and women will find work. On-line developers advance by taking on increasingly more complex projects. Some may become managers while others may become marketers. Experienced on-line developers can also launch consulting firms or create their own on-line service.

THE MARKETERS

THE CYBERMARKETPLACE IS no different from any other. Businesses that succeed are the ones that market quality products to a broad base of consumers. The Internet is an especially powerful marketing tool since it invokes a "halo effect," generating sales that carry over into the traditional marketplace.

Toy and game manufacturers, for example, have discovered that putting electronic versions of their products on the Internet increases sales of both the CD-ROM version and the "real" thing at the retail level. Check out the newsstand Web sites of *Essence*, *Ebony*, and *Vibe*, among others, which promote their on-line and print products at the same time.

Frasernet, for example, gives me an entirely new forum for plugging my services and enhancing the image of my company and products. I use my Web site to publish information, gather data, and sell my products and services (books, tapes, and speaking engagements). We're talking synergy here.

Companies and individuals are promoting themselves right in your home. The entertainment industry has been remarkably aggressive in seeking out consumers in their living rooms by using the Internet to publicize their music, films, magazines, games, and whatever else they've got coming down the pike.

Visit any of the Warner Music Group sites and you'll see what I mean. Warner has created a family of sites, including Warner Bros. Records Black Music Division (www.wbr.com/Black), Elektra Entertainment Group (www.elektra.com), WarnerActive CD-ROM games (www.warneractive.com), and Radio Aahs (www.pathfinder.com), a music 'zine for children.

DefJam has created a site where you can "chat" with artists, learn the history of this volatile company, get tickets for upcoming concerts, and see an update of album release dates. That's just for starters. Hardcore fans can get tour schedules, artists' biographies, and audio and video samples.

Advertisements are also a potential source of income, although most Web sites have not yet built a profitable advertising base because of the difficulty in tracking site usage. Today, the only way to gather demographics is to force users to manually register answers to marketing queries. Rather than using expensive tracking methods, most Webmasters are using such efficient tools as electronic certificates, which are expected to increase the appeal of purchasing electronic billboard space on the Net.

Keith Clinkscales, the publisher of *Vibe* magazine, has created a sizzling hip-hop site that gets more than a million hits a week. Advertisers line up to sponsor one or more of the slick, interactive sub-sites on his electronic pages. NetNoir's alliance with America Online and the joint venture of Black Entertainment Television (BET) and Microsoft have resulted in new Web sites that offer arts and entertainment, public affairs, and merchandising targeted to Black consumers.

But Web site designers, beware! Don't let your castle in the sky turn into the impossible dream. The reality today is that the average Web site doesn't even try to make money. Only one in twenty sites generates more than one million dollars a year. To be that one, be cool, be cautious, and be in love with what you're doing, but do it smart!

One inspired tactic Web entrepreneurs have perfected is renting out space to other vendors for a fee. NetNoir and other content providers, like MelaNet and AfroNet, have created Afrocentric outlet stores that sell everything you can buy at your local mall, without making you leave the comfort of your armchair.

The amount of information available on NetNoir, the soul of cyberspace, is mind-blowing. There are listings for products, business links, African-American directories, cultural activities, chat rooms (termed "drums"), dialogues with Black personalities and celebrities— the list goes on and on. Just type "Netnoir" into the keyword section of the Internet and get ready for a long, enjoyable, and educational ride.

THE MANAGERS

LIKE ALL COMPANIES, computer and telecommunications systems need managers—to monitor and oversee databases and the local and wide-area networks that connect people and departments within a company or organizational group.

Corporate Network Managers (LAN/WAN)

LOCAL AREA NETWORKS (LANs) and wide area networks (WANs) link defined work groups within an organization or group of organizations to provide employees with instant access to corporate data. For companies big and small, these networks can create virtual conference rooms or convention centers where employees, clients, vendors, and staff meet, exchange ideas, attend conferences, and make cutting-edge decisions from their office desks or even their kitchen tables.

Networks will highlight the best and the worst aspects of the systems you already have in place. Companies that refuse to embrace technological change will miss out on the cost-cutting, business-building opportunities that a high-tech workplace can offer—but don't join up until you understand why the move makes sense.

Take the experience of Jake Oliver, CEO of the newspaper chain Afro-American, which has kept Baltimore's African-American community informed for more than a century and now publishes newspapers in Richmond, Virginia, Washington, DC, as well as in Baltimore, where the company is headquartered. Oliver had been wading slowing into high-tech waters without knowing whether technology made sense for his business, until he discovered that his readers were searching his Web site for the fast-breaking news his weekly newspaper couldn't deliver.

In a published interview in *Black Enterprise*, Oliver stressed that "Black folks want to go to a Black source for news about things that happen in our communities," a niche he realized he could fill if he upgraded his antiquated computers to a WAN. The move also appealed to his business sensibilities since the high-tech system he envisioned would reduce the time and costs involved in layout, pasteup, and simple office tasks.

Riding the info-road was not a smooth trip, and Oliver had several costly bumps along the way, including the installation of an expensive data transmission system that ultimately cost almost four thousand dollars a month in telephone bills. Things got better, however, when he began working with an AT&T division created specially to find data networking solutions for small businesses.

AT&T brought in a data networking specialist who linked the computers in the Richmond, Washington, and Baltimore offices. As Oliver explained, "By going to the wide area network, we could save on travel by keeping the Richmond people in Richmond and the DC people in DC, the flat rate would be cheaper, the time to proof ads would be much shorter, and life would be easier."

Oliver's offices, which had operated as independent units, now instantly share information about ad sales, newsstand sales, and subscriptions. His Web site (at http://www.afroam.org) runs independently on a twelve-thousand-dollar SGI server. His desktop publishing equipment and software allows the paper to compete. He can transmit digitized layouts to the printer over the phone lines instead of using messenger or overnight delivery services.

The move to high-tech made sense for this business that sells information. But Oliver is careful to do a cost-benefits analysis every step of the way. For him, riding the information highway is paying off.

Data Processing Managers

A LAWYER IS working against the clock to complete a brief due in court the next day. She E-mails her partner, who is on a conference call, with specific questions about the case. The partner receives her message and downloads a brief from an earlier case that contains pertinent legal arguments. The lawyer logs onto Lexis, the legal database, to search for additional cases relevant to her argument. While she is writing the brief, a paralegal checks the accuracy of the case citations on his computer. For several terrifying moments, the lawyers screen freezes, then blacks out. The system has crashed and apparently lost all the buyer's work. Within minutes, the data processing manager has retrieved the lost files and the lawyer resumes her work. This scenario is played out every minute in law firms and all manner of corporations around the world.

Data processing managers oversee database activity to make sure that corporate computer systems are up and running, that information and documents are stored and accessible, and that sensitive data remain secure. Their responsibilities depend on the nature of the corporation and the data it uses. The data processing manager of a law firm, for example, would have to design or purchase computer systems that tracked the status of each case, stored and retrieved briefs and other corporate documents, and provided access to the legal networks like LEXIS/NEXIS. An important part of the job is regularly backing up data and recovering lost or damaged data.

Black Data Processing Associates has taken advantage of the growing need to install, upgrade, and manage network databases by providing forums that link Black business owners who want to automate their operations with Black technology consultants. These linkages forge lucrative alliances. Joe Jameson, for example, owner of a New York–based software consulting firm, got contracts worth fifteen thousand dollars from the New York Urban League by networking through BDPA. For more information and for a chapter near you, call 800-727-BDPA.

CORPORATE NETWORK AND data processing managers usually get their start as programmers or analysts. Employers favor applicants with top computer skills and a master's degree in management science. However, as in most high-tech jobs, someone with experience and proven expertise can often slip in the door without having the prerequisite degree.

Managers must be able to think logically and to work well with people. They must also have good oral and written communication skills. With a little luck and a lot of diplomacy, mid-level managers often move up the ladder to top executive and managerial positions. These positions are a firm grounding for entrepreneurs itching to start their own software or computer consulting companies.

THE TECHNICIANS

AS INTERNET AND telecommunications technology takes off, opportunities on established career tracks will continue to grow at above-average rates. The following are just a few of the positions you might consider.

Computer Engineers

COMPUTER ENGINEERS DESIGN and test the electronic components in computers, such as the integrated circuits, that are the nuts and bolts of the overall system. Engineers are increasingly being called upon for advice by the research and development departments of major corporations striving to solidify their foothold in the global marketplace.

Computer engineers usually have a bachelor of science degree in electrical or materials engineering from a university or technical college. Prior work experience in data processing is good background for people interested in pursuing this career. If you have an administrative knack, your job as a computer engineer could well lead to management, where the financial rewards are much higher.

Computer Repair Technicians

THE NEED FOR computer repair experts will grow fast as the number of homes and businesses that are either becoming automated or upgrading their existing systems increases. Three out of every five computer repair technicians are employed by computer wholesalers; others work for retail establishments or with organizations that service their own equipment. People interested in engineering should consider this line of work.

Computer repair technicians often get their start through apprenticeship programs or formal training in electronics offered by vocational schools, technical institutes, junior and community colleges, and some high schools. The military also offers formal training and work experience. While in training school, students become proficient in mathematics, physics, electricity, and electronics and may specialize in computer equipment repairs. Once employed, technicians must keep abreast of technological advances by taking advanced training courses.

Repair technicians may become specialists or troubleshooters who assist other repairers in diagnosing and fixing a problem. Repair work is also a good basis for experienced workers to open their own service firms or shops.

Telecommunications Technicians

A MULTITUDE OF career opportunities will expand to meet the needs of the technologic revolution. Currently, most telecommunications technicians are employed by cable television and telephone corporations. But the advent of fiber optics lines, a technology that merges data and voice communications, will create an explosive demand for experts to maintain, repair, and install voice lines and other equipment that facilitates the transmission of computer data.

To be a fast hire, a telecommunications technician should come to the job interview with a bachelor of science degree in electrical engineering or computer science in hand. A two-year associate degree, combined with appropriate work experience, such as a stint in technical training in the military, also works. Telecommunications technicians with leadership skills can advance to managerial positions and launch their own firms or consulting businesses.

Black entrepreneurs may lack the capital and relationships necessary to launch their own firms. Not all of us can tap into the resources that

WHERE WE ARE ON THE NET

So now you want to meet your brothers and sisters on the Internet. Where do you find them? One way is simply to type "African American" or "Blacks" in the keyword section of whatever on-line service you use to access the Internet. This will bring up a multitude of Web sites. The more you dig, the more you will find. Here are a few ways to start your search.

When you need a phone number, you look to the telephone book. When you want information about types of Web sites, you use on-line directories. The Universal Black Pages (http://www.gatech.edu/bsga/blackpages.html) is an ideal launching pad for your journey through Afro-centered Web sites. The Conduit (http://www.imhotech.com) also provides links to Black-oriented sites, as does Black on Black Communications (http://www.i-media.com/BOBC) and BlackAmerica Online (http://www.Blackamericaonline.com). Web sites for people of color that offer a broad base of information, ranging from business networks to entertainment news to chat rooms, include: NetNoir (www.netnoir.com); World African Network (http://www.world-africannet.com); MelaNet (www.melanet.com); AfriNet (http//www.afrinet.net); and BET Networks (http.//www.betnetworks.com).

Sites focused on Black entertainment are expanding at exponential rates. Type in the company that interests you as a keyword to see if it has a site. You will find entertainment-related information on most of the networks listed above.

Also, check out the following:

- For Black-focused job banks, check out Minorities Job Bank (http://www.minorities-JB.com)
- For Black-oriented music, art, and history, surf to the African American Haven (http://www.auc.edu)
- For Black film guides, hit the Black Cinema Network (http://infor-amp.net/ashleyma/Blackcine.html).
- Black culture and politics are at Meanderings (http://www.webcom.com)
- Urban culture is at the Hitlist (http://www.cldc.howard.edu/%7aja/hitlist/htmls/index.html)

- Read about your favorite magazines on-line, including *Essence, Black Enterprise, Vibe,* and *Ebony,* among others.
- And don't forget Frasernet at http:/www.frasernet.com

Remember, each of these sites can lead you to a multitude of other Black-oriented Web sites. Just hop aboard the Web and start surfing.

Microsoft has offered BET in their joint venture on the Net. To jump-start opportunities for African Americans, a triad of Black-owned firms has formed an alliance to provide advisory services, venture capital, and private equity funds to minority entrepreneurs looking to stake their claim in the telecommunications industry.

The players are Bandwidth Consulting Inc., Pryor, McClendon, Counts & Co., and Ark Capital Management. In addition, the Telecommunications Development Fund has committed to providing small businesses with the funds necessary to compete in the telecommunications marketplace. The catch? To access these funds, a business must be able to produce a solid business plan and a strong management team with the potential to earn a 30 to 40 percent return on investment.

Most of the leading computer companies are located in California's Silicon Valley and outside Boston in corporations located on the famed Route 128. New centers are springing up in Atlanta, Dallas, and Northwest areas like Seattle and Redmond, Washington, the location of Microsoft. Software companies, which are generally smaller and can be cottage industries, are located all over the country.

The best job prospects in high-tech fields are in biotechnology, health care, pharmaceuticals, financial services, utilities, insurance, and entertainment. Government agencies, universities, and manufacturers of computers and electronics are other frequent employers of computer service professionals. Of course, opportunities for computer jobs are most plentiful in firms that design and install computer systems, integrate networking systems, develop packaged software, or even run an entire computer facility. Opportunities also abound in companies specializing in data processing and database management.

8

PUBLISH OR PERISH

If anyone's gonna write about me, I reckon it be me/myself.
— LANGSTON HUGHES

The world does not know that a people is great until that people produces great literature and art.
— JAMES WELDON JOHNSON

RODNEY REYNOLDS
FOUNDER/PRESIDENT
AMERICAN LEGACY MAGAZINE
NEW YORK, NEW YORK

Rodney Reynolds must have ink in his veins. At thirty-eight, it seems he's been in the publishing business practically half his life. His career got started with the printing courses he took in high school, progressed during his college days at the University of Cincinnati, and blossomed with his first major publication, a slick maga-zine about Black professional life in Cleveland.

But his venture as a cutting-edge publishing magnate came crashing down when advertisers shunned the new publication. Down, but not out, he tried several new ideas, gained valuable experience, and made high-level contacts. Each friendship led him to new opportunities, until one day his idea of producing a magazine called *American Legacy,* with Black history as its editorial theme, caught the attention of Steve Forbes. The rest is history.

Rodney believes that there are three criteria needed to enter the world of magazine publishing today: "Money, access to money, and more money. You have to have a high-quality idea, a solid business plan, an attractive mock-up, a defined niche, and, finally, nerves of steel." A solid business background and strong communications skills are his prerequisites for success in the fast-paced world of media. "Every day you've got to get up and go out and sell something. Most of the decision-makers you will come in contact with are white, so being flexible and adaptable is required," says Rodney. He feels the biggest obstacle is getting advertisers to look at the African-American market seriously, seeing it as comprising different and varying tastes and interests.

Ultimately, Rodney believes in the principle of "activity" knowledge: You learn by doing, and by trial and error.

"Never give up on your ideas," he advises. "Hold on, press on."

FAVORITE BIBLICAL PASSAGE:

*I can do all things through Christ
which strengtheneth me.*

—Philippians 4:13

I HAD JUST finished speaking to a group of Black college students about the positive impact of networking within our community. As the applause died down, I shuffled my notes together and got ready for a sprint to the airport. A small crowd waited for me at the edge of the stage and I took a few minutes to talk with them, hoping to learn. A young woman reached up to shake my hand and blurted out, "Mr. Fraser, how can I get my book published?" She looked at me expectantly, as though I held within my notes the secrets to producing a bestseller.

I am asked this question all the time, and it got me thinking about the importance of getting our words into books and magazines. We have always been storytellers and writers, but until fairly recently, our stories have been largely inaccessible in the mainstream marketplace because many publishers did not believe that they were of interest to a wider audience. But the times they are a-changing and we can seize the opportunity not only to write but to publish books, edit and design magazines, tell the stories that we want to tell, make sure our words are read.

There are so many ways to become part of this exciting industry—as a writer, agent, publisher, editor, designer, and sales rep. Let's not waste another moment.

The book and magazine publishers are seeking out our voices as they realize that we not only read and write, we buy! Books written by Black authors are flying onto bestseller lists and Black-oriented magazines are crowding the newsstands. This emerging Black literary renaissance gives us the opportunity to get our feet into the publishing industry's doors.

BOOK PUBLISHING

BOOK PURCHASES BY Blacks grew from $181 million in 1990 to $296 million in 1995 as major book publishers began to capitalize on the popularity of a growing group of Black authors who have tapped into the commercial market. Walter Mosley (*Devil in a Blue Dress, Black Betty, White Butterfly, Gone Fishin'*), Terry McMillan (*Waiting to Exhale, Disappearing Acts, Mama*), and Susan Taylor (*Lessons in Living, In the Spirit*) have become household names with bestseller status, joining Alice Walker and Toni Morrison, whose books introduced white readers to Black heroes. The number of Black-oriented publishers and bookstore retailers has also expanded, from a handful in the 1960s to hundreds today.

Major publishing houses are creating divisions (also called imprints) and lines of books targeted at African-American readers. Back in 1991, editor Cheryl Woodruff, the first African-American woman to be named vice president at a major commercial house, helped develop and launch Ballantine Books' One World imprint which is devoted to publishing "multicultural" lines by Black and Latino authors.

Publishers and bookstores are also increasingly sensitive to marketing strategies aimed at African-American readers. In December, windows and display tables are stacked with books about Kwanzaa, while February book displays celebrate Black History Month. Publicity and marketing departments are selling Black-oriented books in beauty parlors, through street vendors, and at church fairs, Black expos, and bazaars.

Publishing's enthusiasm for reaching Black readers does not automatically translate into greater opportunities for job opportunities within the industry. Some industry insiders, Black and white, worry that although the exploding market has created an appreciation for African-American authors, there is a danger they will be segregated from the mainstream.

Despite the crossover success of marquee writers like Walter Mosley, Toni Morrison, and Terry McMillan, most Black authors face an uphill battle getting their books published. Part of the struggle is inherent in the publishing process—new authors rarely have an easy time finding a publisher, no matter what color they are. But it's also true that editors choose books that appeal to their own tastes, and Black editors are still a rarity within the ranks of major publishers.

In book publishing overall, African Americans are only 3.4 percent of the managers, editors, and professionals, as compared to the newspapers where we make up 6 percent of comparable positions. For further comparison, the general work force in the New York area is 21.9 percent Black.

"The question of why there are so few minorities has lingered for years in New York's literary industry, which has long regarded itself as something of a liberal bastion despite its color line," a *New York Times* article noted in 1996. Low starting salaries, which typically begin at $19,500 or less, are said to discourage talented minority applicants who are often aggressively sought by industries with richer pay scales. Many African Americans are also unaware of opportunities available in publishing, although publishers are now trying to reach out to us. Employee diversity makes "good business sense," according to Andrew Giangola, director of corporate communications at Simon & Schuster, one of the largest publishing companies in the country. Simon & Schuster has implemented an aggressive recruiting program to hire minority candidates for the company's trade, reference, business, and education divisions. As a result, one quarter of the company's new hires last year were minorities. Such aggressive recruiting spells a tremendous opportunity for African Americans willing to tackle a career in publishing.

Books are generally categorized as textbooks, academic books, and trade books, and may be published as hardcovers or paperbacks. Trade books are the ones you see in the bookstores and on bestseller lists. They cover every conceivable topic and include fiction and nonfiction titles on history, religion, science, politics, cooking, or self-help.

The majority of trade houses are owned by multimedia conglomerates with wide-ranging business interests that may include books, magazines, music, motion pictures, and videos. Rupert Murdoch's News Corp., for instance, owns HarperCollins Publishers, Fox Television, scores of newspapers and magazines, plus a multitude of other media concerns.

Each publishing company may also be divided into several divisions, or imprints, devoted to particular lines of books, such as classics, literary fiction, religion, sports, romance, mysteries, true crime, science fiction, children's literature, and poetry. Random House (owned by Advance Publications), is composed of a number of individual divisions or imprints, including Ballantine Books, One World, Vintage Books, Alfred E. Knopf, Villard, Fawcett, Pantheon, Schocken, Shambhala, Crown, Harmony, Modern Library, and others.

A good way to get a feeling for the many facets of book publishing is to follow the progress of a book from its arrival as a proposal or manuscript to its birth as a bound copy that will hopefully find its way into a reader's hands. Along the way, keep your creative eyes and ears open—maybe you'll bump into a career that makes sense to you.

Literary Agents

ONCE A WRITER comes up with an idea for a book and prepares a book proposal or manuscript (more on that later), an agent enters the picture. Agents are essential in the book publishing world today—nurturing new authors, helping them prepare their proposals and manuscripts, and shepherding the material to the best editors for a given project. They also serve the publishers by screening out many inferior projects. As you can imagine, literary agents are often extremely powerful, since they control the means of access to the publishers as well as to the creative talent.

In my experience, nine times out of ten an editor will reject a proposal that is not agented. Agents make their living by constantly meeting with and speaking to editors to find out who is buying what and by watching for trends that may signal the next hot market. Once they find an interested editor for a given project, agents negotiate the terms of the contract, ranging from the advance payment to whether the author has the right to consult on jacket design. They also handle any problems that may arise after contract signing and throughout publication. Not only do agents develop, solicit, and pitch book projects to publishers, they are an author's advocate and voice within the publishing world.

Although agents typically charge 15 percent of a client's earnings, good agents negotiate much better deals for their clients than most could do on their own. There are several established Black agents in the publishing industry, including Marie Dutton Brown, Lawrence Jordan, Faith Childs, and Denise Stinson, but Black agents may represent white authors just as white agents represent Black Authors. I have the utmost faith in my agent, Barbara Lowenstein, who is white, and she delivers "big time."

There is no set route to becoming an agent, although many learn the business by starting out as assistants to established agents and working their way up until they have their own list of clients. Some agents begin by working in publishing companies. Others have fled law firms for the agenting world. Faith Childs left her job as a lawyer to become an apprentice agent and later founded her own firm.

Top agents know the publishing landscape as though it were their own backyard and forge close relationships with the major players who can green-light top deals. The best are tenacious and won't back down until they get the deal they think their client deserves.

Once a book is sold to a publisher, the acquiring editor and other publishing employees work with the writer to complete, produce, and market the book, a process that requires the coordinated efforts of an army of people, each with unique talents, skills, and areas of expertise.

- The contract and legal departments draw up the book contracts and handle legal issues that may arise before and after the book is published.
- The editorial department solicits and edits manuscripts.
- The art department designs the cover and artwork for the book.
- The subsidiary rights department negotiates sales for the right to publish the book in various formats, including softcover, electronic, audio cassettes, magazine excerpts, film, and foreign translations.
- The publicity department creates awareness for a book.

- The marketing department develops promotions to attract buyers.
- The sales department sells to chain and independent bookstores.

Editors

THE TERM "EDITOR" is a misnomer. Today's editors do not simply sit at their desks reading and marking up manuscripts. As one editor put it, "We work from nine to five and read from five to nine." During their long workday, editors perform a diverse and complex set of tasks necessary to turning manuscript pages into a bound volume.

In trade houses, editors are under pressure to acquire books that will sell big. They read proposals and manuscripts in the evenings, on weekends, on vacation. They also work with authors to make a concept more commercial or more interesting.

Editors are also looking to create lines of books that appeal to the tastes of a diverse reading public. Kensington Publishing's Monica Harris challenges editors to expand the base of minority readers by publishing new voices. These days, as publishers are scrambling to meet budget and sales targets, editors cannot wait for the next hot title to land on their desks. Instead, they take an active role in seeking out and developing books that the reading public will be willing to buy at steadily rising prices. They must be aware of cultural trends and keep track of the types of books being shopped by agents and published by other houses. They must also be aware of what books are selling and which ones have bombed. "You have to be a cultural junkie to survive in this business," says literary agent Jay Acton, who has seen 109 of his books climb up the bestseller lists.

Once editors find a proposal or manuscript they like, they have to convince their colleagues that the book is worth the company's investment. They must decide how large an advance to pay the author and how much money to budget to produce the book. That means estimating potential sales and converting projected gross earnings into net.

Although advances can range from five hundred dollars to seven figures, first-time writers consider themselves lucky to get published and lucky still to be offered more than ten thousand dollars. Most front-page stories of publishers shelling out millions of dollars for a first novel are wildly out of proportion to the truth.

Beyond working directly on the manuscript, editors are also involved with every other aspect of bringing the book out. "I am the point person for each stage of the process," explains one editor. "I suggest and approve jacket copy and design and sign off on the interior look and feel of the book. I am expected to develop marketing plans for my books and to convince the sales department that my books and authors are important. In short, I am the author's advocate."

Rookie editors go through a kind of editorial boot camp, generally enduring several years of working long hours for miserable wages. For minorities, the difficulty of working long hours on meager wages may be compounded by the challenge of being one of a few Black faces within the company. For those who persevere, however, the rewards can be worth the wait. Monica Harris, who at twenty-five was already developing her own list, encourages young editors to "make a concerted effort to stick with it." Harris received a career achievement award from the New York chapter of the NAACP in recognition of her role in developing one of the industry's first Black romance genres.

Most editors begin the business as editorial assistants, performing secretarial and clerical duties while learning their craft. Most change employers several times as they climb up the career ladder. Creativity, curiosity, a broad range of knowledge, self-motivation, and perseverance are valuable assets within the editorial department. You must be able to collaborate and work with people from a broad variety of backgrounds and to cope with the stress of juggling a staggering number of responsibilities while motivating the writer, as well as colleagues, to do what it takes to produce a quality book.

Production and Design

ONCE A MANUSCRIPT has been accepted by the editor and cleared by the legal department (which vets the text for plagiarized and defamatory material), it is turned over to the production department, which begins the process of shaping the manuscript pages into the book that you ultimately see in the stores. At this stage, artists and designers consult with the editors to produce the jacket design and the look and feel of the book, including the typeface and the layout of photographs, artwork, and maps that may be included with the text. Books targeted to Black audiences may incorporate special design elements to alert readers that the author and content are African-American.

Production and design people are good at managing the flow of materials streaming through their offices and have to have the skills to make every piece of the puzzle fit together—on time. Deadlines and teamwork are the name of their game.

Publicity As a book goes into production, the publicity department is already making plans to promote and sell the book. What and how much they do depends on each book's budget. Bestselling books by authors like Walter Mosley and Terry McMillan may command large promotional budgets in excess of one hundred thousand dollars, but most budgets are quite modest. To market books aimed at Black readers, publicists may target unique media and community outlets.

"We use the same techniques that we would for any other book but we focus on different resources," explains Tara Watts of St. Martin's Press. To publicize *Chocolate Star*, for example, Watts is promoting the author as a "Black Jackie Collins" who she hopes will appeal to the Black women that read about the book in magazines like *Essence*, *Today's Black Woman*, and *Upscale*, in addition to mainstream magazines like *Elle*, *Vogue*, and *Working Woman*. "Top publicists are familiar with each magazine, radio station, and TV show's market and needs," says Watts, who plans to pitch *Chocolate Star* to BET and several Black radio shows.

Black publicists generally understand the best way to widen the promotional net to capture as many African-American readers as possible. "We bring to the table stuff our white colleagues have never heard of," says Watts, who was incredulous to learn that coworkers knew little about rapper LL Cool J, whose book is being published by St. Martin's Press. She comments, "I knew from my personal experience which magazines, TV and radio shows we should hit with the book," which added a lot to the publicity machine.

The lack of Black publicists within the industry had led several African-American authors to take charge of their own promotional campaigns or to hire freelancers like Julia Shaw of the Shaw Literary Group of New York; who have special knowledge of strategies that would appeal to Black readers. Julia works with publishers, the media, and bookstores to generate publicity for Black authors.

A good publicist needs to have excellent writing skills and know how to schmooze with the media. In an interview with *Black Enterprise*, Marilyn Ducksworth, vice president, associate publisher, and executive director of publicity for Putnam Berkley Group, explained, "Publicity is about relationship-building and I love establishing relationships with the media." She has established quite a few contacts in her career, having handled annual campaigns for some 225 adult and children's titles and promotions for Bill Cosby, Patti LaBelle, and Tom Clancy.

Tara Watts adds, "If I had to use one word to describe a good publicist, I'd say tenacious." Once you learn the skills, you can transfer your experience to virtually any PR department in and outside of book publishing. Tara started in sports and entertainment PR. "The tools are the same," she says, "no matter what you're selling."

Sales

SALESPEOPLE SELL BOOKS to retailers, wholesalers, chains, schools, and libraries, and occasionally directly to the consumer. Each year, salespeople, publicists, and editors converge on the Frankfurt Book Fair and the American Booksellers Association's Bookexpo America, trade shows where publishers present their lists to booksellers.

Sales, marketing, and public relations departments have traditionally hired more Blacks than their editorial counterparts. According to industry insiders, these positions are more accessible since they attract those with experience from other industries. Because sales mean dollars, publishers value employees who can execute profitable marketing and sales promotions.

Sales reps must be well versed in the list of books they are selling, with a sense of each author's market and prior sales history. They should also be thoroughly knowledgeable about each of their accounts' businesses and be able to read their needs "like a book." Like sales reps everywhere, publishing reps should be enthusiastic about their product and persistent in their approach.

CUBA GOODING, JR., made "Show me the money!" a household phrase. That phrase struck home with all of us for a very good reason: In this age of skyrocketing expenses, we are all interested in careers that pay the bills. Publishing has a reputation for being low-paying, so what can you expect salarywise?

Salaries in publishing generally reflect the publisher's size and the commercial appeal of its books. As a rule, the publishing conglomerates pay higher salaries than the small presses, and commercial or trade publishers pay more than academic presses. Top management, editorial directors, and sales and marketing directors make the most.

Jobs with major book publishers are concentrated in New York City, Chicago, Los Angeles, Boston, Philadelphia, San Francisco, and Washington, DC. Smaller presses are located throughout the country. Literary agents are concentrated in New York City and Los Angeles, although a few agents have offices in other locations.

If you love books and like what you've read about the industry, this is an ideal time to get started. In general, entry-level editorial positions have a high rate of turnover because they are so low-paying; this is where virtually everyone in publishing starts and "pays their dues." A year or two as an editorial assistant in a publishing house will tell you enough about the available opportunities to allow you to make critical decisions about moving up, or moving on.

One way to get a sense of the business and to develop contacts that may lead to a job is by taking a publishing course. Publishing programs are offered to college graduates by Radcliffe College, New York University, and the University of Colorado. These programs also provide special assistance to minority candidates to help them get their foot in the door; Radcliffe provides scholarships to minorities. Experience and contacts are also critical to entering and advancing in the publishing industry. The more people you know, the better your chances of finding a position.

Many people just start right in, learning as they go, but if you can, take advantage of the publishing programs available. Find out if your college placement center has information on potential publishing internships. Above all, network! Many people I've spoken to say that they got their start in the business through someone they knew; make it your business to get to know and talk to people engaged in all aspects of publishing. People are always happy to lend a hand.

SO YOU WANT TO BE AN AUTHOR?

I'VE DESCRIBED SOME of the jobs available in the world of book publishing. But before we leave this area, I'd like to go back to the young woman who asked me how to get her book published. This is really a separate book because, except for staff writers at magazines, becoming a published author is unlike all other career goals. A great deal more luck, creativity, and perseverance are involved, and most people who become authors only do so after having established some other, more secure way of generating an income.

Despite these caveats, I will tell you that in my travels, when people ask me for advice, it is often information about being an author that they're after. Every week I get fifteen to twenty calls and letters from people who want to write a book. My advice is always the same— please do. We need many more African Americans committed to writing. The most frequently asked questions are: How do you come up with a book idea that will sell? How do you get a publisher? Do I need an agent?

I'll do my best to give you some capsule answers, based on my own experience, as well as the experience of several personal friends who are writers.

Writers write. Pretty basic. If you are interested in writing as a career, crystallize in your own mind the type of writing that appeals to you. Most writers have the ability to write anything they set their minds to, ranging from screenplays to magazine articles to books. Some are good at everything their pen touches, but most begin by concentrating on a field that appeals to them. Writers write because they want to, and they become good at their craft because they work hard at it. Just because it's simple to buy paper and pens does not mean writing is an easy way to make a living. In fact, it's one of the hardest.

If you have an idea that you want to turn into a book, how should you proceed? First, find out what's being published. A short walk through a bookstore reveals a wide range of literature—everything from literary fiction to health care. Walter Mosley is known for writing literary mysteries; Terry McMillan for writing popular novels; Dennis Kimbro for describing strategies we can use to succeed in America. How did those books get onto the shelves? Because a publisher believed the book was good enough to read and would be popular enough to sell.

Content and timing are everything in this business. The experience of Linda Villarosa, a bestselling author and executive editor of *Essence* magazine, epitomizes how changes in the industry's outlook can turn an idea or a book proposal that has been gathering dust into the next hot property. "I first took [an] idea for [a] book to an agent eight years ago who said it wouldn't sell," she recalled in an interview with *Black Enterprise*. "Two years ago, that same agent came back to me with the exact book I had proposed." The book—*Body & Soul: The Black Woman's Guide to Physical Health & Emotional Well-Being*—ultimately sold to a publisher for six figures.

Not every idea will be rewarded with such a lucrative deal, but take the point to heart; no matter how dear your idea is to you, it is a hard sell if the concept doesn't fit into the current marketplace. My own experience with *Success Runs in Our Race* may help you understand the process of getting your own idea into the bookstores.

On February 4, 1993, I was in a meeting with my staff when my secretary announced that my literary agent, Barbara Lowenstein, was on the line and it was urgent. Every call from Barbara is urgent and usually worth taking. I thought perhaps my proposal for a new book on networking in the Black community needed some fixing. Just twenty-four hours earlier, we had thought it was in good enough shape to submit to several large New York publishing houses. What was so urgent now?

I picked up the phone and greeted her with "Hey, girl, what it be about?"

I could almost hear a grin in her New York voice: "Are you sitting down?"

"Yes."

"I got you a deal."

"On what? A truckload of collard greens?"

"A book deal."

I was shocked. "How's that possible? You only sent out the proposal yesterday."

"Several key people really like the idea, so we got a little bidding war going and here's where we are: three hundred thousand dollars cash advance, one hundred thousand dollars for marketing and promotions, and one hundred thousand dollars in performance bonuses for reaching certain sales marks." She paused. "I think you ought to take it . . . don't you?"

I couldn't think at all. I just hung onto the phone in stunned silence. Then the celebration began and has been going on ever since. Writing *Success Runs in Our Race* changed my life and fulfilled one of my grandest dreams.

Within the past decade, the success of Black-oriented titles has generated scores of authors churning out books for African-American readers. If you are interested in joining these ranks as a writer, you should try, regardless of whether you get a megadeal or not. As African Americans, I believe we have a duty to fill the bookshelves with writings that reflect our experience, our culture, and our hopes.

Here are some tips I've picked up along the way that could help you get the words in your head or on your hard drive into the bookstores:

Prepare a proposal. In the book world, a proposal is a cross between a business plan and a chapter-by-chapter, step-by-step outline. You must have done your basic research and thought out how you will develop the story before even putting pen to paper. To write a successful proposal, you must already have written the book, at least in your head. Think of a theme or idea that you are very comfortable with, that you know a lot about.

If you are not a professional writer, you may need help putting the proposal into tip-top shape. But at this stage, just make sure that your idea is clearly stated so it will catch the attention of the person who will ultimately get you the deal—the agent.

Find a literary agent.   The agent's primary job is securing a publishing deal for you. It's not easy to get an agent to review your proposal. They are generally swamped with manuscripts and proposals from potential writers trying to break into the business. Established agents generally seek out established writers. They rarely take on authors they find in the "slush pile"—the reams of unsolicited material agents and editors receive from would-be authors. If you are not a professional writer, and even if you are, my best advice is to connect with an agent by networking. Think about who you know that might have a good relationship with an agent, writer, or publisher. I met Barbara Lowenstein, well known as one of the top agents in the business, through Sherry Winston, a close friend who, in turn, was a close friend of cookbook authors Mel and Cheryl London. Sherry arranged for me to meet with the Londons over lunch, convinced that I had a marketable book idea, they set up an introduction to Barbara. You know the rest. I can't stress strongly enough how important personal contacts are in this business. Without such an introduction, you will have a much more difficult time getting your proposal read.

Even so, certain steps can help your proposal jump over the loads of letters that stream into agents' offices every day.

First, research which agency might be appropriate for your idea. Many agents develop an area of expertise—for example, nonfiction genres such as religion, health, sports, or science, or works by African-American and Latino writers. One way to find the best agent for your particular idea is to look in the acknowledgment section of popular books similar to the one you have in mind. Authors usually give a heartfelt "thank you" to the agent who made their deal. You can also check your local library for *Literary Marketplace*, an industry reference book that lists hundreds of agents.

Next, write a solid letter, explaining your credentials and the reasons your book idea is hot. Sell, sell, sell!

After sending your material to the agent, follow up with a telephone call within two or three weeks to make sure it has been received and reviewed. Do not pester the agent for a response. This is the quickest way to get rejected. Even if the agent is not ready to sign you, if you are polite and respectful of the agent's time, you might get some helpful feedback on the proposal or a lead to another agent who might be interested in your project.

Get a professional writer involved. Agents may suggest, or insist, that you work with a professional writer who specializes in celebrity or expert collaborations, especially if this is your first book. These days, publishing professionals often distinguish between writers and authors—authors are the professionals, business owners, community leaders, and other personalities who have compelling stories to tell but do not make a living writing. There are writers who can help you, and the agents know them. Making a good match between author and writer is crucial. In my experience, you will know immediately if the relationship is one you can live with over the several months, or years, it can take to get the book written.

MAGAZINE PUBLISHING

WITHOUT GROWING NUMBERS of African-American publications, we would be nearly invisible in the magazine world. Despite some movement within the industry, so far not much is happening to pull in minorities. "African Americans do not consider magazine publishing a promising career avenue," says Charles F. Whitaker, a professor at the Medill School of Journalism at Northwestern University. In 1995, Whitaker released the first statistical report on industry demographics, which demonstrated that Blacks have clustered in entry-level positions as assistant and associate editors.

Two years later, he does not see much change, although Charles does not believe the industry is overtly racist. "It's more that publishers haven't extended themselves to welcome minorities." He believes that mainstream magazines need to adopt more aggressive hiring strategies to overcome feelings of "subtle racism" that discourage Black candidates from entering the business. Although magazine executives use the excuse that qualified minority candidates are in short supply, others recognize the industry's tendency to hire look-alikes. "We tend to

HOW TO BE A SUCCESSFUL AUTHOR

The Competition
- Over 50,000 books are published each year
- 95 percent sell fewer than 5,000 copies
- 120 books make the *New York Times* bestseller list each year
- 100 books by Black authors make the Black bestseller lists each year

Write Anyway
- Identify a gap and fill it
- Be open and honest; write in your voice, from your experience
- Have a clearly defined vision, philosophy, and story
- Know your audience, Black or white
- Get some help with the proposal and/or book
- Do your research; what do people want or need?
- Know when the book is finished

Powerful Packaging
- Make your title provocative
- Suggest bold graphics for the book jacket

Good Public Relations
- It's free
- Use Black radio, newsprint, and magazines
- Use mainstream media, too—don't let them forget us

Speak Writing
- Put your story on tape
- Speak anywhere, anytime—at churches, meetings, conferences
- Hand-sell—get the word out

Support Black Bookstores
- They keep our books in stock and hand-sell them
- Hold book signings
- Build relationships

hire ourselves over and over again," one editor told *Folio*, the industry bible.

Magazines are "clubby" by nature. 4/Color, a multicultural trade association, was formed to encourage outreach and advocacy for minorities in the industry, and several publishers, including Time Warner and Condé Nast, have established policies to recruit and hire Black employees. The shifting demographics of the American population are also pushing management to diversify, because publishers that target the general audience are eager to attract an increasingly ethnic readership and advertising base.

Yet efforts at diversification seem painfully slow. As one editor put it, "Blacks are not knocking down doors to get into the business, and magazines aren't exactly knocking down doors to bring them in."

While department heads may be sincere in their intentions, without support at the corporate level they often lack the resources to actively seek out qualified candidates. "I would jump at the chance to bring a qualified Black journalist into my department," an executive editor of a small trade magazine told me, "but I don't have the time to actively look for candidates on my own." Out of fifty applicants the editor remembers interviewing over the past five years, only four were Black.

Because efforts to recruit minorities are sporadic, many Blacks either do not view magazine publishing as a career option or are unaware of opportunities to enter the field. We may also hesitate to seek magazine positions because we don't see ourselves represented within the pages and therefore conclude that writing and publishing are inherently "white" occupations.

Even within Black publishing, some African Americans feel put off by old-line magazines like *Ebony* and *Black Enterprise*, which tend to focus on phenomenal success stories celebrating Black achievement, rather than dealing with issues that impact the underclass. However, we all know that mainstream media handles that niche with depth and zeal.

Right now, the growing African-American press still presents our best opportunity in the magazine industry. Indeed, were it not for *Ebony, Essence, Jet,* and *Black Enterprise,* and their younger siblings, including *American Legacy, Upscale, Vibe, Emerge,* and *Heart & Soul,* a large pool of talented journalists would have nowhere to turn.

The magazine industry's predicted growth in the upcoming years is a slow two to three percent. With the consumer's ability to get fast-breaking news off television and computer screens, niche publishing— magazines targeted at special-interest areas—is the wave of the future.

This is a great opportunity for African Americans. *Health Quest* promotes itself as a health information source for African-American men
and women; *Successful Black Parenting* focuses on child-raising issues
of primary concern to African-American parents; *Heart & Soul* covers
Black women's health and fitness; *Signature* is one of several Black
bridal magazines; and *Minority Golf* combines articles and instruc-
tional tips about the game with personality profiles, as well as advice
on which greens are most welcoming to Black players.

Circulation and size varies, with some publications reaching millions
of readers and others a limited market. This variety provides room for
a vast array of talents at every level of employment.

Career opportunities fall within the broad categories of publishing,
editorial, advertising and sales, circulation, promotion and publicity,
and production. Each area provides a range of jobs and demands a
diverse set of experiences and skills.

Publishers run the business, and in many magazines they are also
the hands-on bosses. They ensure that the magazine is fiscally stable,
promoted to advertisers and subscribers, and sold. Advertising and
sales, circulation, promotion, and production fall under the publisher's
direction.

Advertising

ADVERTISING BRINGS IN the revenue by soliciting and selling advertising. While *Black Parenting* might target its efforts at a specialized
group of advertisers interested in reaching its readership, a general-
interest magazine will seek advertising from a broad range of clients.

Sales representatives must be thoroughly knowledgeable about the
magazine's editorial policies and readership. They also must understand the needs and goals of potential marketers. This presents a
special opportunity for Blacks who can draw upon their insights into
African-American consumers and businesses to develop new accounts.

Within the Black magazine industry, soliciting advertisers can be an
uphill battle. *Ebony* founder and publisher John H. Johnson is credited
with discovering the Black consumer market as part of his pioneering
efforts to attract advertisers to his magazine pages.

Despite the huge consumer base of *Black Enterprise*, Earl Graves,
BE's founder and publisher, says that penetrating the advertising market requires breaking new ground all the time. This challenge not-

withstanding, *Black Enterprise* has demonstrated that advertising dollars can be generated: According to *Folio, Black Enterprise* posted a 30 percent increase in ad pages in 1995, compared to the same period for the previous year.

The success of established magazines like *Ebony, Essence,* and *Black Enterprise* has made it more difficult for newer arrivals to solicit ads. Advertisers may be reluctant to spend in new venues in the belief that all Black magazines are essentially alike. "Advertisers lump all the Black magazines together without looking at their audiences," Cheryl Todmann says. Cheryl is a former publicist with *Essence* who now works as a copywriter at *TV Guide.* She believes that most advertisers really don't see much difference between *Essence, Black Enterprise,* and *Jet.*

Sales has traditionally been a difficult profession for Blacks to excel in. A recent article in *Sales & Marketing Management* uncovered deep and pervasive racism within the sales industry as a whole and reported that vendors may be openly hostile to Black sales representatives or may refuse a sale based simply on the seller's color. Charles Whitaker also sees sales as a difficult career path for African Americans in the magazine industry.

On the other hand, sales is an important, high-paying segment of the industry. If you're willing to take on the challenge, be prepared to work twice as hard to reach quota and steel yourself against personal rejection. The good part is that sales skills are transferable to any number of industries and careers.

Circulation

CIRCULATION IS RESPONSIBLE for pumping the magazine onto newsstands and into homes in the most efficient and cost-effective way possible. Increasing or establishing a circulation base within the African-American community is perceived as a major obstacle among mainstream publishers. Innovative publishers are using specialized marketing techniques, such as distributing their publication to our churches, museums, educational and charitable groups, and universities and colleges. Tapping into the huge network of Black fraternities and sororities has also yielded profitable results. *Essence* built its circulation on this rich source of Black readers.

Promotion

PROMOTION AND MARKETING departments develop campaigns that draw advertisers and readers to the magazine.

African Americans can infuse promotion campaigns with valuable insights. While working at *Tennis Magazine*, Cheryl Todmann helped develop a promotion aimed at reaching young Black athletes interested in tennis. A tennis player herself, Cheryl knew from her own experience whom to bring to the table to develop the promotion and take the steps necessary to get the project moving.

To work in promotions, you have to have the ability to gather information in a heartbeat. The Internet makes accessible reams of information that can help develop a profile of the magazine's target readers and advertisers, including such demographics as age, income, and education level. This information puts a face on the reader who is most likely to buy the magazine, a picture that advertisers want to see before sinking dollars into ad space.

The chance to be creative and to see the results of your work almost immediately makes promotions a dream job for people who enjoy a fast pace and crazy deadlines.

A background or degree in marketing is a plus, although much of the learning comes on the job. Cheryl Todmann fell into her career after taking a marketing course in college. Her favorite magazine was *Essence*, and through persistence she got a job in the marketing department, where she learned everything from special-events management and writing to developing promotions and public relations. People who succeed in promotions are generally proactive, strategic thinkers, and good talkers and writers, with the ability to work well under pressure.

Editorial Department

EDITORIAL AND ART plan the content and overall look of the publication. They work together to ensure that each issue is chock-full of information that will appeal to the magazine's target reader. The pace is fast and exciting up to each deadline, when all the pieces must fit together. At most magazines, the editor-in-chief and executive editor plan the articles and features for each issue, then work with the editorial staff to make sure each piece is thoroughly researched and written in a clear and engaging style that reflects the magazine's "personality."

The editors must have a thorough knowledge of their market and a feel for upcoming trends. They must be team leaders, with the ability to motivate the staff to produce top-quality material on deadline. Good editors are not only talented researchers and writers, but they have the energy, enthusiasm, and commitment to do what it takes to produce on deadline and to accept criticism from the editors and staff they report to. On magazines, teamwork and collaboration are critical to success.

For Bobby Clay, his job as an editor at *Sports Illustrated* is a dream come true. "I have access to all sorts of people and places and can present major athletes' stories by making them seem like people, not just idols." Bobby also relishes the chance to delve into explosive issues involving the sports industry. He says that he has gotten used to being on a mainstream magazine, and that a mutual love of sports breaks down barriers between him and his colleagues. "Most sportswriters are frustrated ex-jocks, which means we share a bond—we all appreciate the same fights and the same games."

Bobby's advice to African Americans interested in journalism is to remember that getting started is hard. "You have to work your way up," he says, "covering small-town events on meager pay." He recommends taking advantage of internships and getting experience by working on school newspapers. "People doing the hiring are professionals and you have to have your act together."

Career paths vary, but most writers and editors begin as fact checkers or editorial assistants. From there, they can move up to writing and managerial responsibilities, although the competition for upper-level positions can be keen.

Art Department

"IF YOU LIKE stress and have no life, become an art director," advises my friend Victoria Beerman, who is an art director at a relatively small trade magazine. Victoria really does enjoy the challenge of creating a new magazine from scratch every month. She works closely with the editorial staff to create art and designs that communicate the magazine's image and each story's theme. "We see art as business," Victoria says. "We take art and make sure that it communicates something specific, instead of just hanging on a wall."

Art directors must cope with rigid deadlines made more stressful by having to make last-minute changes even as the magazine is sent to the printer. "Getting along with others is key," Victoria says. There is also the stress of planning the next issue, a phenomenon that she describes as "white paper terror." Nevertheless, the job is exciting if you can balance the rest of your life against its demands. "I love my work," says Victoria. We should all be so lucky.

Production

PRODUCTION IS WHERE it all comes together—the articles, artwork, ads, and photographs. The whole works is funneled together and merged into the publication that is stuffed into your mailbox or displayed on the newsstand.

If you are a computer whiz, production may be a great place for you. Computers have taken over every aspect of the process, and the systems are continually updated. Production is invigorating, since the staff works with every other department of the magazine to create the final product.

Most production people find that the stress of making deadlines at odd hours of the day and night is made up for by the "instant gratification" that comes with producing an entirely new product on a weekly, monthly, or quarterly basis.

WORKING CONDITIONS WITHIN the magazine industry vary, depending on the size and location of the publication. Hours can be long and irregular, especially near deadline, and pressure can be intense as writers, artists, and editors scramble to put an issue to bed. For people who enjoy the challenge, putting out a quality publication is exciting; they are committed to doing whatever it takes to get the magazine out on schedule.

Overall, magazine publishing is not considered a high-paying profession, although top executives at big-time publications can bring in six-figure salaries. Salary levels vary, depending on factors such as the size of the magazine's circulation and advertising revenues, an employee's years of experience, job title, and the geographic region in which the magazine is headquartered. *Folio* magazine has noted a gender gap, with men often receiving more money than women for the same work, but it did not examine whether race has any impact on earnings.

Editorial offices of most magazines are based in New York City, with satellite advertising offices in other large cities. The top African-

American magazines located in New York include *Essence* (the Hollingsworth Group, Inc.), *Black Enterprise* (Earl G. Graves Publishing Co.), and *Emerge* (Black Entertainment Television). *Ebony*, *Ebony Man*, and *Jet* (Johnson Publishing Co.) have offices in Chicago.

Internships and reporters' positions on college and high school papers are good ways to gain firsthand experience. There are also summer courses in magazine publishing that are helpful networking tools, although they do not offer much in the way of hands-on experience. Condé Nast and *Sports Illustrated* both offer minority internships. Getting started may also require beginning a career at a small-town magazine, covering local issues. African Americans who have gained experience on Black-oriented magazines may have an easier time finding work in higher-level positions with mainstream publications.

Remember, in magazines, as in every business, the best way to get started and to get ahead is to NETWORK. Talk to as many Black industry insiders as you can, and you will get help finding a way into a business where who you know counts more than a stack of advanced degrees.

9

REBUILDING OUR NEIGHBORHOODS

Start where you are and move to positions of control in your own community.

— HAKI MAHABUTI

Community cannot feed for long on itself, it can only flourish with the coming of others from beyond, their unknown and undiscovered brothers.

— HOWARD THURMAN

LEON HOGG
PRESIDENT
HALLMARK MANAGEMENT
CLEVELAND, OHIO

Leon was a serious student at Ohio University, majoring in economics and political science. Upon graduation he immediately went to work with football Hall-of-Famer Jim Brown in his new community-based organization, the Black Economic Union. Begun in 1968, the organization's mission was to help improve economic and housing conditions for Black people in urban America. Their venture started out slow but soon blossomed into a booming business of new housing development, rehabilitation, and management. Now, after nearly thirty years in the business, BEU and Leon's second company, Hallmark Management, own and/or manage three thousand units of property in several different markets.

Leon's focus has never wavered—quality homes, apartments, and condominiums, regardless of income. "Many of my tenants are on public assistance," he says, "but it doesn't matter. They deserve a decent and clean place to raise their family. They deserve dignity and respect, and I make sure everyone on my ninety-person staff understands that."

Much of Leon's training came on the job, but while putting in ten- to twelve-hour days he got his real estate brokers license and the prestigious CPM (Certified Property Management) designation. Leon says, "Today the business is far more complicated than ever before because when dealing with city, state, and federal governments, the bureaucratic red tape is endless. You have to pay attention to hundreds of details and have the patience of Job."

He recommends a solid educational background in economics, political science, and/or law for anyone contemplating a career that requires navigating complex bureaucratic waters. "Fortunately," Leon says, "I love people and I've developed good writing, oral, and listening skills—tools necessary for anyone entering the world of urban development.

"There is no better way to create wealth in America than through real estate, but you've got to be entrepreneurial and have your own niche or hook."

Leon's first "hook" into the business was his friend Jim Brown, whom he had known for three years prior to the founding of BEU. Brown gave him a chance to cut his teeth in the trenches. His second "hook" was his willingness to work in an area of urban market management and development that few people wanted to bother with. Today, Leon believes, his "hook" is his experience and his track record, one that few can equal in the rapidly changing market of urban redevelopment.

THE LAST TIME I was in New York City, I headed uptown to see for myself the changes I had heard were taking place in Harlem. Harlem is the center of the African-American universe and still inspires awe and reverence among Black folks. I've often visited Harlem through the writings of Langston Hughes, Dorothy West, and James Baldwin, and I can almost hear the echoes of Louis Armstrong's trumpet when I pass the historic Apollo Theater.

I took the long route, beginning at Third Avenue and 96th Street, the line of demarcation between the Upper East Side's silk-stocking district and the projects to the north. The transformation between downtown and uptown is immediate.

Luxury high-rises give way to brick projects and clusters of abandoned town houses and walk-ups with boarded-up windows and crumbling facades. Salsa, merengue, and hip-hop music pour from project windows and bodegas. Children play stickball in empty lots strewn with broken glass and garbage. About 60 percent of the residents in this area of East Harlem are Latino, the rest African-American.

Above 96th Street, gypsy cabs are the primary mode of transportation. I hailed one and directed the driver to 125th Street and Seventh Avenue, Harlem's main commercial and political concourse. In the past, local gentry would put on their Sunday best before venturing onto Seventh Avenue, then known as "Harlem's Park Avenue." Drugs, poor planning, and depressed economic conditions turned that heyday into yesterday. On 125th Street buildings are run-down and sidewalks cracked.

Government and privately sponsored efforts to revitalize inner cities, where most of us live, have not led to sustained urban rebirth. Relief programs serving personal needs for income assistance, housing subsidies, food stamps, and child care are stale. Housing programs have produced few homes; welfare checks did not become paychecks; food stamps did not create jobs.

The result? Billions have been poured into antipoverty programs, yet inner-city residents remain stranded in impoverished communities overwhelmed by crime, family dissolution, and joblessness. Government is struggling to find solutions that do more than just keep the poor afloat, living on welfare payments and food stamps, without learning a marketable set of skills.

Most welfare recipients I've spoken with are thirsting for jobs but don't have the education, experience, or support necessary to find even the most rudimentary work. Many have no idea how to write a resume. One woman I spoke with, who had had no success finding work on her own, was excited about working a clerical job as mandated under the new welfare reform act. "This way, I can at least get some experience so I can get another job down the line," she said, after enthusiastically showing me a government form directing her to report to the welfare office for employment.

Contrary to popular belief, people on welfare want jobs. Although the welfare reform act is not perfect, it's a start toward getting people off the rolls and into the workplace. But clearly politics alone cannot solve urban blight. To reenergize our communities, we must infuse government spending with the same success-oriented principles that drive business and finance. Entrepreneurs and financiers have the know-how to create and sustain small- to grand-scale developments, from urban vegetable gardens to multimillion-dollar enterprises capable of supporting thousands of jobs. Politicians and businesspeople can join forces to bring new businesses into urban settings and grow the businesses already in place. As depressed neighborhoods rebuild, they will attract middle- and upper-income residents who will pump wealth back into the community.

At the same time, a booming market means little to those who lack the skills to do more than sweep streets. Inner-city residents need a way to acquire the education and skills to participate in rebuilding their own neighborhoods.

It's a complex process, but there is already evidence of an economic renaissance on 125th Street. National chains like Ben & Jerry's Ice Cream, Blockbuster Video, and The Body Shop have opened stores in between neighborhood delis, bodegas, and discount stores. Banks share the block with neighborhood cash exchanges where residents cash checks, pay bills, and take care of immediate financial needs. Banners promoting the Harlem Business Improvement District (BID) are draped across the street.

These signs of change hold promise for Harlem and other urban areas that have suffered from years of neglect and ineffective government programs. Businessmen and women are joining with politicians to bring new businesses, jobs, and quality housing into the 'hood. Old war zones are developing into thriving neighborhoods and business centers.

The need to upgrade our housing stock, to develop small businesses, to improve our schools, and to create financial bases within the community is there. People skilled in crafts, real estate development, finance, and teaching will be critical to effecting these changes. Look to the needs within our inner cities and determine whether the jobs and opportunities available appeal to you. Here it is easy to find a way to do well while doing good.

Urban planning knits together sociology, philanthropy, economics, and education. We will need bankers and financiers to loan or produce the capital necessary to build infrastructure, entrepreneurs to establish thriving businesses capable of serving the larger city as well as the local neighborhood, and educators to teach our children the skills to take part in building their own economies.

We also need people with the vision and staying power to see the grand plans to completion. Wall Street may structure the bond deal that raises money for public housing, but once the check has cleared, someone has to build and maintain the homes. We have got to learn to do for ourselves.

We are learning that good hearts aren't enough to end poverty. We need good business minds and skilled workers, too. Throughout the United States, success stories show that we can make a positive and lasting change in these communities. Empowerment zone funds, established by the Clinton administration, have provided seed money and tax incentives to spur urban growth; housing programs have integrated, rather than segregated, the poor within the surrounding community; neighborhoods have pooled their resources to build businesses without relying solely on government support. Each of these ventures is succeeding by blending government initiatives, private funding, and human resources.

Eight major cities were selected as empowerment zones by HUD, which carries a federal commitment of one hundred million dollars in assistance. The idea is to take empowerment zone funds and leverage them with private monies to encourage business development and to attract commercial investment. The empowerment zone also offers federal tax incentives to businesses that hire local employees. Zone sites include New York's Harlem, Washington Heights, and Inwood neighborhoods, Atlanta, Cleveland, Baltimore, Chicago, Detroit, and the Philadelphia-Camden, New Jersey area.

With this cash infusion Harlem is primed for a business explosion. A massive three-hundred-million-dollar program, funded by empowerment zone monies plus state and city commitments, has attracted megacorporations like Magic Johnson Theaters, Viacom, and Barnes & Noble. These and other businesses are part of Harlem USA, the largest private commercial investment ever made in an inner-city neighborhood. Harlem USA broke ground in mid-1997.

The potential for profits is clear when you consider that Harlem residents spend over two hundred million dollars on clothing and thirty-three million dollars on books, much of it outside the community. Awareness of Harlem's spending power has already sent some private investors scurrying uptown. Inspired by the promise of funding support, a new generation of entrepreneurs is itching to get moving, and many are moving into the neighborhoods where they are building their own businesses. This new generation is unlikely to put up with the political shenanigans of the past. They are interested in getting the job done, and done right.

Deborah Wright, who at thirty-eight is the president and CEO of New York's empowerment zone, has a head for business and a keen understanding of the political scene, which reflects her experience at First Boston and as part of the Dinkins and Giuliani mayoral administrations. In an interview with *New York Magazine*, Wright stressed the importance of bottom-line economics: "The private sector has a whole different set of criteria for investment than what's been used up here in the past. It's not about who owes whom or who's friends with whom. The numbers have to pencil out, and that, by itself, will fundamentally change Harlem."

The potential for profits is epitomized by the success enjoyed by Blockbuster Video, which opened on 125th Street in March 1996 in what turned out to be one of the highest-grossing locations in the city. The success that national chains are experiencing on 125th Street shouldn't really surprise anyone when you consider that Harlem, with a half million residents, is the size of a large city. Would anyone be surprised if the only ice cream store in Atlanta earned some profits?

Despite enthusiasm for ambitious undertakings like Harlem USA, there is concern that local mom-and-pop stores will lose out to national corporations, which are largely owned and managed by outsiders.

When Pathmark announced plans to open a large store in Harlem, the community was fiercely divided among residents who wanted the store's broader array of grocery staples and bodega owners who feared the supermarket giant would put them out of business. Yet development is the only way to create meaningful jobs and keep cash within the community.

Van Woods, the president of Sylvia's Restaurant (and Sylvia's son), told *New York* magazine that Black business people must take the leadership role. As he put it, "None of [our] energy went toward starting our own businesses and employing our own people. Thirty years after the civil-rights movement, we don't own one national retail chain. Not one."

Business leaders like Van Woods and Deborah Wright are setting the example of how we can invest in our own futures instead of subsisting on services provided by a government that has run itself into the ground trying to spend away social ills. Harlem is one example of how a depressed community can begin to create a business environment where we can truly "do for ourselves."

For small business entrepreneurs, the empowerment zones offer a unique opportunity to obtain support. Interested parties can contact their local empowerment zone representatives to learn about possibilities in these areas.

My own hometown, Cleveland, has designated its first twelve million dollars in empowerment zone funds to ten businesses and a new Job Match. In its first year, Job Match will screen, train, and find jobs for three hundred and fifty empowerment zone residents. The empowerment money has attracted another eight million dollars in private funds, which is expected to create and retain nearly five hundred new jobs, in addition to developing dozens of new housing units. Several suburban businesses have been inspired to "reverse migrate" into downtown Cleveland.

Cleveland's success in turning blighted neighborhoods into thriving communities has been recognized by Andrew Cuomo, assistant secretary of HUD, who praised the city for the number of economic development loans it has made to businesses. "The game in the empowerment zone," Cuomo told the Cleveland empowerment zone's newsletter, "is who can catch up to what Cleveland is doing?"

Good leadership, a solid working and middle class, and a conglomeration of public and private sector partnerships have set Cleveland on its course toward urban revitalization. A cast of Black politicians and city council members have pushed Cleveland's development plans by working effectively with the business, civic, and educational communities. Cities across the nation can learn from this example.

PUBLIC HOUSING

INNER CITIES ARE plagued by the disastrous consequences of building huge high-rise dumps, also known as "projects." Cheaply built and poorly maintained, these concrete monoliths are the result of a postwar government policy of housing low-income families in clusters of high-rise buildings that are magnets for drugs and violence.

My friend Inge Hanson, who runs a nonprofit organization out of a project store front, hears rats scurrying in the walls, smells raw sewage spewing through the back courtyard, and faces monster flies swarming in from the sanitation department next door. "I only spend twelve hours a day here—imagine what it's like for the people who live here day in and day out," she says. Drug busts on the street outside her office are commonplace. "It's almost like watching a TV show, except it's real and the kids who are being picked up are kids you know. Most of them have never had a chance to do anything but deal, and once they're out of jail they'll be doing it again. They're not bad kids. But look where they live."

Crowding low-income families into densely populated buildings is a surefire way to generate violence. On top of that, projects isolate the poor from surrounding communities, intensifying suspicion and animosity between neighborhoods. Crime rates and poverty have chased all but the most dedicated merchants from these blocks, reducing job opportunities and increasing welfare rolls.

To revitalize neighborhoods, housing authorities and developers are razing high-rises and replacing them with smaller town houses that blend public housing with surrounding neighborhoods, making these buildings less prone to criminal takeover. This new style of housing also creates more usable space for businesses. In addition, housing officials are concentrating on creating community support centers within these developments that will provide children and adults with a variety of enrichment classes and activities. In East Harlem, several projects have thriving community centers offering "Rites of Passage" classes, drug rehabilitation support, recreational activities, SAT and GED prep, parenting classes, and much more.

To support this urban renewal, HUD has awarded $477 million in grants and targeted one hundred thousand of the nation's worst public housing units for demolition by the year 2000. My research indicates that over five billion dollars will be spent from 1996 through 2006 by government, banks, and private foundations to address the overall urban housing problem. That commitment will create hundreds of millions of dollars in goods and services, supplies, labor, and skills.

In three years, the Newark public housing authority leveled more than 2100 units and built one thousand single-family town houses, creating hundreds of jobs for inner-city residents. Newark's experience is being replicated in other cities across the country. In just five years, Cleveland's Cuyahoga Metropolitan Housing Authority (CMHA) renovated four thousand urban housing units through an infusion of more than $318 million raised by government, private sector, and service organizations.

According to Claire E. Freeman, CMHA's chief executive officer, the development created thousands of new inner-city jobs. CMHA is considered a national model, having turned what Claire deemed "life-threatening housing conditions" into award-winning town houses. The authority also provides on-site health, education, family, and career counseling, among other services. Under Claire's guidance, residents who had previously been unable to find jobs are starting businesses.

"We are dealing with the people problems that come hand in glove with the condition of extreme poverty," Claire says. "If we can't treat the total fabric of the person and the neighborhood, it's like a bad apple in a barrel. One very troubled or violent teenager can, for example, seriously impair the quality of life of a family, a CMHA development, or an entire neighborhood."

During my tour of the site, I saw why CMHA is such a success. CMHA stands in stark contrast to the public projects I have visited where elevators stink of urine, parents escort their children from the ground floor to their apartments, and drug deals are carried out in the stairways. The architectural design provides private entrances that Claire calls "defensible space." Removing interior public stairs and hallways has virtually eliminated crime in the renovated homes. Outdoor gardens encourage friendly interaction and also increase the sense of space so necessary to quality living.

CMHA's commitment to providing residents with more than just housing is paying off. Urban residents are learning skills that will get them jobs and make them self-sufficient even if Washington were to eliminate all forms of public assistance. Claire's holistic approach aims to teach residents how to seek out and even create their own paycheck, instead of waiting for the postman to deliver it. Don't get me wrong—I firmly believe that government should continue to help the very poor. But I also believe that through public and private partnerships we must design programs like Claire's that teach people how to value and make money.

Claire Freeman sees public housing as a transitional solution to provide people with enough stability to maintain a job and to become self-sufficient. On average, after spending about six years living in public housing, most residents of her urban community are able to rent or buy on their own. Claire is an example of what one person can do to turn decaying urban housing projects into livable habitats that help people take charge of their lives.

BUILD-IT-YOURSELF COMMUNITIES

COMMUNITIES MADE UP of affordable housing can stimulate minimigrations from the suburbs into the cities, which means new customers for inner-city entrepreneurs and new jobs for professionals and blue-collar workers.

In the 1970s, a small group of Black residents came up with the idea for Marin City USA, a forty-five-acre redevelopment project intended to create jobs, business contracts, affordable housing, and community facilities in a predominately Black neighborhood outside of Oakland, California. They brought together twenty-one social service agencies to plan and develop the $110-million four-year building project.

I visited the site a year after groundbreaking. Al Fleming, the project director, and Betty Times, the executive director, have made sure that African Americans are involved in every phase of the development. I saw African Americans employed in the front offices, in the retail centers, and on the construction site. Fifty percent of all available jobs and 22 percent of all contracts went to minorities. A job training facility trains workers who hold the four hundred permanent jobs that support the project.

Within the community, a retail outlet houses a grocery store, drugstore, clothing store, fast-food restaurants, cleaners, and a microenterprise center that trains potential entrepreneurs.

Forty percent of the town houses and rental apartments are rented to low- and moderate-income residents who receive financial assistance, tax credits, and an opportunity to attend home buyers' workshops and credit counseling.

The road has been hard, but with the grace of God and a powerful vision, Al Fleming and Betty Times are helping to create a community that will improve the condition and well-being of all of its residents.

NEW CAPITAL STRATEGIES

ALTHOUGH GOVERNMENT PROGRAMS like empowerment zones and HUD's HOPE IV provide the framework for rebuilding our neighborhoods, some communities have taken charge of their own development. In New York City's Brownsville section, chains like Payless Shoes, Dunkin' Donuts, and Martin Paints have opened outlets. Banks have written millions of dollars' worth of mortgages. Prosperity here has grown out of the entrepreneurial spirit of a small group of Caribbean immigrants who took one of the city's most blighted and feared neighborhoods and turned it into a thriving community.

Immigrants from Jamaica, Haiti, and a dozen other Caribbean nations have brought with them the zeal for work instilled by the threat of starvation at home. As Dr. Wldaba Stewart explained to *Forbes* magazine, "The typical immigrant is willing to take any job, many times jobs that other Americans are not willing to take. In hospitals they end up taking janitor jobs, disposing of medical waste, or lifting a 200-pound patient." Unpleasant, difficult work that may pay less than twenty thousand dollars a year can add up when it is combined with incomes from several family members.

Banks are actively seeking business from these immigrants who pool their savings in a network called a "su-su," which is similar to the Korean "keh" club or our own "Christmas savings club." Each su-su partner contributes a set amount of about one hundred dollars per week to the su-su, which is loaned out in pots totaling thousands of dollars as down payments on housing or business start-ups.

Because real estate in depressed areas like Brownsville is often cheap, immigrants can quickly save up the amount necessary to buy real estate and homes. Development has decreased crime and filled abandoned lots with town houses that are growing in value. *Forbes* reported that one Jamaican immigrant paid fifty thousand dollars for a three-bedroom town house in 1987; ten years later it was assessed at $125,000.

How can you get involved in these exciting new opportunities in America's inner cities? The economic boom created by su-su networks promises to stimulate many different types of careers, several of which have been highlighted in earlier chapters of this book: bankers and financiers are needed to put together deals to underwrite rebuilding the infrastructure; educators will be in demand to teach skills; and small business entrepreneurs will have the golden opportunity to launch and grow businesses.

JOBS IN THE 'HOOD

EXPERTS IN SKILLED trades and crafts will be in demand to build housing, industrial complexes, sewers, and roads. This work demands people with a range of talents and educational backgrounds—managers, clerical workers, skilled and semiskilled craft and trade workers. Opportunities will boom for trade contractors, masons and carpenters, painters and plasterers, roofers, plumbers, electricians, and sheet-metal workers.

Construction jobs and trades make up one of the nation's largest industries and offer many opportunities for starting small businesses. With a moderate financial investment, you can start a contracting business from your own home, hiring workers as needed for specific projects. One friend of mine scraped together twenty-five dollars to buy a set of brushes to paint a friend's bathroom for one hundred dollars. Two years later, he was winning thirty-thousand-dollar contracts to paint Park Avenue apartments in New York City.

Earnings in construction can be significantly higher than average for other industries. Experienced construction managers can earn from $35,000 to $110,000, while skilled craftsworkers charge upwards of $35 per hour

You don't need a college degree, which makes skilled trades and crafts a great career for the 85 percent of us who don't earn four-year degrees. (By the way, 75 percent of whites don't earn college degrees, either.) No reason to be ashamed of earning thirty-five dollars an hour and up as an electrician, plumber, or carpenter, even if you don't have a degree.

How much you make depends on your experience and training. Skilled workers, like carpenters, bricklayers, plumbers, and electricians, generally spend several years in on-the-job or apprenticeship training, which is administered by local employers, trade associations, and trade unions. Nearly a quarter of all workers are union members or are covered by union contracts. Historically, union membership has been rigidly restricted, and in many instances membership still depends on who you know.

With a booming economy, new construction is way up. My friend Stuart Deicher, owner of Stuart Construction, is building new homes in Cleveland as fast as he can find skilled tradesmen and apprentices to do the work. There is a shortage. The opportunities for entry-level apprenticeships are abundant, but according to Stuart, "the work is hard, and very few young people are willing to pay the price to learn a construction craft. I would put to work, today, any person regardless of color, in any one of the skilled crafts, if I could find them. Within three to five years they could earn $40,000 to $75,000 per year as a journeyman, and start their own small business if they wanted to." Twenty-five years ago that offer was not open to Blacks.

If you are already in one of these trades or want to get started, make an effort to network with individuals and organizations instrumental in urban redevelopment projects. Contact your local chamber of commerce for resource lists.

VOLUNTEERING TO BUILD THE NEIGHBORHOOD

ALTHOUGH THE FEDERAL government has made a commitment to America's inner cities in the form of the Empowerment Zones, other government programs are being downsized. Volunteers are a key component for rebuilding our communities. Even if you have no college degrees or work experience, your community can benefit from your contribution. We need mentors, tutors, parks and recreation volunteers, and Little League coaches. Our communities require neighborhood cleanups, as well as volunteers to assist our elderly and housebound residents and to support hospital and nursing home staffs. You are needed.

Nonprofit organizations serving our inner cities also desperately need an array of supplies and equipment to operate efficiently. They would welcome functioning computers and other types of office equipment (photocopy machines, fax machines, postage meters), as well as office furniture from computer workstations to sofas and folding chairs. Don't discount the importance of of paper clips, photocopy paper, and staplers, either. Look around and remember: Your trash is their treasure.

I hope that you will join in the effort that not only will improve our communities but will be financially and spiritually enriching for you as well.

ECONOMIC DELIVERANCE THROUGH THE BLACK CHURCH

ON ANY GIVEN Sunday, twenty-one million African Americans are worshiping in one of the forty-three thousand Black churches spread across this country. Over the past few years, Black pastors have been actively mixing religion with free enterprise to enrich church membership in material ways and provide communities with such services as day care, substance abuse counseling, and after-school programs.

Kirbyjon Caldwell, a bright Wharton School graduate and former municipal bond trader for First Boston Corp., combines financial wizardry with a dedication to serving the spiritual needs of his community. In 1982, he abruptly resigned from his high-paying profession to become the pastor of Windsor Village United Methodist Church in Houston, Texas. The struggling church had only twenty-five members, but today the congregation has grown to nine thousand members, worshiping in a newly constructed church building.

Reverend Caldwell's crowning achievement is the Power Center, a 104,000-square-foot facility that is home to a branch of Texas Commerce Bank, Houston Community College, a nutrition program, a health clinic, a pharmacy, and a 1,900-seat banquet facility. And, oh, yes, a private grade school founded by Reverend Caldwell.

How did he do it? Reverend Caldwell's background in banking and finance helped him refinance a $2.3-million bond offering the church had made years earlier. With church donations, federal and private grants, and new loans, Reverend Caldwell secured the four million dollars needed to renovate an old Kmart into the Power Center. As Reverend Caldwell told *The Wall Street Journal*, "Unless there is economic justice, you won't have peace in the community. The Old Testament speaks of that."

To me, Reverend Caldwell is a bridge between the community building we can do on Wall Street and in the pulpit to achieve economic freedom and equality.

Author Dennis Kimbro says that churches fall into three categories: "entertainment churches, containment churches, and liberation churches." Liberation churches are the ones that get involved in creating African-American businesses, and we need more of them.

Reverend Dennis Dillon of Brooklyn, New York, offers his members one of the most aggressive, biblically based economic development programs in America. He built from scratch The Economic Revival Center, a 12,000-square-foot conference facility that provides the congregation and the community with instruction on small business start-ups, real estate development, investment clubs, and business networking strategies. On Saturdays, the center holds special spiritual services that attract nearly 1200 people to hear Reverend Dillon's biblical sermons that teach economic strategies for wealth creation and debt reduction.

Wheat Street Baptist Church in Atlanta is another center of religious capitalism, collecting fifty thousand dollars annually in rent from the ten businesses operating in two malls owned and developed by the church. The pioneering Wheat Street Church has had its economic development program in place for twenty-five years! Under the guidance of church leaders skilled in economics and business development, Wheat Street's two-thousand-member congregation opened a credit union that has over one million dollars in assets and a real estate portfolio worth approximately thirty-three million dollars. Wheat Street's real estate holdings include Wheat Street Towers, a senior citizens home, and Wheat Street Gardens, a low-income family housing development. Wheat Street's business manager, Eugene Jackson, told *Black Enterprise*, "Our mission is about creating economic opportunities for the people in our community."

Wheat Street is far from being the only religious establishment serving up a mix of Scripture and economic empowerment. Reverend James Walleye Edwin Dixon II, senior pastor of the 2,500 member Northwest Community Baptist Church in Houston, helped his congregation develop a 36,000-square-foot shopping center that is home to the Deliverance Grocery and Deli Institute, a grocery store training center. Not bad for a pastor who took over the church in 1981 when he was just old enough to vote.

These are deeds that epitomize the belief articulated by former Congressman and Reverend Floyd H. Flake, of the Allen AME Church in Queens, New York, who sees the church as the last best hope for a deteriorating community and believes firmly that ministers have a moral obligation to help create businesses and provide jobs and social services for our poor. To that, I say amen and amen again.

10

LET US ENTERTAIN YOU

Music is not only a reflection of the values of Black culture, but
... the basis upon which it is built. ...

— BEN SIDRAN

Music is to Black people what oil is to Arabs.

— MELBA MOORE

RONITA HAWES-SAUNDERS
FOUNDER
RADIO STATIONS WROU-FM
DAYTON, OHIO

After nearly twenty years of working in
the radio and televison industry,
RoNita Hawes-Saunders attended a
communications seminar on a lark.
There she learned that her hometown,
Dayton, Ohio, was underserved by
radio stations. After the seminar she
peppered the presenter with questions.
Impressed by her interest, he walked
her through the steps needed to apply for an FCC license. A few days
later, RoNita called an old college friend who was a practicing

communications attorney and began the lengthy and expensive process of getting a radio license. Few people believed it was possible. Working three jobs to pay her legal bills and having faith that God would help to provide all that she needed, when it was needed, RoNita pressed on. Ten years and several hundred thousand dollars later, RoNita opened radio station WROU-FM in Dayton, Ohio.

As a liberal arts student at Denison University, RoNita had learned to think and to understand how the world really works. "All obstacles in life have a purpose," she says. "The ten years it took to get my license gave me the time and the insight on how to run a radio station profitably. I volunteered, asked questions, built relationships in the industry so that when the inevitable happened, I was ready!"

Within two years the station was profitable, and within five years she purchased a second station. "Those who pursue opportunities in radio or TV must have good technical skills," RoNita advises. They should know how things work and have a solid feel for the business side of the business. Good selling and interpersonal skills are a must because of the variety of personalities that you must deal with every day—including on-air talent, sales personnel, administrative help, community groups, and the almighty advertiser.

"Several times a month I talk to aspiring media moguls. I always ask them three questions: How bad do you want it? What are you willing to sacrifice for it? Who do you plan to help when you get it? I can tell by the sincerity of their response who's going to make it, and who's not.

"My advice to all those who begin down this entrepreneurial path is that there are no excuses for failure when you are in charge of your life. If you achieve your dreams, credit others. If you fail, shoulder the blame."

FAVORITE BIBLICAL PASSAGE:

To every thing there is a season,
and a time to every purpose under the heaven:
A time to be born, and a time to die;
a time to plant, and a time to pluck up
that which is planted.

—Ecclesiastes 3:1–2

ENTERTAINMENT IS A two-edged sword for African Americans. Our achievements in arts and entertainment are viewed largely in terms of our contributions as entertainers, while we are turned away from the power centers controlling the industry—despite the fact that we spend more time watching films and television than any other segment of the population!

Representation at the employment level is also low. In 1993, the *Hollywood Writers' Report* showed that 95% of all television writers were white males, and only six Black television directors consistently found work.

Black artists are still stereotyped within the 'hood and sitcom genres. Although these shows score at the box office and in the Nielsen ratings, they also narrowly portray Black images on screen.

However, things are beginning to change. Black actors like Eddie Murphy, Whoopi Goldberg, Laurence Fishbourne, and Wesley Snipes are snapping up color-blind roles. Although Black actors such as Sidney Poitier and James Earl Jones have been a commanding presence for decades, never have this many Black stars taken on major parts that could just as easily have been offered to whites. Tom Hanks and Harrison Ford were passed over in favor of Denzel Washington for the starring role in *Courage Under Fire*. (Denzel was paid ten million dollars, the highest amount ever paid to a Black actor for a dramatic role.)

Expanding markets created by multimedia and cable television are bringing African Americans into starring roles in the executive suites and independent studios. Bill Cosby, Quincy Jones, and Oprah Winfrey, as well as a whole new bumper crop of baby moguls—the Hughes brothers, John Singleton, Keenen Ivory Wayans—are assuming control in areas that span all facets of the entertainment business.

Spike Lee's Forty Acres and a Mule production company took Hollywood by storm in 1987 with *She's Gotta Have It*, a movie without guns or gangs that cost just $175,000 to make. Lee followed up with a slew of films that encompassed Black history (*Malcolm X*), race relations (*Do the Right Thing, Jungle Fever*), family life (*Crooklyn*), the inner city (*Clockers*), and the historic Million Man March (*Get On the Bus*). Perhaps even more important than the quality of the films themselves is Lee's ability to make them on his own terms.

Spike Lee's contributions reach beyond translating his vision of Black life and culture to the screen. Like director John Singleton (*Boyz N the Hood, Poetic Justice, Higher Learning, Rosewood*), Lee uses his clout to ensure that African Americans work on his productions. He also takes financial responsibility for his work—he funded *Get On the Bus* with investments from Black financiers who were taken with the film's message of self-reliance.

Hollywood is slowly opening its doors under pressure from groups like the NAACP, and talented young brothers and sisters with enthusiasm and creativity are edging their way up from entry-level positions into areas of greater responsibility at major studios. A case in point is Stephanie Allain, senior vice president of production at Columbia Pictures, who spearheaded movies such as *Jason's Lyric* and *I Like It Like That*. Stephanie began her career as a story analyst in 1988 and climbed to the top. Another example is Andre Harrell, now CEO of Motown Records, who coproduced *New York Undercover*, a television series that consistently tops the charts for Black viewing audiences. Harrell now plans to produce two independent films each year.

The climate has never been better for African Americans to gain a measure of control in a business that once picked Ava Gardner, a white actress, to play the part of Julie, a Black woman, in *Showboat*, a part that Lena Horne had set her sights on for years. One way to keep the momentum going is to learn from those who are paving the way. Let's get busy!

GETTING YOUR START IN FILM

BREAKING INTO TELEVISION or film requires, above all, persistence and a willingness to take on any job to get a foot in the door. One way or another, you have to pay your dues. Everybody does. Many start out working on industrials, low-budget productions, and videos. Documentaries and educational or government films are other entry points.

Most entry-level jobs require little or no formal training. College students or recent graduates may seek unpaid internships to get in, while others start out by taking gofer positions (as in "go-for this, go-for that"). Universities, technical schools, and many private institutes offer training programs in the various aspects of filmmaking, screenwriting, directing, and acting.

Despite the difficulty of breaking in, jobs within the film industry are expected to blossom over the next decade. Globally, 1997 was the busiest year ever in the history of movie production. Entertainment spending is projected to zoom, fed by the new technologies that will create hundreds of television channels and produce an insatiable demand for new product. The Department of Labor has projected a 61 percent increase in jobs in the motion picture industry over the next ten years. You don't have to be a math professor to figure out this is much higher than the growth rate for jobs overall. Job opportunities are also projected to soar in related industries, including film reproduction, distribution, and rentals. The turnover rate is also astronomical, providing new jobs every minute.

The film and television industry is divided into three categories that reflect the phases of production: preproduction, production, and postproduction. In small independent studios, some jobs cut across all three phases. Within large Hollywood studios, responsibilities are more stratified.

PREPRODUCTION

PREPRODUCTION IS JUST another word for advance planning. This includes budgeting, casting, location search, set design and construction, special effects preparation, costuming, and scheduling. If you have a talent for detail and are a visionary, able to imagine what does not yet exist, this may be the place for you.

Writers

WRITERS COME FIRST, because nobody can do anything until they provide the script. Screenwriters may work from an original idea, a news article, or a literary property such as a book or play. Using these sources, the writer produces either a screenplay or a script for a television pilot (a sample episode of a proposed television series).

A screenplay often goes through numerous rewrites before being accepted for production. If it is accepted, that is. (Some screenwriters make a comfortable living without ever seeing their scripts produced.)

Scripts may be revised again during production. Years ago, during filming of his first television series, I Spy, Bill Cosby objected to a joke made about his character's color. The director eliminated it from the script. So, writing for television or film requires not only creativity but the flexibility to rewrite according to the needs of others.

The Writers Guild of America sets stringent minimum rates that must be paid for each phase of screenwriting. Since several writers may ultimately work on a given script, which job you perform can be fiercely contested. Have your lawyer on call and your heart filled with peace and strength. Fees paid to established screenwriters are negotiable, depending on their experience and measure of success. Top screenwriters may earn upwards of six hundred thousand dollars per script.

Novelists and magazine writers whose works form the basis of a script—for example, Terry McMillan, whose bestseller *Waiting to Exhale* was adapted into a hugely successful film—may adapt their own work for the screen or simply sell the rights to option the literary property and to develop it into a motion picture or teleplay. The savvy novelist or writer will negotiate points of the gross profit and will usually garner additional book sales as a result of the buzz from the movie.

Scriptwriting often leads to directing and producing. Take Bentley Kyle Evans: at thirty, he is making his mark as producer and writer for the Fox comedy *Martin*, which stars Martin Lawrence. Although Evans got his start with small acting gigs, he moved behind the scenes to learn the dynamics of television writing. Since the show's debut, he's been promoted from writer to executive story editor, to coproducer, to producer. Incidentally, Evans also cowrote *A Thin Line Between Love and Hate*, which grossed more than forty million dollars.

Story Analysts/Editors

ANOTHER SOLID OPPORTUNITY is to become a specialist in finding promotable material. Story analysts and editors seek out and develop the scripts, ideas, and properties upon which motion pictures and television shows are based. If you read a lot and have an instinct for the next trend, this may be the job for you. Analysts are hired by studios or celebrities on a full-time or freelance basis to scour newspapers and magazines for ideas and to cultivate relationships with book editors and literary agents. This position is excellent training for entry into other aspects of the business.

Script "Girls"

ONE SPECIAL OPPORTUNITY I'd like to alert you to is that of "script girl." Naturally, this job may be held by a man or a woman. The qualifications: great attention to detail, good writing skills, and the ability to work hard under pressure. People in the industry call this one of the most "insanely insane" jobs. The reward: membership in the Writers Guild.

The script girl's responsibility is to keep track of every word and direction in the script. She (or he) sits behind the director's shoulder and takes a Polaroid photo of every scene for the record. She reminds actors if they forget a line and notes every variation from the script—including whether an actor has changed the color of his socks, or if his hair was flattened down in one scene but nappy in the next.

Producers

SO YOU WANT to be a bigwig? To be a producer, no matter what you're feeling on the inside, it's what you're showing on the outside that counts. So, first of all, wardrobe. Second, a thick skin. You can't be the one with the temperament; you're the one who calms other people's tempers. When it comes to the finish line, everything rides on your ability to get the job done. It's your money or money you've borrowed. That's the deal.

Producers are responsible for all money matters regarding a project, including financing the production. The executive producer may be an investor living in another country who never sets foot on the set, but the line producer works closely with the director to select the script and stars, and may even specify the shooting location, because these are issues that affect the film's bottom line. The producer also oversees the development of a detailed budget.

Make no mistake, producers are in the game to make money. They look for properties themselves and also rely on story analysts to discover potential projects. Within the television industry, producers assume different roles and responsibilities, depending on the type of show being produced.

African Americans with the clout and the financing to form their own production companies can shape the way people of color are portrayed on the screen. They also can hire Black actors and crews who might otherwise be overlooked. Independent production companies are often tied to major studios that distribute their work, but they retain decision-making and control over the content of their pictures.

Denzel Washington formed Mundy Lane Entertainment when he nabbed the rights to the popular Easy Rawlins detective novels written by Walter Mosley. Mundy Lane has forged close working relationships with major studios including Tri-Star, Warner, Columbia, and Disney, ensuring that its projects are financed and distributed in the high-profile manner they deserve.

BEHIND THE SCENES:
PRODUCTION JOBS TO CONSIDER

Production Manager
Oversees day-to-day operations on the set, including budgeting, managing schedules for the crews, arranging travel, lodging, and meals, setting up casting schedules, and ensuring that the proper equipment is available

Location Scout
Scouts locations, negotiates with landlords, cleans up after everyone's gone, deals with property damages

Line Producer
Set coordinator, coordinates and schedules crew

Production Assistant
Does whatever told to, e.g., pops bottles and fills coolers with ice, parks cars, keeps people off sidewalk

Producers enter the business from all varieties of careers. What you need is persistence, persistence, and some more persistence, disguised as charm and self-assurance. Kim Greene and Camille Tucker, who have upcoming feature film projects at major studios, were secretaries when they convinced director Bill Duke to serve as executive producer for the forty-minute short, *Sweet Potato Ride*. Duke's participation helped the duo raise the twenty-two-thousand-dollar budget necessary to shoot the project. The opportunity is there; the question is whether you have the desire and energy to seize it.

PRODUCTION

PRODUCTION MEANS ACTUALLY making the film. Simple. What's complicated is that production may involve relatively few people or several thousand, depending on the scope of the project. For example, the cast and crew in *She's Gotta Have It* was minimal in comparison to the number of professionals employed in the production of *Malcolm X*.

Directors

DIRECTORS ARE TOP dogs in the movie business, and the door's open for African Americans with plenty of talent. The director is responsible for the entire cast and crew, all technical and artistic elements of the production, every shot and every nuance of the story. With the director of photography (DP), the director blocks out each shot. Below the director are three more directors, all of whom may earn a percentage of the gross. The first director works with the leading players, runs the set, and is usually the one who yells "action." The second director "wrangles" the other actors, and the third director wrangles the extras.

Just about everyone wants to be a director, and the casualty rate is high. One flop and your career may be over. If you've got the sensibility of an artist and the skills of an administrator, salesperson, diplomat, and psychotherapist, you just might have a shot. In today's Wild West film environment, the director must be a Renaissance person, assuming the role of writer, writer-producer-director, and sometimes even star. The classic example is Spike Lee, who is in charge of almost every element that goes into developing and creating his films.

As is true with producers, there are no straight path or training prerequisites to become a director. Vision, discipline, business acumen, the ability to deal with many kinds of people in stressful situations— these are some of the director's key attributes.

Where do directors come from? Just about anywhere. Some of the most respected directors come up through the ranks, as film editors, top cameramen, assistant directors, or even business managers. Then you have actors, whose clout and connections can sometimes lead to their being given the opportunity to direct. A lucky few get their first jobs after formal training in directing at respected film schools such as New York University, Columbia University, UCLA, or after working in low-budget or industrial films.

One of the hottest sources of directing talent is music videos. Take twenty-something F. Gary Gray, who got his start working as a cameraman for BET and Fox. Gray nabbed his first directing job by convincing the rap group W. C. and the Maad Circle to give him a shot at the helm for their next music video. When you're hot, one good thing leads to another, and Gray was soon directing videos for other rap and soul groups, including TLC and Mary J. Blige. Ice Cube brought him in to direct *Friday*, which turned out to be a huge commercial success, grossing forty million dollars on a three-million-dollar budget. One of Gray's success stories is *Set It Off*, starring Queen Latifah.

Art Directors

ART DIRECTORS ARE responsible for creating a physical environment that embodies the mood called for in the script. If you're a sensitive visualist, this may be the career for you. Many art directors get their experience by working in live theater productions and then move on to higher-paying film and television projects. Related occupations in this area include scene illustrators, set designers, model makers, carpenters, painters, costumers, and makeup- and hairstylists, all of which can provide experience, as well as serving as a point of entry to the television and motion picture industry.

Actors

ACTORS DREAM THE impossible dreams. As everyone knows, the competition in this field is superthick, but at least more and more roles are being offered to African Americans these days in both television and film.

For the few who make their way to the big screen, acting is a highly visible and lucrative profession. However, most actors struggle to pick up parts wherever they can. For stage actors, this may include a long tour in Japan or in the boondocks in road shows and dinner theaters. To make a living, even successful actors continue to accept small roles, including commercials and product endorsements.

A few lucky actors make an excellent living working as character actors. A classic example is the highly respected Hollywood veteran Bill Duke, who has played bad guys for years, from the drug dealer in *Superfly* to a pimp in *American Gigolo*. Actors always say it's more fun to be bad than good, on screen at least.

According to one highly successful actor I know, most actors and actresses have formal dramatic training and experience, which can be obtained in over five hundred colleges and universities that offer degrees in dramatic and theater arts, or in dramatic arts classes taught by experienced professionals in New York and Los Angeles. Many get their first professional experience working as extras or in television commercials. Other routes are acting in Off-Off-Off-Broadway shows and summer stock. Once they reach a certain plateau, actors rely on

THE PERFORMANCE ARTIST:
FROM DOWNTOWN TO BIG TIME

If you want to be in on stage, try starting as a performance artist. Record companies and publishers are scrambling to sign up spoken-word artists as audiences all over the country flock to cafes to hear the latest. Spoken-word poet Sapphire, who propels audiences to their feet with her roof-shattering material, signed a five-hundred-thousand-dollar contract with Knopf to publish her books. *Push,* her first novel, was reviewed by *The New York Times*! Veteran performance artist Hattie Gossett has been knocking them off their feet for years with her red-hot originals, such as *King Kong.*

> if king kong had been home
> with his kids and his old lady and his neighbors
> helping to protect their turf from the invaders
> he never would have gotten hauled across the ocean
> and ended up getting shot off the top of the empire state
> building
> and what was that boy doing up there
> in the dark
> with that woman
> anyway

To get your start, sign up to strut yourself at the poets' venues. In New York, that would be the Nuyorican Poets Cafe, where it all began.

agents to find them parts, although they are always hustling to make their own connections to bring in work.

Camera crew

THE CAMERA CREW, from the director of photography to the gaffer (lighting technician), are the artisans behind the scenes who work together to capture the scenes in the script on film. The cinematographer, or director of photography, is the visionary who composes the film shots to reflect the mood the director wishes to create. You'll usually find the director and the DP talking softly off in the corner, creating the setup for the actual filming.

Moving the camera is the responsibility of the camera operator, who

THE SCOOP ON SHOOTERS

Camera Operator
Looks through viewfinder, moves camera, frames shots

Assistant Camera Crew
First assistant focuses each shot, marks tape for actors
Second assistant helps mark tape, checks equipment, operates slate and
  clapsticks
Third assistant loads camera, takes care of equipment

Gaffer
Sets up lighting for each scene

coordinates with the first assistant, who pulls focus as the operator pans the lens to frame the shot. A great camera operator can compensate for a haphazard actor.

There are a few crack African-American shooters, as camera operators are known, out there now, but the industry is screaming for more, and this is one area where enterprising types should rush in. Camera operators may be owner-operators, which means they own their rig (harness and an arm) or, rarely, the entire camera. A rig costs about sixty thousand dollars and a camera from one million to five million dollars. Operators will contract their services and equipment to the production company. Owners of steady-cams, rigs with a balanced arm and harness, are in demand now, so go ahead, mortgage the house. It's been done, and paid back within a year.

Until recently, few Blacks have studied to be in control of the camera because they felt they couldn't get these kinds of jobs. But today, even if an all-Black production company wants to hire an all-Black crew, there aren't enough of us working in this area. What does this say to you? Run to hone your technical skills, then let everybody in town know you've got them.

Working with the camera is a lifetime craft that requires tremendous teamwork. Everyone from the camera operator on down does what the DP says to do, even if it makes no sense. The same camera crew often works together on many jobs, developing a flawless instinct to work as a single unit to get the job done under tremendous pressure. For these technicians, the camera is their life. As my buddy in Hollywood says, they are "100 percent geeked out" and passionately consumed by their work.

Most camera technicians have either completed college or technical school or gone through an apprenticeship program. Experience is usually the best way to learn how to operate the sophisticated equipment. Cinematographers often begin as assistant camera operators and come up through the ranks. Many get started just by helping out on productions—running errands, moving things, and doing whatever else is needed. One assistant I know drove the truck delivering the equipment to the set, just so he could make those crucial contacts.

Sound Crew

IF YOU ARE one of the few who appreciate just how crucial sound is to the success of a production, a job on a sound crew might be a career to consider. The sound crew works with the director to create everything you hear during a film, television show, or live broadcast. Sound engineers, audio recordists, and boom operators (the guy or gal holding the microphone) record dialogue and music during the shoot. Sounds, music, and special effects are usually laid in during postproduction.

CAMERA CREW, SOUND engineers, and audio recordists may be union members who work on an on-call basis. Minimum pay rates are set by the International Alliance of Theatrical Stage Employees and Motion Picture Machine Operators (IATSE), the union that controls this segment of the industry.

This work allows for great autonomy, travel, and all the benefits of a flexible schedule, but it also pretty much guarantees a fluctuating income and requires a never-ending, time-consuming, and stressful search for new gigs. You will always be hustling work. It's all about staying in touch with people.

On the other hand, television studios tend to hire employees on a full-time basis at a pay scale dictated by union regulations. This employment is secure but may not be as interesting.

Special Effects Technicians

SPECIAL EFFECTS TECHNICIANS are the magicians of the industry, creating virtually anything that the script requires from talking dolls and animals to living dinosaurs and exploding volcanoes—all made

TECH TAKE IN TV*

Operator technician
average annual salary	$24,260
range	$16,422 in small markets to $45,158 in large markets

Technical director
average annual salary	$25,962
range	$18,444 to $44,531

Maintenance technician
average annual salary	$32,533
range	$24,210 to $50,235

Chief engineer
average annual salary	$53,655
range	$38,178 in small markets to $91,051 in large markets

*According to a survey conducted by the National Association of Broadcasters and the Broadcast Cable Financial Management Association

possible by the wizardry of their imagination combined with highly specialized computer technology, carpentry, plumbing, and electronics. Special effects wizards and makeup artists turned Eddie Murphy into a four-hundred-pound blob for his role in *The Nutty Professor*.

Special effects technicians are jacks of all trades, although the field also relies heavily on advanced computer techniques. George Lucas is Industrial Light & Magic. The company has become the center of special effects technology, visited by producers, directors, and technicians from around the world. To work in special effects today, I recommend becoming a computer whiz in the latest software used to create the effects. A special tip for enterprising African Americans— stop by an industry job fair in New York or LA to find out the latest high-tech software crying out for skilled users. You can find where the next one is by reading industry magazines such as *Videomaker, Location Update,* or *Interactive Week.*

POSTPRODUCTION

POSTPRODUCTION IS THE laborious process of shaping the film from hours of individual shots into a final movie that mesmerizes us in the theater. While the shoot itself takes weeks or months, postproduction can last up to a year.

Editors

FILM EDITORS HAVE one of the most important roles in the film industry, because until they've finished their magic tricks, all you've got is raw footage. To call them editors is actually a misnomer, because what they really are is storytellers. An editor at the peak of his or her artistry creates a movie that has you sitting on the edge of your seat by virtue of its exquisite pacing and dramatic continuity. On the other hand, the best-shot film can be ruined by poor editorial production. Few viewers realize just how important the rhythm of the movie is.

After the footage is shot and processed by a lab, an editor will study it for days. From shelves of reels, the editor selects the best shots and pieces them together into a 1 ½-hour movie. One of the toughest parts of being an editor is all the beautiful footage you must cut in order to strengthen the film's narrative line.

Assistant editors select sound elements, including voice-overs, music, and special noises such as crickets or lightning strikes, that give the film the final combination of sight and sound. They help with the technical aspects of the editing, including splicing, patching, rewinding, coding, and film storage. A film librarian is the script girl of the postproduction realm: He or she keeps track of each reel of footage and has it ready the second the film editor calls.

Editors often begin as assistants or librarians and work their way up. Editors may also go on to other occupations within the industry.

Motivated would-be editors will get an editing internship or take an inexpensive course at a nonprofit urban film center; Downtown Community Television (DC TV) is one well-known hands-on training facility in New York that provides artist-in-residence grants to individuals or groups coming up with snappy ideas that speak for and to our community.

Audio Recording Engineers

THE RECORDING ENGINEERS lay in sound during postproduction, adding sound effects and background music and dubbing in dialogue that could not be recorded during filming. Experience relevant to this occupation can be acquired through work at radio stations, with music groups, or on music videos.

Promoter

WITHOUT PROMOTION AND marketing, a film may die a quick and expensive death. Effective publicity is extremely important, especially for Black filmmakers whose work is often mismarketed, or worse, not marketed at all. We are also vulnerable to the danger that the major studios will focus efforts on narrow filmmaking genres with proven audience appeal. I call this the *Boyz N the Hood* sequel phenomenon. Such a single-focus approach has contributed to the perception that our community is monolithic. We have to make films for a variety of audiences or risk being pigeonholed into another period of "blaxploitation" (the era in the '70s when Black film-making was almost exclusively identified with popular supergangster and action-hero flicks like *Superfly*, *Shaft*, and *Coffy*).

Promoters who don't understand Black audiences will miss the mark when developing their marketing plans for Black films. Publicists should be thoroughly familiar with the Black media outlets that reach the largest percentage of potential viewers, such as BET, *Ebony*, *Essence*, and *Jet*. A devastating example of poor promotion is the movie *The Five Heartbeats*, directed by Robert Townsend. The movie received rave reviews but was targeted to a young crowd, who failed to appreciate its nostalgic depiction of 1960s pop groups such as the Temptations.

Last but not least, the key point I'd like to make: Black filmmakers will not get their films on the market in a manner that best serves the ideals and needs of our community unless we form our own alliances to finance, distribute, and market African-American films. Just do it!

MAKE YOUR MARK IN MARKETING

Marketing personnel
Develop marketing strategy: estimate demand for film and probable audience
Implement advertising plan: decide when and where to release the film, create plan

Unit Publicists
Prepare press releases, including bios, about directors and stars
Set up print interviews and TV appearances

Sales Staff
Sell the film through distribution deals, leases, and sales to theater owners, TV networks, and foreign markets

THE POWER BROKERS

THE CHAIN OF command can be complex, as film and television studios, record companies, and cable channels often reside under the same corporate roof. Within the Black entertainment world, highly placed corporate executives are few and far between. One standout is Robert Johnson, founder, chief executive officer, and largest stockholder (46 percent) of BET Holdings Inc., of Washington, DC, a publicly held company that is among the fastest growing media-entertainment companies in America. Starting with a fifteen thousand-dollar personal loan, Bob has built a company with a current market value of more than five hundred million. BET includes four cable channels, two magazines, a major web site, a restaurant, a clothing line, a credit card, and a forthcoming two-hundred-million-dollar, one thousand-room resort in Las Vegas, called the BET SoundStage Hotel and Casino. (By the way, the Black travel and tourism industry has one of the most active lobbies in Washington right now, helping make this another fast-growing economic opportunity for African Americans.) "Quality entertainment is colorblind," Bob Johnson recently told the Associated Press. "We plan to target Blacks but appeal to everybody." Bob's partners in his new hotel venture are Hilton Hotels and his Black movie- and sports-star friends. Now, that's entertainment leverage.

Another standout is Richard D. Parsons, who oversees all corporate staff functions at Time Warner Inc., the world's leading media and entertainment company. As CEO, Parsons reports only to the board of directors and stockholders, while all other managers, such as financial managers, accountants, and attorneys, report to him.

Most entertainment executives work their way to the top after holding other positions in the industry. Actors, directors, producers, agents, and lawyers may make the switch to executive office suites.

Most Black entertainment executives began by leveraging their clout as entertainers to create their own production companies with alliances to major studios and television networks. Such moguls as Bill Cosby, Michael Jackson, Quincy Jones, Eddie Murphy, and Oprah Winfrey, among others, have formed their own media conglomerates that control their own products, including production, recording, and publishing.

THE AGENTS

JUST LIKE THE man behind the curtain in *The Wizard of Oz*, entertainment agents and lawyers operate behind the scenes, often calling the shots that may mean birth or death to a film, television pilot, or series. In effect, they function as high-priced employment agencies for the actors they represent. They will proffer advice and solicit work for any money-making human property they can get their hands on, including actors, directors, screenwriters, composers, and costume designers.

Agents frequently start as attorneys with entertainment law firms or work their way up the ranks from the basement at a talent or management company. The best agents have the uncanny ability to spot and develop new talent and breathe life into a faltering career.

One example is Dolores Robinson, of Dolores Robinson Entertainment, whose management firm represents Jada Pinkett, Rosie Perez, and her own daughter, Holly Robinson.

Instinct is what you need here. I'm talking about a high-stakes poker game where you bluff the producers and studios into the best deal for your clients. Agents must also possess the poise and stability to soothe volatile clientele on a daily basis. The sky's the limit in this career but you must earn every penny. Your income, generally 10 percent of the deals you sign, will depend on the length of your client roster as well as the magnitude of the deal itself. Top agents may earn well over the seven-figure mark.

In the film and television business, you may find yourself working with a bunch of ruthless, goal-oriented personalities who would sell your grandma to get a job. Watch out! Keep your morals! At the same time, film and television sets can be very familial and supportive. My good friend in the industry says, "Everywhere else I'm a freak except here."

In television, the highest-paying and most specialized jobs in all segments are concentrated in New York City, Los Angeles, Chicago, and Washington, DC. However, most cities have television stations where you can get your start. Motion picture production jobs are concentrated in Los Angeles and New York City. The power brokers, including producers, entertainment lawyers, and agents, also tend to be concentrated in Los Angeles and New York. And of course if you're an actor or technician with big ambitions, you're going to have to go to one of those cities to get work.

THE MUSIC BUSINESS

OUR MUSIC IS our power, connecting us to our past and drawing us into the future, pulling us together and sometimes driving us apart. Black music expresses our fears and despairs, as well as our love and joy. As Quincy Jones has written, "No other form of communication has had the transcending power of music, with its chameleon-like ability to connect itself to everyone and everything."

With just twelve notes and a beat, Blacks created and shaped gospel, the blues, jazz, rock, R&B, reggae, rap, hip-hop—music that put an indelible stamp on American culture. Yet the music industry suffers from a racial divide. Black music dominates the charts and accounts for nearly 25 percent of the profits in a twelve-billion-dollar industry, but most Black record labels are run by entertainment conglomerates controlled by white executives. Ninety percent of the music we listen to and buy is produced by the Big Six record and distribution companies: Warner Elektra Atlantic, Polygram Group Distribution, Cema Distribution, UNI Distribution Corp., BMG Distribution, and Sony Music Entertainment Inc. In these megacorporations, African Americans are often wedged into "Black music" divisions where they may lack full autonomy. Although they are executives, they are largely excluded from production and marketing, packaging, and distribution centers where deals are spun into gold and platinum sales.

But here, too, things are changing. The most enduring and inspiring example I can give you is that of a twenty-year veteran of the industry, chair and CEO of Warner's Elecktra/East West Records, Sylvia Rhone. She climbed to the top of the industry ladder the tough way by anyone's standards; today, her title is unadorned by the "Black music" moniker. Her success has opened the door to other Black executives, including Denise J. Brown, senior vice president of the Black Music Division at Warner Bros. Records, Lisa Cortes of Loose Cannon Records (distributed by Polygram), and Tracey Edmonds of Yab Yum Entertainment (who also received a push from her husband Babyface).

Joining their ranks is an emerging corps of young entrepreneurs who were toddlers when Rhone entered the industry as a secretary. What sets the "baby" moguls apart is their ability to leverage profits from the Big Six by launching sublabels, which enables them to earn a greater share of the royalties on the records they produce.

These new financing arrangements have allowed young start-ups to make a name for themselves with a virtually interest-free loan from the major label, which is paid back from earnings generated from the sublabel's recordings. Why did we get this deal? Because Black producers are churning out hits! And in an industry where hits mean clout, we can wield power.

GETTING YOUR START

COMPETITION FOR JOBS in the record industry is fierce. If you want to break in, you'll need perseverance, enthusiasm, and talent to the nth degree. Even entry-level secretarial jobs are hard to get, so think carefully about how you can sell your skills in the music marketplace. And have fun! Because the places where you may be "chillin'" could be spawning the trends and superhits of tomorrow.

Most music industry jobs do not require any special training, although a college or advanced technical degree can catch someone's eye. The beauty of this business is that the most crucial qualifications are personality and talent, plus the willingness to do whatever it takes to get ahead. If you belong in the recording industry, you'll know it.

To help yourself along, get to know the industry and focus on the type of music you want to pursue. Read record reviews and subscribe to 'zines specializing in our community's take on our musical culture, such as *Billboard, Jazziz, Vibe,* and *The Source.*

You never know who you're going to find in a record store, so make one of them your second home. And take advantage of all opportunities to talk with industry insiders. Take unpaid internships and part-time and summer jobs in local recording studios or on road tours. What they say is true: The more experience, contacts, and knowledge you gain, the closer you will be to achieving your goals.

A&R *(Artists and repertoire)*

DO YOU LOVE chasing down new acts to hear the latest sound? Are you always up on the latest trends and adept at predicting the next hot riff? Is haggling for a better deal one of your fortes? With hard work, you might be able to turn your interests into a profitable career by joining a label's A&R department, the division that scouts new talent.

At independent labels, the A&R department is far more active than at the majors, covering new artists and less mainstream types of music. These young African Americans are on their toes with the razor-sharp instinct to pick up on every new "flavah" that Black music is kickin'. And this is the key reason why major labels love to make sublabel deals with them.

A&R staffers are out there in the clubs or attending concerts or scene-making events where talent may be discovered. Now wouldn't you like to get paid to go out at night? Staffers also listen to recordings sent to the department, plan production of a recording, and assist in recording sessions.

Most A&R executives and staff start at the bottom and look for ways to soar to the top as quickly as possible. To get in, well, just get in, as a receptionist, assistant, or clerk.

Producers/Executives

IN THE MUSIC industry, and especially in the Black music trade, the executives and producers are generally young, hip-to-the-music-scene surveyors who are ready to do whatever it takes to get in and move up in the industry. The top producers spend their days and nights scouring clubs and concerts for new talent. They have a knack not only for following but for setting the trends.

If you can bring a hot act to the table, so much the better. A hit can give the budding entrepreneur leverage to command multimillion-dollar joint ventures or sublabel deals.

Producer Jermaine Dupri became one of the youngest music industry executives in the country at age twenty when he parlayed his success as a producer of platinum-plus rap groups into a three-million-dollar deal with Sony to start So So Def Recordings.

Or take Sean "Puffy" Combs. At nineteen he was named vice president of A&R at Uptown Records. At twenty-four he cut a one-million-dollar deal with Arista to distribute his Bad Boy Entertainment record label, and at twenty-six he negotiated a seventy-five-million-dollar joint venture.

All this started from producing parties in high school and during his college years at Howard University. Combs's climb to fame and fortune came with hard work, a keen ear for tomorrow's big hit, and some luck. Known for being a hard driver, Combs rarely takes a break, even to sleep. He has also put some of his millions back into the community that he acknowledges launched his career. Daddy's House, a nonprofit organization run by rapper Sister Souljah, provides a multitude of services for inner-city youth.

Engineers

ONE OF THE most important jobs in the music industry is the sound engineer. On the road, the engineer makes the stars sound like their records (one of the biggest challenges is having to service the sound equipment as the live show is in progress). By far the biggest responsibility is in the studio, when the recording engineer works with the producer to mix the different tracks into the best version of the song.

During the session, numerous tapings are made of the song, with each instrument and voice recorded separately. Selecting and mixing the tracks together to produce the best version is one of the most important jobs in the business, and generally engineers can literally write their own tickets.

Production engineers and technicians must have a deep understanding of the music they record and also the technical skills necessary to operate and repair the sound and recording equipment. Although some have learned their trade on the job, there are trade or vocational schools that offer courses or two-year degrees in this field.

Rebekah Foster left college, where she was majoring in sports med-

THE PECKING ORDER AT THE
RECORDING SESSION

Executive Producer
In charge: works directly with the artist; selects studio musicians, engineers, and technicians

Recording Producer
In charge of all aspects of taping: supervises technicians; controls all factors influencing the sound quality, including microphone, placement, tracks used

Recording Engineer
Operates the control consoles, modulates volume and intensity of the recorded sound, helps direct the artist's performance, services sound equipment

Setup Worker
Selects, arranges, and hooks up all equipment needed in the session, including microphones, amplifiers, tape recorders, isolation booths, instruments, and music stands

icine, when she realized that her dream was to produce music. Now she records such hot acts as Queen Latifah, Naughty by Nature, and Whitney Houston. She has also worked for her heroes Dizzy Gillespie, Sarah Vaughan, and the Count Basie Orchestra. Sound good? Be prepared to work hard if you want to reach Rebekah's level. After leaving college, she drove a bus to subsidize her on-the-job training and learned the ropes by taking small jobs with everybody from rap groups to a tiny acoustic folk company. She has toured as an engineer, tour manager, and production manager and gets paid handsomely for her time. Not one to keep the fruits of her success to herself, Rebekah formed Ujima Sound Productions Limited, a networking group of her Black colleagues.

Packagers

SO YOU CAN'T sing or play a note. Lucky for you, the music industry has use for a variety of other skills and talents. If you are an artist,

ENGINEERING EGGHEADS

Sound mixer
Blends the sounds of the various tracks made during the recording session

Tape transferor
Operates the equipment that reproduces recordings from the master

Quality-control inspector
Using optical and audio equipment, inspects the metal record produced from the master for defects

Record tester
Uses optical and audio equipment to test sample recordings

photographer, writer, graphic designer, or video director, you can combine your skills and interests in music into a career. The look and feel of a CD must convey an image that jibes with and enhances the artist's own persona in appearance and in sound. In this business, consumers do judge tapes and CDs by their covers.

Meet Tar—you may not know his name or recognize his face, but if you've spent any time in the R&B section of a music store, you know his work. His photographs grace the covers of CDs by artists including Boyz II Men, George Clinton, and Brandi. Tar honed his lensing skills by taking pics of the cheerleaders and football players at his high school. Realizing that few Black photographers were involved in the music business, he had an inkling that his hobby might be profitable as well as intriguing. Tar's hunch paid off. As *Black Enterprise* reported, today Tar's New York studio bills more than $450,000 annually.

Promoters

THE BEST WAY to promote a song or rap is to get it onto the airwaves, which means that the promotion staff must be up to date on the target audience for each radio station and how best to promote the new release to that audience. What radio stations do you listen to? Rap, hip-hop, soul, gospel? Each station and show develops programming for a specific audience that broadcasters hope will tune in. Think of how shocked you would be if you flipped the dial to your favorite R&B station and heard Chopin instead.

The promotion and publicity staff develop the plans, make the contacts, and prepare all the written information necessary to generate publicity for their label's recordings. They arrange interviews, autograph sessions, and concerts. And most important, they cultivate relationships with the radio executives and disc jockeys who are likely to give airtime to their artist.

Bestselling albums appeal to several different target audiences. Groups like TLC and The Fugees get airplay on pop, R&B, and hip-hop stations, as do performers such as Whitney Houston and Toni Braxton.

Promotion people need to have excellent oral and written communication skills. A background in advertising or public relations is also helpful, especially if you are seeking a higher than entry-level position.

To get in, you can start as a receptionist, assistant, or clerk. That's what Grammy-nominated jazz flutist Sherry Winston did. She started her career in music promotion as a receptionist for Electra/Asylum Records, then worked her way up to director of jazz promotion for Columbia Records. Her journey took ten years, with several stops and her own business venture along the way.

Music-video makers

THE MUSIC VIDEO began in the early 1980s as an art form shown at New York and LA clubs in the wee hours of the morning. Today it's imperative that a recording artist have a video to accompany the release. In fact, videos now have their own award category at the Grammys. A demand for videos has spawned a new generation of producers, visualists, editors, and shooters and inspired a new visual language. On average, videotape editors make a cut about every three seconds.

Managers and Lawyers

THE MANAGER IS the artist's voice in the marketplace: managers arrange and negotiate contracts with the label, set up performance schedules, handle commercial endorsements and promotional presentations, and do whatever else is necessary to build the artist's image and fan base. A manager's fees are paid by the artist and are normally 15 to 20 percent of the gross.

Quadri El-Amin, who helped make Boyz II Men an R&B phenomenon, was an assistant to the group's first road manager, Khalil Roundtree, who was shot on tour in what may have been an attempted robbery. El-Amin devoted himself to launching the group's career; it still dominates the charts and is considered the act that breathed new life into Motown. El-Amin parlayed his success with Boyz II Men into the formation of Southpaw, a management company handling international tours, endorsements, and recording contracts for several artists. Not bad for a young man who started in entertainment by throwing basement parties and charging twenty-five cents a head. This New Jersey native majored in business administration at Rutgers, where he promoted on-campus concerts.

These careers demand excellent oral and written communication skills, but most important is a keen ability to aggressively negotiate and secure career opportunities for clients. The ability and desire to network and a deep interest in music are also important.

A legal career is the perfect demonstration that the music game is not all glitter and glamour. Entertainment lawyers work hard to negotiate the deals that send their clients to the top. As one music lawyer put it, "We're paid to make deals, not spend time backstage with the stars."

If you love music, however, and are unhappy spending long hours drafting briefs, you might be able turn your interest into a career where you enjoy the results of the work. The experience can also lead to executive positions outside the legal department but inside the industry.

A case in point is Denise J. Brown, formerly a partner at Mayer, Katz, Kaber, Leibowitz & Roberts, one of the most prestigious entertainment law firms in the business. She left her partnership to become senior vice president of the Black Music Division of Warner Brothers Records. Brown has no question about why she was chosen. She told *Essence*, "I was the best person for the job." Her background in entertainment law has been a tremendous asset in understanding the legal subtleties that permeate complex negotiations and a fine foundation for forming alliances with the broad group of executives in the business.

Networking and persistence plus a proven interest in the music business will help neophyte attorneys get their foot in the door.

MONEY DEPENDS ON success in this business. Highly successful artists, producers, and agents can rake in millions of dollars, while others may not make enough to survive. Recording, production, and editorial work is also paid according to the employee's level of experience and the size of the corporate employer.

Most music industry jobs are centered in New York City, Los Angeles, Atlanta, and Nashville, as Blacks have begun to break through into the country music scene.

In the entertainment industries, Blacks should seek out African-American mentors and look for entry-level positions in companies that produce Black-oriented programming or films. The best advice is to be tenacious and never give up. We also must make a concerted effort to learn as much as we can about every facet of the industries and the corporations that employ us. A broad breadth of knowledge is critical to moving forward.

There's something they forgot to tell you in high school: You may not get that glamorous job without an internship. Intern experience—and this means unpaid—is the way to gain experience and to prove how devoted to entering the business you really are. So you were saving up for college. Consider using that money to support yourself while you take an internship.

Internships can provide a wealth of experience and contacts. Entertainment conglomerates and recording studios aren't stupid. Why pay out thousands of dollars when they can get a bright, starry-eyed intern who just might turn out to be the next Rebekah Foster for free?

Several music and entertainment companies offer internships targeted at college and graduate students that provide credit toward a degree. Internships are available at cable TV stations, magazines, recording studios, and Fortune 500 entertainment conglomerates. If you don't see the internship you want, make one up. Call up the company of your choice and offer . . . yourself. You'll be surprised how many takers there are.

Because most jobs in the entertainment and music industry are temporary, intermittent, part-time, or on a contract basis, advancement can be difficult. Networking is a big plus, since people in the industry tend to hire those they know and have already worked with.

Executives with the experience and contacts may prefer to launch their own label rather than endure the frustration of stagnating within the Black music divisions of entertainment conglomerates. One example is Eddie Pugh, who was Columbia's Black music division senior VP. In 1995 Pugh left to form Our Turn Records. The work is hard, but the rewards, in terms of personal satisfaction and financial success, can make the move worthwhile.

11

SPORTS: KICKING DOWN
THE REMAINING DOORS

Sports were the way for the Negro, the way to
respectability, acceptance by white folks, and most of all,
the way to make money, to own something.
— HENRY EDWARDS

What Jackie Robinson reminded people
of, and should remind them of today,
is the tremendous untapped
potential in this country.
— FORMER NEW YORK GOVERNOR
MARIO CUOMO

WAYNE EMBRY
GENERAL MANAGER
CLEVELAND CAVALIERS
CLEVELAND, OHIO

Wayne Embry is a big man—big on
the basketball court, big in stature,
and big when it comes to taking care
of business. As America's first Black
general manager of a professional
basketball franchise, he not only
managed the Cleveland Cavaliers
to numerous winning seasons, he

managed a successful small business and helped to manage several corporate and civic organizations while serving on their boards. But if you want to see a big man cry, sit next to Wayne in church on Sunday and watch him well up as he listens to "Precious Lord, Take My Hand."

Wayne's eleven-year all-star NBA career, a solid education in business at Miami University of Ohio, plus some Dale Carnegie courses gave him the skills to face the challenges of professional sports management. But it was his grandfather who inspired him the most.

"People loved and respected Granddad. He worked his way up to foreman in the plant, which was very unusual for a Black man in those days. I learned a lot just observing how he treated people."

After retiring from his own pro career, Wayne landed his first management job with the Milwaukee Bucks as assistant to the president; then, when he was thirty-three, he was named general manager of the Cavaliers. His strong work ethic, excellent interpersonal skills, and reputation for integrity helped him balance the needs of players, agents, and owners. Comments Wayne, "The business of big-time sports management is one of endless speculation, second-guessing, and the demands of proving yourself every day. It requires tremendous self-confidence, and you earn the trust of others over time. Your image is everything. My advice for anyone entering the sports management area is to know the game inside and out, but bring to the table a strong set of principles and the ability to build solid relationships. This is truly a relationship business, one that requires rational judgment at all times."

All the money in the world won't get the job done in pro sports without good leadership. As an inspiring business and community leader, Wayne continues to prove that when the door opens, Blacks can rise to the occasion, no matter the odds, be it on the playing field or in the front office. Wayne has opened the door for many to come in.

FAVORITE BIBLICAL PASSAGE:

And we know that all things work together for good to them that love God, to them who are the called according to his purpose.

—Romans 8:28

SEVERAL YEARS AGO I was speaking before a group of executives in the pharmaceutical industry about the success of diversity in American business. I reminded them of an American businessman, Branch Rickey, who was president of the Brooklyn Dodgers fifty years ago.

Branch Rickey was a knowledgeable and visionary leader. He started the farm system of bringing along players for major league teams. He was a religious and moral man, and the idea that minority athletes were excluded from the major leagues rankled him. He was also a businessman, and he thought that bringing paying minority customers to the ballpark would make him richer.

A good judge of people, he chose Jackie Robinson as the man to break the color barrier in major league baseball. We know today that Jackie was the ideal person to do this. He was more than a great ball-player, he was a great human being. When he joined the Brooklyn Dodgers fifty years ago in 1947, he changed much more than base-ball—he changed America.

The American sports industry is a gigantic $156 billion-a-year success story according to *Fortune* magazine, thanks in large part to African Americans. Much of its growth has occurred during the past fifty years and includes not only professional sports but the burgeoning fitness business and such facilities as bowling alleys, skating rinks, tennis clubs, golf courses, and all of the equipment and clothing that goes with recreational sports.

Given the achievements of African-American athletes and the newness of sports as an industry, employment opportunities for Blacks should be excellent. But sports in America have historically been segregated and have systematically denied opportunity to African Americans on the field, on the production line, and in the boardroom. It is a history that is only now beginning to fade.

Today a quiet revolution has been going on that is changing the complexion of the American sports industry. Blacks are finally getting into the executive offices and joining the ownership ranks of top sports enterprises. With the strong growth and increasing popularity of sports, Blacks are positioned to make their voices heard and get a significant share of the astronomical earnings sports are generating.

The industrialization of America changed sports from competition among gentlemen to a major entertainment industry with a worldwide audience. Workers pouring into the country's industrial centers from Europe and the rural South in the early years of the twentieth century needed a form of recreation that didn't require a sophisticated knowledge of language to be enjoyed. Sports, which had previously been considered a diversion for the elite or simply a pleasant way to get some exercise, were organized and professionalized by America's entrepreneurs.

In its early days, professional sports was a ladder for minority athletes to climb out of poverty. Irish, German, Slavic, Scandinavian, and Italian Americans came to dominate the sports world. This was not true for Black Americans. Although Moses Fleetwood Walker and his brother Welday briefly played baseball for the Toledo Blue Stockings in 1884, bigoted owners and players banned Black athletes from participating in professional team sports. When a Black man, Jack Johnson, KO'd Tommy Burns in 1908 and won the heavyweight boxing title, there was a hue and cry throughout the country for a "white hope" to bring the championship back to the white race.

Yet there was a large Black audience for professional sports, and the Negro baseball and basketball leagues were formed and gave Black audiences a very high-quality athletic performance. Some Black entrepreneurs profited from the segregated system forced upon them, and the system was responsible for some great teams, such as the Homestead Grays, Birmingham Black Barons, Kansas City Monarchs, and Toledo Crawfords, as well as many great players like Josh Gibson, Satchel Paige, "Cool Papa" Bell, and Buck O'Neil. These great teams and players, however, were not allowed to participate fully in the national pastime.

But times were changing. In 1937, when Joe Louis won the heavyweight crown, there were no calls for a new "white hope." And on June 22, 1938, a year after the Brown Bomber first took the title, he demolished Adolf Hitler's favorite fighter, Max Schmeling, in one minute and ten seconds of the first round and became not only a "credit to his race" but a true American hero.

Aside from prizefighting, horse racing, and major league baseball, professional sports were small and disorganized before World War II. There was a fledgling NFL with teams in Green Bay, Chicago, New York, and other places. Most players were white, but Blacks occasionally played. The great African-American singer Paul Robeson, who had been an All-American football player in college, played professional football for a short time. But it wasn't until 1946 that Black players became teammates of whites on both the Los Angeles Rams and the Cleveland Browns. The first of these players were Marion Motley, Woody Strode, Kenny Washington, and Bill Willis.

In basketball, Chuck Cooper was the first Black player drafted by an NBA team—the Boston Celtics in 1950. In the same year, the New York Knicks signed Sweetwater Clifton, who had been playing with the Harlem Globetrotters, and Earl Lloyd, who played college ball at West Virginia State, joined the Washington squad.

Professional golf is only now becoming interesting to African Americans with the emergence of Tiger Woods as a genuine superstar, but it remains difficult for many African Americans to get the chance to learn and play the game because equipment is prohibitively expensive, most golf courses belong to private clubs, and public courses are crowded. Even so, African-American professional golfers such as Charlie Sifford, Lee Elders, and Calvin Peete led the way for Tiger Woods.

Another sport that had restricted Black participation was tennis. Tennis was primarily an amateur sport until the 1970s. In the 1950s, Althea Gibson became the first African American to compete, and in the 1970s Arthur Ashe became both a champion (at Wimbledon in 1975) and a leader in the struggle for human rights.

Segregation in American sports was finally vanquished by World War II, when America fought against countries whose racist policies were more venal than her own. When Jackie Robinson joined the Brooklyn Dodgers in 1947 and broke the color barrier, however, the battle was just beginning.

Since 1987, there have been increases in opportunities in major league baseball for Blacks, largely due to the notoriety brought to the issue when Los Angeles Dodger executive Al Campanis startled and provoked television viewers with his statement that Blacks didn't have the ability to manage in professional sports. The Reverend Jesse Jackson wasted no time in bringing the industry's poor hiring records to the attention of the media.

Al Campanis was fired, but somebody should have given him an award. As a result of the fracas, major league teams began to adopt or implement affirmative hiring policies and make a concerted effort to bring African Americans into front office and management positions.

Hall-of-Famer Hank Aaron said in 1997, "It is tragic to me that baseball has fallen so far behind . . . in terms of racial leadership. . . . It is certainly not the national standard it once was. Here's hoping that on the fiftieth anniversary of Jackie Robinson's historic breakthrough, baseball will honor him in a way that really matters. It could start more youth programs, giving tickets to kids who can't afford them, become a social presence in the cities it depends on. It could hire more Black umpires, more Black team doctors, more Black concessionaires, more Black executives."

Blacks are beginning to assume important positions in the sports industry as executives, franchise owners, agents, managers, and coaches, although the Center for the Study of Sports in Society reported a downturn in this trend during the 1995–96 season: "There were declines in the percentage of general managers in the NBA, as well as in the percentage of vice presidents on NBA and Major League teams. Additionally, the percentage of minority players declined in all three leagues for the first time in the 1990s."

Black sports professionals have the power to influence and change industry policies and trends. With more Blacks part of the corporate decision-making process, African Americans are ready to take advantage of opportunities the sports industry offers as the market seems poised for a new spurt of growth over the next decade.

This market explosion is partly a result of America's increased awareness of the benefits of physical fitness. Consumer obsession with health and exercise has spurred the growth of athletic teams and fitness centers, all of which generate new job opportunities. Also, the percentage of leisure time and disposable income that Americans can allocate to attend or participate in a sport is increasing. I feel certain that as the industry grows, there will be a continuing growth of job slots and new kinds of jobs.

Expansion teams at the professional level offer increased opportunity for employment in a diverse array of sports. The major team sports are baseball, football, basketball, hockey, and soccer. There are also such individual sports as tennis, golf, boxing, wrestling, horse racing, running, and race car driving. Sports that were once barely noticed have also become increasingly popular. Soccer, swimming, ice-skating, gymnastics, and women's basketball, are drawing greater numbers of spectators and television audiences, increasing these sports' financial appeal to corporate and media sponsors.

INDUSTRY SEGMENTS

WITHIN THE SPORTS industry, there are many potential career choices. The industry is highly diversified, made up of athletes, agents, and coaches, executives and groundskeepers. The sports industry also includes managers and scouts, as well as companies that produce uniforms and equipment. Another big part of the industry lies in getting the stories out to the public: Public relations professionals and the sports press keep interest in sports at a fevered pitch. In addition, the role of agents who represent the athletes has also become an important element of the industry.

The industry broadly divides into six segments:

- On the Field (and Sidelines)—Athletes, coaches, trainers, officials
- Administrators—Owners, general managers, executives, financial directors, front and back office personnel
- Agents—in a world of their own
- Promotors—Events planners, public relations and sports event marketing experts
- Service Providers—Protection and security, building services and groundskeepers, ushers and ticket takers, equipment managers and front-office personnel
- The Sports Press—Reporters, editors, camerpeople, analysts

Within each segment there are obstacles, but opportunities are many and increasingly bright.

ON THE FIELD

Athletes

THE FIRST OF those involved in sports that come to mind are, of course, the athletes—the highly paid pros who not only exert themselves on the field or the court but also make product endorsements to the tune of millions of dollars. In fact, *U.S. News & World Report* noted that nearly seventeen hundred Black athletes earned approximately $1.7 billion in salaries and nearly $1 billion in endorsements in 1995. This income was earned largely by baseball, basketball, and football players. The activities of celebrity-athletes such as Tiger Woods, Michael Jordan, and Muhammad Ali blur the lines between sports and entertainment.

Room for such celebrity-athletes is limited, as are slots available to any athlete trying to make it in the pros. According to a report in *U.S. News & World Report* on March 24, 1997, the odds against any high school athlete playing on a professional level are ten thousand to one. If you truly believe you have what it takes to become a professional athlete, then right on! No one wants to deny you your dream. But be smart and give serious thought to getting a good education and developing some other skills along the way. (I recommend that all you young athletes hoping to work your way up to the pros take an evening and rent the video documentary *Hoop Dreams*. It shows that the road to the pros, even for the gifted, is far from glamorous and often impossibly frustrating.)

However, many other professionals also play crucial roles in making the game happen—from high-profile coaches and managers to athletic trainers to the umpires and referees. Within each group, job opportunities are available for Blacks, but entry into the professional world is intensely competitive and demands a high level of talent and a tremendous desire to succeed.

Coaches

THERE ARE MORE minorities in the coaching ranks than in any other sports field, and opportunities for coaching jobs exist throughout the United States—from elementary and junior high schools and the YMCA and Little League organizations to colleges and universities and right up to the pros.

At the professional level, coaches are highly paid and highly visible. Many have either played professional sports themselves or were outstanding college players. Coaches must have a thorough knowledge of the game, be able to work with and motivate athletes, and have the ability to deal with the press and front office personnel. At every level, the job is highly pressured, since coaches are responsible for the team's won-loss record, which translates to the bottom line. In schools, a winning season is just a winning season. In the pros, a winning season means millions of dollars in revenues from sources ranging from ticket sales to lucrative television contracts, product endorsements, and licensing revenues.

But coaching, particularly at amateur and school levels, can be highly rewarding on a personal level as well. It is only within the last ten years that coaching jobs in three of the major professional sports have opened up for minorities. From 1989 to 1993 there were thirteen African-American head coaches or managers in the NFL, NBA, and MLB, out of a total of eighty-three positions. However, in 1995, that number declined to twelve Blacks filling eighty-eight available slots. Black assistant coaches fill 152 of 628 jobs (24 percent), with the NBA showing the highest percentage among the three leagues (41 percent).

Head coaching jobs for minorities are hard to come by, especially away from basketball. In its seventy-five-year history the NFL has had only two Black head coaches. Division 1 college football is just as difficult to enter, with only four Blacks serving as head coaches last season among the nation's 107 Division 1-A programs. Major league baseball had six managerial openings recently but did not fill any of the vacancies with a minority applicant.

Basketball, on the other hand, continues to offer opportunities at all levels. There are now four Black head coaches in the NBA, earning anywhere from three hundred thousand to eight hundred thousand dollars per year. The 1994–95 college basketball season began with approximately fifty Black head coaches at the Division I level. One was Cheryl Miller, who left a broadcasting career to lead the University of Southern California women's basketball team. The average salary for head coaches of women's Division I basketball is about forty-five thousand dollars. For men's basketball, it's seventy-seven thousand dollars.

The opportunities for minorities are greater at the junior high and high school levels, where salaries for teacher-coaches range from nineteen thousand to eighty-five thousand dollars.

The requirements are the same for all coaches: Know your sport inside and out, be a good communicator and a strong motivator, and have thick skin. "It's a people kind of job. You have to be able to relate," says Miller, thirty-one, a communications major (USC, 1986) and a part-time assistant coach at USC from 1986–1991. "I know coaches who can coach Pat Riley out of a game, but have the personality of a rock."

Trainers

TRAINERS FALL WITHIN the category of fitness and medical experts and work with athletes at all levels to keep them healthy and in good physical shape. Trainers must be highly skilled in the practical everyday area of the sports medicine field. They must be able to quickly evaluate an athlete's level of conditioning and recommend diet and exercise programs that will bring the athlete to the peak of conditioning. In the case of injury, the trainer may act as a physical therapist in treating strains and muscle pulls. And it may be the trainer who is responsible for treating cuts and bruises on the spot during a game.

At the professional level in the NBA, NFL, and MLB, few top trainer positions are filled by minorities. Medical staff, which includes trainers, assistant trainers, and strength and conditioning coaches, are predominantly white men. In 1995, only five out of seventy-nine head trainers were Black (6 percent), but this was still an improvement over 1992, when only two out of seventy-seven were Black (3 percent). MLB teams have the worst hiring record in this category: in 1997 none of their trainers or assistant trainers were Black. The low percentage of Blacks in the profession suggests a tremendous opportunity waiting for African Americans interested in this career who are willing to fight for it.

Athletic trainers who work for professional baseball, football, basketball, or hockey teams earn from one thousand five hundred to four thousand dollars per month; some trainers work all year, others only during the playing season. Trainers who work for schools usually earn a teacher's salary plus an additional amount for training.

A bachelor's degree is the minimum requirement for certification. The test consists of a written, practical, and oral examination of your knowledge of anatomy, physiology, kinesiolgy, hygiene, nutrition, conditioning, taping, bracing, emergency procedures, prevention of injury, injury evaluation, and rehabilitative procedures.

A good way to break in is to work as a student trainer or manager within your school's athletic program.

A trainer I know predicts steady job growth in the field as more secondary schools start mandating that a trainer attend every sports contest. I believe that if you want to be in sports medicine, you won't find any more highly motivated patients than athletes. They don't like to be hurt and definitely don't like not being in the game.

Scouts

PROFESSIONAL SPORTS SCOUTS evaluate the athletes from amateur ranks and from other teams and advise management of professional teams about the athlete's skills, temperament, and suitability for the team and program they represent. Often, scouts are retired former team members and coaches, and scouting has in the past come out of the "old boy" network. But today there is a lot riding on scouting the opposition and new prospects. It is a field that may present many new possibilities for the knowledgeable and observant.

Officials

UMPIRES AND REFEREES officiate at various athletic events. They are responsible for enforcing the rules of the game and for calling plays. Their specific duties depend on the sport with which they are associated. Baseball umpires, for example, call balls and strikes, decide whether balls are fair or foul, determine whether a runner is safe or out, and, in general, ensure that the game is played fairly. In basketball, not only must officials have a comprehensive knowledge of the game, they must be in almost as good shape as the players themselves.

Overall, Black officials and referees represent a high percentage of Blacks relative to the population, with an average of 34 percent within the NFL/NBA/MLB.

Major league baseball umpires earn between twenty-two thousand and fifty thousand dollars, and while traveling receive a small amount of expense money per day; umpires in the rookie leagues earn around one thousand dollars a month plus expense money; college and high school umpires earn considerably less and are often paid on a per game basis. Professional football referees may earn between three hundred and five hundred dollars for each regular-season game; postseason games pay more.

Umpires and referees must have at least a high school diploma and often attend special schools for officials in their sport. They must have a comprehensive understanding of all rules and regulations before being certified to become an umpire at the professional level.

THE ADMINISTRATORS

REQUIREMENTS FOR KEY administrative positions vary. Ownership obviously requires the financial ability to invest in the team. Top administrative positions demand a knowledge of the sport and experience in the particular area of focus. In general, these positions require college and often advanced degrees.

Owners

OWNING A TEAM is often the dream of businessmen with the money to invest in an exciting, high-profile industry or of retired athletes who want the chance to see their former team play from the owner's box.

Make no mistake. The price of entry is exorbitant. Yet the high price tag of purchasing even a slice of team ownership has increased the opportunities for potential Black investors and has helped make sellers color-blind.

Black Enterprise reported that "when Orlando Magic General Manager Pat Williams sought investors to purchase the team, he told the Orlando *Sentinel* that he didn't care what color they were. 'Regardless of what race you're talking about, there just aren't a lot of people who can afford to take on a project of this magnitude . . . Even to buy a piece of a club, you're talking about putting up $20 million or $30 million,' Williams said."

Athletes and businessmen with money to risk are finding opportunities to take a piece of a club for themselves. With ownership comes leverage. When Isiah Thomas invested "a reported $12.5 million in the Toronto Raptor franchise," he also acquired the position of chief of basketball operations.

Thomas is not alone, although the percentage of Black owners is still small. In professional basketball, three (or 7 percent) Blacks hold the title of chairman of the board, president, or chief executive officer.

The percentage of limited Black partners, however, is on the rise. Other Blacks with ownership stakes in major league sports include Devon Cherry (Jacksonville Jaguars), William Simms (Carolina Panthers), Norman Francis (New Orleans Saints), and Hank Aaron and Rubye M. Lucas (Atlanta Braves). There are also many Black owners and investors in minor league professional sports.

General Managers/Top Executives

THE PRICE BARRIER to ownership precludes most people from entry. However, some African Americans are achieving management positions in the industry. Twenty-eight percent of the NBA's general managers are Black. But, as of 1997, Bob Watson of the New York Yankees was the only Black general manager in major league baseball, and only four Blacks served in this capacity in the NFL.

The general manager's job is tough. He or she must negotiate player contracts, make trades with other clubs, develop long-range strategies, and negotiate contracts for TV and radio rights. The general manager also works closely with the team's manager and with the club's personnel director.

The general manager must have in-depth knowledge of the game with an understanding of each player's abilities, the strengths and weaknesses of other teams and individual players, and a comprehensive view of the market for the sport. In short, the general manager must be intimately familiar with the sport and the team from the big picture down to the most minute detail.

Former major-leaguer Bob Watson spent five years as an assistant manager with the Houston Astros before getting a chance to run the show. Other former athletes who have risen to the top include Willis Reed of the New Jersey Nets, Elgin Baylor of the Los Angeles Clippers, Billy McKinney of the Detroit Pistons, and Calvin Hill of the Washington Redskins.

Athletic Directors

THE JOB OF college athletic director has usually been closed to minorities. The tendency has been to groom head coaches into the athletic director's role, which essentially eliminates minorities from serious consideration. Today, however, college presidents are focusing more on candidates with sound financial management and fund-raising abilities, especially those with degrees in sports management or sports administration.

In the 1993–94 academic year, the NCAA reports there were thirty-two Black athletic directors out of a total of 897. At the Division I level, African Americans held thirteen of 296 positions. The numbers are better in the high school programs. In smaller school districts, the athletic director may also coach and teach classes.

Salaries range from twenty-five thousand dollars at secondary schools to $140,000 at the Division I level. In a 1992 report, the U.S. General Accounting Office listed the average base salary of Division 1 athletic directors at around eighty thousand dollars.

The difference between Division I and Division III, however, "is like night and day," says Roy Anderson, now in his ninth year as athletic director at Division III Medgar Evers College in Brooklyn, New York.

"In Division III you're not in a vacuum just dealing with athletics," says Anderson, who earned a B.A. in journalism from New York's Fordham University. "Everything we do affects another department. We only have one gym at Medgar Evers and it's also used for classes, so there are certain days we can't play games at home. TV rights, scholarships, recruiting? I don't even think about stuff like that."

Anderson supervises twenty-five employees at Medgar Evers and says that as athletic director he has done everything from coaching to sweeping the floor. Still, he advises potential athletic directors not to turn up their noses at Division II, Division III, and junior college programs. "If you're a self-starter," he says, "there are some good opportunities."

A master's degree in sports management is becoming almost mandatory for entry into this career.

Sports Information Directors

EVERY SPORTS TEAM, league office, and conference worth its salt now employs a public relations or sports information director (known as SID). In effect, they are the publicity arm for professional, college, and high school programs. On game days, sports information directors attend athletic events and see to it that the media has all the information it needs. On non-game days, sports information directors attend practices, prepare advance material, and process requests for interviews and credentials.

Most SIDs have a degree in journalism or communications. Salaries can range from twenty thousand to more than one hundred thousand dollars. "No two days are alike. It's seven days a week, lots of night work and lots of travel," says *Black Enterprise.*

Financial Directors

FINANCIAL DIRECTORS MUST have a thorough understanding of financial and business management in addition to experience running sports organizations. A degree in business and/or sports administration is a help.

Community Relations Directors

THE COMMUNITY RELATIONS director oversees team efforts to build fan support and to improve relations between the team and the community. They often work with the public relations or sports information director to plan events and promotions that will generate publicity for the team and increase goodwill.

Community relations directors often coordinate their efforts with the publicist, so a good understanding of marketing is a plus. This position is frequently held by minorities, since teams often focus their efforts on communities that consist of a large minority population. Within the NFL/NBA/MLB, 25 percent of community relations directors are Black.

THE AGENTS

VIRTUALLY EVERY MULTIMILLION-DOLLAR sports deal bears the mark of the industry's power players, the sports agents who wheel and deal behind the scenes to secure the eye-popping contracts for superstar athletes. Agents wield enormous power in the sports world, since their clients are the magnets that draw fans into the stadiums and spur consumers to buy player-endorsed products.

They arrange for Michael Jordan to drink Gatorade and for Penny Hardaway to wear Nikes, and they make sure that Deion Sanders remains a "prime-time" household name.

Through perseverance, hard work, and creative deal-making, several African-American sports agents have made big names for themselves. One top deal-maker is David Ware, who owns his own Atlanta-based law firm and sports management company. Ware helped put together Pro-Bowler Barry Sanders's $17.5-million contract with the Detroit Lions, a deal that remains the largest nonquarterback contract in the NFL.

The question remains, however, whether Black agents can attract top athletes to their fold. According to Ware, even Black athletes tend to think that white agents and lawyers produce better contracts.

But William Strickland's reputation for crafting "monster" contracts convinced Patrick Ewing, Dominique Wilkins, and Michael Jordan to join ProServe, a management company he worked with until 1992. Strickland, currently with IMG, the largest sports management company in the world, stresses that attracting Black clients takes more than having the same skin color. Competence and a portfolio of success stories draw top players.

Raymond Anderson, who formed AR Sports with partner Larry Reynolds, recalls that when he was starting out, Black athletes were advised against working with Black agents because management wouldn't take them seriously. But Anderson does not believe skin color alienates front office management. As more Blacks negotiate high-profile contracts, the doors into deal-making rooms are opening wider.

Agents put in long hours on the phone, in the office, and on the road to scout potential clients and to bring them into the fold. They must also keep current on the strengths and weaknesses of their clients, of teams, and of other players within the sport. Moreover, agents must be thoroughly versed in the complex technicalities of union agreements, which one lawyer has described as "more confusing than the federal tax code."

THE PROMOTERS

THE TREMENDOUS BOOM in sport-related events and products has made sports marketing and publicity a critical part of the industry.

Sports Events Marketing

SPORTS EVENTS PLANNING, management and marketing is a fast-growing industry segment with greater-than-average growth projected over the next ten years. Marketers create special events tying a sports tournaments or game series to a corporate sponsor. One purpose of special events in sports is to attract more and more people to the stadium. For example, the AT&T Tennis Challenge and the Pizza Hut One-on-One Basketball Program are two sporting events tied to corporate sponsorship. These events create visibility and hefty profits for corporations, sports management companies, and the teams and athletes involved. State-of-the-art stadiums, product marketing, and corporate and media relationships combine to generate billions in revenues. In fact, a 1990 study reported that corporate America spent a total of $23.52 billion on sports marketing. Although challenging to break into, the field continues to expand.

Planners and marketing and promotions specialists need a solid business background. They must possess good writing and oral communication skills and the gift of persuasion.

Larry Lundy began managing an event portfolio that included the Rolando Blackman 3-On-3 Weekend and a youth basketball program. He made a deal with NBC to televise the annual Bayou Classic football game between Grambling and Southern universities, creating over $1.5 million in network sales for the broadcast. Today he manages account activity for the NFL, Drew Pearson Companies, and marketing activities for active and retired pro athletes.

"We're in the business of building our client's business," Lundy told

Black Enterprise. "When I help Drew get a new account or reach sales goals, I know I've been a part of the team."

Sports marketing is a mini-industry unto itself. The *IEG Directory of Sponsorship Marketing* features 1,500 agencies, suppliers, and services, in addition to more than four thousand sports events and sponsorship opportunities. Special event marketing has become such an important part of the sports industry that many teams have created departments or positions that coordinate special events in-house.

Job opportunities range from top-level planners to support and administrative staff. Special events create a virtually endless stream of jobs for sales media reps, advertisers, food vendors, public relations specialists, laborers or union help, caterers, hotels, airlines, and more.

Salaries vary, depending on the level of the sports organization represented and on the nature of the event produced. Sales commissions, bonuses, and other incentives can add to the salary base.

Managers must be willing to put in long hours during a season and/ or event under extreme pressure and tight deadlines. They must also be prepared to travel extensively, since events and games are held throughout the country. These things are also true for public relations people working for the team. Sports events marketers and public relations staff who are employed by a team or sports organization work at team or league headquarters. Outside firms are located throughout the country.

Thousands of sporting events require volunteer or part-time help, and this can be a good way to get experience in this highly competitive business. Persons interested in breaking into the business should contact not-for-profit organizations, schools, clubs, and professional event management firms to seek paid or non-paid positions in sporting events.

Think about events that take place near your home. Often local people are hired to run an event that is on tour in different cities, such as the Virginia Slims tennis tournament.

Formal study is another way to learn the ropes. Over one hundred colleges offer programs in sports management. A combination of both experience and formal study is ideal.

Public Relations

PUBLIC RELATIONS IS closely tied to sports event marketing. Publicists are responsible for generating publicity for the team and its players.

Teams generally hire outside public relations specialists to handle the press, to create or deflect media coverage of the team and its players, and to generate publicity for special events such as a play-off series or tournament. But teams generally have their own in-house public relations office which coordinates day-to-day publicity matters.

They are critical in the determination of which players are presented to the media and how they are presented. As sports have become a top television draw, the role of the public relations director has become increasingly important in building a fan base and viewing audience, which affects the team's bottom line.

Employees in the public relations department often have a background in communications, as well as plenty of knowledge about a particular sport. Public relations, marketing, and advertising degrees are often recommended for applicants looking for publicity work.

Sports event planning, marketing and public relations demand a broad variety of skills. Coordinating events and publicity requires a high degree of organizational skills and attention to detail. Employees must also be extremely flexible and creative to work out kinks and unexpected problems that may occur during an event. These jobs also require a strong ability to lead and motivate others. The most successful marketing and public relations specialists are self-motivators capable of intense concentration under stressful conditions.

THE SERVICE PROVIDERS

THERE ARE A multitude of service positions available in sports, including arena services such as security building and groundskeepers, ushers and ticket takers and equipment managers; office workers include secretaries, mail room workers, filing clerks, receptionists, and other typical support jobs. Getting your foot in the door—in almost any capacity—is often the best first step toward realizing your ultimate goal. Even seemingly insignificant jobs can give you an opportunity to learn the business from close up and possibly to make the right contacts or impress a potential mentor. So put yourself in the environment in which you wish to succeed, and then work like hell to show 'em what you've got!

THE SPORTS PRESS

WHEN BRANCH RICKEY was asked why he didn't conclude a profitable deal to televise the Dodger home games, he replied, "Radio stimulates curiosity, television satisfies it." Many sports people in the late 1940s believed that television would be a bad thing for spectator sports. "Why would people come to an event and pay, when they could see it free at home?" went the thinking. It hasn't worked out that way. Today television is the dominant financial factor in professional sports, but most major sports events sell out as well. A multitude of television and radio shows, newspapers, and magazines devoted solely to sports or to a particular sport crowd the airwaves and the newsstands. Some commentators and writers, such as Bill Russell, Bryant and Greg Gumbel, and Ahmad Rashaad, are as well known as most star athletes.

The market continues to grow, owing not only to the growing popularity of sports but to the technological advances that have led to the licensing of new cable channels, which have in turn spawned a variety of sports-oriented channels and shows. In addition to a great deal of sports coverage on both network and local television, there are channels dedicated to twenty-four-hour-a-day, seven-day-a-week sports programming. ESPN 1 and 2, Sports Channel, and MSG are premium cable channels that attempt to satisfy what seems to be the American public's insatiable appetite for sports.

On top of all this coverage of actual sporting events, we now also have the popular show *American Gladiators*, in which entirely new forms of one-on-one competition are dreamed up to provide viewers with yet another sports spectacle.

Despite television's dominant role in the sports media, the print press continues to hold a wide readership among sports fans. Simons Market Research Bureau reported that 84 percent of all men surveyed in 1992 read the daily sports section.

Sports have also become a popular feature on the Internet, which provides up-to-date information and news about teams and individual athletes. Many teams have their own home page and Web site. There are also a variety of chat rooms devoted exclusively to sports topics. Internet subscribers spend large amounts of time browsing sports-related sites.

In addition, many teams have their own broadcasting production companies that prepare special programs about the organization and its players. Major League Baseball, for example, owns Phoenix Communications, which broadcasts stories about the leagues and also prepares documentaries about special events, such as the play-offs and World Series.

Although competition for positions in all facets of the television industry is fierce, there are a large variety of career and job opportunities available for writers, researchers, publicists, producers, directors, and announcers. Blacks have made inroads into the sportscasting business, where people like Greg Gumbel, Robin Robinson, and others have become household names. Many retired Black athletes, such as Lynn Swann and Walt Frazier, have entered the business as (no pun intended) color commentators.

Jobs available within the television industry are wide-ranging and include announcers and newscasters, program directors, soundmen, camera crews, and other technical positions.

Sportscasters

ANNOUNCERS WHO COVER sports events for a viewing audience are known familiarly as sportscasters. This is a highly specialized form of announcing, since sportscasters must have extensive knowledge of the sports they are covering, plus an ability to describe quickly and accurately what is going on.

They must also be comfortable on camera and must have the ability to entertain viewers with statistics, anecdotes, and conversation between plays. The personality and on-screen presence of the announcer are all-important. Often the sportscaster will spend several days with team members, observe practice sessions, interview individuals, and do research on the history of the event or of the teams to be covered. The more information a sportscaster can acquire about individual team members, the institution they represent, the tradition of the contest, the ratings of the team, and the community in which the event takes place, the more interesting coverage is to the audience.

Sports Program Directors

PROGRAM DIRECTORS PLAN and schedule program material, including sportscasts, for television stations and networks. They decide what material is broadcast and when it is scheduled, work with other staff members to develop programs, and buy programs from independent producers. Their duties are determined by such factors as whether they work for a small or large organization, for one station or a network, or in a commercial or public operation.

Print Journalists

NEWSPAPERS AND MAGAZINES devote a tremendous amount of available space to sports. *USA Today* allots 50 percent of the paper to the sports section and publishes *Baseball Weekly*, which covers major league, minor league, and college play.

Dozens of publications are devoted entirely to sports, such as *Sports Illustrated, Sport,* and *The Sporting News,* and also many publications cover a specific sport, such as *This Week in Baseball, Baseball Weekly, Golf, Tennis,* and *Boxing News.* Black sports journalists have risen to the top of the profession at several major newspapers and magazines. These writers include Claire Smith and William Rhoden of *The New York Times.* Roy Johnson, formerly at *Sports Illustrated* and now editor-at-large at *Fortune Magazine,* and Bobby Clay, one of the magazine's editors, are top-notch sports reporters.

Sports journalists may cover a particular team or sport, or they may be responsible for covering one or two sports, reviewing the events and competitions across the country and the world. They may travel with a particular team and report on its successes and failures. Journalists often spend years covering the same team and acquiring extensive knowledge about the team, its operations, and its players. Sports columnists may also write opinion or editorial pieces regarding an aspect or controversy impacting the sporting world. Sports journalism is considered more creative than other types of reporting because writers are given more leeway to inject colorful and descriptive prose than reporters writing straight news stories.

Sports Photographers

MOST MAJOR PAPERS have at least one photographer who specializes in sports, and the major wire services operate extensive photographic services with bureaus worldwide. National sports publications normally staff all major events with their own photographers, as well as stringers.

JOBS WITHIN THE sports media profession are available in every town and city that has a newspaper and television station. The most prestigious and high-paying jobs, however, are found in major cities with respected television and newspaper organizations. National television shows are produced in New York.

There are no formal educational requirements for entering the field of television announcing, although many stations require employees to have a college education. Sports announcers must have a broad interest in and knowledge of sports. Poise and a pleasing voice and personality are essential.

Although some schools offer broadcast training, the best way to prepare is through experience. Most broadcasters begin their careers in an entry-level position at a small station and work their way through the ranks. Internships also offer valuable job experience.

Network jobs are few, and the competition for them is great. An announcer must have several years of experience as well as a college education to be considered for these positions. Training and experience for other positions within the industry is also best gained through internships and entry-level positions.

Print journalists usually have college degrees in journalism, English, creative writing, or communications. Working on college newspapers, stringing, and any writing in sports coverage while in school are good ways to start.

Reporters generally get their first real jobs with a small town or local paper and work their way to bigger assignments at larger newspapers and magazines. Editorial positions are generally attained after the journalist has spent several years working as a reporter.

Sports is definitely a growth field, so if you think you'd like to be part of this exciting career instead of just another spectator, set your goals high and start mapping out your route. A bachelor's degree in the right major will help get you inside the industry. From there, you'll need dedication, hard work, and a dash of chutzpah to grab one of those sought-after jobs in sports management, sports medicine, or journalism. Don't be discouraged if it takes many years to work your way up to your ideal. Remember, this is a business built on competition, exertion, and toughing it out, and, as philosopher Yogi Berra once observed, "It ain't over till it's over," or, as Les Brown says, "It ain't over till I win."

Go for it . . . and good luck!

12

HEALTH CARE: TAKING CARE
OF OUR OWN

Health is a human right,
not a privilege to be purchased.
— SHIRLEY CHISHOLM

You have not seen many civil rights groups
marching for medical and nutrition rights for children.
— ARTHUR ASHE

CECELIA WOOTEN
FOUNDER
ADULT MEDICAL DAYCARE CENTER
BALTIMORE, MARYLAND

Cecelia Wooten was born and raised in Baltimore, Maryland, where she still lives. Cecelia got an associate's degree and became a registered nurse. It was something she had loved from her youngest days—helping and caring for others. "There was something innately moral and spiritual about it," she says. Her four sisters were just like her, and her aunt, who owned a nursing home for thirty years, was a role model for all of them.

It was inevitable that Cecelia and her sisters would follow in their aunt's footsteps. When the opportunity came, the sisters joined together and took over their aunt's business, then remodeled, refinanced, and restructured it to meet the new needs of a community that was growing older. They opened their Adult Medical Daycare Center, which has expanded over the last twelve years to six locations. Business is booming, and new plans to grow are in the works.

"It's a tough business," Cecelia says, "but you can make a decent living while helping others to live a better life. That's what I really love about what I do. The problem is that sometimes you get so attached to your senior citizens, they become like family. Then they may take a downward turn in health and die, and it hurts."

Another major, albeit less emotionally stressful, problem is the lack of standardization in care from various government bureaucracies that provide the financial support for many of her clients. "The business is confusing and fraught with red tape and inequities," Cecelia says. But, all in all, neither she nor her sisters would trade in their business plan and nurses' caps for anything else.

Cecelia feels that college training in nursing and geriatric work experience in a hospital setting are the prerequisites for going into this business. Business and communications courses would also be especially helpful. She also feels that "You must truly love people, be compassionate, patient, and empathetic to make it in the world of care-giving."

The seniors who reside in Cecelia's nursing homes are all colors; in some of her facilities they are predominantly Black, in others they are predominantly white. "When people need care," Cecelia says, "they don't care what color you are and you should not care what color they are. I live by the Golden Rule, and it has enabled me to navigate the valleys of life, as well as helped run a growing and successful business. Anyone could do it, if they put their heart into it."

FAVORITE BIBLICAL PASSAGE:

And though I bestow all my goods to feed the poor,
and though I give my body to be burned,
and have not charity, it profiteth me nothing.

—I Corinthians 13:3

INGE HANSON, THE director of an East Harlem youth program, told me about her experience with a crew of emergency medical technicians (EMTs). She was working at her computer one afternoon, trying to focus on the monthly accounts, when the door to the storefront office sprang open and a tangle of kids pushed through, shouting in a mixture of English, Spanish, and street slang. She managed to work out that a boy had been hit by a car on the street, and as she jumped up to check it out, a tall, bearded man with ear-locks and a wide-brimmed black hat walked slowly into the office, half-carrying a fourteen-year-old Puerto Rican named Rick. Freddy, a dark-skinned Dominican teen, was holding onto Rick's other arm, trying to explain that Rick had jumped in front of the bearded man's car as a joke but had tripped and fallen across the hood. The force of the fall had knocked Rick across the street.

The tall man kept repeating that he had been driving down the block to avoid traffic and hadn't expected this. Inge dialed 911, then helped the man lay Rick on the office's one rickety couch. The boy seemed dazed but coherent.

The EMTs got to the office in seconds—the hospital was literally around the block—and took in the scene. "What is this, the UN?" one paramedic asked, looking around at the conglomeration of ethnic types, including Inge, who is a pale blonde. "The tall, bearded man looked like he had been transported onto our street from another century," she said, "and we're all hovering over Rick, who can't seem to remember how to speak English or Spanish."

The EMTs took all of this in stride and convinced them that Rick would be fine, all the while cracking jokes as they prodded and poked him to make sure he had no broken bones or sprains. By this point, the office had filled with parents from the block, who had rushed in to make sure that Rick was all right. Assured that he was more shaken than bruised, they began to harangue him for acting the fool, throwing himself in front of the car and frightening the poor driver. Two of the mothers took the man by the arm, dragged him away from Rick's side, and forced him to sit down and relax while they poured him a glass of water.

The EMTs laid Rick on a stretcher and carried him off, followed by the mothers who kept scolding him for being so "estúpido" as to have gotten himself hit by a car. "I think Rick was pretty relieved when the EMTs got him into the ambulance and shut the doors," Inge remembered. "The whole episode didn't take more than thirty minutes, but it felt like a two-hour sitcom or disaster movie—I'm not sure which."

Not all of our health crisis stories end on such a positive note. Accidents at home and on the streets are common in our inner-city communities, much more common, in fact, than in other communities. So are illnesses and disease. And yet we are less likely to receive quality diagnosis and treatment.

Nearly half of America's thirty fastest-growing occupations are in the health services area. This field is in the midst of rapid change, yet major problems continue to plague the health-care delivery system in predominantly Black communities. There are strong and disturbing reasons for us to take action: Not surprisingly, we are often reluctant to seek help from a system where care is still provided mostly by non-Blacks and services in our poorer communities are diminishing. Many of us, rich and poor alike, put off checkups and treatments because we fear or distrust the medical establishment.

How do we change these depressing trends? One way is to improve cross-cultural communications among all of us; another is to recruit more Black health-care professionals. For even as the importance of careers in health care is increasing, the presence of African Americans in the industry is dwindling. We are only 6 percent of the medical student population and 4 percent of nursing staffs; at the same time, we make up 27.7 percent of nurse's aides, orderlies, and attendants.

To rectify this disparity and take part in an industry so vital to our community and individual well-being, we must penetrate and advance among the upper ranks of health-care workers. Our own tradition of independence and self-healing is key to our progress in this area.

The strong impetus we feel to seek help from within our community is a powerful incentive to create our own family of professionals within the health-care system, infusing their ranks with the hallmarks of our traditional health practices—kinship, mental and spiritual healing, and nutritional and herbal remedies. Clearly, if we are to help overcome the nation's health-care crisis, we must begin by taking care of our own.

There is room for people of every educational, economic, and cultural background in this rapidly growing industry, and I encourage you to consider a career that appeals to you and that draws upon your strengths and interests. Jobs range from unskilled positions requiring little to no education or training to careers that demand an array of advanced educational degrees and training that makes health professionals one of the most highly educated sectors of all industries.

Because of their locations in inner cities, hospitals provide a large number of employment opportunities for Blacks at the entry levels, with a built-in system of upward mobility for those willing to go for additional training and education. This makes health care the perfect market-place for a career that is "pay as you grow."

Opportunities are so plentiful in the health-care industry that you can set your sights high and find a way to get there. There are numerous scholarships available to bright, dedicated African Americans interested in medicine and science. For example, Merck, the international health products company, recently inaugurated a twenty-million-dollar scholarship and internship program to encourage African Americans to enter careers in the sciences. Administered by the United Negro College Fund, the new program awards thirty-seven fellowships annually.

The trend toward managed health care is also bringing innovations in job opportunities. With shortened hospital stays, for example, nursing will shift from primarily hospital-based settings to home- and community facility-based settings. Nurses will become more independent, more accountable, and more comfortable in an unstructured work environment.

Primary care physicians are also in great demand due to the emergence of HMOs (health maintenance organizations), where they are the "gatekeepers" responsible for the overall well-being of individual patients. On the downside, these physicians will have larger patient loads and will have to function with strict cost limitations on their services.

Nonphysician providers—physician's assistants, nurse practitioners, clinical nurse specialists, and nurse midwives—will be in demand. In a 1994 survey, the American Medical Association found that 56 percent of group practice physicians employ one or more of these specialists, thereby increasing the efficiency of their practice.

About fifteen-thousand new health-care jobs are created each month. Overall, jobs should increase by 47 percent by the year 2005. There are far too many individual occupations to cover them all here, so I'll concentrate on the segments projected to have the fastest growth and the ones that I believe are most important for our community.

THE DOCTORS

WE NEED MORE Black physicians and dentists. Simple. We account for only a tiny percentage of the doctors practicing today and the number of African Americans applying to medical and dental schools is declining. In 1995, for example, only 40 percent of the 3,595 African Americans who applied to medical school were accepted.

Fortunately, several programs are being designed to seek out and encourage minorities to attend medical and dental schools. In 1991, the Association of American Medical Colleges (AAMC) launched Project 3000 by 2000, whose name encompasses the program's mission to graduate three thousand minority doctors from medical school by the year 2000.

Black colleges are fertile ground for budding doctors, offering them the sound educational training they will need. Xavier University in New Orleans is the recognized leader, with over 70 percent of its pre-med students being accepted into medical schools. Howard, Spelman, and Morehouse also rank ahead of the Ivy League when it comes to preparing Blacks for admission to medical schools.

Minority scholarships are another impetus for helping Black youngsters prepare for a future in sciences, medicine, and dentistry. The Meyerhoff Scholarship Program at the University of Maryland puts its emphasis on high achievement, realizing that young Blacks may be criticized by their peers for trying to "act white" if they hit the books instead of the streets. "In most inner-city settings in this country, it is not cool to be a high-achieving African-American, especially for young males," University of Maryland Baltimore County president Freeman A. Hrabowski III told *Black Enterprise*. "We take a comprehensive approach that emphasizes working with the whole person." The Meyerhoff program has sent most of its alumni into medical or graduate school.

For those with the scientific aptitude and inner strength essential to become a physician or dentist, the future is bright. With HMOs dominating health care's future, the need for primary care specialists (family practitioners, pediatricians, and internists) is enormous. Rural and inner-city hospitals are wooing medical residents with sign-on bonuses, while HMOs are actively soliciting their services. An aging population is also driving the need for physicians who specialize in geriatric care and ailments common in the elderly, such as Alzheimer's and osteoporosis.

Choosing the path of a physician requires a commitment to long and taxing hours, with the burden of heavy loans (as much as one hundred thousand dollars or more) at the end of the academic road. Hours are generally irregular, and half of all physicians say they spend sixty hours a week or more on the job, not to mention the late-night calls or beeps that can send them back to the hospital or office or to a patient's home. Doctors who work within an HMO or group practice get some backup that may ease the stress of being "on call" and may also get more time off. No matter how you do it, however, practicing medicine is one of the most daunting and challenging careers you can choose, so make sure you have the inner commitment to follow through on your dream.

If all you see are dollar signs in the diploma, you need to rethink your priorities. The lure of money and prestige is a strong, but misplaced, motivator. Most young doctors today will tell you they are motivated by altruism and commitment. Tanya Savage, a medical student at Howard University College of Medicine, recently told *Black Enterprise* that she chose to become a doctor because she once received painful and unnecessary dental work from a dentist looking to increase his billings.

To inspire her when the going gets rough, rather than dreaming of dollars, Tanya draws upon her intense desire to be a good doctor. "Every time someone asks for you because you're a good doctor, or you give somebody hope, those are the times when I know that I'm doing what I'm supposed to do," she said.

All that being said, there is of course plenty of money to be made, although the trend to consolidate medical services within HMOs and other types of group practices has somewhat depressed pay scales. In 1993 the American Medical Association reported the average income for doctors as about $189,300; incomes varied according to number of years in practice, geographic region, and specialty. According to the Association of American Medical Colleges, in 1994–95 first-year residents earned an average salary of $30,753, while eighth-year residents (yes, there are such things) brought in $41,895.

Where can you expect to go, once you've got your medical degree in hand (and a sheaf of loans to boot)? It might seem that a medical diploma would be a ticket to anyplace, but choices can be limited if you're looking to land a prestigious residency. Grades and, more important, recommendations from your medical school professors and deans make all the difference when it comes to these plum positions. "We have to play by the rules, get the best grades, and go to the best

Median net income of MDs after expenses (1993)	
All physicians	$156,000
Radiology	$240,000
Surgery	$225,000
Anesthesiology	$220,000
Obstetrics/Gynecology	$200,000
Pathology	$170,000
Emergency medicine	$164,000
Internal medicine	$150,000
Psychiatry	$120,000
Pediatrics	$120,000
General/Family practice	$110,000

Source: American Medical Association

schools in the hopes that we are selected," one doctor told *Black Enterprise*. "We don't have the fathers and grandfathers—those generations of doctors who can open the doors for us and be mentors."

If you're willing to tackle inner-city hospitals, the opportunities are more plentiful, although working conditions are generally worse. Overcrowded facilities and shortages in staffing, equipment, and funding can exacerbate the stresses inherent in the profession. But people receiving their health care from these hospitals desperately need quality medical attention, and if they are African Americans, they will especially benefit from being cared for by professional brothers and sisters they can trust and relate to.

For the most part, however, hospitals and clinics are as varied as the cities, towns, and rural counties in which they are located. Before settling on a choice, think carefully about your strengths, interests, and preferences. If you enjoy excitement and pressure, a big-city hospital may be for you. If you prefer climbing mountains or trekking country roads in your free time, look for a small-town or rural facility. In medicine, the choices can be as multifaceted as your needs and talents, so take some time to consider the type of lifestyle you envision for yourself when making your decision about where to settle down.

The road to a medical degree is an arduous, expensive, long-term commitment. Plan to spend eleven years acquiring the education, skills, and training necessary to become a full-fledged physician, to wit:

- 4 years undergraduate school
- 4 years medical school
- 3 years residency

If you specialize, your residency may stretch to eight years. And just when you thought it was safe to pick up a stethoscope, you will also need to be licensed to practice, a requirement in all states, Washington DC, and the U.S. territories. Board certification in one of twenty-four medical specialties requires another final examination and one or two years of practice.

That's a long trip around the board game of life before you pass "Go." And once you cross the finish line and earn your license, the race has just begun. To succeed, doctors must be prepared to constantly educate themselves about the rapid changes in the profession. They must be willing to burn the midnight oil, yet keep their wits sharp to respond to the emergencies that are part of daily practice. And, above all, they must have a powerful desire to serve and heal others.

Career growth is endlessly varied and constantly challenging. Some doctors form their own practice or partner with other physicians to establish group practices. Others may pursue research or academia. Still others assume more and more responsibility at hospitals and health facilities. Whatever your area, becoming a doctor requires energy, dedication, and persistence.

Physician Assistants

IF YOU LOVE taking care of people but don't want to undertake the long haul of becoming a physician, consider becoming a physician assistant (PA). Like doctors, PAs respond to emergencies that can require a split-second diagnosis and response. This job was born on the battlefields of Vietnam, where medical corpsmen became skilled at treating their comrades in the most adverse conditions imaginable. During the 1960s, these veterans were recruited by the medical profession to increase patients' access to high-quality health care in rural and inner-city hospitals where the few doctors available were being overwhelmed by increasing numbers of patients.

Although much of the work can be routine, PAs employed in areas where doctors are scarce are charged with tremendous responsibilities, often providing most of a patient's direct care. PAs can take a patient's medical history, prescribe drugs, and perform minor surgery.

Job prospects within this category are excellent, with the Department of Labor predicting above-average growth based on the growing emphasis in the medical industry to contain costs. By the end of the decade, there will be nearly four million new jobs in the field, while today there are seven openings for every graduating PA and more than forty thousand unfilled positions in the nation's medical laboratories.

PAs are in especially high demand in inner-city and rural clinics. (About one third of all PAs work in communities having fewer than fifty thousand residents.) Like doctors, PAs usually work long, often irregular hours.

Although PAs don't make as much as the physicians they work with, potential earnings are relatively high. In 1994, median annual salaries were $53,284, although income depends on specialty, where you work, and the number of years of experience you have.

Becoming a PA takes far less time and money than going to medical school, but you still need a lot of education. More than seventy accredited PA programs are located throughout the United States, most of them affiliated with colleges and university schools of medicine. Entry into a two-year PA program usually requires two years of college and some work experience in the health-care field. All states except Mississippi have their own laws governing the qualification of PAs.

Like doctors, PAs must be self-confident and emotionally stable, in addition to being committed to helping people. To advance within the profession, some PAs pursue additional education in a specialty area, such as surgery or emergency medicine. The more experience and skills gained, the higher the salary and the greater the responsibility.

THE NURSES

"DOCTORS DON'T SAVE lives, nurses do," proclaimed *Nurse*, a national bestseller several years ago that later became a popular television series. Nursing and saving lives has a long and rich history within the African-American community, dating back hundreds of years to the "grannies" who provided help to pregnant women and the gifted women healers who ministered to ailing slaves with recipes for secret homespun cures.

That tradition continues today with the Black nurses, medical assistants, and nurse practitioners who tend the sick in rural, urban, and suburban health facilities across the United States.

"I've always loved nursing and the feeling that I'm caring for others," Jennifer Shirley told me. Jennifer is a registered nurse and the assistant director of nursing at Alps Manor Nursing Home in New Jersey. She brings to her career the respect for home remedies and natural healing that were part of her Jamaican upbringing.

Despite this rich heritage, our nursing numbers are dwindling dramatically. In the 1970s, 17 percent of nurses were African-American, while today we make up only 4 percent of all registered nurses.

Worse yet, Dr. Betty Smith Williams, president of the National Black Nurses Association, reported in *Black Collegian* that half of the Black registered nurses are undereducated, lacking basic professional competencies.

Despite these disturbing statistics, there is reason to hope African Americans will return to nursing as a profession. The number of men—and Black men in particular—who choose nursing as a career is beginning to rise. The National Black Nurses Association is also taking an active role in maximizing career opportunities for African Americans in nursing through active recruitment into educational programs, the creation of scholarship opportunities, a national network of chapters, and the advocacy of equity and equality for Black nurses and their patients.

Nursing is attracting not only high school and college graduates but workers who are seeking a second career either by choice or by necessity. Some nurses are entrepreneurial, building their profession into a comfortable business doing what they love. Liz Pettiford Pfeiffer, who lives in New Hampshire, spent twenty-eight years as a registered nurse, ultimately specializing in gerontology. Realizing that her aging patients often had nowhere to go after they left the hospital, Liz decided to establish a quality residential share home for the elderly.

These homes, also known as supportive care homes, are usually large houses that have been converted into residential units for about twenty people. Their nurturing, family environment contrasts dramatically with institutional nursing homes.

Liz's voice warms with pride as she describes Wadleligh House, the supportive care home she founded on April 1, 1996. Wadleligh is an antique colonial, built in 1827. It is decked out with ornate woodwork and maple floors, three working fireplaces, and thirteen rooms that accommodate six elderly women and one man.

Residents are cared for by Liz, her husband, Ron, a part-time staff of four medical professionals, a cook, and a housekeeper. Love is a job requirement, Liz told me. "I only hire people who love working with the elderly," she said. "Our residents feel security, warmth, and love here. For them, Wadleigh House is not the end of the road, but the beginning of another new experience."

One of Liz's "ladies," whose son was worrying that his mother would be upset about moving in, finally told him after two hours, "You can leave now, I'm home."

Liz Pfeiffer encourages people who enjoy working with the elderly and who also have a strong independent streak to emulate her efforts. "There is a tremendous need for this type of home all across the country—by the year 2000, over half the population will be over sixty-five years old. Nursing homes are already packed and expensive. Residential care is a wonderful alternative."

Liz and Ron are role models for the Black community, and I hope some of you will follow their lead. They are not only filling a need, they are having the time of their lives. "I can't tell you what joy the home brings me," Liz said. "I'm in this because I love it."

Everyone should be able to feel that way about their work. And I believe that we can, if we serve the community and do what we passionately believe in.

Nurses are hard at work in all facets of health care—in emergency rooms, operating rooms, intensive care units, maternity wards, and general care areas of hospitals, in private homes, nursing homes, and public health clinics. No matter where they work, or in what capacity, they share a common goal: to help and to heal.

According to Barbara Taylor-Young, a registered nurse who spent twenty-eight years at Columbia Presbyterian Hospital in New York City before retiring, the most enriching experiences in her career were "seeing patients who were near death get better and go home."

Registered nurses often begin their careers as medical assistants or nurse's aides, progress to licensed practical nurses, and then acquire the education and training necessary to become full-fledged registered nurses. Registered nurses (RNs) spend thousands of hours learning much more than simply how to treat diseases and injuries. Nurses minister to the patient as a whole, providing for the physical, mental, and emotional needs of their charges and often for family members as well.

"We have more time to spend with patients and families than doctors," Barbara Taylor-Young said. "That's the part of the job that is most rewarding to me."

NURSING CAREERS

Virtually every job on the nursing career path, from medical assistant to registered nurse, is targeted for way-above-average growth over the next decade.

JOB TITLE	GROWTH RATE
Medical assistants	74%
Nurse's aides and attendants	42%
Licensed practical nurses	42%
Registered nurses	43%

Jennifer Shirley, who specializes in nursing the aging, said she meets with patients and families, reviews lifestyle changes, and makes sure "it is all working—that their needs are addressed, from nutrition, recreation, and personal care to social interaction.

"Nursing can be most meaningful in the lonely hours of the night," Jennifer said, "when a patient just needs to be with someone after family and friends have gone home."

Nurse's Aides and Medical Assistants

BECOMING A NURSE'S aide is a good way to get a feel for nursing, and the job itself is important. Aides often spend the most time with patients, helping with basic care and soothing fears that doctors and nurses may not have the time to address or notice.

Nursing-home aides, particularly, may have more contact with patients than any other member of the staff; they develop warm and nurturing relationships that literally give older folks a new lease on life.

Medical assistants are a specialized group of hospital aides who handle clerical and clinical tasks that often swamp nurses and administrators. When you make an appointment for a laboratory test or rush to a hospital for a medical emergency, the first person you meet is probably a medical assistant. Their duties include answering phones, scheduling visits, filling out insurance forms, and arranging for hospital admission and laboratory services. The medical assistant job is one of the fastest-growing occupations around and requires little to no training to get started.

*　　*　　*

NURSES IN EVERY job category spend long hours working on their feet, coping with people who are suffering from pain and often fright. "I gave 110 percent, all the time," Barbara Taylor-Young told me, which is probably why she was so loved and respected by her patients and colleagues that hundreds of people showed up at her retirement party.

Nurses are on the front lines. The job requires physical and emotional stamina, plus close attention to detail, even after an exhausting day or night. They must be caring, sympathetic, and focused, often when they are so bone-tired that even walking is an effort. In addition to their personal dedication to their patients, they also must painstakingly complete their charts and other paperwork accurately at the end of each day.

Emotional stability is crucial. Nurses confront the most extreme levels of emotion on a daily basis. Barbara Taylor-Young still has a small statue of a water buffalo given to her by an eighteen-year-old heart patient just before he died. She had cared for him since he was first admitted to the hospital as a five-month-old baby. "I think about him every time I see that water buffalo. He wouldn't eat unless I was there to feed him. It was rough when he died, but I knew I had helped him. And that's what kept me going."

If you are up for the challenge, you can virtually write your ticket to anyplace in the world. Job settings range from bustling urban hospitals to cozy clinics nestled into suburban and rural communities.

RNs may also find employment in elementary schools, universities, and factories. It might actually "pay" to volunteer in various settings to see which type of working environment most appeals to you.

The nursing field offers job security for life, which can translate into a comfortable income if you put in the years necessary to earn a nursing degree.

Nursing jobs are located in virtually every town, suburb, and city throughout the United States in every conceivable type of setting. If you want to work in smaller cities and towns, jobs are especially plentiful in the Southeast and Midwest, while jobs based in the inner city are found throughout the United States.

Of all the nursing categories, registered nurses have to put the most time and money into their education. Students must graduate from an accredited nursing school and pass a national licensing examination; individual states often have additional licensing requirements.

There is more than one way to become a registered nurse. You can

NURSING SALARIES*

Median annual nursing salaries vary according to years of experience, responsibilities, and area of specialization.

RNs

Staff nurses	$35,256
Head nurses	$50,700
Clinical nurse specialists	$47,674
Nurse practitioners	$47,432
Nurse anesthetists	$73,444
Licensed practical nurses	$23,394
Medical assistants	$17,000–$24,000
Nurse's aides	$14,612

*Occupational Outlook Handbook, 1996–97 Edition

earn an associate's degree, which takes two years to complete, a bachelor of nursing degree, which takes four to five years, or a nursing diploma, which takes two to three years to earn through a hospital diploma program. My advice is to get as much education as you can. There's a move afoot in the industry to increase educational requirements for nurses, and it goes without saying that the more education you have, the better your chances for success.

Practical nurses must have a high school diploma and complete a state-approved program which conveys a license. Nurse's aides and medical assistants do not need special training, although employers often prefer hiring people who have had some previous experience in the field.

PHYSICAL AND OCCUPATIONAL THERAPISTS

LIKE IT OR not, folks, we are all getting older, and I hope we will be fit enough to celebrate a lot more birthdays, a goal these health-care professionals can help us achieve. Medical advances also make it possible for more people to survive life-threatening injuries and illnesses and resume independent and productive lives. That's what this segment of the health-care industry is about: helping people with physical and mental disabilities recover, or maintain, basic motor functions and reasoning skills—anything we do with our bodies and brains.

The range of jobs is broad. Occupational therapists help people learn, or relearn, how to dress, walk, eat, and use a computer. They may teach special exercises to strengthen muscle groups and improve dexterity and teach those with permanent disabilities how to operate adaptive equipment, such as motorized wheelchairs and specialized computers. For people suffering from memory loss or cognitive problems, therapists may use mental games and exercises to stimulate different parts of the brain. Computer programmers with knowledge in this field have developed software that improves a brain-injured person's ability to make decisions and solve problems.

Physical therapists work with accident and burn victims, as well as people suffering from multiple sclerosis, cerebral palsy, amputations, and arthritis.

The joy a therapist feels, knowing he or she has helped someone take a first sip of water or first bite of food, can be exhilarating. A friend who was hospitalized for several weeks after breaking his neck choked up as he described to me an emotional celebration party the ward held for his roommate, a paraplegic who had finally managed to grasp a fork and feed himself a single mouthful of food. A team of physical therapists had spent eight months training this young man to do something we all take for granted. By the way, my friend was lucky—he recovered fully from his injuries, although he spent several months strengthening his neck muscles with a series of exercises the resident physical therapist had taught him to perform.

Physical therapy is the fifth-fastest-growing occupation in the country, and occupational therapy is ranked eighteenth. I hope many of you will consider these careers. Our heritage of caring for and nurturing our own makes us prime candidates to take on this work that, for me, epitomizes what we must do for ourselves—get up on our feet and make our presence known, respected, and admired.

Working conditions vary, depending on the nature of the therapy practiced. The job is physically demanding, since therapists usually need to bend, stand, crouch, and stoop along with their patients, lift heavy equipment, and even lift patients. Therapists work indoors and outdoors, in swimming pools and gymnasiums.

Like other health professionals, occupational and physical therapists can work wherever the sick and disabled are treated. You'll find them in hospitals, clinics, nursing homes, private offices, and schools, in urban and rural settings. The choices are there—it's up to you to determine what setting suits your interests.

LaShae Anthony, a young brother determined to get ahead in this world, likes to tell me, "If you want to get to work, you gotta get yourself some skills, man." You need to know a lot about the body, both inside and out, before you can even think about tweaking your first patient. At a minimum, occupational therapists must have a bachelor's degree in occupational therapy. Most states require a license to practice, which means passing a national examination given by the American Occupational Therapy Certification Board. Physical therapists must graduate from an accredited physical therapy program and pass a state licensure exam.

Lots of people are interested in becoming physical therapists, so competition is intense. Make sure you get good grades and take all those courses people say we can't do—like science, biology, mathematics, and physics.

You should also get some firsthand experience by volunteering at a hospital or clinic. You'll need to keep up with the profession by participating in continuing education courses and workshops; in some states, this is a requirement for maintaining your license.

Patience, patience, patience. Let me say it again—patience. And determination. You'll have to be patient to work with your clients and enjoy savoring gratification over the long haul. Remember the party the hospital staff held for the man who spent eight months learning how to bend his fingers around a fork and raise food to his mouth? These folks just don't give up.

MEDICAL TECHNOLOGISTS

IT'S SUMMERTIME, AND softballs are jumping off bats and gloves during a Fourth of July family cookout. "Yo, you're out," squeaks a pint-sized umpire as a huge teammate crashes home and literally knocks herself out against a large stone near home plate. The neighborhood listens for the siren that means help is on the way. A pair of EMTs (emergency medical technicians) checks the player for injury, all the while calming anxious parents and friends.

Medical technology is evolving and diversifying as fast as rabbits. I'll touch on only a few of the vast array of careers within this field, namely the four that the U.S. Department of Labor projects as the fastest growing: radiological technologists and technicians, surgical technologists, EEG technologists, and EMTs.

Growth in these areas is projected from an onslaught of aging baby boomers whose geriatric illnesses and conditions will provide ample business for the health-care industry as a whole. Advances in surgical techniques, radiological imaging equipment, and high-tech ambulances are also fueling the need for individuals fluent with novel, complex technologies.

Because of the high price tag, innovative equipment is usually introduced at large urban hospitals that have the money to underwrite installation and training costs. This gives African Americans living in these areas an opportunity to give back to our own in an exciting field with a future. What a great way to meet the millennium.

Radiological Technologists and Technicians

SUPERMAN'S X-RAY VISION seems commonplace in a career rated as the ninth-fastest-growing in the country. X-rays are most widely known for producing the hazy black-and-white photographs doctors and nurses examine to set broken bones. Radiographers are the technicians who prepare you for an X-ray and operate the equipment.

Ultrasound technologists, known as sonographers, beam high-frequency sound waves into areas of the body hidden deep beneath your skin. Sonogram images show your innards at work, allowing medical professionals to trace the flow of your blood while watching your heart beat. Mothers and fathers can gaze in wonder at their developing child's first strokes through a pool of amniotic fluid. Some sonographers specialize in capturing images of parts of the body, such as the brain (neurosonography), blood flow (vascular sonography), the heart (echocardiography), and the eye (ophthalmology).

Radiation is also a popular weapon in the fight against cancer. Radiation therapy technologists administer radiation to specific body parts over the course of a patient's treatment.

Radiological technologists attend one- to four-year programs leading to a certificate, associate's degree, or bachelor's degree. Two-year programs are most prevalent, but a bachelor's or master's degree is necessary if you want to advance to supervisory and teaching positions. Additional training is needed if you want to specialize in ultrasound and magnetic resonance imaging.

Surgical Technologists

OPERATING-ROOM TECHNICIANS SET up the operating room, check that equipment is sterile and operating correctly, and prepare patients for surgery. They also help the surgical team dress and get ready for action. Surgical technologists must have the ability to work well under pressure and to withstand the sight of blood. Surgical technologists attend formal programs that combine classroom study with on-the-job training. One- or two-year programs are offered by community colleges, vocational-technical institutes, and hospitals.

EEG Technologists

AN ELECTROENCEPHALOGRAM IS a neurodiagnostic test that records electrical impulses transmitted by the brain and the nervous system to diagnose diseases such as Alzheimer's, epilepsy, strokes, brain tumors, and sleep problems.

EEG technologists must complete a certificate training program in a hospital or receive an associate's degree from a two-year community college. With additional experience and training, EEG teckies can advance to chief or manager of an EEG lab or assume teaching and research positions.

EMTs (Emergency Medical Technicians)

EMTS GIVE APPROPRIATE emergency care, which may include restoring breathing, controlling bleeding, treating for shock, and a slew of other lifesaving tasks, before transporting the victim to an emergency room where other professionals are waiting to spring into action.

EMTs probably experience the most on-the-job stress. They must be able to cope with the extreme pressures of treating the seriously ill and wounded with no time to spare. They work indoors and outdoors in all kinds of weather and face all manner of crises. These individuals should also be good at calming victims and bystanders and must have the physical strength necessary to clear an accident scene and transport a patient to a treatment facility. Good eyesight and quick reactions are also critical, since these drivers must weave through traffic at high speeds without becoming accident victims themselves.

EMTs need one hundred to one hundred and twenty hours of basic classroom work, plus a period of emergency-room training. EMTs may advance to seek supervisory positions, and some become police officers or firefighters. Turnover rates are high, since the job is extremely stressful without much chance for advancement and is often low-paying.

OTHER TECHNOLOGISTS SPEND long hours standing, which can be wearing, especially since they must produce quality results while calming and instructing patients who may be seriously ill. It's stand and deliver for this crowd. Median annual salaries for technologists are between twenty thousand and thirty thousand dollars.

What kind of person most enjoys getting an inside view of the body? Someone who is meticulous about details and follows procedures to a T. Technicians should be people-friendly, since they need to put seriously ill patients at ease and explain complex procedures that can be frightening. They also need the manual dexterity and vision to operate precision equipment, plus good working skills to maintain their records and reports in tip-top condition. Radiation therapists need the emotional strength to work with extremely ill and dying patients.

STATISTICS ABOUT DISEASE and death rates among Blacks are sobering, to say the least. Our life expectancies are shorter than the national average, and we lead the mortality rate from the nation's six biggest killer diseases. Cause for concern? You bet, unless we help take charge of our own health care. I hope the people you have met in this chapter have inspired you to consider taking the roads they have traveled to enjoy exciting, well-paid careers. Health is a heaven-sent blessing, but we can't sit around and expect God to keep us physically fit. We need to take the actions that will ensure our present and future well-being. To your health!

13

GLOBAL COMMERCE: SEIZING OPPORTUNITIES IN THE NEW WORLD ORDER

An old world is dying, and a new one, kicking in the belly of its mother, time, announces that it is ready to be born. The birth will not be easy, and many of us are doomed to discover that we are exceedingly clumsy midwives.

—JAMES BALDWIN

Pioneers are special people. "First" is always difficult. We don't know that things can be done, that dreams can be fulfilled, that great accomplishments can be realized until somebody takes that first step.

—GERALDINE NECKIMAN

The modern world must remember that in this age when the ends of the world are being brought so near together, the millions of Black men in Africa, America and the Islands of the Sea, not to speak of the brown and yellow myriads elsewhere, are bound to have a great influence upon the world in the future, by reason of sheer numbers and physical contact.

—W.E.B. DU BOIS

EUGENE D. JACKSON
PRESIDENT/CEO WORLD AFRICAN
   NETWORK
ATLANTA, GEORGIA

In 1968, the assassination of Dr. Martin Luther King, Jr., sent shock waves through the streets of the nation. Eugene Jackson's hometown of Kansas City was in turmoil. While he worked in the streets to keep peace on that April day and the days that followed, out of the chaos emerged a new direction for his life. It was then that Jackson knew that he was not only driven to use his training as an electrical engineer but was also compelled to apply his skills as a "social engineer," working in business to benefit people in his community.

Three months after the riots, he left his position as an electrical engineer at Colgate-Palmolive and began a path that led to a series of successful entrepreneurial endeavors that today comprise a business that spans from the United States to Africa. His company began with the launch of the first radio news network designed for African Americans and now includes Internet development in the United States as well as the only African-owned cellular telephone franchise in South Africa. The overarching mission of World African Network is to use communications technology to connect people of African descent worldwide.

Problem solving, according to Jackson, is a crucial element for functioning successfully in any entrepreneurial setting. "The earlier you begin to exercise the ability to look for and find solutions, the better the chances of succeeding independently, in business and in life," says Jackson. "As a child I observed the business owners in my community and worked side-by-side with my uncle, who owned and farmed land for a living. Seeing people who looked like me solving problems in their own respected businesses helped me develop an early sense of entrepreneurial independence. By seeing them, I understood what was possible."

Jackson believes that nothing compares with the drive you gain through exposure and experience. However, his formal education at the University of Missouri-Rolla was a vital step in his development. Whatever the field of endeavor, Jackson suggests that at least an understanding, if not formal computer training, is important to the success of any business owner. In addition to the age-old distinctions based on skin color, today the growing and more important distinction that exists is between those with access to information and those without. Computer-based education allows one to use the latest high-tech tools to research and market a business and to keep pace with competitors, quickly and inexpensively.

Obtaining capital has been Jackson's greatest business hurdle. An unrelenting belief in the art of the possible and the faith to pursue a vision, no matter how many rejections, are key elements for overcoming financing hurdles. "In this respect, global commerce is no different. It requires that you apply the same highly developed skills that you use at home as well as the good common sense to learn about other cultures. You must spend time on the ground," says Jackson. "You cannot assume that you have an American or an African-American advantage. Brotherhood doesn't take you far if you don't have the competence, the commitment, or the capital to achieve your objectives."

Jackson's advice to entrepreneurs: "Get ready now . . . Africa will be the center of economic development in the twenty-first century. By preparing now, you put yourself in a position to contribute to the economic future of people of African descent everywhere. Worldwide respect can be gained through independent business in an independent Africa, resulting in great economic leverage for Africans everywhere. Business opportunities in Africa are greater than ever. They are bigger than any one of us."

FAVORITE BIBLICAL PASSAGE:

For I consider the suffering of the present time is not worthy to be compared with the glory which shall be revealed in us.

—Romans 8:18

WHEN I WAS growing up, on warm summer Sunday mornings the church up the street would have its windows flung open, and we'd hear them singing that old favorite, "He's Got the Whole World in

His Hands." I found the evocative memory of that timeless music rushing back to me recently when I attended a conference on new global business opportunities, except now I heard the words as, "We've got the whole world in *our* hands."

That's right. With the advent of lightning-quick communications technology and international air freight, a relaxation in trade regulations, and the collapse of Cold War antagonisms, the 1990s are a time of exciting new markets opening up around the globe. And the people taking advantage of these opportunities are no longer just the big multinational companies, but regular folks.

Until fairly recently, doing business outside your own backyard was looked on as the specialty of huge international corporations. International markets were thought to be out of reach of most small entrepreneurs, including African Americans. But that's been changing. In Eastern Europe, Central and South America, and South Africa, capitalism is the key for a healthy economic future, and Black American entrepreneurs have jumped into international business waters with both feet.

Lou Collier, president of the Institute for the National Black Business Council, says, "The growing 'Global Economy' that corporate America is seeking to capitalize on also means more participation of people of color as Africa, Asia, Eastern Europe, the Caribbean, Central and South America become more prominent players in this global economy as consumers of products and services, producers of products, and eventually as providers of business services." The question is: Will a critical mass of African Americans uproot and disperse (like other cultural groups) to distant countries long enough to establish the strong friendships and business relationships necessary to maximize the opportunities? It may take a generation, along with some amount of permanent relocation, to make contacts and establish lines of distribution. We are already beginning to do this among African Americans living in South Africa and in certain developing countries.

BASIC INFORMATION

OF COURSE, TO do business in the international market, you need to fully understand basic international trade practices. You've got to know the territory. Read, read, and then read some more. Understand the rules, learn who is there to help you and how to get the information you need, and put that knowledge into action.

As a matter of fact, trade information is plentiful, and much of it is available to you at absolutely no cost. Your initial resource is the U.S. Department of Commerce's Export Hotline and Trade Data Bank (800-USA-XPORT). Here you can find five-thousand market reports on seventy-eight countries and industries. The Trade Bank lists more than ten thousand companies looking to buy and sell products overseas.

Your local chambers of commerce are ready to help you. And there are a number of trade organizations that offer seminars on how to tap into international trade markets.

One of these is the Association for Minority Exporters and Importers (MEXIM), of which Lloyd Pilgrim-Spooner is president. Lloyd offers this advice:

1. In developing your marketing plan, it's most important to obtain trade data on exports. With this information, you will be able to do a market analysis and get a picture of the size of the potential market, the existing competition, and your potential customers.

2. While a federal license is *not* required for an import/export business, state or local licenses may be needed. Check with the offices of your city and county clerks.

3. Take advantage of international trade events. These may be trade fairs, trade missions, shows, catalog shows, foreign buyer missions, and similar programs. They give you a chance to size up the competition, make connections, and establish relationships with people who may be eager to buy what you have to sell. To find out about trade events and similar marketing opportunities, contact the U.S. Government Trade Information Center (800-USA-TRADE).

4. If you want to test products, or ideas, before visiting the country you've earmarked for distribution, you can contact the International Trade Administration. Their trade opportunities program (TOP) can provide names of overseas companies wishing to represent American products and services.

5. If the prospect of high overseas shipping costs seems overly daunting, it is possible to use a freight consolidator, who ships the products of several exporters on a shared-cost basis.

6. Use your bank to verify the credit status of potential overseas customers and to process payment. Transactions can be insured by

doing a background check on your purchaser. Payments can be handled through your bank.

MEXIM's personalized information service, available to minority firms and individuals, can locate foreign import agents and distributors.

There are also several trade journals and magazines to help you keep up to date on global opportunities. Among them are *International Business*, *The Exporter*, *World Trade*, and *Export Today*. If your local library doesn't stock them, look them up in the current periodicals file and invest in your own subscription.

Once you have chosen a country that seems a likely prospect for your product or service, contact its embassy or consulate, as well as the mayor's office in your city, for information about sister city programs or foreign visitor hospitality. Ask to be placed on the mailing list for news about future conferences or programs.

Suppose you want to import products from another country and then ship them overseas. Then you should contact the National Customs Brokers & Forwarders Association of America at 212-432-0050.

Assist International at 212-725-3311 offers a cornucopia of resources, such as videotapes, books, databases, and consulting services. Among them is *The Export Tools Handbook*. A phone call will place you on their mailing list.

One good example of a smart guy who used his head to create an overseas business is Warren Anderson, who lives in Ohio and is doing big business in South Africa. Warren was in his mid-thirties when he gave up his high-paying management job in Connecticut to apprentice at McDonald's—yes, the Golden Arches McDonald's.

With a partner, Stephen Dubose, he acquired a McDonald's distributorship: Every item that a McDonald's prepares for a customer—from the napkins to the fries to the kiddie toys—comes from a distributorship. They were the first African Americans to own a distributorship for a major fast-food chain. Within a year, Warren bought out his partner. He subsequently became a member of the Young Presidents Association, an international group of under-forty executives in charge of corporations.

Last year, his eighty-five-worker Ohio distributorship supplied 259 restaurants in the tri-state area, all of which amounted to sales of $118 million. Warren thinks of himself as a nomad, commuting every few weeks between his ventures in Ohio and South Africa, where he supplies McDonald's franchisees. He makes it a point to build relationships with his customers. "They know I come to them as another businessman, not an employee representing a huge conglomerate. I am truly a small businessman, and they can relate to that."

Fascinated by airplanes since childhood, Lex Nigel Barker got his pilot's license at age seventeen. With a BA in business administration and a master's degree in aeronautical science, he worked in aircraft sales for many years before going out on his own. Born in Guyana and educated in Brazil, he also speaks Spanish and Portuguese.

Seeing that competition in the saturated U.S. market was increasingly intense, Lex concentrated on building relationships in Asia, Eastern Europe, Latin America, and the Caribbean. His company, International Aircraft Trading, Inc. (IAT), buys, sells, manages, operates, and maintains aircraft of all kinds. "A client might call from South America and need a helicopter spare by tomorrow. We get it down there. That makes a name for us."

How does he know what's happening in his industry? He uses information provided by the Federal Aviation Administration to track individuals and corporations buying and exporting aircraft. He and his six employees get in touch with these prospective customers, and then they stay in touch.

"A deal can take a day, or it can take four years," he says. "The key to completing any sale is credibility and persistence. If you tell them you're going to call next week, you make sure you do it."

Such persistence has led to annual sales of $1.6 million.

NEW FRONTIERS FOR BLACK ENTERPRISE

GOVERNMENT COMMITMENT TO the support of minority- and women-owned business has been helpful in allowing us to focus on the long-term prospects of the global marketplace.

One place where our ethnicity is a definite advantage is in cosmetics. According to the Chicago-based American Health and Beauty Aids Institute (AHBAI), all of their Black-owned member companies are selling products abroad at a growing rate. One such company, Pro-Line Corp., is active in forty-three countries! Its strategy is to put the products in the hands of beauty salon operators and enter into distribution agreement with local vendors. They also work with distributors to translate their instruction sheets into the local language.

Television, too, is seeking new outlets, as Robert Johnson, founder of the cable network Black Entertainment Television (BET), has realized. With BET reaching 85 percent of cable households, he's created BET on Jazz, a completely separate cable network. Music, of course, doesn't have to be translated for foreign audiences, and jazz already has a substantial international audience. Add satellite capability, and a new opportunity pops.

Chicago-based publisher John H. Johnson has started *Ebony, South Africa.* Johnson wanted to launch the magazine years ago, but South African tariffs—100 percent of costs—make that country the most expensive market in the world. To get around this obstacle, he teamed with five South African publisher-partners.

At the magazine's new editorial offices in Johannesburg, seven South African employees work under the direction of D. Michael Cheers, who was formerly at *Ebony* and *Jet* in Washington, DC. The initial issue projected fifty pages of advertising; eighty were sold. Clearly, corporate South Africa knows this is the publication that covers the market.

Johnson readily admits that forming the strategic partnership with South Africans has been the key to creating this international version of the publication. "You have to have access to enough capital," Johnson says, "but it's not the sole thing you need to be successful. Whenever you go into a foreign country, you need someone who has an understanding of the foreign market. I don't think I could have done this alone."

The Calvert Group is becoming the first U.S. investment firm to establish offices in postapartheid South Africa and has established the New Africa Fund. A recent Fund conference was attended by ambassadors representing half of the African continent. This is the first fund to look for stocks throughout Africa. One of the fund's lead managers is Maceo Sloan, who is founder of Sloan Financial Group in Durham, North Carolina, which has assets of three billion dollars. He says, "Africa will be one place where everyone will smile when we show up instead of scratching their heads and saying, 'What are you doing here?' "

The World African Network is a growing telecommunications company founded by Eugene D. Jackson. The mission is to use communications technology to connect our peoples worldwide through broadcast, cellular, and emerging technologies. In this effort Eugene is aided by his wife, Phyllis M. Jackson, a former NBC network programming executive, and by Motown Records chairman Clarence Avant,

Sydney Small, a former partner in the Unity Broadcasting Network, and New York media executive Percy Sutton.

One theme that emerges from the experiences of African American global businesspeople is that it can be invigorating to work in a business environment where one's race is essentially a nonfactor. "Competence counts more than skin color," says John R. Robinson, CEO of the New York City–based National Minority Business Council. He encourages Black Americans to focus on "virgin territories, which small minority and other firms can get into before they become saturated."

As usual, knowledge and preparation count most of all. Cheryl J. Dobbins, president of Basic Technologies Information, managed to visit the world's largest market, China, as part of an Energy Department trade mission; she came away with ideas on how to sell her company's technical management skills and plenty of contacts to establish relationships with. Both the U.S. and China are working to lower barriers to trade and services.

Emerging Markets

LET'S TAKE A look at a few BEMs—that's what global businessmen call Big Emerging Markets.

Brazil, the world's tenth-largest economy, is hungry for American products, observers report—anything and everything from computer software and peripherals to security equipment, sporting goods, plastics, and Snickers candy bars.

Because access to Brazil's telecommunications, petroleum, and utilities industries is limited, most U.S. initiatives have been in manufacturing, where nearly all sectors are open. One note of advice: If you're thinking of doing business in Brazil, study up on this nation's history, culture, and social mores. Social niceties and interactions there are of major business importance. For one thing, there's an emphasis on conducting business in person and with the utmost civility.

South Africa, with its population of forty-one million, is the largest target in sub-Saharan Africa for U.S. goods and services. It's a place of stark contrasts—many first-class world businesses and affluent swimming-pool suburbs posed against a background of squalid townships and sparsely populated rural areas where people live in nearly primitive conditions.

This new free market needs telecommunications, health care, electrification, and housing. But while business and investment opportunities abound, investors should be aware that the country does not yet have a skilled, educated labor pool.

San Diego builder Dennis L. Russell has already opened branches of DLR Construction in Capetown and Johannesburg. The firm makes concrete blocks for housing. His investment in equipment and training has already reached the million-dollar mark, but that doesn't appear to trouble him. "Sometimes you have to do things that put people to work," he explains.

In all, there are few trade barriers. Partnerships with American entrepreneurs are welcomed, and many are flourishing.

Among the well-known corporations venturing into South Africa's marketplace, in addition to Johnson Publishing with its *Ebony, South Africa* magazine, and Luster Products of Chicago, are Levi Strauss, which just opened a factory outside of Capetown, Ford Motor Company, and Dell Computer.

India's more than 915 million inhabitants include a consumer class of about three-hundred million people and an upper middle class of about seventy-five million, all eagerly seeking U.S. products in the wake of trade regulation liberalization. It is no wonder that more than two hundred U.S. firms have already reached trade agreements and made investments in India. Half of these are in manufacturing industrial and consumer products. At this point, the United States is India's largest trade partner.

As expected, the busiest industries are telecommunications, power, information technology, electronics, transportation, food processing, financial services, and hydrocarbons.

Mexico's recently wild economy looks as if it's in the process of recovery, fueled by the North American Free Trade Agreement (NAFTA) which did away with trade barriers, the privatization of former state enterprises, and other economic reforms. Major growth sectors are telecommunications, pollution control—Mexico City rates high on the list of the world's most polluted environments—and auto parts.

Al's Turbo Exchange, a Santa Monica, California auto repair business whose specialty is rebuilding turbochargers and superchargers, had the idea of advertising in international newspapers and magazines. Within five years owner Tony Haywood noticed that sales to Mexican customers represented 20 percent of his business. His advice to other businessmen: Go global.

Indonesia consists of three thousand islands inhabited by 193 million people whose principal industry, until recently, was agriculture. The country is rich in oil, and its major exports are now textiles, airplanes, electronics, and chemicals. The Indonesian government intends to make a major investment in modernizing the infrastructure with new impetus in energy, environmental technology, aerospace, health care, and telecommunications.

The government, which maintains tight control of many industries, is often criticized for its rigid stand on human and worker rights, although some of that justifiable criticism is beginning to be focused on the corporations involved. Nike, for one, has come under fire for allowing sweatshop conditions to exist there.

Nevertheless, tariff barriers were lowered in 1995, and foreign ownership restrictions were removed in many areas. Indonesia receives more loans from the Export-Import Bank of the United States than any other country and boasts the first U.S. Commercial and Information Center in Asia. If human rights problems can be addressed and corrected, Indonesia will become a hot market in the global world of business.

South Korea's forty-five million people enjoy a per capita income of $8,530 (compared with $874 in Indonesia, for example). The country's rapid transition from an agricultural to a manufacturing economy has been incredible. Korean automobiles and electronics are commonplace in the United States. Other expanding industries are aircraft, telecommunications equipment, architecture, construction and engineering services, computers, peripherals, and transportation.

Korea has historically stayed clear of foreign imports. To succeed, foreign companies need to keep up constant communication with public- and private-sector officials and be able to show long-term commitment.

Thailand is an economically stable, free-market state that welcomes foreign investment. It has been a magnet for Japanese manufacturing investment.

Thailand imports U.S. chemicals, ships, aircraft, nonelectrical machinery, and appliances. High import duties and copyright, patent, and trademark piracy are also facts of economic life here. To sell to the private sector, American companies have to have a Thai representative. Also, foreign control of local companies can only be done through joint ventures with Thai-based companies.

Argentina has been able to lower its inflation rate from an incredible

5000 percent to a relatively normal 9 percent. The per capita income of its thirty-four million people is a healthy $8,400. The country has vast agricultural and mineral resources, and its workforce is highly skilled, with a literacy rate of 96 percent. Privatized companies in the fields of construction, heavy machinery, mining, and telecommunications have attracted investors. Additional growing markets include cellular phones and other forms of wireless equipment, electronic components, and environment and pollution control. There are few tariff barriers, and foreign companies are allowed to participate fully in government contracts.

However, 50 percent of the country's wealth is controlled by twenty-five Argentine holding companies. For that reason, foreigners are advised to conduct detailed investigations and then to pursue joint ventures.

Poland is one of Europe's fastest-growing countries, and with its population of thirty-nine million, it's also one of the biggest. The government is committed to free markets and economic reform. Consumer goods, broadcasting equipment, pollution control, and automotive products are good prospects for us. Banking services, telecommunications, and hospitality should also be looked at.

Doing business with the Polish government is not so much tricky as complicated; tariffs and regulations vary from one sector to another. What is clear, however, is that foreigners can invest in any Polish privatization.

GLOBAL INVESTING

THE INVESTMENT COMMUNITY agrees that overseas markets, which have long lagged behind domestic markets, are ready for growth. Analysts believe that mutual funds offer the best vehicles for diversification. Fund managers are able to allot their large portfolios to many more products than the small investor can sensibly purchase. By investing globally in emerging markets, investors can maximize their returns.

In addition to the Calvert Group's New Africa Fund (which I mentioned earlier), a number of global funds have produced fine results. Among these are Aim Global Growth Fund and Aim International Equity Fund. The John Hancock Global Marketplace fund was rated numero uno on the *Black Enterprise* list of global funds in 1995. Another top performer was the Hotchkiss and Wiley International Fund; T. Rowe Price, Vanguard, and Scudder all have international funds.

You ought to look for a fund with a network of analysts who personally visit the companies they invest their clients' money in. And you have to know that investing in the global market is for the long haul. All transactions should be part of a comprehensive investment program that reflects the client's needs, financial situation, and goals.

WORKING IN THE GLOBAL MARKETPLACE

ACCORDING TO A survey taken by the National Foreign Trade Council (NFTC), the number of Americans working overseas went up by 30 percent in 1995. And the majority of companies taking part in the NFTC survey reported that they expect the trend to continue.

People who work overseas see it as an opportunity to live a glamorous life in countries rich in culture and tradition. The life may not be all that glamorous, but foreign lands are surely rich in culture and tradition—which means we have to understand that the rest of the world doesn't always do or say things the way we do. New management and communication skills have to be learned before you go out into a world where colors, flowers, business cards, and even handshakes mean different things than they do in the U.S. Our handshake and informal ways may offend people in other cultures.

It's better to be more formal than too familiar. There are two books that tell you about this subject: *Dos and Taboos Around the World* by Roger E. Axtell, and *Kiss, Bow, or Shake Hands: How to Do Business in Sixty Countries.*

Getting Started

HERE ARE SOME suggestions for anybody who wants to get on the international career track:

1. Look for courses, conferences, and seminars that focus on the international aspects of your present career. Join organizations with international branches.
2. Ask business associates who have been overseas to help you.
3. Rework your resume—emphasize your cultural experience, the languages you speak, and the travel you have done. Volunteer for pro-

jects or assignments that can give you international awareness or additional exposure.

4. Consider investing in additional training—possibly an advanced degree in international affairs, business management, or languages. It's possible that your company might pay for you to upgrade your training.

When you get that assignment overseas, follow the advice of J. Eric Wright, manager of international capital markets for Citibank in Johannesburg. He joined in the social doings of the Soweto families instead of hanging out with his coworkers at the bank. This helped him understand the people better and learn how the marketplace worked.

Belinda Miller, who comes from Norfolk, Virginia, was assigned to Beijing by the Swissotel corporation. She was surprised at the way Chinese employees reacted to her directions. They thought she was being harshly critical. When she took some language classes, she found out that the Mandarin word for "question" is the same as the word for "problem." Like J. Eric Wright, she made sure to go to local social events. This made her more popular, showed that she had respect for their culture, and made her relationship with native Chinese far better.

FOR AFRICAN AMERICANS, overseas assignments can offer more than monetary rewards. A Black senior executive in China told an interviewer that for the first time in his life he felt that his success was based 100 percent on his own efforts.

Visiting Thailand, Hermene Hartman of the magazine *N'Digo* was surprised that the people there knew nothing about Black Americans. When she told her guide about slavery, his response was, "You must be very valuable people because someone bought you."

The experience works the other way, too. Many white Americans get their first taste of being on the receiving end of racism when they go overseas. Suddenly aware of what minorities have been going through for years, they frequently become active in the EEO programs of their companies back home.

SOUTH AFRICA

ONE YEAR AFTER a group of white executives from Sanlam Properties, a South African development company, drove their minivan through the impoverished territory of Soweto, the biggest, most modern shopping center any Black township had ever seen opened there. After years of commuting to stores on the edge of the enclave or paying the inflated prices charged by the tiny convenience stores that the apartheid government allowed, the native South Africans—there are three million of them in the city—wept tears of joy as they pushed their carts through the wide aisles of a Shoprite supermarket (no relation to the American markets of the same name), then strolled out to the steakhouse and then over to see what movies were playing at the triplex.

The restoration of political peace has opened the eyes of developers to the abundance of Soweto and the other townships. Gas stations, fast-food chains, banks, developers, and retailers are busily scouting the territories.

However, the new interest from white retailers has created bitterness among Black businessmen in the township. After years of serving the ghetto and weathering the ordeal of apartheid, they are being pushed aside by outsiders with big bucks.

Blacks in South Africa have never had the same access to capital, or credit, as whites. Nor have they been able to gain similar expertise in business management. They have no relationships with suppliers to buy in bulk. South Africa's Blacks argue that white entrepreneurs becoming businesspeople in their townships should be compelled—by political pressure, if not by law—to take local partners.

Native Entrepreneur

MAMA'S JAZZ JOINT —a home away from home. That's what the sign says outside the club at 263 Jan Smuts Avenue in Dunkeld West. When I visited Mama's it reminded me of the old Brooklyn jazz spots I used to hang out in. Mama—actually owner Charmain Modjadji— has a telephone and a fax and a management team of twelve, including an entertainment director, a community liaison person, a chef from Soweto and a retired professional chef, a garden manager, and a pair of financial advisors. Mama's functions on a membership basis and offers personal, corporate, and gold card memberships. Upcoming events are described in Mama's brochure. There are fashion shows, fund-raising dinners, planned political discussions, celebrations of public holidays, and on Sundays jazz from 2:00 to 8:00 P.M.

Second home to a host of businessmen, politicians, and movers and shakers from all sectors of South African society, Mama's is the first

African social establishment to serve the needs of people who are serious about networking and their own development in a relaxed and informal setting.

In addition, Mama's is actively providing employment for semi-skilled and professional people. Beyond the club staff, Mama's advertises the services of young, brilliant, and talented hairdressers to give you a most remarkable braiding style to suit your image. Swimming lessons for adults and children are offered by established professionals with lifesaving skills.

In essence, Mama's is a meeting place in the suburbs for people of all classes, colors, and creeds who wish to enjoy themselves and share ideas on business and social levels in a warm and comfortable atmosphere in a spirit of peace, cooperation, and understanding. "Joburg" could use many more spots like this one. A savvy New York nightclub owner looking for a new world to conquer could do quite well in this emerging market.

South Africa After Apartheid

TO OVERTURN THE effects of more than a century of laws aimed at limiting Blacks in every area of endeavor will require a great deal more than the equivalent of waving a magic wand. Journalist Newton Kanhema, a reporter for South Africa's major newspaper, the *Star*, estimates that it will take at least two generations for Blacks to reach the level of education needed to compete in the job market. The attitudes inherent in apartheid were established with the passage of the Masters and Servants Act in 1856. The act was abolished only in 1986.

The need for affirmative action can hardly be questioned. A recent survey of South Africans in technical fields found there were only 30 Black engineers (versus 17,840 white engineers), 31 Black pharmacists (versus 2,021 white pharmacists), 4 Black geologists (versus 731 white ones), 60 Black accountants out of a total of 14,036, and fewer than 20 Black architects out of 2,650. You can read more about the shameful story of discrimination in Christine Ounta's eloquent book, *Who's Afraid of Affirmative Action?* The end result of apartheid is that all of South Africa has been robbed of generations of talented professionals.

The country is unprepared to serve its people. South Africa's Department of Health has admitted that the majority of its Black population is worse off now than before. According to a survey carried out by the Community Agency for Social Enquiry, only about 20 percent of South African Black households have running water inside the home; 16 percent have no toilets of any kind; nearly 60 percent have no electricity. Public health services, such as childhood immunization programs, are also lacking.

AFRICA

WHAT WE CAN clearly see from here is opportunity: for trained African Americans to take their talents to South Africa to build on the ruins of what the world recognizes as failed policy. The man who has taken it on himself to lead the assault on the remains of apartheid is the Reverend Leon H. Sullivan, whose Third African-African American Summit, held in Dakar, Senegal, brought together one thousand Black Americans and four thousand African government officials and business executives to discuss solutions for Africa and South Africa's economic problems. Together they represented twenty-one nations. Reverend Sullivan characterized the summit as the first step toward building a movement for American Blacks to help Africa.

"We're going to build bridges to Africa," Reverend Sullivan told an interviewer. "We're going to put our skills and training to work to help Africa. African-American businessmen might have more to do with shaping the future of Africa than anybody." And he added, "America will no longer concede the African marketplace to Europeans."

Among those present at the conference was Secretary of Commerce Ron Brown. The death of Ron Brown, whose efforts at enlarging global markets were innovative and tireless, means the rest of us will have to work a lot harder.

Reverend Sullivan's people-to-people programs have so far succeeded in training one thousand new teachers, some of whom are already establishing new schools in Africa. Some African bankers and technicians are currently in training, doing work on the continent. Many interested civic groups have donated thousands of dollars' worth of supplies to schools where the children previously had no books at all.

His plan is to amass a group of one million supporters in the United States, who will build a self-help network for Black Africa and Black America. The crown jewel of Reverend Sullivan's program is SHIPS, a program in which small groups of investors pool networks of cash, which Sullivan's corporate friends then match. You should know that three quarters of that money will be earmarked for investment in America's inner cities, while the rest is for building projects in Africa.

Reverend Sullivan is also the founder of the Opportunities Industrialization Centers that operate in one hundred U.S. cities and in sixteen African countries. He has trained more Blacks than any nongovernment agency in the world.

For information about the many activities under the Reverend's leadership, you can write SHIPS, 5040 E. Shea Blvd., Suite 260, Phoenix, AZ 85254-4610 or call 800-835-3530.

CHINA

WITH A POTENTIAL market of more than one billion people, China has insisted on swapping jobs for market access. By placing illegal trade duties of 100 percent on American automobiles, for example, the government convinced General Motors to build factories and cars in China, using Chinese workers. Similarly, Boeing Aircraft is shifting parts of its 737 construction to Xian, China, where workers' monthly wages barely equal the hourly rate of Boeing's Seattle-based machinists. That China is acting illegally seems to have little effect upon the outcome. According to the AFL-CIO, more than half a million American jobs were exported to China last year. The Economic Policy Institute in Washington, DC, predicts that another 250,000 jobs in the aerospace industry will be lost to China. Are we looking at a global marketplace or a global job drain?

Hermene D. Hartman, reporting in her Chicago publication, N'Digo, on the imminent turnover of Hong Kong to the People's Republic of China, was struck by the way the massive economy operates. There is no concept of credit. Whatever you buy, you pay for in cash—that includes a house or a car, as well as shoes. She was also impressed by the deep respect all Chinese show the elderly and the fact that family life is at the very center of their culture.

However, a panel of experts on a Chinese television show criticized their own educational system. While their children happen to be the world's top achievers in math and science, the experts said they were not creative. Ms. Hartman agreed that Hong Kong's shops offered the best copies of everything, but that there was little originality in the designs. She wondered about the possible benefits a collaboration of

Asian exactness and Black creativity might produce. Who knows what exciting possibilities exist when cultures collaborate?

ASSIGNMENT FOR THE FUTURE

WHAT CAN WE do to reap the advantages of the growing marketplace?

As I said earlier, the global marketplace is a reality. Pursue some of the areas mentioned in this chapter, and find out all you can about those nations where you too might find a profitable niche. Work with others who have gone before and with government and trade offices to get the best overview of what possibilities are out there.

For example, Stanford University alumnus Kathryn Leary, of the Leary Group Inc., has spent years traveling back and forth between the States, Japan, and South Africa. She has developed strong contacts, as well as a deep understanding of the opportunity niches for Blacks and for American businesses in general. If you are seriously considering venturing into either market, it would be a wise investment to seek her consultancy (see Resources Guide).

Whether you seek only an income-producing situation or feel up to the moral commitment of investment in a place like South Africa, you may wind up discovering an extremely challenging and exciting career.

14

FUTURE WEALTH

The pessimist sees the difficulty in every opportunity; the
optimist sees the opportunity in every difficulty.

— L.P. JACK

WHILE WE ARE free, we are not yet equal—at least not until we bring
to the table of democratic capitalism an accumulated wealth equal to
or greater than that of other cultural groups who use their wealth for
political power and ownership in the American dream. Dr. Claud Anderson of the Washington, DC–based Harvest Institute made the
point clear in his insightful book *Black Labor, White Wealth*: "To
achieve self-sufficiency, Blacks must master the principles of capitalism
and group economics. Civil rights, social rights and integration cannot
produce group wealth and power."

We must always be vigilant in our fight for human rights, because
they are the foundation for our new mission of economic freedom. But
there is a new price to pay for this freedom. We must invest in a new
program of economic literacy. This requires revamping networking disciplines to include supporting our own businesses and professions first.
There is a greater need to live within our means, or even below our
means, in order to have resources to invest wisely and strategically,
thus accumulating wealth for our families and future generations.
Wealth creation through debt reduction and living smaller but more
fruitful lives will be the new mantras for the twenty-first century.

Our time has come. The next one hundred years will be a century of tremendous progress. All the signs are evident. Our needs are great, but the opportunities to serve, to invest, and to capitalize are even greater. The opportunities are so great that we are stumbling over and into them rather than taking full advantage of them. To bring future wealth to Black America, we need to experience more than a shift of consciousness; we need a shift in conscious action. Guidance is all around us. More and more Black people are speaking and writing about it—daily, weekly, monthly. There is a new buzz in the air, a new song, and a new vision. All you need to do is listen, learn, and join in. There is room for everyone at this table. Pick what excites and moves you, search for and discover your purpose and passion in life, and then start down a new path. There are a thousand helping hands waiting for you, but you must leap first, and the net will appear. Not one minute too late or too early.

Many see opportunity as a mountain. Some envision themselves enjoying the beautiful view from the summit, and some see themselves wandering aimlessly in the valleys below, lost, tired, and afraid. Seeing and leveraging opportunity requires the wisdom of Solomon, the endurance of Job, and the baseball bat of Hank Aaron. My own motivation to endure the pain of opportunity is based on my personal needs as well as the needs of my community. Doing well while doing good has always been my career objective. There is nothing more important to me than the success of our people and our businesses, for they are the basis of our moral, spiritual, and financial freedom.

NEEDS AND OPPORTUNITIES

BALANCING NEED AND opportunity sometimes requires uncompromising sacrifice and a self-serving agenda. All great achievers understand this and find a way to reconcile it in their hearts and minds. In the field of **education**, for example, teachers must find a way to teach, even though many of their urban students come from homes and neighborhoods where parents must struggle to feed them and maintain a value system. There is a decline in the number of Black teachers, especially males. We have to find a way to stop the decline and increase the number of Black teachers guiding and nurturing our children. Teaching is an honorable and fulfilling profession. The need is great at all educational levels to share and market our knowledge for a greater good. For at the core of the problem of our "image of incompetence" lies the greatest opportunity. Each time a Black person stands before an audience to teach, consult, or speak, that image changes. While most who enter this realm will not become rich, they will be enriched in the same way the farmer enjoys the fruits of his labor. Some will see a career in education as a sacrifice, others as a joy. Either way, as the need to improve education, provide after-school care, teach basic skills to those transitioning from welfare and reeducate all sectors of America's workers increases, the opportunities and budgets for education will continue to grow.

Thousands of African Americans will also be needed in the areas of **finance and banking**. The focus will be on economic development strategies. We need expertise in capital market investment instruments, venture funds, and banking. The manifestation of Black power will be driven by the level of sophistication we use to leverage our enormous wealth, which is estimated to be over one trillion dollars within twenty years. When we master the playing field of banking and finance, we will earn global respect and dominance in selected markets.

Creating new jobs is a top economic priority. We are in the process of changing the mantra of the 1950s and 1960s—"Get a good education, then get a good job." "Get a good education and create a job" dominates our new thinking. The corporate brain drain of the 1960s and 1970s will diminish, and many more will be focusing on **small business development** by starting new businesses, buying existing businesses, and marketing their skills through franchise opportunities, multilevel marketing, and home-based businesses.

Self-employment and Blacks working for Blacks should climb from the one million plus today to three to four million (20 to 25 percent of our workforce) in the next twenty years. Black colleges are gearing up for this quantum leap.

Cashing in on the **technology** revolution will play a major role in helping to create future wealth. The trendsetting power of urban young people and the creative prowess of Black advertising agencies will help make computers "cool." Just as sneakers, jeans, pagers, and portable radios were made stylish and cool, urban culture will help mainstream the computer and the accompanying software. With easy access to vast amounts of information via the Internet, productivity will skyrocket, leveling the economic and opportunity playing fields.

Expanding our output in the **publishing** world with more books and magazines and developing new venues such as a national Black weekly newspaper will present a wealth of new information and opportunities and a point of view presently little known in America. Those who seize new opportunities in mainstream publishing will tell our story in a more balanced and enlightened way.

Billions of dollars will be spent on **rebuilding our neighborhoods**. Opportunities in the construction trades and crafts, as well as in sales, marketing, loans, management, and development, are awesome. Major urban centers like New York, Chicago, Detroit, and Philadelphia are planning to spend hundreds of millions over the next ten years to build new homes, upgrade public housing, and rehabilitate old housing stock and also to build new centers of commerce on some of the most valuable and strategically located land in America. Center-city locations and downtown living and entertainment are on the way back. This is where we live, and it's time to cash in.

Dr. Claud Anderson suggests that we employ vertical integration business strategies to control industries in which we are disproportionately represented (entertainment and sports, for example) or consumer products which we disproportionately purchase (athletic wear, electronic equipment, movies, etc.).

Vertical integration means to control the raw materials, production, distribution, and retailing of a product or service. Progress has been slow but incremental, and the money, management skills, and vision are now in place. We have seen it with the recent financing of our own films (Spike Lee's profitable *Get On the Bus*), movie theaters (Magic Johnson/Sony Theaters), sports franchises (Isiah Thomas's investment in the Toronto Raptors), and ownership of numerous television and radio stations, and in greater control in rap and gospel music. More opportunities will come as we gain expertise in the variety of jobs now available in the **entertainment** and **sports** worlds.

But Geannine Amber, writing in *Essence*, warns that we "must never let violence become a marketable commodity, a Rite of Passage and a badge of authenticity for our young people." We don't need violence to create wealth at any level in Black America, and we must resist the corporations who tempt us with millions of dollars to act up, act out, and act crazy in the name of "keeping it real."

As the **health-care** industry is downsized and restructured, Black physicians and dentists must protect their customer base by forming new alliances and venturing into smaller communities where Black doctors are underrepresented and Blacks are underserved. Black doctors are needed, and Black nurses and technicians will be in demand in a society growing older and increasingly oriented toward wellness and home care. Small business opportunities are everywhere in this category, and many entrepreneurs will gradually become rich.

Just as other cultures moved to America from their homelands to start new businesses and set up pipelines of distribution for merchants back home, we must begin to do the same. **Global commerce** is the order of the day. Opportunities in the motherland are slowly evolving, with South Africa leading the way. The concept of vertical integration can start here, where raw materials and channels of distribution will be controlled by Blacks. Sub-Saharan Africa is another place where our color can work to our advantage. South America, the Caribbean, and the Pacific Rim are other geographical regions where we heavily influence the music, entertainment, and sport products. Exporting and controlling commodities related to these industries must become part of our strategy for financial freedom in America.

Succeeding in any one of these areas begins with personal decision-making and coming to terms with oneself. I have been there myself, that crossroads where you are forced to look at your life and make a choice for the future.

PRINCIPLE-CENTERED

IT WAS 1989 and one of those cold and gloomy winter days in Cleveland. I was sitting in my big chair at home, recovering from a painful full-mouth periodontal treatment. It was quiet. My wife, Jean, was at work, the boys were at school. The phone rang. "Mr. Fraser? I'm Scott's English teacher. I'm calling because your son was rude, crude, and offensive in class today, and he will not be permitted in class tomorrow if his obnoxious behavior doesn't change. I've reported him to the assistant principal and would like you to talk to him when he gets home."

I asked for a few details and agreed to have some words with Scott. This was not the first call from school for either of the boys.

I shook my head, took a sip of some strong coffee, popped an aspirin, and put an ice pack on my jaw.

I began to pout. Could it get any worse than this, I asked myself? Here I am, I thought, living large in a big house, financially over-extended, my new business is struggling, and I don't feel good. Never mind that I hadn't exercised in years and was overweight by twenty pounds, and my designer jogging suit was screaming. I was working fourteen hours a day and hadn't read a meaningful book in a year or been to church in recent memory.

What the hell was I doing? Sure, the boys were a little screwed up, but who wasn't? My life was out of balance. My family culture was at war with my business culture. I was afraid to admit it or even talk about it.

I leaned back in my chair, and my eyes fell upon the magazine rack that sits beside my chair. In it was a Bible, something I hadn't read in years. I picked it up, and the pages fell open to Genesis, Chapter 6, the story of Noah. I read it word for word at least three times. God was not happy with what He had created, so He recruited Noah to save that which was worthy, then He destroyed all the rest.

I needed some Noah in my life. I needed to separate what was worthy from what was destructive. I had made resolutions before, without success. Was it time to try again? I grabbed a yellow legal pad and wrote down seven New Year's resolutions, each one having to do with some screwed-up part of my life.

Over the next few years, several succeeding iterations of those resolutions became guideposts to a more balanced and productive life. I described them in an earlier chapter:

1. Seek Spiritual Growth
2. Give First, Share Always
3. Discover Your Unique Purpose
4. Find Inspiration in Your Suffering
5. Support Your Race and Culture First
6. Maintain Ties to Extended Family
7. Achieve Success with Dignity

Slowly, with much help from friends and family, I applied these basic principles and soon my life began to take on a new shape.

My story is really the story of my generation. The civil rights laws enacted in 1964 opened new opportunities, the likes of which our parents had never dreamed. We aggressively stepped up to the plate and prepared ourselves to hit a home run. The growth of the Black middle class during the late sixties and seventies was the largest in our history. But what became clear during this period was that our homegrown African-American culture and values would have to give way to the corporate culture of mainstream workplaces and that there was not a whole lot of compatibility between the two.

We seized the opportunities, learning new skills, speaking and writing a certain way, and dressing according to a specific standard. It also meant becoming competent in the subtle world of corporate bureaucracy and politics, and some of our successes were remarkable.

The reality is that millions of African Americans are succeeding because their conscious and subconscious moral and spiritual underpinnings are intact and fully functioning in every aspect of their lives. Whenever and wherever I meet African Americans in the process of achieving and also contributing to their communities, I find many of the seven principles that were so useful to me in place and actively engaged. That's surely no coincidence, because they are universal values that have served humankind well for millennia.

We can recognize those who have strayed from these principles. They are dissatisfied with their lives and have no larger sense of community. They may have money in their pockets but no mantle of dignity.

These principles provide a road map for individual success. They are as effective for a ten-year-old child trying to work his way out of South Central Los Angeles as they are for the fifty-year-old CEO looking for meaning in his or her life. They embody our greatest strengths—and meet our greatest needs. They build upon and reinforce one another. They are part of our collective memory as people of African descent.

THE SPIRIT OF UBUNTU

ON MY FIRST trip to Johannesburg, South Africa, I was befriended by a bright and energetic Black newspaper reporter named Newton Kanehama. He generously gave me a comprehensive tour of the Johannesburg landscape and psyche.

How had so many Black people managed to survive and psychologically overcome apartheid? Through hours of discussion and meeting countless impoverished families in their homes and schools, I was introduced to the word "Ubuntu," a South African term meaning "the quality of being human."

Newton loosely defined Ubuntu for me: "A person is a person through other people, we owe our selfhood to others, we are first and foremost social beings." Every place I went, I could see and feel the spirit of willing participation, unquestioning cooperation, warmth, trust, empathy, and personal dignity. We see these qualities in Nelson Mandela and Archbishop Desmond Tutu.

Newton himself was my model. He embraced me, a stranger, and was willing to share with me all that he had. Clearly, he had committed himself to the service of his people and country.

I was forced to reflect on my own privileged position as part of an extended Black family, which badly needed a similar commitment from the Black middle class. Glenn Loury has stated, "All Blacks are connected—by bonds of history, family, conscience and common perception in the eyes of outsiders—to those in the urban slums. Black politicians, clergy, intellectuals and businessmen and ordinary folk must create hope in these communities; they must become their brothers' keeper. Only then will change be possible."

Or as brother Spike Lee has said, "Uplift the race!"

We definitely have a full agenda—to engage with society, reconnect with our African-American history and community, and deepen our personal sense of dignity and self-worth—as we move individually and collectively toward our Future Wealth. By "Future Wealth," you who have read this book now certainly know, I mean not only material self-enrichment but personal reevaluation and a decision to emphasize sharing, meaning and purpose wherever possible in all our actions.

The vectors of your dreams and your reality merge somewhere just beyond the horizon at a place called The Future. The journey toward that destination begins now, with a single step.

> When we come to the end of all that there is,
>
> and we stand at the brink of eternity, and
>
> there is nothing before us but darkness, we
>
> must believe that God will give us something
>
> firm to stand on, or teach us how to fly.

✳ RESOURCE GUIDE ✳

NETWORKING FOR INFORMATION
AND CONTACTS

Whenever I receive a letter or a phone call asking for information or contacts, I compliment the person for taking the initiative to seek the knowledge, and I recommend a book or two. Then I ask the person to call me back after reading the book. At that point, I refer them to additional sources, contacts, professional organizations, and Web sites. By the time we're finished, the person can say he or she has successfully networked for information.

Information is power. Our research team has developed this comprehensive resource guide to save time, money, and frustration as you seek additional contacts and information to find your path. The guide is also designed to give you deeper knowledge about your personal interests. There are literally hundreds of people and organizations waiting to help you live your dream. All you have to do is read what they have written, then call and ask for guidance.

Hundreds of hours have gone into the preparation of this resource guide. Most of the books listed in the suggested readings sections I've personally read. I invite you to do the same. My life has been enriched by the information and contacts contained within, and I now eagerly share them with you.

Here is how the Resource Guide is organized:

PART I
**General Career Development
Sources**

PART III
Regional Job Outlook Information

PART II
Resources Available for Each Chapter:
- **Organizations and Professional
  Associations**
- **Suggested Reading**
  General
  Reference
  Magazines
- **Contacts**
- **On-line Services**

PART I
GENERAL CAREER DEVELOPMENT SOURCES
LOOKING FOR CAREER ADVICE, ROLE MODELS, OR MENTORS? TRY
NETWORKING WITH THESE ORGANIZATIONS.

Black Professional Organizations

Alliance of Black Entertainment
  Technicians
1869 Buckingham Road
Los Angeles, CA 90019
213-933-0746

American Association of Blacks in
  Energy
927 15th Street NW, #200
Washington, DC 20005
202-371-9530

American Association of Black
  Women Entrepreneurs Corp.
815 Thayer Avenue, #1628
Silver Spring, MD 20910
301-565-0258

American Association of Minority
  Businesses, Inc.
222 S. Church Street, #220
Charlotte, NC 28202
704-376-2262

Association for Multi-Cultural
  Counseling and Development
5999 Stevenson Avenue
Alexandria, VA 22302
703-823-9800

Association of Black Ambassadors
310 Somer Lane Place
Avondale Estates, GA 30003
404-299-6803

Association of Black Foundation
  Executives
1828 L Street NW, #300
Washington, DC 20036
202-466-6512

Association of Black Psychologists
PO Box 55999
Washington, DC 20040-5999
202-722-0808

Association of Black Sociologists
Department of Sociology
Central Michigan University
Mount Pleasant, MI 48859
517-774-4000

Association of Black Sporting Goods
  Professionals
PO Box 772074
Coral Springs, FL 33077-2074
888-294-7020

Association of Mom and Pop Food
  Stores
117 Broadway
Jack London Waterfront
Oakland, CA 94697-3715
510-444-5741

The Black Caucus of the American
  Library Association
5 Washington Street, #333
Newark, NJ 07102
504-596-2601

Black Entertainment and Sports
  Lawyers Association
1502 Fairlakes Place
Mitchellville, MD 20721
301-333-0003

Black Flight Attendants of America
1060 Crenshaw Boulevard, #202
Los Angeles, CA 90019
213-299-3406

Black Professionals in International
Affairs
PO Box 11675
Washington, DC 20008
301-953-0815

Black Psychiatrists of America
866 Carlston Avenue
Oakland, CA 94610
510-834-7103

Blacks in Government
1820 11th St. NW
Washington, DC 20001-5015
202-667-3280

Black Women in Publishing
P.O. Box 6275
FDR Station
New York, NY 10150
212-772-5951

Coalition of Black Trade Unionists
PO Box 66268
Washington, DC 20035-6268
202-429-1203

Conference of Minority Public
Administrators
PO Box 3010
Fort Worth, TX 76113
817-871-8325

Congressional Black Caucus
House Annex II
Ford Building, Room 344
Washington, DC 20515
202-675-6730

Congress of National Black Churches
1225 I Street NW, #750
Washington, DC 20005-0908
202-371-1091

Consortium of Information and
Telecommunications Executives
Inc.
Bell Atlantic
540 Broad Street, 10th fl.
Newark, NJ 07102
201-649-6881

Council on Career Development for
Minorities
1341 W. Mockingbird Lane, #412E
Dallas, TX 75277
214-631-3677

International Association of Black
Professional Firefighters
8700 Central Avenue, #306
Landover, MD 20785
301-808-0804

International Black Buyers and
Manufacturers Expo and Conference
312 Florida Avenue NW
Washington, D.C. 20001
202-797-9070

Multicultural Food Service
and Hospitality Alliance
P.O. Box 1113
Minneapolis, MN 55440
612-540-3267

National Alliance of African American
Athletes
1112 Linkside Drive
Baltimore, MD 21234
410-821-1629

National Alliance of Black School
Educators
2816 Georgia Avenue NW
Washington, DC 20001
202-483-1549

National Alliance of Postal and
Federal Employees
1505 11th Street NW
Washington, DC 20001
202-667-4040

National Association of Black
Accountants Inc.
7249-A Hanover Parkway
Greenbelt, MD 20770
301-474-6222

National Association of Black Book
Publishers
PO Box 22080
Baltimore, MD 21203
210-358-0980

National Association of Black
  Consulting Engineers
2705 Bladensburg Road NE
Washington, DC 20018
202-333-9100

National Association of Black Owned
  Broadcasters Inc.
1333 New Hampshire Avenue, #1000
Washington, DC 20036
202-463-8970

National Association of Blacks in
  Criminal Justice
North Carolina Central University
PO Box 19788
Durham, NC 27707
919-683-1801

National Association of Black
  Journalists
3100 Taliaferro Hall
University of Maryland
College Park, MD 20742
301-405-8500

National Association of Black Social
  Workers
8436 West McNichols Avenue
Detroit, MI 48221
313-862-6700

National Association of Black
  Telecommunications Professionals
1025 Vermont Avenue NW, #910
Washington, DC 20005
800-946-6228

National Association of Black Women
  Attorneys
724 9th Street NW, Suite 206
Washington, DC 20001
202-637-3570

National Association of Black Women
  Entrepreneurs Inc.
PO Box 1375
Detroit, MI 48231
810-356-3686

National Association of Fashion and
  Accessories Designers
6309 Cranston Lane
Fredericksburg, VA 22407
540-891-5432

National Association of Health
  Services Executives
8630 Fenton Street, Suite 126
Silver Spring, MD 20910
202-628-3952

National Association of Investment
  Companies
1111 14th Street NW, #700
Washington, DC 20005
202-289-4336

National Association of Market
  Developers Inc.
6 North Michigan Avenue, #909
Chicago, IL 60602
312-874-3773

National Association of Minority
  Automobile Dealers
1250 Connecticut Avenue NW
Washington, DC 20036
202-637-9095

National Association of Minority
  Contractors
666 11th Street NW, #520
Washington, DC 20001
202-347-8259

National Association of Minority
  Media Executives
1401 Concord Point Lane
Reston, VA 22091-1307
703-709-5245

National Association of Real Estate
  Brokers Inc.
1629 K Street NW, #602
Washington, DC 20036
202-785-4477

National Association of Securities
  Professionals
1212 New York Avenue NW, #210
Washington, DC 20005-3987
202-371-5535

National Association of Urban Bankers
1010 Wayne Avenue, #1210
Silver Spring, MD 20910
301-589-2141

National Bar Association Inc.
1225 11th Street NW
Washington, DC 20001
202-842-3900

National Beauty Culturists' League
25 Logan Circle NW
Washington, DC 20005
202-332-2695

National Black Association for Speech,
   Language and Hearing
PO Box 50605
Washington, DC 20091
202-274-6162

National Black Caucus of Local
   Elected Officials
1301 Pennsylvania Avenue NW, #705
Washington, DC 20004
202-626-3168

National Black Chamber of
   Commerce
2000 L. Street NW
Washington, DC 20036
202-416-1622

National Black Data Processing
   Associates
1250 Connecticut Avenue NW, #610
Washington, DC 20036
800-727-2372

National Black MBA Association
180 N. Michigan Avenue, #1515
Chicago, IL 60601
312-236-2622

National Black Media Coalition
1120 New Hampshire Avenue, #204
Silver Spring, MD 20904
301-593-3600

National Black Nurses' Association
1511 K Street NW, #415
Washington, DC 20005
202-393-6870

National Black Police Association
3251 Mt. Pleasant Street NW
Washington, DC 20010
202-986-2070

National Black Public Relations
   Society
6565 Sunset Boulevard, #301
Hollywood, CA 90028
213-856-0827

National Business League
1511 K. Street NW, #432
Washington, DC 20005
202-737-4430

National Coalition of Black Meeting
   Planners
8630 Fenton Street, #126
Silver Spring, MD 20910
202-628-3952

National Conference of Black Lawyers
1875 Connecticut Avenue NW, #400
Washington, DC 20009
202-234-9735

National Conference of Black Mayors
   Inc.
1422 West Peachtree Street, NW
Atlanta, GA 30309
404-892-0127

National Council of Black Engineers
   and Scientists
1525 Aviation Boulevard, Suite C424
Redondo Beach, CA 90278
213-896-9779

National Dental Association
5506 Connecticut Avenue NW, Suite
   24–25
Washington, DC 20015
202-244-7555

National Dental Hygienists
   Association
5506 Connecticut Avenue NW, Suite
   24–25
Washington, DC 20015
202-244-7555

National Federation of Black Women
Business Owners
1500 Massachusetts Avenue NW,
Suite 34
Washington, DC 20005
202-833-3450

National Food Service Association
3737 Canterbury Street
Harrisburg, PA 17109
717-652-1723

National Insurance Association
PO Box 53230
Chicago, IL 60653-0230
773-924-3308

National Medical Association Inc.
1012 10th Street NW
Washington, DC 20001
202-347-1895

National Minority Supplier
Development Council Inc.
15 West 39th Street, 9th floor
New York, NY 10018
212-944-2430

National Naval Officers Association
40 Lake Edge Drive
Euclid, OH 44123
800-772-6662

National Network of Minority Women
in Science
c/o American Association for the
Advancement of Science
1333 H Street NW
Washington, DC 20005
202-326-7017

National Newspaper Publishers
Association
3200 13th Street NW
Washington, DC 20010
202-588-8764

National Optometric Association
1489 Livingston Avenue
Columbus, OH 43205
614-253-5593

National Organization for the
Professional Advancement of Black
Chemists and Chemical Engineers
525 College Street NW
Washington, DC 20059
800-776-1419

National Organization of Black Law
Enforcement Executives
4609 Pinecrest Officer Park Drive, 2nd
floor, Suite F
Alexandria, VA 22312
703-658-1529

National Pharmaceutical Association
12510 White Drive
Silver Spring, MD 20904
301-622-7747

National Sales Network
909A Broad Street, #258
Newark, NJ 07102
201-799-2478

National Society of Black Engineers
1454 Duke Street
Alexandria, VA 22314
703-549-2207

National Society of Real Estate
Appraisers
1265 East 105 Street
Cleveland, OH 44108
216-795-3445

National Technical Association, Inc.
6919 North 19th Street
Philadelphia, PA 19126
215-549-5743

National Urban League Inc.
120 Wall Street
New York, NY 10005
212-558-5300

100 Black Men of America Inc.
141 Auburn Avenue
Atlanta, GA 30303
404-688-5100

Organization of Black Airline Pilots
PO Box 5793
Englewood, NJ 07631
201-568-8145

Organization of Black Designers
300 M. St. SW, #N110
Washington, DC 20024
202-659-3918

SUGGESTED READING/LISTENING/VIEWING

General

The Black Manager: Making It in the Corporate World, Floyd Dickens, Jr., and Jacqueline B. Dickens (American Management Association, rev. 1991).

The Black Woman's Career Guide, Beatryce Nivens (Doubleday, rev. 1987).

The Career Decisions Planner, Joan Lloyd (John Wiley & Sons, 1992).

Careering and Re-Careering for the 1990's: The Complete Guide to Planning Your Future, 2nd ed., Ronald L. Krannich (Impact, 1991).

Careers Without College (Peterson's Guides, current edition).

The Colorblind Career, Ollie Stevenson (Peterson's, 1997).

Compendium of Resources for Teaching About the Non-Profit Sector, Volunteerism and Philanthropy, Nancy L. Crowder, Virginia Hodgekinson (Independent Sector, 202-223-8100).

The Complete Job-Search Handbook: All the Skills You Need to Know to Get Any Job and Have a Good Time Doing It, Howard E. Fiogler (Henry Holt & Co., 1988).

The Crystal-Barkley Guide to Taking Charge of Your Career, Nella Barkley and Erick Sandburg (Workman Publishing, 1995).

Discover What You're Best At, Barry Gale (Simon & Schuster, 1990).

Empowering Yourself: The Organizational Game Revealed, Harvey J. Coleman (Kendall/Hunt Publishing).

Every Young Person's Guide to Winning the Job Hunt Game, Yolonda Gayles (Inner Workings Books, 1993).

How to Help Your Child Land the Right Job (without being a pain in the neck), Nella Barkley (Workman Publishing, 1993).

The Hundred Best Companies for Blacks to Work for in America. (In press.)

Inside Corporate America: A Guide for African Americans, Wilson Simmons II (Berkley Publishing Group, 1996).

Making Vocational Choices: A Theory of Vocational Personalities and Work Environments, John L. Holland (Prentice-Hall, 1985).

What Makes the Great Great: Strategies for Extraordinary Achievement, Dennis Kimbro (Doubleday, 1997).

Success Gems: Your Personal Motivational Success Guide, Jewel Diamond Taylor (Quiet Time Publishing, 1995).

Success Runs in Our Race: The Complete Guide to Effective Networking in the African-American Community, George Fraser (William Morrow and Company, 1994).

What Color Is Your Parachute?, Richard Nelson Bolles (Ten Speed Press, 1997).

What's Next? Career Strategies After 35, Jack Falvey (Williamson Publishing Co., 1987).

You Can Make It Without a College Degree, Roberta Roesch (Prentice-Hall, 1986). Practical strategies for the non-graduate.

Reference

The African American Network, Crawford B. Bunkley (Plume, NAL, 1996).

The African American Yellow Pages, National Edition, edited by Stanton F. Biddle, Ph.D. (OWL Books, 1996). (See your White Pages for local edition.)

The Black Resource Guide, 1990 (Black Resource Guide, 1990).

The Career Guide—Dun's Employment Opportunities Directory (Dun and Bradstreet Corp., published annually in November).

Career Guide to America's Top Industries (JIST Works, Inc.).

Career Guide to Professional Associations (Garrett Park Press, current edition).

Careers Encyclopedia, Craig T. Norback, ed. (VGM Career Horizons, 1991).

Diaspora Design Directory, 800-989-5147.

Dictionary of Occupational Titles (U.S. Department of Labor, current edition).

Encyclopedia of Associations (Gale Research, Inc., 1993).

Guide to Black Organizations, Current edition (Manager of Public Programs, Philip Morris Companies, Inc., 120 Park Avenue, New York, NY 10017, 1997).

International Jobs: Where They Are and How to Get Them, Eric Kocher (Addison-Wesley, 4th ed.).

Macmillan Directory of Leading Private Companies (Macmillan, published annually in March).

Occupational Outlook Handbook (compiled by the U.S. Department of Labor, published in May of even years).

1,999 Facts About Blacks: A Sourcebook of African-American Accomplishment, Raymond M. Corbin (Beckham House, 1996).

SuccessGuide: The Networking Guide to Black Resources—Atlanta, Chicago, Cincinnati/Dayton, Cleveland, Detroit, New Orleans, New York, Washington D.C., George C. Fraser (SGP, 1994), 216-691-6686.

Who's Who Among Black Americans (Gale Research, Inc., 835 Penobscot Building, Detroit, MI, 48226-4094, 313-91-2242).

Internships, Volunteer Work

Great Careers: The Fourth of July Guide to Careers, Internships, and Volunteer Opportunities in the Non-Profit Center, Devon Smith, ed. (Garrett Park Press, 1990).

Internships (The Career Press, 1990). A five-volume series on internships.

Magazines/Newsletters

Kennedy's Career Strategist, Marilyn Moats Kennedy.
1150 Wilmette Avenue
Wilmette, IL 60091
847-251-1661

CONTACTS

Executive Recruiters

LOOKING FOR THE RIGHT JOB?
THESE BROTHERS AND SISTERS CAN HELP YOU.

Sheila Brooks
Personnel Executive Placement
1511 K Street NW, #1157
Washington, DC 20005
202-783-4340

Eral Burks
Minority Executive Search
PO Box 18063
Cleveland, OH 44118
216-932-2022

Wendell L. Johnson
Associates, Inc.
12 Grandview Drive
Danbury, CT 06811
203-743-4112

William Burgess III
Corporate Environments
160 E. 26th Street, #6G
New York, NY 10010
212-686-5598

Software

Career Design Software
PO Box 95624
Atlanta, GA 30347
800-346-8007
Fax: 404-321-6474

On-line Services

AFAMNET
http://www.afamnet.com

The Black Collegian Online
http://www.black-collegian.com

Career Placement Registry
Career Placement Registry, Inc.
Swann Avenue
Alexandria, VA 22301
800-368-3093
Fax: 703-683-0246

Minorities Job Bank
http://www.minorities-jb.com

Moody's Corporate Profiles
Moody's Investors Service, Inc.
Dun and Bradstreet Corp.
99 Church Street
New York, NY 10007
800-342-5647
Fax: 212-553-4700

PART II
CHAPTER ONE: TEN TRENDS MOVING BLACK AMERICA FORWARD

BLACK PROFESSIONAL ORGANIZATIONS

The Association for the Study of Afro-
American Life and History, Inc.
1407 14th St. N.W.
Washington, DC 20005-3704
202-667-2822

Black Enterprise Magazine
Market Research Dept.
130 Fifth Avenue
New York, NY 10011
212-886-9540 or 9541

Harvest Institute
730 11th Street NW, 4th Floor
Washington, DC 20001
202-496-1622

Joint Center for Political and
Economic Studies
1090 Vermont Avenue NW, Suite
1100
Washington, DC 20005
202-789-3500

Moorland-Springarn Research Center
500 Howard Place NW
Washington, DC 20059
202-806-7241

NAACP Legal Defense and
Educational Fund
99 Hudson Street, #1600
New York, NY 10013
212-219-1900

Schomburg Center for Research in
Black Culture
515 Malcolm X Boulevard
New York, NY 10037-1801
212-491-2202

Morehouse Research Institute
830 Westview Drive, SW
Atlanta, GA 30314
404-215-2676

WEB Du Bois Institute for Afro
American Studies
Harvard University
12 Quincy Street
Cambridge, MA 02138
617-495-4113

SUGGESTED READING/LISTENING/VIEWING

General

Job Shift: How to Prosper in a Workplace Without Jobs, William Bridges (Addison-Wesley, 1994).

Megatrends 2000, John Neisbitt (Avon Books, 1991).

Popcorn Report, Faith Popcorn (HarperCollins, 1992).

The Third Wave, Alvin Toffler (Bantam Books, 1980).

The World in 2020: Power, Culture, and Prosperity, Hamish McRae (Harvard Business School Press, 1994).

CHAPTER TWO: OUR EDGE: INNER POWER

SUGGESTED READING/LISTENING/VIEWING

Business as a Calling: Work and the Examined Life, Michael Novak (Free Press, 1996).

Care of the Soul: A Guide for Cultivating Depth and Sacredness in Everyday Life, Thomas Moore (Harper Perennial, 1992).

The Centering Moment, Howard Thurman (Friends United Press, 1969).

Conversations with God: An Uncommon Dialogue, 2 vols., Neale Donald Walsch (Putnam, NY, 1995, 1996).

Deep River and *The Negro Spiritual Speaks of Life and Death*, Howard Thurman (Friends United Press, 1975).

Disciplines of the Spirit, Howard Thurman (Friends United Press).

Don't Believe the Hype: Fighting Cultural Misinformation about African-Americans, Farai Chideya (A Plume Book, 1995).

The Growing Edge, Howard Thurman (Friends United Press, 1956).

Howard Thurman: His Enduring Dream, George K. Makechnie (Boston University Press, 1988). (Boston University, Howard Thurman Center, 19 Deerfield St., 3rd Floor Boston, MA 02215; 617-353-4045)

In the Spirit: The Inspirational Writings of Susan L. Taylor (Amistad, 1993).

The Inward Journey, Howard Thurman (Friends United Press, 1961).

It's Not Over Till You Win, Les Brown (Simon & Schuster, 1997).

Jesus and the Disinherited, Howard Thurman (Friends United Press, 1981).

King James Bible: Original African Heritage Edition, Rev. Cain Hope Felder, Ph.D., ed. (Winston Publishing).

Loving Yourself First: A Woman's Guide to Personal Power, Linda Coleman-Willis (WLW Publishing).

Meditations of the Heart, Howard Thurman (Friends United Press, 1976).

My Soul Looks Back, 'Less I Forget: A Collection of Quotations by People of Color, Dorothy Winbush Riley, ed. (HarperCollins Publishers Inc., 1993).

The Nibble Theory and the Kernel of Power: A Book About Leadership, Self-Empowerment and Personal Growth, Kaleel Jamison (Paulist Press, 1984).

Of Water and the Spirit: Ritual, Magic, and Initiation in the Life of an African Shaman, Malidoma Patrice Somé (Penguin, 1994).

The On-Purpose Person: Making Your Life Make Sense, Kevin W. McCarthy (Pinon Press, 1992).

Power of Associations: Success Through Volunteerism and Positive Associations, Henry E. Ford (Kendall/Hunt Publishing Co., 1996).

The Power of Myth, Joseph Campbell with Bill Moyers (Anchor Books, 1991).

Ritual: Power, Healing and Community, Malidoma Patrice Somé (Swan Raven & Company, 1993).

The Search for Common Ground, Howard Thurman (Friends United Press, 1981).

The Seven Spiritual Laws of Success: A Practical Guide to the Fulfillment of Your Dreams, Deepak Chopra (Amber-Allen Publishing, 1994).

Sister Power: How Phenomenal Black Women Are Rising to the Top, Patricia Reid-Merritt (John Wiley & Sons, 1996).

Substance of Things Hoped For, Samuel Proctor (G. P. Putnam's Sons, 1996).

Transform Your Life: A Woman in Ministry, Barbara Lewis King, A. B., M. S. W., D. D (DeVorse & Co., 1989).

The Twelve Universal Laws of Success, Herbert Harris (The LifeSkills ® Institute, P.O. Box 181069, Cleveland, OH 44118; 800-775-0712 ext. 8140).

Upon This Rock: The Miracles of a Black Church, Samuel G. Freedman (HarperCollins Publishers Inc., 1993).

The Value in the Valley: A Black Woman's Guide Through Life's Dilemmas, Iyanla Vanzant (Fireside, 1995).

Visions for Black Men, Na'im Akbar (Mind Productions, 1991).

Who Are You? And What Are You All About? A Self-Evaluation Handbook, Arlene T. Dyer (Reyd Publications, 1995).

The Wisdom of Joseph Campbell: In Conversation with Michael Toms (Audio Cassettes, New Dimensions Foundation, 1991).

With Head and Heart: The Autobiography of Howard Thurman (A Harvest/HBJ Book, 1979).

CHAPTER THREE: KEY BUILDING BLOCKS FOR ECONOMIC SUCCESS

BLACK PROFESSIONAL ORGANIZATIONS

Association for Multicultural
   Counseling and Development
5999 Stevenson Avenue
Alexandria, VA 22302
703-823-9800

National Association of Black
   Accountants
7249-A Hanover Parkway
Greenbelt, MD 2077
301-474-6222

National Association of Urban Bankers
1010 Wayne Avenue, #1210
Silver Spring, MD 20910
301-589-2141

National Association of Securities
   Professionals
1212 New York Ave NW, #210
Washington, DC 20005
202-371-5535

National Urban League, Inc.
120 Wall Street
New York, NY 10005
212-310-9000
Fax: 212-344-8925

General Organizations

The Foundation for Ethnic
   Understanding
17 East 45th Street
New York, NY 10017
212-297-0323

LOOKING TO START AN INVESTMENT CLUB?

National Association of Investors
   Corp.
PO Box 220
Royal Oak, MI 48068
810-583-NAIC

SUGGESTED READING/LISTENING/VIEWING

Beyond Race and Gender, Roosevelt Thomas (AMA, 1992).

Black Labor, White Wealth: The Search for Power and Economic Justice, Claud Anderson, Ed.D. (Duncan & Duncan, inc., 1994).

Black Lies, White Lies: The Truth According to Tony Brown, Tony Brown (Quill/ William Morrow, 1995).

The Black Woman's Guide to Financial Independence, Cheryl D. Broussard (Penguin, 1996).

Breaking Down Walls: A Model for Reconciliation in an Age of Racial Strife, Raleigh Washington and Glen Kehrein (Moody Press, 1993).

Challenge to Succeed in the 90's, Jim Rohn (214-401-1000, audio cassettes).

Color-Blind: Seeing Beyond Race in a Race-Obsessed World, Ellis Cose (HarperCollins Publishers Inc., 1997).

5 Minute Mutual Fund Investor: A Basic Guide to Investing in Mutual Funds, Dana V. C. Mervin (M. Systems-Publishing Group, 1994).

Killing Rage: Ending Racism, bell hooks (Owl Books, 1995).

Leadership, James MacGregor Burns (HarperCollins Publishers Inc., 1978).

Money: Who Has How Much and Why, Andrew Hacker (Scribner, 1997).

Principle-Centered Leadership, Stephen R. Covey (Summit Books, 1990).

Racial Healing: Confronting the Fear Between Blacks and Whites, Harlon L. Dalton (Doubleday, Anchor 1995).

Redefining Diversity, Roosevelt Thomas (AMA, 1996).

Smart Money Moves for African Americans, Kelvin Boston (Putnam 1996).

Talking Dollars and Making Sense: A Wealth-Building Guide for African Americans, Brooke M. Stephens (McGraw Hill, 1997).

Two Nations: Black and White, Separate, Hostile, Unequal, Andrew Hacker (Ballantine Books, 1992).

Valuing Diversity: New Tools for a New Reality, Lewis Brown Griggs and Lente-Louise Louw, eds. (McGraw-Hill, 1995).

Wake Up America—Regain Your American Heritage: Become Financially Fit Through Debt Elimination, Carol Walker (Financial Freedom Enterprises, 1997)

Magazines/Newsletters

*Next Step Magazine, a Publication on
    Multiculturalism and Diversity*
PO Box 38584
Philadelphia, PA 19104
215-387-2387

Issues and Views
PO Box 467
New York, NY 10025
212-655-7847

Multicultural Marketing News
332 Bleecker Street, #G41
New York, NY 10014
212-242-3351

CONTACTS

LOOKING FOR ECONOMIC LITERACY TRAINING FOR YOUR FAMILY, ORGANIZATION, OR CHURCH?

Cheryl Broussard
Broussand/Douglas Inc.
Financial/Investment Advisors
499 Hamilton Avenue, #140
Pala Alto, CA 94301
415-688-1188

Morris B. Mann
Mann Associates
Economic Literacy Training
702 Cornell
Ypsilanti, MI 48197
313-481-0546

Brooke M. Stephens, CFP
Financial Consultants
43 Vanderbilt Avenue
Brooklyn, NY 11205
718-875-2575

Carol A. Walker
Financial Fitness Centers
2696 North University Avenue,
  Suite 180
Provo, UT 84604
800-669-8815

CHAPTER FOUR: EDUCATION AND TRAINING

BLACK PROFESSIONAL ORGANIZATIONS

Association of Black Women in
  Higher Education
c/o Nassau Community College
Nassau Hall, Room 19
One Education Drive
Garden City, NY 11530-6793

Institute for Independent Education
1313 North Capitol Street NE
Washington, DC 20002
202-745-0500

National Alliance of Black School
  Educators
2816 Georgia Avenue NW
Washington, DC 20001
202-483-1549

National Association for Equal
  Opportunity in Higher Education
Lovejoy School Building

400 12th Street NE, Suite 207
Washington, DC 20002
202-543-9111

National Citizens Commission for
  African American Education
2141 Industrial Parkway
Silver Spring, MD 20904
301-680-8804

National Urban Coalition
1875 Connecticut Avenue NW
Suite 400
Washington, DC 20008
202-986-1460

Toussaint Institute Fund
20 Exchange Place, 41st Floor
New York, NY 10005-3201
212-422-5338
Fax: 212-422-0615

General Organizations

American Association of School
Administrators
1801 North Moore Street
Arlington, VA 22209
703-528-0700

American Council on Education
1 Dupont Circle NW
Washington, DC 20036
202-939-9300

American Federation of Teachers
555 New Jersey Avenue NW
Washington, DC 20001
202-879-4400

Association for Childhood Education
International
11501 Georgia Avenue, Suite 315
Wheaton, MD 20902
301-942-2443

College and University Personnel
Association
1233 20th Street NW, Suite 503
Washington, DC 20036
202-429-0311

Council for Advancement and
Support of Education
11 Dupont Circle NW, Suite 400
Washington, DC 20036
202-328-5900

National Association for the
Education of Young Children

1834 Connecticut Avenue NW
Washington, DC 20009
202-232-8777

National Association of Women in
Education
1325 18th Street NW
Washington, DC 20036
202-659-9330

National Education Association
1201 16th Street NW
Washington, DC 20036
202-822-7200

National School Boards Association
1680 Duke Street
Alexandria, VA 22314
703-838-6722

National Speakers Association
1500 South Priest Drive
Tempe, AZ 85281
602-968-2552

Teach for America
P.O. Box 5114
New York, NY 10185
800-832-1230

Toastmasters of America
800-993-7732
(Check your White Pages for local
chapter)

SUGGESTED READING/LISTENING/VIEWING

General

American Speaker (Georgetown Publishing House, 1101 30th Street NW, Washington, DC 20007; 800-915-0022).

At the Essence of Learning: Multicultural Education, Geneva Gay (Kappa Delta Pi, 1994).

Be Prepared to Speak, Video (Toastmasters International, Kantola Productions, 55 Sunnyside Avenue, Mill Valley, CA 94941; 800-989-8273).

Classroom in Conflict: Teaching Controversial Subjects in a Diverse Society, John A. Williams (SUNY Press, 1994).

Consultant's Kit: Establishing and Operating Your Successful Consulting Business, Dr. Jeffrey L. Lant (JLA publications, 1986).

Different and Wonderful: Raising Black Children in a Race-Conscious Society, Dr. Darlene Powell Hopson and Dr. Derek S. Hopson (Fireside/Simon & Schuster, 1990).

The Dreamkeepers: Successful Teachers of African American Children, Gloria Ladson-Billings (Jossey-Bass, 1994.)

For Professional Speakers Only, Mike Frank (Speakers Unlimited, Box 27225, Columbus, OH 43227; 614-864-3703).

How to Get Your Point Across in 30 Seconds or Less, Milo Frank (Pocket Books, 1986).

The Miseducation of the Black Child—The Hare Plan: Educating Every Black Man, Woman and Child, Nathan Hare, Ph.D., and Julia Hare, Ed.D. (Black Think Tank, 1991).

Raising Black Children: Two Leading Psychiatrists Confront the Educational, Social and Emotional Problems Facing Black Children, James P. Comer, M.D., and Alvin F. Poussaint, M.D. (Plume, 1992).

Speaker's Sourcebook II: Quotes, Stories, and Anecdotes for Every Occasion, Glenn Van Ekeren (Prentice-Hall, 1994).

Speaking with Power and Passion, Les Brown, audio cassette (1350 S. Ridge Road, Wichita, KS 67209; 800-733-4226).

Winning When It Really Counts, Arch Lustberg (Simon & Schuster, 1988).

Reference

Academic Labor Markets and Careers (Falmer Press/Taylor & Francis Inc., 1988) (1900 Frost Road, Suite 901, Bristol, PA 19007; 800-821-8312).

The Black Students' Guide to Colleges, Barry Beckham (Beckham Publications, 1997).

The Black Students' Guide to Scholarships, Barry Beckham (Beckham Publications, 1997).

Encyclopedia of African American Education, Faustine C. Jones, ed. (Greenwood, 1996).

Job Search Handbook for Educators (ASCUS, Evanston, IL).

100 Best Colleges for African-American Students, Erlene B. Wilson (Plume, 1993).

Requirements for Certification of Teachers, Counselors, Librarians, and Administrators for Elementary and Secondary Schools and Junior Colleges (University of

Chicago Press, current edition) (11030 South Langley Avenue, Chicago, IL 60628; 800-621-2736).

Magazines/Newsletters

American Educator
555 New Jersey Avenue NW
Washington, DC 20001
202-879-4420

American School and University
Intertree Publishing Co.
1400 North Providence Road,
Bldg. 2, Suite 1040
Media, PA 19063
610-566-7080

The Black Collegian
140 Carondelet Street
New Orleans, LA 70130
504-523-0154

Black Issues in Higher Education
10520 Warwick Avenue, #B-8
Fairfax, VA 22030-3108
703-385-2981

The Chronicle of Higher Education
1255 23rd Street NW
Washington, DC 20037
202-466-1000

Educational Leadership
1250 N. Pitt
Alexandria, VA 22314
703-549-9110

Learning
1111 Bethlehem Pike
Springhouse, PA 19477
215-646-8700

Wilson Library Bulletin
950 University Avenue
Bronx, NY 10452
800-367-6770

CONTACTS

Consultants

**WOULD YOU LIKE TO BE A CONSULTANT?
TALK TO SOME OF AMERICA'S BEST.**

Richard Orange
Richard Orange and Associates
Portsmith Consulting Group
"Diversity Strategy and Consulting"
163 Washington Park
Brooklyn, NY 11205
718-855-1172

Josie Lindsey
Bell and Lindsey and Associates
"Organizational Development"
8536 Crow Drive, #GL40
Macedonia, OH 44056
216-468-3130

Ramon Williamson
"Sales Training"
2010 Corporate Ridge, #700
McLean, VA 22102
703-749-1400

Iris Randall
New Beginnings
"Executive Coaching"
30 Main Street
Danbury, CT 06810
203-790-0011

Cynthia Jones
Jones Worley Design Inc.
"Environmental Graphics"
723 Piedmont Avenue, NE
Atlanta, GA 30365
404-876-9272

Cathy Nedd
Cathy Nedd Detroit
"Public Awareness"
300 River Place, Suite 5350
Detroit, MI 48207
313-567-NEDD

Edward Jones
Corporate Organizational Dynamics
"Organizational Change"
302 Grove Road
South Orange, NJ 07079
201-763-0176

Carol Patterson
Correct Communications
"Marketing and Communications"
105 Lock Street
Newark, NJ 07103
201-242-3305

Roosevelt Thomas
R. Thomas and Associates
"Understanding Diversity"
4535 Flat Shoals Parkway, #302
Decatur, GA 30034
404-212-0070

Amy Hilliard-Jones
Hilliard-Jones Marketing Group
   Incorporated
4823 South Kimbark Avenue
Chicago, IL 60615
312-924-9997

Julius C. Dorsey, Jr.
Dorsey and Company
"Strategic Consulting to
   Management"
2000 East Ninth Street
Cleveland, OH 44115
216-621-5252

Lafayette Jones
Segmented Marketing Services, Inc.
4265 Brownsboro Road, Suite 225
Winston-Salem, NC 27106
919-759-7477

Pat Tobin
Tobin and Associates
"Public Relations Consultants"
6565 Sunset Boulevard, Suite 301
Hollywood, CA 90028
213-856-0827

James H. Lowry
James H. Lowry and Associates
"Management Consultants"
211 West Wacker Drive, Suite 950
Chicago, IL 60606
312-223-9570

WOULD YOU LIKE TO START YOUR OWN FOUNDATION AND/OR
SCHOLARSHIP FUND LIKE NOEL E. HORD OF DANBURY, CONNECTICUT?
SEND FOR INFORMATION.

The Cleveland Foundation
1422 Euclid Avenue, Suite 1400
Cleveland, OH 44115

The Hord Foundation Inc.
Noel E. Hord, Samuel R. Hyman—
   Chairman
P.O. 4671
Danbury, CT 06813

WOULD YOU LIKE TO BE A SPEAKER?
TALK TO SOME OF THE YOUNG STARS.

Willie Jolly
5711 13th Street NW
Washington, DC 20011
202-291-7631

Valada
"Storyteller"
P.O. Box 2351
Longwood, FL 32752
407-444-2095

Marlon Smith
Success by Choice
The "High-Tech" Motivator
25125 Santa Clara Avenue, Suite 321
Hayward, CA 94544
510-887-1311

Otis Williams
Otis Williams Limitless
P.O. Box 53391
Cincinnati, OH 45253
513-731-0077

Desi Williamson
Impact!! Seminars Unlimited
Business Development Consultant
4505 North Avenue
Edina, MN 55436
612-926-5100

Robert L. Wallace
The Bith Group Incorporated
Creating Competitive Advantage via
    Training and Technology
8950 Old Annapolis Rd., Suite 236
Columbia, MD 21045
410-730-0077

Melvin J. Gravely II
PO Box 62126
Cincinnati, OH 45262-2126
513-769-4200

Marvin E. Montgomery
Professional Sales Training
1455 East Schaff Road
Cleveland, OH 44131
216-459-2650

Ivory Dorsey
Golden Eagle Business Services, Inc.
Training and Consulting Services
PO Box 43447
Atlanta, GA 30336-0447
404-881-6777

Traci Lynn
Traci Lynn International
"Making Your Life Work"
45 E. City Line Avenue, Suite 494
Bala Cynwyd, PA 19004
215-248-3016

Linda Coleman
Speaker/Trainer
P.O. Box 90369
Los Angeles, CA 90009
213-243-8258

Jewel Diamond Taylor
Motivational Speaker
4195 Chino Hills Parkway, #180
Chino Hills, CA 91709
213-964-1736

Paul Harris
Chrysalis Consulting Group
"Valuing Diversity"
2201 St. Paul Street
Baltimore, MD 21218
410-889-4700

Hattie Hill
Hattie Hill Enterprises, Inc.
"Encouraging Wisdom Through
  Instruction"
5025 Arapaho Road, Suite 512
Dallas, TX 75248
972-702-9788

Barbara Brown
Seminar Connections
"Conflict Management"
5160 Baltimore National Pike
Baltimore, MD 21229
410-455-0300

INDEPENDENT BLACK PRIVATE SCHOOLS
WANT TO START YOUR OWN SCHOOL? ASK THEM HOW.

Hans Hageman
East Harlem School at Exodus House
309 E. 103rd Street
New York, NY 10029
email:hhag@aol.com

Institute for Independent Education
  (IE)
1313 North Capitol Street NE
Washington, DC 20002
202-745-0500

Toussaint Institute Fund
20 Exchange Place, 41st Floor
New York, NY 10005-3201
212-422-0615

S. R. Martin College Prep School
2660 San Bruno Avenue
San Francisco, CA 94134
415-715-0102

Open a Learning Center

Sylvan Learning Centers (franchise)
1000 Lancaster Street
Baltimore, MD 21202
800-627-4276

Kumon Math and Reading Centers
  (franchise)
Kumon USA Inc.
Midwest Office
2 Continental Towers, #109

1701 Gold Road
Rolling Meadows, IL 60008
800-222-MATH

Bedford Kumon Math and Reading
  Center
Mable Griar
755 Broadway Avenue
Bedford, OH 44146
216-439-6282

CHAPTER FIVE: FINANCE AND BANKING

BLACK PROFESSIONAL ORGANIZATIONS

American League of Financial
  Institutions
900 19th Street NW, Suite 400
Washington, DC 20006
202-857-3176

National Association of Black
  Accountants
7249-A Hanover Parkway
Greenbelt, MD 20770
301-474-6222

National Association of Investment
  Companies
1111 14th Street NW, Suite 700
Washington, DC 20005
202-289-4336

National Association of Securities
  Professionals
1212 New York Avenue NW, #210
Washington, DC 20005-3987
202-371-5535

National Association of Small Business
  Investment Companies
1199 North Fairfax Street, Suite 200
Alexandria, VA 22314
703-683-1601

National Association of Urban Bankers
1010 Wayne Avenue, Suite 340
Silver Spring, MD 20910-5600
301-589-2141

National Bankers Association
1802 T Street, NW
Washington, DC 20009
202-588-5432

National Black MBA Association
180 N. Michigan Avenue, #1515
Chicago, IL 60601
312-236-2622

National Insurance Association
PO Box 53230
Chicago, IL 60653-0230
773-924-3308

General: Securities

American Financial Services
  Association
919 18th Street, 3rd Floor
Washington, DC 20006
202-296-5544

Association for Investment
  Management and Research
PO Box 3668
Charlottesville, VA 22901
804-977-6600

Financial Analysts Federation
5 Boar's Head Lane
Charlottesville, VA 22903
804-977-8977

Financial Executives Institute
10 Madison Avenue
PO Box 1938
Morristown, NJ 07962-1938
201-898-4600

Securities Industry Association
120 Broadway, 35th Floor
New York, NY 10271
212-608-1500

General: Banking

American Bankers Association
1120 Connecticut Avenue NW
Washington, DC 20036

Bank Administration Institute
500 North Michigan Avenue, Suite
  1400
Chicago, IL 60611

Financial Institutions Marketing
  Association
111 East Wacker Drive
Chicago, IL 60611
312-938-2570

Independent Bankers Association of
America
One Thomas Circle NW, Suite 950
Washington, DC 20005

General: Insurance

Independent Insurance Agents of
America
127 South Peyton Street
Alexandria, VA 22314

Insurance Information Institute
110 William Street
New York, NY 10034

Life Insurance Marketing and
Research Association
PO Box 208
Hartford, CT 16141

National Association of Independent
Insurance Adjusters
300 West Washington Street, Suite 805
Chicago, IL 60606

National Association of Life
Underwriters
1922 F Street NW
Washington, DC 20006

The Institute of Financial Education
111 East Wacker Drive
Chicago, IL 60611
312-946-8800

National Association of Professional
Insurance Agents
400 North Washington Street
Alexandria, VA 22314

Society of Certified Insurance
Counselors
3630 North Hills Drive
Austin, TX 78731
(800) 633-2165

Society of Chartered Property and
Casualty Underwriters
720 Providence Road
Malvern, PA 19355

CONTACTS

Selected Black Securities Firms

M. R. Beal & Co.
565 Fifth Avenue
New York NY 10017
212-983-3930

Pryor, McClendon, Counts and Co.
3 Penn Central, 1515 Market Street
Philadelphia, PA 19102
215-569-0274

W. R. Lazard
14 Wall Street, 18th Floor
New York, NY 10005
212-406-5855

Ariel Capital Management, Inc.
307 North Michigan Avenue, Suite
500
Chicago, IL 60601
312-726-0140

Jackson Securities Inc.
100 Peachtree Street, NW, #2250
Atlanta, GA 30303
404-522-5766

SBK-Brooks Investment Corp.
25 Prospect Avenue West, #700
Cleveland, OH 44115
216-861-6950

Utendahl Capital Partners
30 Broad Street, 31st Floor
New York, NY 10004
212-797-2500

Selected Black Banks

The Boston Bank of Commerce
133 Federal Street
Boston, MA 02110
617-457-4400

Carver Bancorp Inc.
75 West 125th Street
New York, NY 10027
212-876-4447

Citizens Trust Bank
75 Piedmont Avenue, NE
Atlanta, GA 30302
404-659-5959

First Independence National Bank
44 Michigan Avenue
Detroit, MI 48226
313-256-8400

Founders National Bank
3910 W. Martin Luther King, Jr.
  Boulevard
Los Angeles, CA 90008
213-290-4862

The Harbor Bank of Maryland
25 West Fayette Street
Baltimore, MD 20221
410-528-1800

Independence Federal Savings Bank
1229 Connecticut Avenue NW
Washington, DC 20036
202-628-5500

Seaway National Bank of Chicago
645 E. 87th Street
Chicago, IL 60619
773-487-4800

United Bank of Philadelphia
714 Market Street
Philadelphia, PA 19106
215-829-2265

Selected Black Insurance Companies

Atlanta Life Insurance Co.
100 Auburn Avenue
Atlanta, GA 30301
404-659-2100

Booker T. Washington Insurance Co.
P.O. Box 697
Birmingham, AL 35201
205-328-5454 or 800-288-4180

Golden State Mutual Life Insurance
  Co.
1999 West Adams Boulevard
Los Angeles, CA 90018
213-731-8271

North Carolina Mutual Life Insurance
  Co.
411 West Chapel Hill Street
Durham, NC 27701
919-682-9201

Universal Life Insurance Co.
480 Linden
Memphis, TN 38126
901-525-3641

SUGGESTED READING/LISTENING/VIEWING

General

The Negro as Capitalist: A Study of Banking and Business Among American Negroes, Abram L. Harris (Urban Research Press, 1992).

Business Week/Top 200 Banking Institutions
McGraw-Hill Inc.
1221 Avenue of the Americas, 39th Floor
New York, NY 10020
212-512-4776

Financial Services Report
Philips Publishing
7811 Montrose Road
Potomac, MD 20854
301-340-2100

Financial World
Financial World Partners
1328 Broadway, 3rd Floor
New York, NY 10001
212-594-5030

Magazines/Newsletters

Barron's National Business and Financial Weekly
Dow Jones & Co.
200 Liberty Street
New York, NY 10281
212-416-2700

Institutional Investor
488 Madison Avenue
New York, NY 10022
212-303-3300

Investment Dealers' Digest
2 World Trade Center
New York, NY 10048
212-227-1200

Moody's Bank and Finance Manual
Moody's Investor Service, Inc.
99 Church Street, 1st Floor
New York, NY 10007
212-553-0300

CHAPTER SIX: SMALL BUSINESS LEADS TO BIG BUSINESS

BLACK PROFESSIONAL ORGANIZATIONS

American Association of Minority Businesses, Inc.
222 South Church Street, Suite 220
Charlotte, NC 28202
704-376-2262

Association of Black Women Entrepreneurs
P.O. Box 49368
Los Angeles, CA 90049
213-624-8639

Association of Mom and Pop Food Stores
117 Broadway
Jack London Waterfront
Oakland, CA 94697-3715
510-444-5741

Institute for the National Black Business Council, Inc.
1100 Wayne Avenue, Suite 850
Silver Spring, MD 20910
301-585-NBBC

International Black Buyers and
  Manufacturers Expo and
  Conference
312 Florida Avenue NW
Washington, DC 20001
202-797-9070

Interracial Council for Business
  Opportunity
51 Madison Avenue, Suite 2212
New York, NY 10010
212-779-4360

Minority Business Enterprise Legal
  Defense and Education Fund
220 I Street NW, Suite 240
Washington, DC 20002
202-543-0040

National Association of Investment
  Companies
1111 14th Street NW, Suite 700
Washington, DC 20005
202-289-4336

National Association of Minority
  Automobile Dealers
1250 Connecticut Avenue NW
Washington, DC 20036
202-637-9095

National Association of Negro
  Business and Professional Women's
  Clubs, Inc.
1806 New Hampshire Avenue NW
Washington, DC 20009
202-483-4206

National Black Chamber of
  Commerce
2000 L. Street NW
Washington, DC 20036
202-416-1622

National Black MBA Association
180 N. Michigan Avenue, #1515
Chicago, IL 60601
312-236-2622

National Business League
1511 K Street NW, Suite 432
Washington, DC 20005
202-737-4430

National Council of Negro Women
  Inc.
633 Pennsylvania Avenue, NW
Washington, DC 20004
202-737-0120

National Food Service Association
3737 Canterbury Street
Harrisburg, PA 17109
717-652-1723

National Minority Business Council
235 East 42nd Street
New York, NY 10017
212-573-2385

National Minority Supplier
  Development Council
15 West 39th Street, 9th Floor
New York, NY 10018
212-944-2430

United States African American
  Chamber of Commerce
117 Broadway
Jack London Waterfront
Oakland, CA 94697-3715
510-444-5741

General Organizations

National Association for the Self-
Employed
PO Box 612067
Dallas, TX 75261
800-232-NASE

National Foundation for Teaching
Entrepreneurship
120 Wall Street, 29th Floor
New York, NY 10005
212-232-3333

Small Business Administration
Office of Information
Advocacy Department, Room 7800
Washington, DC 20416
202-606-4000

Young Entrepreneurs Organization
1010 North Glebe Road, Suite 600
Arlington, VA 22201
703-519-6700

Franchises

American Association of Franchisees
and Dealers
P.O. Box 81887
San Diego, CA 92138-1887
619-235-2556 or 800-733-9858

The American Franchisee Association
53 West Jackson Boulevard, Suite 205

Chicago, IL 60604
312-431-1467 or 800-334-4232

International Franchise Association
1350 New York Avenue NW, Suite
900
Washington, DC 20005
202-628-8000

BUSINESS INCUBATORS

Birmingham Business Assistance
Network
110 12th Street
Birmingham, AL 32503
205-250-8000

Franklin Business Center
1433 East Franklin Avenue
Minneapolis, MN 55404
612-870-7555

Fulton-Carroll Center
2023 North Carroll Avenue
Chicago, IL 60612
312-421-3941

Houston Small Business Development
Corp.
5330 Griggs Road
Houston, TX 77021
713-845-2400

Oakland Small Business Growth
Center
675 Hegenburger Road

Oakland, CA 94621
510-444-4495

Redwood Development Center
c/o Sam McDaniel
815 East Mound Street, Suite 200
Columbus, OH 43205
614-252-0057

San Francisco Renaissance Micro
Business Incubator
404 Bryant Street
San Francisco, CA 94107
415-541-8580

West Charlotte Business Incubator
617 North Summit Avenue
Charlotte, NC 28216
704-377-0048

West Philadelphia Enterprise Center
4548 Market Street
Philadelphia, PA 19139
215-895-4000

SUGGESTED READING/LISTENING/VIEWING

General

Black Economics: Solutions for Economic Empowerment, Jawanza Kunjufu (African American Images, 1991).

The Black Entrepreneur's Guide to Success, Melvin J. Gravely II (Duncan & Duncan, Inc.).

Black Entrepreneurship in America, Shelly Green and Paul Pryde (Transaction Books, 1996).

Black Folks' Guide to Business Success, George Subira (609-641-0776).

Black Wealth Through Black Entrepreneurship, Robert Wallace (Duncan & Duncan, 1994).

Bottom-Up Marketing, Al Ries and Jack Trout (Plume, 1989).

Consultant's Kit: Establishing and Operating Your Successful Consulting Business, Dr. Jeffrey L. Lant (JLA publications, 1986).

E Myth, Michael Gerber (HarperCollins Publishers Inc., 1995).

Entrepreneurship and Self-Help Among Black Americans, John Sibley Butler (University of New York Press at Albany).

Franchising: The How-To Book, Lloyd T. Tarbutton (Prentice-Hall, Inc., 1986).

Getting Black Folks to Sell, George Subira (609-641-0776).

Guerrilla Marketing Weapons: 100 Affordable Marketing Methods for Maximizing Profits from Your Small Business, Jay Conrad Levinson (Plume, 1990).

Hazards of Entrepreneurship: A Guide to Business Success, Blossom O'Meally-Nelson, Ph.D. (Stephenson's Litho Press, 1995).

Highway to the Electronic Goldmine: How to Profit from Direct Response TV Advertising, Rodney H. Buschser (FMS Direct 861 Seward Street, Hollywood, CA 90038; 213-465-2363).

How to Master the Art of Selling, Tom Hopkins (Warner Books 1980).

How to Succeed in Business Without Being White: Straight Talk on Making It in America, Earl Graves (HarperBusiness, 1997).

Innovation and Entrepreneurship: Practice and Principles, Peter E. Drucker (Perennial Library, 1986).

Islam's Climate for Business Success, W. Deen Mohammed (The Sense Maker, 1995).

Jewish Power: Inside the American Jewish Establishment, J. J. Goldberg (Addison-Wesley, 1996).

The Noble Art of Vending: An African Centered Guide to Vending Success, Al Parinello (The Career Press, 1992).

101 Best Businesses to Start, Sharon Kahn and The Philip Lief Group (Doubleday, 1992).

The Personal Touch: What You Really Need to Succeed in Today's Fast-Paced Business World, Terrie Williams with Joe Coney (Warner Books, 1994).

A Piece of the Action: How Women and Minorities Can Launch Their Own Successful Businesses, Suzanne Caplan (Amacom, 1994).

The Psychology of Selling, Brian Tracy, audio cassettes (619-481-2977).

Small Business Troubleshooter, Roger Fritz (Career Press, 1995).

Streetwise Small Business Start-up, Bob Adams (Adams Media Corporation, 1996).

Strike It Rich: 49 Hottest Home Business Tax Strategies, David D'Arcangelo (800-876-0030).

The 22 Immutable Laws of Marketing, Al Ries and Jack Trout (HarperBusiness, 1993).

250 Home-Based Jobs, Scott C. Olsen (Atlantic Richfield Company, current edition).

The Work at Home Sourcebook, Lynie Arden (Live Oak Publications, 1990).

Working Solo, Terri Lonier (Portico Press, 1996).

References

African American Yellow Pages, edited by Stanton F. Biddle, Ph.D. (Owl Books, 1996). (Check your local white Pages for local editions; there are nearly 60 versions published.)

National and Regional Minority and Women-Owned Business Directory
Business Research Services
1990 M Street NW, #400
Washington, DC 20036
202-331-8840

National Memo: The Corporate Guide to Minority Vendors
National Business League
1511 K Street NW, Suite 432
Washington, DC 20005
202-737-4430

Small Business USA
National Small Business United
1156 15th Street NW, Suite 1100
Washington, DC 20005
202-293-8830

SuccessGuide: The Networking Guide to Black Resources
(Atlanta, Chicago, Cleveland, Cincinnati/Dayton, Detroit, New York, New Orleans, Washington, DC, 1995)
2940 Noble Road, #103
Cleveland, OH 44121
216-691-6686

Magazines/Newsletters

Black Enterprise Magazine
130 Fifth Avenue
New York, NY 10003
212-242-8000

Entrepreneur Magazine, newsstand

Executive Female
National Association for Female
  Executives
30 Irving Place, 5th Floor
New York, NY 10016
212-477-2000

Inc. Magazine, newsstand

Minority BusinessNews USA
11333 N. Central Expressway, #201
Dallas, TX 75243
214-369-3200

Success Magazine, newsstand

Target Market News
228 S. Wabash, #410
Chicago, IL 60604
312-408-1881

Upline Magazine
Business Building Tools for Network
  Marketers
400 E. Jefferson Street
Charlottesville, VA 22902
804-979-4427

Urban Call
The Trade Magazine for Urban
  Retailers
Lafayette Jones, Publisher
4265 Brownsboro Road
Winston Salem, NC 27106-3425
910-759-7477

The MLM Insider Magazine
Network Resources
3529 NE 171 Street
North Miami Beach, FL 33160
305-947-8655

CONTACTS

WANT TO JOIN A NETWORK MARKETING ORGANIZATION?

Raymond King, Jr.
Black Heritage Products, Inc.
1315 Headquarters Drive
Greensboro, NC 27405
910-379-7505

Shirley and Delmar Carmack
Golden Neo-Life Diamite
2760 Pleasant Wood Drive
Decatur, GA 30034
404-284-6272

AESOP Direct 2000
6245 Coffman Road
Indianapolis, IN 46268
888-882-3767

Gary O. Shelton
GlobalCom
243 West Congress, #350
Detroit, MI 48226
313-961-2647

Les Brown, Kym Yancey
The People's Network (TPN)
2045 Chenault Drive
Carrollton, TX 75006
800-876-0030

Marc Campbell
Driver's Seat Network
Credit Development International
L.A. Network Center
1100 S. LaBrea Boulevard, Suite 200
Los Angeles, CA 90010
213-934-8205 x140

Ivey Stokes
MAXXIS 2000, Inc.
1080 Holcomb Bridge Road
Building 100, Suite 135
Roswell, GA 30076
770-552-4766

Ken Bridges, Al Wellington
Matah Network
215 W. Clinton Avenue, #4
Oaklyn, NJ 08107
609-854-1859

WANT TO START A LOCAL BLACK CHAMBER OF COMMERCE?

Mike Butler, Doris Polite
Tucson Black Chamber of Commerce
1690 North Stone Avenue, #113
Tucson, AZ 85705
520-742-7713

Roy A. Hastick, Sr.
Caribbean-American Chamber of
    Commerce and Industry
Brooklyn Navy Yard
Brooklyn, NY 11205
718-834-4544

WANT TO START A SMALL BUSINESS?

American Association of Minority
    Businesses, Inc.
Charles Kelly
222 S. Church Street, Suite 220
Charlotte, NC 28202
704-376-2262

Carole Joy Creations Inc.
Carole J. Gellineau
107 Mill Plain Road, #200
Danbury, CT 06811
203-798-2060

Church's Fried Chicken
Leon J. Oldham
Six Concourse Parkway, Suite 1700
Atlanta, GA 30328-5352
770-391-9500

Delta Planning
Robert Donaldson
P.O. Box 22618
Beachwood, OH 44122
216-831-2521

The Fresh Club, Inc.
Phil Davis
P.O. Box 20947
Cleveland, OH 44120
216-791-3245

The Harlem Venture Group
Bret Leonard
2840 Broadway, #200
New York, NY 10025
212-722-0600

KBK Enterprises, Inc.
"Business Development"
Bernard W. Kinsey
301 Mt. Holyoke Avenue
Pacific Palisades, CA 90272
310-454-2521

McDonald's Corporation
Frank Gihan
711 Jorie Boulevard
Oak Brook, IL 60523
630-623-3429

Uncle Noname
Wally "Famous" Amos
P.O. Box 897
Kailua, HI 96734
808-261-6075

NEED A LOAN ON YOUR PURCHASE ORDERS?

Prin. Vest Corp.
1061 Natchez Point, #182
Memphis, TN 38103
901-578-4508

University Advancement Inc.
Equipment Leasing—Business Loans
1700-203 Oaktree Road, Suite 115
Edison, NJ 08820
908-381-8537

ON-LINE SERVICES

Business Start-ups

http://www.melanet.com
http://www.portraits.com/
http://www.cqws.com/webguide.phtml
http://www.megasuccess.com/
http://www.cweb.com/ecenter/
  howtodo.htm
http://www.bizopp.com/mailord.html
http://www.arrowweb.com/borfil/
  page3.html
http://www.cochenille.com/index.htm
http://www.ourstuff.com
http://www.musicblvd.com/
http://www.hothothot.com/
http://www.virtualvin.com/
http://www.virtualflowers.com/
http://www.classicmovieart.com/
  about.html
http://galaxy.einet.net/hytelnet/
  OTH053.html
http://www.lowe.org/smbiznet/sites/
  111.htm

http://www.idimagic.com/
  avgrants5.html
http://www.sb2000.com/newbus.html
http://www.wp.com/fredfish/
http://www.smartbiz.com/sbs/cats/
  startup.htm
http://www.smartbiz.com/sbs/cats/
  startup.htm#NET
http://www.sba.gov/
  business_management/
  StartingYourBusiness.html
http://www.smartbiz.com/sbs/books/
  book888.htm
http://www.frsa.com/womenbiz/
http://earth1.epa.gov/oar/oaqps/sbap/
  index.html
http://www.att.com/press/0793/
  930728.bsb.html
http://www.cftech.com/BrainBank/
  GOVERNMENT/SBA.html

Entrepreneurs/Entrepreneurship

http://www.undp.org/undp/news/
  newpress.htm
http://www1.pbs.org/newshour/forum/
  june96/ets_6-26.html

http://www.incomeops.com/online/
  contents9602/urban/urban.html
http://www.umich.edu/~ilir/
http://www.uhsa.uh.edu/ush/hub.htm

http://www.freshcom.com/fresh/
about.html
http://journal.wharton.upenn.edu/
v40n1/gn-wmy-panels.html
http://bizserve.com/ten/
http://www.enterweb.org
http://www.slu.edu/eweb/
http://www.home2.net/net2/business/
entrepreneur.html
http://www.aybc.org/entreprn/
entrepr.html
http://library.wustl.edu/~listmgr/devel-l/
Sep1995/0021.html

http://wally.rit.edu/pubs/guides/
entrep.html
http://www.netday96.com/btw/
http://www.netday96.com/info_usa/
netday_description.html
http://www.netday96.com/kits_usa/
toolkit.html
http://www.netday96.com/
marketplace_usa/
http://www.netday96.com/partners_usa/
patrons.html
http://www.svi.org/netday/
http://www.IBBMEC.com

Venture Capital

http://www.accel.com/how2win.htm
http://www.iquest.net/~woode/
vcc.html
http://www.financehub.com/vc/
vcfirms.html
http://www.webequity.com/
http://www.datamerge.com/
venture4.html
http://www.product.com/olympic/
brochure.html

http://www.webdirect.ca/melia/
venture.html
http://catalog.com/intersof/vc/
about.html
http://www.financehub.com/vc/
vconsult.html
http://www.catalog.com/intersof/vc/
about.html
http://www.smartcard.com/

CHAPTER SEVEN: TECHNOLOGY

BLACK PROFESSIONAL ORGANIZATIONS

Consortium of Information and
Telecommunications Executives
Inc.
Bell Atlantic
540 Broad Street, 10th Floor
Newark, NJ 07102
201-649-6881

National Association of Black
Consulting Engineers
2705 Bladensburg Road NE
Washington, DC 20018
202-333-9100

National Association of Black
Telecommunications Professionals,
Inc.
1025 Connecticut Avenue NW, Suite
308
Washington, DC 20036
202-829-8100

National Black Data Processing
Associates
1250 Connecticut Avenue NW, #610
Washington, DC 20036
800-727-2372

National Council of Black Engineers
and Scientists
1525 Aviation Boulevard, Suite C424
Redondo Beach, CA 90278
213-896-9779

National Network of Minority Women
in Science
c/o American Association for the
Advancement of Science
1333 H Street NW
Washington, DC 20005
202-326-7017

National Society of Black Engineers
1454 Duke Street
Alexandria, VA 22314
703-549-2207

National Technical Association,
Inc.
6919 North 19th Street
Philadelphia, PA 19126
215-549-5743

General Organizations

Information Technology Industry
Council
1250 I Street NW
Washington, DC 20005
202-737-8888

Computer and Communications
Industry Association
666 11th Street NW, Suite 600
Washington, DC 20001
202-783-0070

Information Technology Association
of America
1616 North Fort Myer Drive, Suite
1300
Arlington, VA 22209
703-522-5055

National Systems Programmers
Association of America
7044 South 13th Street
Oak Creek, WI 53154
414-768-8000

ON-LINE SERVICE PROVIDERS

America Online
800-827-6364

CompuServe
800-848-8199

Delphi Internet
800-695-4005

Dow Jones News Retrieval
609-452-1511

Genie
888-946-2787

Prodigy
800-776-3449

NETCOM
800-353-6600

Selected Blacks on the Internet

African American Haven
(http: //www.gatech.edu.bgsa/Black
pages.html)

AfriNet
(www.afrinet.net)

AfroNet
(www.afronet.com)

BET Networks
(http: //www.netnetworks.com)

BlackAmerica Online
(www.Blackamericaonline.com)
310-948-1727

Black Cinema Network
(http: //inforamp.net/ashleyma/
Blackcine.html)

Black Enterprise
(http://www.blackenterprise.com)

Black On Black Communications
(www.i-media.com/BOBC)

Black Information Network
(www.bin.com)

The Conduit
(www.imhotec.com.)

CPTiime
home.earthlink.net/-afrolink/)

Cyberwise
E-mail: BETEK@aol.com
http: //www.Blackenterprise.com

Ebony
(http://www.ebonymag.com)

Essence
http://www.essence.com

The Gold Experience
(http: //www.wbr.com/goldexperience)

The Hitlist
(http: //www.cldc.howard.edu/%7aja/
hitlist/htmls/index.html)

Meanderings
(http: //www.webcom.com)

MelaNet
(www.melanet.com)

NetNoir
(www.netnoir.com)

The Network Journal
(www.tnj.com)

SuccessSource/*SuccessGuide*
(http://www.frasernet.com)

The Universal Black Pages
(http://www.gatech.edu/bgsa/
Blackpages.html)

Vibe
(http://www.vibe.com)

World African Network
(www.worldafricannet.com)

On-line Marketing

FAQ: How to Announce Your New
Web Site
(//ep.com/faq/webannlunce.html)

Guerilla Marketing Online
(www.gmarketing.com)

Innovative Solutions
(www.netxpert.com./webwork.html)

Internet Marketing and
Communications
(www.cam.org/'delphig/marketing.htm)

The Online Resource of Network
Marketers
(www.he.net./'image.nwm.imincat.list_
online.htm)

Smart Business Supersite
(//smartbiz.com)

10 Keys to Online Marketing Success
(www.thielenonline.com/tenkeys.htm)

SUGGESTED READING/LISTENING/VIEWING

General

African American Resource Guide to the Internet, Rey O. Harris and Stafford L. Battle (McGraw Hill, 1996).

Being Digital, Nicholas Negroponte (Alfred A. Knopf, Inc., 1995).

Cybercorp: The New Business Revolution, James Martin (Amacom, 1996).

Dictionary of Computer Words: An A to Z Guide to Today's Computers, (Houghton Mifflin, 1995).

The Internet Business Companion, David Angell and Brent Heslop (Addison-Wesley, 1995).

Net Gain: Expanding Markets Through Virtual Communities, John Hagel III and Arthur G. Armstrong (Harvard Business School Press, 1997).

Reference

Directory of Top Computer Executives
Applied Computer Research
P.O. Box 9280
Phoenix, AZ 85068
602-995-5929

Magazines/Newsletters

Computer Reseller
1 Jericho Plaza
Jericho, NY 11753
516-733-6700

ComputerWorld
CW Publishing Company
500 Old Connecticut Path
Framingham, MA 01701
800-343-6474

The Conduit
The Definitive Technological Guide for the African in America
1845 Steiner Street
San Francisco, CA 94115

Data Communications
1221 Avenue of the Americas

New York, NY 10020
212-512-3139

InfoWorld
155 Bovet Road, Suite 800
San Mateo, CA 94402

Inter@ctive Week
100 Quenton Roosevelt Boulevard
Garden City, NY 11530
516-229-3700

PC World Lotus
77 Franklin Street
Boston, MA 02110
617-482-8470

Wired Magazine
16 West 19th Street
New York, NY 10010
212-822-0200

CONTACTS

E. David Ellington
NetNoir
221 Main Street, #480
San Francisco, CA 94105
415-536-6700/David E@NetNoir.Com

Charles Johnson
Globalnet Marketing Group
Distributors of Web-TV
3102 Maple Avenue, #450
Dallas, TX 75201
214-855-0083

Wayne Smalls
Pyramid Computer Services
Software Developers
P.O. Box 23113
Alexandria, CA 22304
703-461-0501

CHAPTER EIGHT: PUBLISH OR PERISH

BLACK PROFESSIONAL ORGANIZATIONS

The African-American Authors
  Network
4275 Donlyn Court
Columbus, OH 43232
614-856-3070

The Black Caucus of the American
  Library Association
5 Washington Street, #333
Newark, NJ 07102
504-596-2601

Black Women in Publishing, Inc.
Box 6275, FDR Station
New York, NY 10150
212-772-5951
Fax: 908-352-8955

National Association of Black
  Journalists
3100 Taliaferro Hall
University of Maryland
College Park, MD 20742
301-405-8500

National Newspaper Publishers
  Association
3200 13th Street NW
Washington, DC 20010
202-588-8764

General Organizations

American Society of Journalists and
  Authors, Inc.
1501 Broadway, #302
New York, NY 10036
212-997-0947

American Society of Magazine Editors
575 Lexington Avenue
New York, NY 10016
212-752-0055

Association of American University
 Presses
584 Broadway, Suite 410
New York, NY 10012
212-941-6610

Authors Guild Inc.
330 West 42nd Street
New York, NY 10036
212-398-0838

Magazine Publishers of America
919 Third Avenue
New York, NY 10022
212-872-3700

Publishing Programs

Howard University Publishing
 Institute
2900 Van Ness Street NW
Washington, DC 20008
202-806-0970

Radcliffe College/Harvard University
Radcliffe Publishing Course
6 Ash Street
Cambridge, MA 02138
617-495-8678

University of Denver Publishing
 Institute
Division of Art and Humanities,
 English Department
2075 South University Boulevard, D-
 114
Denver, CO 80210
202-806-8465

Scholarships

The following organizations have scholarships available for minority students.

The Association of American Publishers
1718 Connecticut Avenue NW,
 Suite 700
Washington, DC 20009-1148
202-232-3335

Stanford Professional Publishing Course
Stanford University Alumni Association
Bowman House
Stanford, CA 94305
415-725-1083

SUGGESTED READING/LISTENING/VIEWING

General

The Artist's Way: A Spiritual Path to Higher Creativity, Julia Cameron (G. P. Putnam's Sons, 1992).

How to Enjoy Writing: A Book of Aid and Comfort, Janet and Isaac Asimov (Walker and Company, 1987).

How to Publish a Book and Sell a Million Copies, Ted Nicholas (P.O. Box 877, Department USA-2, Indian Rocks Beach, FL 33785; 800-730-7777).

How to Write a Book Proposal, Michael Larsen (Writer's Digest Books, 1985).

How to Write a Damn Good Novel, James N. Grey (St. Martin's Press, 1987).

On the Air: How to Get on Radio and TV Talk Shows and What to Do When You Get There, Al Parinello (The Career Press, 1991).

The Self-Publishing Manual, Dan Poynter (Para Publishing, 1996).

A Whack on the Side of the Head: How You Can Be More Creative, Roger Von Oech (Warner Books, 1990).

Writing Your Heritage, Debra Dixon (National Writing Project, 1993).

Reference

Blackboard: African American Bestsellers Inc., 3354 E. Broad St., Columbus, OH 43212; 614-235-5540.

Guide to Literary Agents (Writer's Digest Books, 1997).

Literary Market Place (B. B. Bowker, 245 West 17th Street, New York, NY 10011, annually).

Writer's Market, edited by Mark Kissling (Writer's Digest Books, 1997).

The Writer's Handbook, edited by Sylvia K. Burack (Writer, 1997).

Writer's Guide to Magazine Editors and Publishers, Judy Mandell (Prima Publishing, 1997).

Magazines/Newsletters

The American Poetry Review
World Poetry, Inc.
1721 Walnut Street
Philadelphia, PA 19103
215-496-0439

Publishers Weekly
245 West 17th Street
New York, NY 10011
212-645-9700

Quarterly Black Review of Books
625 Broadway, 10th Floor
New York, NY 10012
212-475-1010

Sisters of the Word
SASE, Rinard Publishing
PO Box 821248
Houston, TX 77282-1248

The Writer
120 Boylston Street
Boston, MA 02116
617-423-3157

Writers' Journal
P.O. Box 25376
St. Paul, MN 55125
612-730-4280

Selected Black Presses

Black Classic Press
P.O. Box 13414
Baltimore, MD 21203
410-654-1050

Duncan & Duncan, Inc.
2809 Pulaski Highway
Edgewood, MD 21040
410-538-5579

One World
Ballantine Books
201 E. 50th Street
New York, NY 10022
212-940-7742

Third World Press
7822 South Dobson
Chicago, IL 60619
773-651-0070

Winston-Derek Publishers
1722 West End Avenue
Nashville, TN 37203
615-321-0535

SAVE 40 PERCENT—PRINT YOUR BOOK IN HONG KONG.

Dan Wong
Tradco USA Inc.
International Industrial Trading and
  Development

6005 Harwich Manor
Oklahoma City, OK 73132
405-722-6006 (F) 405-722-3353
Hong Kong: 011-867555107465

Selected Bookstores

OPENING A BOOKSTORE? WRITING A BOOK?
CHECK WITH THESE STORES.

African American Images
1909 W. 95th Street
Chicago, IL 60643
773-445-0322

AfroCentric Bookstore
333 S. State Street
Chicago, IL 60604
312-939-1956

Afro Mission
104 S. 13th Street
Philadelphia, PA 19107
215-731-1680

Black Images Book Bazaar
230 Wynnewood Village
Dallas, TX 75231
214-943-0142

Eso Wan
900 N. La Brea Avenue
Inglewood, CA 90302
310-674-6566

Folktales
1806 Nueces Street
Austin, TX 78701
512-472-5657

Hue Man Experience
911 Park Avenue, West
Denver, CO 80205
303-293-2665

Marcus Books (San Francisco and
  Oakland)
1712 Filmore Street
San Francisco, CA 94115
415-346-4222

Nia Gallery and Bookshop
7725 W. Belfort Street
Houston, TX 77071
713-729-8400

Roots and Wings Cultural Bookplace
1345 Carter Hill Road
Montgomery, AL 36106
205-262-1700

Shrine of the Black Madonna
(Detroit, Atlanta and Houston)
5317 Martin L. King Jr. Boulevard
Houston, TX 77021
713-645-1071

SisterSpace & Books
1354 U Street NW
Washington, DC 20009
202-332-3433

Tunde-Dada House of Africa
356 Main Street
Orange, NJ 07050
201-673-4446

Vertigo
1337 Connecticut Avenue NW
Washington, DC 10036
202-429-9271

CONTACTS

Selected Black Literary Agents

Marie Dutton Brown
Marie Brown Associates
625 Broadway, Suite 902
New York, NY 10012

Faith Childs
Faith Childs Literary Agency
275 W. 96th Street
New York, NY 10025

Marlen Connor
Connor Literary Agency
7333 Gallery Place
Edina, MN 55435

Lawrence Jordan
Lawrence Jordan Literary Agency
250 W. 57th Street, Suite 1527
New York, NY 10107

Denise L. Stinson
The Stinson Literary Agency
8120 E. Jefferson Street, Suite 6H
Detroit, MI 48214

Gay Young
Gay Young Literary Agency
700 Washington Street, Suite 3B
New York, NY 10014

(other)
Barbara Lowenstein/Madeline Morel
Lowenstein-Morel Associates
121 W. 27th Street, #601
New York, NY 10001
212-206-1630

Selected Black Editors

Make sure you write for editors' guidelines before sending unsolicited
manuscripts.

Malaika Adero, Editor
Amistad Press
1271 Avenue of the Americas
New York, NY 10020

Dawn Daniels, Editor
Simon & Schuster
1230 Avenue of the Americas
New York, NY 10020

Dawn Davis, Editor
Vintage Books
201 E. 50th Street
New York, NY 10022

Deborah Dyson, Editor
Writers and Readers
625 Broadway, 10th Floor
New York, NY 10012

Elias Gebrezgheir, Editor
Wanjiku Ngugi, Editor
African World Press
11-D Princess Road
Lawrenceville, NJ 08648

Carole Hall, Associate Publisher and
  Editor-in-Chief
John Wiley & Sons
605 Third Avenue
New York, NY 10158

Monica Harris, Senior Editor
Kensington Publishing
850 Third Avenue
New York, NY 10022

Janet Hill, Managing Editor
Doubleday
1540 Broadway
New York, NY 10036

Cheryl Willis Hudson, Editor
Just Us Books
356 Glenwood Avenue
East Orange, NJ 07017

David Kelly, Associate Editor
Third World Press
7822 S. Dobson
Chicago, IL 60619

Andrea Lockett, Publisher
Kitchen Table: Women of Color Press
PO Box 40-4920
Brooklyn, NY 11240

Erroll McDonald, Editor
Pantheon
201 E. 50th Street
New York, NY 10022

Jim Moser, Executive Editor
Grove/Atlantic
841 Broadway, 4th Floor
New York, NY 10003

Apryl Motley, Editor
Black Classic Press
P.O. Box 13414
Baltimore, MD 21203

Tracy Sherrod, Editor
Henry Holt and Co.
115 W. 18th Street
New York, NY 10011

Carol Taylor, Editor
Crown Publishers
201 E. 50th Street
New York, NY 10022

Cheryl Woodruff, Editor
Ballantine
201 E. 50th Street, 9th Floor
New York, NY 10022

Miscellaneous Contacts

Julia Shaw
Shaw Literary Group
Publicity and Promotion
11501 Lefferts Boulevard, #2
S. Ozone Park, NY 11420
718-848-7751

Carolina Loren
Golden Eight Associates
A "Turnkey" Self-publishing
  Consulting Service
2778 Hargrove Road, #206
Smyrna, GA 30080
770-436-2210

J. R. Fenwick
Digital Dialogue
"Audio Cassette Your Book"
721 Carlough Street
Landover, MD 20785
301-336-1837

William Byers
AN & I
Multimedia Services
Books on CD Rom
23621 LaPalma Avenue, #426
Yorba Linda, CA 92887
714-693-7065

SO YOU WANT TO PUBLISH? TALK TO SOME OF THE BEST WHO KNOW.

James Crosby
Cleveland Life Tabloid
1729 Superior Avenue
Cleveland, OH 44115
216-771-5433

Preston J. Edwards, Sr.
The Black Collegian Magazine
140 Carondelet
New Orleans, LA 70130
504-523-0154

Hermene Hartman
N'Digo Magapaper
401 North Wabash Avenue, #534
Chicago, IL 60611
312-587-2600

Rachelle Henry
Afrocentric Bazaar
Catalog Sales
PO Box 2774
Antioch, CA 94531
510-757-5385

Melvin Jones
Black Business Directory
1177 Madison, #402
Memphis, TN 38104
504-523-0154

Pat Lottier
The Atlanta Tribune
875 Old Roswell Road, C100
Roswell, GA 30076
770-587-0501

Donald L. Miller
Our World News
201 N. Charles Street, Suite 300
Baltimore, MD 21201
410-385-1696

Rodney Reynolds
American Legacy Magazine
Forbes Inc.
60 Fifth Avenue
New York, NY 10011
212-620-1833

SO YOU WANT TO WRITE A BOOK? TALK TO SOMEONE WHO HAS.

Claud Anderson, Ph.D.
Black Labor, White Wealth
Duncan & Duncan Publishing
Harvest Institute
730 11th Street NW, 4th Floor
Washington, DC 20001
202-496-1622

Kelvin Boston
*Smart Money Moves for African
   Americans*
Putnam Publishing
Boston Media
Fisher Building
3011 W. Grand Boulevard, #458
Detroit, MI 48202
313-875-1200

Don Spears
In Search of Good . . .
Self-published
2220 Freret Street
New Orleans, LA 70113
800-880-2299

Robert Wallace
*Black Wealth Through Black
Entrepreneurship*
Duncan & Duncan Publishing
The Bith Group, Inc.
8950 Old Annapolis Road, #236
Columbia, MD 21045
410-730-0077

Erlene B. Wilson
*100 Best Colleges for African
Americans*
Plume
P.O. Box 343
Radallstown, MD 21133
410-521-1056

CHAPTER NINE: REBUILDING OUR NEIGHBORHOODS

BLACK PROFESSIONAL ORGANIZATIONS

Coalition of Black Trade Unionists
P.O. Box 66268
Washington, DC 20035-6268
202-429-1203

Low Income Housing Information
Service
1012 14th Street NW, Suite 1200
Washington, DC 20005
202-662-1530

National Action Council for
Minorities in Engineering
3 West 35th Street
New York, NY 10001
212-279-2626

National Association of Minority
Contractors
666 11th Street NW, #520
Washington, DC 20001
202-347-8259

National Association of
Neighborhoods
1651 Fuller Street NW
Washington, DC 20009
202-332-7766

National Association of Real Estate
Brokers Inc.
1629 K Street NW, #602
Washington, DC 20036
202-785-4477

National Society of Real Estate
Appraisers
1265 East 105 Street
Cleveland, OH 44108
216-795-3445

General Organizations

American Council for Construction
Education
1300 Hudson Lane
Monroe, LA 71201
318-323-2413

American Institute of Constructors
466 94th Avenue, North
St. Petersburg, FL 33702
813-578-0317

Brick Institute of America
11490 Commerce Park Drive
Reston, VA 22091-1525
703-620-0010

Construction Management
Association of America
7918 Jones Branch Drive
McLean, VA 22102
703-356-2622

The Hamilton Securities Group, Inc.
Street Equity Network
7 Dupont Circle NW
Washington, DC 20036
202-496-6700

International Union of Bricklayers and
  Allied Craftsmen
International Masonry Institute
  Apprenticeship and Training
815 15th Street NW
Washington, DC 20005
202-783-3788

National Association of Home
  Builders of the U.S.
Home Builders Institute
1090 Vermont Avenue NW
Washington, DC 20005
202-822-0200

National Concrete Masonry
  Association
2302 Horse Pen Road
Herndon, VA 22071
703-713-1900

Success 2000 (Construction Trades
  for Minorities)
Washington Humanities Council
1331 H Street N.W.
Washington, DC 20005
202-347-1732

United Brotherhood of Carpenters
  and Joiners of America
101 Constitution Avenue NW
Washington, DC 20001
202-546-6206

For information about the Empowerment Zone opportunities, contact the
Department of Housing and Development at 202-708-0614. You should also
contact your state and local community development office to learn more about
opportunities within your neighborhood.

SUGGESTED READING/LISTENING/VIEWING

General

*Banking on Black Enterprise: The Potential of Emerging Firms for Revitalizing Ur-
ban Economics*, Timothy Bates (Joint Center for Political and Economic Studies, Washington, D.C., 1993).

Competitive Advantage of the Inner City, Michael Porter (Harvard Business Review).

Real Estate Is the Gold in Your Future, Dempsey Travis (Chicago Urban Research
Press, 1988).

CONTACTS

PLANNING A HOUSING DEVELOPMENT?
TALK TO A FEW WHO HAVE DONE IT.

Al Fleming
Marin City Project
620 Drake Avenue
Marin City, CA 94965
415-331-0183
Fax: 415-831-6774

Joshua High
Southlake Properties
4117 NW 78th Avenue
Sunrise, FL 33351
954-746-2251

Leon Hogg, President
Hallmark Management
10510 Park Lane
Cleveland, OH 44106
216-231-0080

Richmond S. McCoy
Chairman and CEO
McCoy Realty Group
375 Park Avenue, Suite #3409
New York, NY 10152
212-832-6767

ON-LINE SERVICES

Neighborhood Networks

http://www.hud.gov/local/bos/
boshsfaq.html
http://www.hud.gov/nnw/
nnwabout.html
http://www.hud.gov/nnw/
nnwsenio.html
http://libertynet.org/community/phila/
natl.html
http://www.hud.gov/local/lou/
loumf2.html
http://www.hud.gov/nnw/nnwlcinf.html

http://www.hud.gov/nnw/nnwnew.html
http://www.hud.gov/nnw/nnwpubs.html
http://131.183.70.50/docs/UUNN/
CDSPPR.htm
http://www.leap.yale.edu/docs/
partners.htm
http://www.tmn.com/civicnet/
index.html
http://www.bev.netl
http://streetequity.net

CHAPTER TEN: LET US ENTERTAIN YOU

BLACK PROFESSIONAL ORGANIZATIONS

Alliance of Black Entertainment
Technicians
1869 Buckingham Road
Los Angeles, CA 90019
213-933-0746
Fax: 213-934-7643
E-Mail: smabet@pacbell.met

Black Awareness in Television
13217 Livernois Street
Detroit, MI 48238-3162
313-931-3427

Black Entertainment and Sports
Lawyers Association
1502 Fairlakes Place
Mitchellville, MD 20721
301-333-0003

Black Filmmaker Foundation
Tribeca Film Center
375 Greenwich Street, Suite 600
New York, NY 10013
212-941-3944

International Association of African
American Music
413 South Broad Street
Philadelphia, PA 19147
215-664-1677

National Association of Black Owned
Broadcasters
1333 New Hampshire Avenue, #1000
Washington, DC 20036
202-463-8970

National Black Media Coalition
11130 New Hampshire Avenue, #204
Silver Spring, MD 20904
301-593-3600

MOBE Institute
Marketing Opportunities in Black
Entertainment
7735 Oak Avenue
Miller Beach, IN 46403
219-938-1888

Vibe Music Seminar
205 Lexington Avenue
New York, NY 10016
212-448-7499

Young Blacks Pursuing a Career in
Entertainment
3658 Perrysville Avenue, Suite 2
P.O. Box 99643
Pittsburgh, PA 15214
412-323-1806

General Organizations

American Federation of Musicians of
the United States and Canada
Paramount Building
1501 Broadway, Suite 600
New York NY 10016
212-869-1330

American Federation of Television
and Radio Artists
260 Madison Avenue
New York, NY 10016
212-532-0800

American Film Institute
John F. Kennedy Center for the
Performing Arts
Washington, DC 20566
202-828-4000

American Guild of Musical Artists
1727 Broadway
New York, NY 10019
212-265-3687

Broadcast Education Association
1711 N Street NW
Washington, DC 20036
202-429-5355

Directors Guild of America
(Assistant Directors' Training
Program)
7920 Sunset Blvd.
Los Angeles, CA 91423
310-289-2000

Entertainment Industry Referral and
Assistance Center
11132 Ventura Boulevard
Studio City, CA 91604
818-848-9997

National Academy of Television Arts
and Sciences
111 West 57th Street
New York, NY 10019
212-586-8424

National Association of Broadcasters
1771 N Street NW
Washington, DC 20036
202-429-5300

National Cable Television Association
1724 Massachusetts Avenue NW
Washington, DC 20036
202-775-3550

Recording Industry Association of
America
1330 Connecticut Avenue NW
Washington, DC 20036
202-775-0101

Screen Actors Guild
5757 Wilshire Boulevard
Los Angeles, CA 90036-3600
213-549-6400

Show Business Association
1510 Broadway
New York, NY 10036
212-354-7600

Society of Broadcast Engineers
Information Office
8445 Keystone Crossing, Suite 140
Indianapolis, IN 46240
317-253-1640

Walter Kaitz Foundation
"Cable's Resource For Diversity"
660 13th Street, #200
Preservation Park
Oakland, CA 94612
510-451-3315

Writers Guild of America, East
555 West 57 Street
New York, NY 10019
212-767-7800

Writers Guild of America, West
7000 West Third Street
Los Angeles, CA 90048
213-951-4000

CONTACTS

John Austin, Mickey Benson
Annual Independent Record Summit
Austin Associates Inc.

9 South Lansdowne Avenue
Lansdowne, PA 19050
610-626-9880

WANT TO BUY A RADIO STATION?
CHECK WITH THESE FOLKS.

RoNita Hawes-Saunders
Hawes-Saunders Broadcast Properties,
  Inc.
211 South Main Street
Fidelity Plaza Suite 400
Dayton, OH 45402-2411
513-222-WROU-FM

Greg Davis
WCCJ
2303 West Moorehead Street
Charlotte, NC 28208
704-358-0211

FOR THOSE INTERESTED IN MUSIC MARKETING/VIDEO PRODUCTION, RECORD-ING, COMPOSING, OR ARTIST MANAGEMENT

David Miller
Assistant to Dean
Nesbitt College of Design Arts
Drexel University

32nd and Chestnut Streets
Philadelphia, PA 19104
215-895-2386

INTERNSHIPS

Arista Records Inc.
Attn: Human Resources
6 West 57th Street
New York, NY 10019
212-830-8483

Black Entertainment Television
Attn: Human Resources
1900 W Place NE
Washington, DC 20018
202-608-2800 ext. 2

The Black Filmmakers Foundation
670 Broadway, Suite 304
New York, NY 10012
212-253-1690

EMI Records Group
1290 Avenue of the America, 35th
Floor
New York, NY 10104
212-492-1700 ext. 3147

The HBO New Writers Project
Wavy Line Production
2049 Century Park E., Suite 4200
Los Angeles, CA 90067
310-201-9351

LaFace Records
One Capital City Plaza
3350 Peachtree Road, Suite 1500
Atlanta, GA 30326-1040
404-848-8050

MTV Networks
1515 Broadway
New York, NY 10036
212-846-2500

National Academy of Television Arts
and Sciences
111 West 57th Street
New York, NY 10019
212-586-8424
Fax: 212-246-8129

PolyGram Holding Inc.
Attn: Human Resources, Internship
Coordinator
Worldwide Plaza
825 Eighth Avenue, 23rd Floor
New York, NY 10019
212-333-8320

Sony Music
550 Madison Avenue, 2nd Floor
New York, NY 10022-3211
212-833-7980

SUGGESTED READING/LISTENING/VIEWING

General

Creative Careers, Gary Blake and Robert Bly (John Wiley & Sons, 1985).

How to Make and Sell Your Own Recording, Diane Sward Rapaport (Prentice Hall, 1992).

How to Be a Working Actor: The Insider's Guide to Finding Jobs in Theater, Film, and Television, Mari Lyn Henry and Lynn Rogers (Back Stage Books, 1996).

Working in Show Business, Lynn Rogers (Back Stage Books, 1997).

Reference

Boom Collective Nine Six: A Visual Arts Directory
P.O. Box 050410
Brooklyn, NY 11205
212-693-1277

International Motion Picture Almanac
Quigley Publishing Company
159 West 3rd Street
New York, NY 10019
212-247-3100

International Television and Video Almanac
Quigley Publishing Company
159 West 53rd Street
New York, NY 10019
212-247-3100

Overground Directory
212-693-1277

Magazines/Newsletters

Back Stage
1515 Broadway
New York, NY 10036
212-764-7300

Billboard
BPI Communications Inc.
1515 Broadway, 14th Floor
New York, NY 10036
212-764-7300

Box Office
6640 Sunset Boulevard, Suite 100
Hollywood, CA 90028
213-465-1186

The Hollywood Reporter
5055 Wilshire, Suite 600

Los Angeles, CA 90036
213-525-2000

Career Moves Newsletter
National Black Media Coalition
11120 New Hampshire Avenue, Suite 204
Silver Spring, MD 20904
301-593-3600

Show Biz News
1505 Fifth Avenue
New York, NY 10036
212-645-8400

Variety
245 W. 17th Street
New York, NY 10011
212-337-7001

CHAPTER ELEVEN: SPORTS

BLACK PROFESSIONAL ORGANIZATIONS

Association of Black Sporting Goods Professionals
P.O. Box 772074
Coral Springs, FL 33077-2074
888-294-7020

Black Entertainment and Sports Lawyers Association
1502 Fairlakes Place
Mitchellville, MD 20721
301-333-0003

National Alliance of African American Athletes
1112 Linkside Drive
Baltimore, MD 21234
410-821-1629

General Organizations

The Athletic Institute
200 Castlewood Drive
North Palm Beach, FL 33408
561-842-3600

American Sports Education Institute
200 Castlewood Drive
North Palm Beach, FL 33408-5696
561-842-4100

Hollywood Golf Institute
10800 Puritan
Detroit, MI 48238
313-832-4965

National Basketball Association
645 Fifth Avenue
New York, NY 10022
212-826-7000

National Football League
410 Park Avenue

New York, NY 10022
212-758-1500

National League of Professional
  Baseball Clubs
350 Park Avenue
New York, NY 10022
212-339-7700

Sporting Goods Manufacturers
  Association
200 Castlewood Drive
North Palm Beach, FL 33408
561-842-4100

Sports Foundation
Lake Center Plaza Building
1699 Wall Street
Mt. Prospect, IL 60056
847-439-4006

Internship

International Management Group
  (IMG)
1 Erieveiw Plaza, Suite 1300

Cleveland, OH 44114
216-522-1200

SUGGESTED READING/LISTENING/VIEWING

In Black and White: Race and Sports in America, Kenneth L. Shropshire (New York University Press, 1996).

The Ultimate Guide to Sport Event Management and Marketing, Stedman Graham, Joe Jeff Goldblatt, Lisa Delpy (Irwin Professional Publishing, 1996).

Magazines/Newsletters

The Sporting News
1212 North Lindbergh Boulevard
St. Louis, MO 63132
314-997-7111

Sports Illustrated
1271 Avenue of the Americas
New York, NY 10020
212-522-1212

CONTACTS

Bill Strickland
President of Basketball
International Management Group
  (IMG)

501 School Street SW, Suite 600
Washington, DC 20024
202-863-9770

CHAPTER TWELVE: HEALTH CARE

BLACK PROFESSIONAL ORGANIZATIONS

Association of Black Psychologists
PO Box 55999
Washington, DC 20040-5999
202-722-0808

Black Psychiatrists of America
2730 Adeline Street
Oakland, CA 94607
510-465-1800

Black Women's Health Project
5021 Baltimore Avenue
Philadelphia, PA 19129
215-474-3066

National Association of Health
  Services Executives
8630 Fenton Street, Suite 126
Silver Spring, MD 20910

National Black Nurses' Association
1511 K Street NW, #415
Washington, DC 20005
800-393-6870

National Black Women's Health
  Project
(National Office)
1237 Abernathy, SW
Atlanta, GA 30310
404-758-9590

National Dental Association
5506 Connecticut Avenue NW,
  Suite 24-25
Washington, DC 20015
202-244-7555

National Dental Hygienists
  Association
5506 Connecticut Avenue NW,
  Suite 24-25
Washington, DC 20015
202-244-7555

National Medical Association
1012 10th Street NW
Washington, DC 20001
202-347-1895

National Optometric Association
1489 Livingston Avenue
Columbus, OH 43205
614-253-5593

National Pharmaceutical Association
12510 White Drive
Silver Spring, MD 20904
301-622-7747

Student National Medical Association,
  Inc.
1012 10th Street NW
Washington, DC 20001
202-371-1616

General Organizations

American Medical Association
515 North State Street
Chicago, IL 60610
312-464-5000

American Academy of Physician
  Assistants
950 North Washington Street
Alexandria, VA 22314
703-684-2782

American Association of Homes for
  the Aging
901 E Street NW, Suite 500
Washington, DC 20004
202-783-2242

American Association of Medical
  Assistants
20 North Walker Drive, Suite 1575
Chicago, IL 60606
312-899-1500

American Health Care Association
1201 L Street NW
Washington, DC 20005
202-842-4444

American Occupational Therapy
  Association
1338 Piccard Drive, Suite 301
Rockville, MD 20850-4375
301-652-2682

American Registry of Radiologic
  Technologists

1255 Northland Drive
Mendota Heights, MN 55120
612-687-0048

American Society of
  Electroneurodiagnostic
  Technologists Inc.
Sixth at Quint
Carroll, IA 51401
712-792-2978

Association of Operating Room
  Nurses
2170 South Parker Road
Denver, CO 80231
303-755-6300

Gerontological Society of America
1275 K Street NW, Suite 3507
Washington, DC 20005
202-842-1275

National Association of Registered
  Nurses
11508 Allecingie Parkway, Suite C
Richmond, VA 23235
804-794-6513

National Commission on Certification
  of Physician Assistants, Inc.
2845 Henderson Mill Road, NE
Atlanta, GA 30341
404-493-9100

SUGGESTED READING/LISTENING/VIEWING

General

The Black Women's Health Book: Speaking for Ourselves, edited by Evelyn C.
  White (The Seal Press, 1990).

*Body and Soul: The Black Women's Guide to Physical Health and Emotional Well-
  being*, Linda Villarosa (HarperCollins Publishers Inc., 1994).

Good Health for African American Kids, Barbara M. Dixon, RD, LDN, and Josleen
  Wilson (Crown, 1996).

Good Health for African Americans, Barbara M. Dixon, RD, LDN, and Josleen Wilson (Crown, 1994).

Pyramids of Power: An Ancient African Centered Approach to Optimal Health, John Chissell M.D. (Ultimate Choice Cassettes, P.O. Box 31509, Baltimore, MD 21207, 410-448-0116).

Reference

AHA Guide to the Health Care Field
American Hospital Association
840 North Lakeshore Drive
Chicago, IL 60611
312-422-3000

Billian's Hospital Blue Book
2100 Powers Ferry Road
Atlanta, GA 30339
770-955-5656

Dun's Guide to Healthcare Companies
Dun's Marketing Services
3 Sylvan Way
Parsippany, NJ 07054
201-605-6000

Hospital Phone Book
Reed Reference Publishing
121 Chanlon Rd.
New Providence, RI 07974
800-521-8110

Nursing Career Directory
Springhouse Corporation
1111 Bethlehem Pike
Springhouse, PA 19477
215-646-8700

U.S. Medical Directory
Reed Reference Publishing
121 Chanlon Road
New Providence, RI 07974
800-521-8110

Magazines/Newsletters

American Journal of Nursing
555 West 57th Street
New York, NY 10019-2961
212-582-8820

Healthcare Executive
840 North Lakeshore Drive
Chicago, IL 60611
312-440-6800

Health Facilities Management
737 North Michigan Avenue
Chicago, IL 60611
312-440-6800

Hospitals
American Hospital Publishing
  Company
737 North Michigan Avenue
Chicago, IL 60611
312-440-6800

Modern Healthcare
740 Rush Street
Chicago, IL 60606
312-649-5341

RN/Medical Economics
5 Paragon Drive
Montvale, NJ 07645
201-358-7200

CONTACTS

INTERESTED IN GOING INTO THE HEALTH-CARE BUSINESS? TALK TO THESE FOLKS

Sherman N. Copelin, Jr.
Health Corporation of the South,
  LTD
107 Harbor Circle
New Orleans, LA 70126
504-246-1166

Gwendolyn Johnson
Geric Home Health Care, Inc.
11811 Shaker Boulevard, Suite 215
Cleveland, OH 44120
800-921-3811

Melvin G. Pye, Jr.
Fairfax Place
Senior Citizens Care and Living
9014 Cedar Avenue
Cleveland, OH 44106
216-795-1363

Dr. Oscar Saffold
Personal Physicians Care Inc.
Family Health Care Plan
1255 Euclid Avenue, #500
Cleveland, OH 44115
216-687-0015

H. Geoffrey Watson, M.D.
Preventive Care Network, Inc.
2582 El Caminito Street
Oakland, CA 94611
510-869-4197

Cecelia Wooten
Ivy Delcia Co.
Adult Medical Daycare
3604 Mohawk Avenue
Baltimore, MD 21207
410-542-5739

CHAPTER THIRTEEN: GLOBAL COMMERCE

BLACK PROFESSIONAL ORGANIZATIONS

Africare (Assistance to Africa)
440 R Street NW
Washington, DC 20001
202-462-3614

Association of Black Ambassadors
310 Somer Lane Place
Avondale Estates, GA 30003
404-299-6803

Black Professionals in International
  Affairs
PO Box 11675
Washington, DC 20008
301-953-0815

TransAfrica, Inc.
1744 R Street NW
Washington, DC 20009
202-797-2301

General Organizations

Association of Southeast Asian
  Nations
Office of East Asia and The Pacific
U.S. Department of Commerce
Washington, DC 20230
202-482-2422

Central and East Europe Business
  Information Center
U.S. Department of Commerce,
  Room 7412
Washington, DC 20230
202-482-2422

China International Exhibition Center
6 Beisanhaun East Road
Chaouyang District
Beijing 10028, People's Republic of
China

Comdex/Sucesu South America
U.S. Department of Commerce
Director of Latin American Affairs
Washington, DC 20062
202-939-9826

Embassy of India
2536 Massachusetts Avenue NW
Washington, DC 20008
202-939-9826

Embassy of Mexico
1911 Pennsylvania Avenue NW
Washington, DC 20006
202-728-1600

Embassy of South Africa
Economic Commercial Section
3201 New Mexico Avenue NW, Suite
300
Washington, DC 20016
202-966-1650

U.S. Government Trade Information
Center
800-USA-TRADE

SUGGESTED READING/LISTENING/VIEWING

General

Competitive Frontiers: Women Managers in a Global Economy, Nancy J. Adler and Dafna N. Izraeli, editors (Blackwell Publishers).

Connecting People: Discovering Peace and Power Through Cultural Flexibility, Thomas S. Watson, Jr. (Nuff Publishing, 1994).

Global Assignments: Successfully Expatriating and Repatriating International Managers, J. Stewart Black, Hall B. Gregersen, and Mark E. Mendenhal (Jossey-Bass).

Global Paradox: The Bigger the World Economy, the More Powerful Its Smallest Players, John Naisbitt (William Morrow & Company, 1994).

International Jobs: Where They Are and How to Get Them, Eric Kocher (Addison-Wesley, 4th ed.).

Kiss, Bow, or Shake Hands: How to Do Business in Sixty Countries, Terri Morrison, Wayne A. Conaway, and George A. Borden (Adams, 1994).

Megatrends Asia, John Naisbitt (Simon & Schuster, 1997).

Out of America, Keith Richberg (Basic Books, 1997).

Reference

The Big Emerging Markets Outlook and Sourcebook
U.S. Department of Commerce
Bernan Press
4611-F Assembly Drive
Lanham, MD 20706-4391
800-865-3457

Chinese Business Guide
U.S. Department of Commerce
U.S. Printing Office
Washington, DC 20402-9328

Doing Business in Argentina
Price Waterhouse & Company
Distribution Center
P.O. Box 30004
Tampa, FL 33630
813-348-7000

Doing Business in Brazil
(monthly updated binder)
Pinheiro Neto & Co.
Matthew Bender Co.
Customer Service Department
1275 Broadway
Albany, NY 12201
800-833-3630

Doing Business in India
Price Waterhouse
1301 K Street NW
Washington, DC 20005
202-414-1890

Doing Business in Indonesia
Harvest International
Wisma Metropolitan I, 10th Floor
Jalan Jendral Sudirman
KAV 29
Jakarta Pusat, 12920
Indonesia
62-21-525-1641

Doing Business in Mexico
(Video Guide)
Big World Inc.
1350 Pine St., Suite 5
Boulder, CO 80302
800-682-1261

Doing Business in Turkey
Price Waterhouse & Co.
PO Box 30004
Tampa, FL 33630
813-348-7000

United States Investments in Indonesia
Harvest International
Wisma Metropolitan I, 10th Floor
Jalan Jendral Sudirman
KAV 29
Jakarta Pusat, 12920
Indonesia
62-21-525-1641

CONTACTS

THEY'RE DOING BUSINESS IN SOUTH AFRICA.

Eugene Jackson
World African Network
400 Perimeter Center Terrace, #900
Atlanta, GA 30346
404-365-8850

Warren Anderson
Anderson/Dubose Company
6575 Davis Industrial Parkway
Solon, OH 44139
216-248-8800

HE'S DOING BUSINESS IN CHINA.

Herbert C. Smith, Ph.D.
Smith International Enterprises, Ltd.
20600 Chagrin Boulevard, #200
Shaker Heights, OH 44122
216-921-3500

SHE'S DOING BUSINESS IN JAPAN.

Kathryn D. Leary
The Leary Group, Inc.
625 Broadway, #902
New York, NY 10012
212-673-0736

NEED A BUSINESS CONTACT ABROAD?

Dr. Henley W. Morgan
Caribbean Applied Technology Center
13 Caledonia Avenue
Kingston 5, Jamaica
809-926-0523
Rose Christian
Small Business on the Move
P.O. Box 304385
St. Thomas, VI 00803
809-774-9529

Sam Alexander
Strive Foundation
P.O. Box 32510
Braamfontein 2017, South Africa
011-643-3011

PART III
REGIONAL JOB OUTLOOK INFORMATION

Job and career information is available regionally from two primary sources:

State employment security agencies, which forecast job opportunities

State Occupational Information Coordinating Committees, which provide job and career information

Alabama

Chief, Labor Market Information
Alabama Department of Industrial
  Relations
649 Monroe Street, Room 422
Montgomery, AL 36131
205-242-8855

Director
Alabama Occupational Information
  Coordinating Committee
Alabama Center for Commerce,
  Room 364
401 Adams Avenue
P.O. Box 5690
Montgomery, AL 36103-5690
205-242-2990

Alaska

Chief, Research and Analysis Section
Alaska Department of Labor
P.O. Box 25501
Juneau, AK 99802-5501
907-465-4500

Executive Director, Research and
  Analysis Section
Alaska Department of Labor
P.O. Box 25501
Juneau, AK 99802-5501
907-465-4518

American Samoa

Statistical Analyst
Research and Statistics
Office of Manpower Resources
American Samoa Government
Pago Pago, AS 96799
684-633-5172

Director
American Samoa State Occupational
  Information Coordinating
  Committee
Office of Manpower Resources
American Samoa Government
Pago Pago, AS 96799
684-633-4485

Arizona

Research Administrator
Arizona Department of Economic
  Security
P.O. Box 6123, Site Code 733A
Phoenix, AZ 85005-6123
602-542-3871

Executive Director
Arizona State Occupational
  Information Coordinating
  Committee
P.O. Box 6123, Site Code 897J
1789 W. Jefferson Street, 1st Floor
  North
Phoenix, AZ 85005-6123
602-542-6466

Arkansas

Manager, Labor Market Information
Arkansas Employment Security
  Division
P.O. Box 2981
Little Rock, AR 72203-2981
501-682-3198

Executive Director
Arkansas Occupational Information
  Coordinating Committee
Arkansas Employment Security
  Division
Employment and Training Services
P.O. Box 2981
Little Rock, AR 72203
501-682-3159

California

Chief, Labor Market Information
  Division
Employment Development
  Department
P.O. Box 942880, MICA 57
Sacramento, CA 94280-0001
916-427-4675

Executive Director
California Occupational Information
  Coordinating Committee
1116 9th Street, Lower Level
P.O. Box 94244-2220
Sacramento, CA 95814
916-323-6544

Colorado

Director, Labor Market Information
Colorado Department of Labor and
  Employment
393 S. Harlan Street, 2nd Floor
Lakewood, CO 80226-3509
303-937-4947

Director
Colorado Occupational Information
  Coordinating Committee
State Board Community College
1391 Speer Boulevard, Suite 600
Denver, CO 80204-2554
303-866-4488

Connecticut

Director, Research and Information
Employment Security Division
200 FollyBrook Boulevard
Wethersfield, CT 06109
203-566-2120

Executive Director
Connecticut Occupational Information
  Coordinating Committee
Connecticut Department of Education
25 Industrial Park Rd.
Middletown, CT 06457
203-638-4042

Delaware

Chief, Office of Occupational and
  Labor Market Information
Delaware Department of Labor
P.O. Box 9029
Newark, DE 19702-9029
302-368-6962

Executive Director
Office of Occupational and Labor
  Market Information
Delaware Department of Labor
University Office Plaza
P.O. Box 9029
Newark, DE 19714-9029
302-368-6963

District of Columbia

Division of Labor Market Information
District of Columbia Department of
  Employment Services
500 C Street NW, Room 201
Washington, DC 20001
202-724-7213

Executive Director
District of Columbia Occupational
  Information Coordinating
  Committee
Department of Employment Security
  Services
500 C Street NW, Room 215
Washington, DC 20001
202-639-1090

Florida

Chief, Bureau of Labor Market
  Information
Florida Department of Labor and
  Employment Security
2012 Capital Circle SE, Suite 200
Tallahassee, FL 32399-2151
904-488-1048

Manager, Florida Department of
  Labor and Employment Security
Bureau of Labor Market Information
2012 Capital Circle SE
Hartman Building, Suite 200
Tallahassee, FL 32399-0673
904-488-1048

Georgia

Director, Labor Information Systems
Georgia Department of Labor
148 International Boulevard North
  East
Atlanta, GA 30303
404-656-3177

Executive Director
Georgia Occupational Information
  Coordinating Committee
Department of Labor
148 International Boulevard North
  East
Atlanta, GA 30303
404-656-9639

Guam

Guam Administrator
Department of Labor
Bureau of Labor Statistics
Government of Guam
P.O. Box 9970
Tamuning, GU 96911-9970

Executive Director
Guam State Occupational
  Information Coordinating
  Committee
Human Resource Development
  Agency
Jay Ease Building, 3rd Floor
P.O. Box 2817
Agana, GU 96910
671-646-9341

Hawaii

Chief, Research and Statistics Office
Department of Labor and Industrial
  Relations
P.O. Box 3680
Honolulu, HI 96813
808-548-7639

Executive Director
Hawaii State Occupational
  Information Coordinating
  Committee
830 Punchbowl Street, Room 315
Honolulu, HI 96813
808-586-8750

Idaho

Chief, Research and Analysis
Idaho Department of Employment
317 Main Street
Boise, ID 83735-0670
208-334-6169

Director
Idaho Occupational Information
  Coordinating Committee
Len B. Jordan Building, Room 301
650 W. State Street
Boise, ID 83720
208-334-3705

Illinois

Director, Economic Information and
  Analysis
Illinois Department of Employment
  Security
401 S. State Street, Room 215
Chicago, IL 60605
312-793-2316

Executive Director
Illinois Occupational Information
  Coordinating Committee
217 E. Monroe, Suite 203
Springfield, IL 62706
217-785-0789

Indiana

Program Manager, Labor Marker
  Information
Indiana Workforce Development
10 N. Senate Avenue
Indianapolis, IN 46204
317-232-7460

Executive Director
Indiana Occupational Information
  Coordinating Committee
309 W. Washington Street, Room 309
Indianapolis, IN 46204
317-232-8528

Iowa

Supervisor, Audit and Analysis
  Department
Iowa Department of Employment
  Services
1000 E. Grand Avenue
Des Moines, IA 50319-0209
515-281-8181

Acting Executive Director
Iowa Occupational Information
  Coordinating Committee
Iowa Department of Economic
  Development
200 E. Grand Avenue
Des Moines, IA 50309
515-242-4890

Kansas

Chief, Labor Market Information
  Services
Kansas Department of Human
  Resources
401 SW Topeka Avenue
Topeka, KS 66603-3182
913-296-5058

Director
Kansas Occupational Information
  Coordinating Committee
401 SW Topeka Avenue
Topeka, KS 66603
913-296-2387

Kentucky

Branch Manager, Research and
  Statistics
Department for Employment
  Services
275 E. Main Street
Frankfort, KY 40621
502-564-7976

Information Liaison/Manager
Kentucky Occupational Information
  Coordinating Committee
Workforce Development Cabinet
500 Mero Street
Capital Plaza Tower, Room 305
Frankfort, KY 40601
502-564-4258

Louisiana

Director, Research and Statistics
  Section
Louisiana State Department of Labor
P.O. Box 94094
Baton Rouge, LA 70804-4094
504-342-3141

Acting Director
Louisiana Occupational Information
  Coordinating Committee
P.O. Box 94094
Baton Rouge, LA 70804-9094
504-342-5149

Maine

Division of Economic Analysis and
  Research
Maine Department of Labor
Bureau of Employment Security
20 Union Street
Augusta, ME 04330
207-289-2271

Acting Executive Director
Maine Occupational Information
  Coordinating Committee
State House Station 71
Augusta, ME 04333
207-624-6200

Maryland

Maryland Director
Office of Labor Market Analysis and
   Information
Economic and Employment
   Development
1100 N. Eutaw Street, Room 601
Baltimore, MD 21201
410-333-5000

Director
Maryland State Occupational
   Information Coordinating
   Committee
State Department of Employment
   and Training
1100 N. Eutaw Street, Room 205
Baltimore, MD 21201
410-333-5478

Massachusetts

Director of Research
Massachusetts Department of
   Employment and Training
19 Staniford Street, 2nd Floor
Boston, MA 02114
617-727-6868

Director
Massachusetts Occupational
   Information Coordinating
   Committee
Massachusetts Division of
   Employment Security
Charles F. Hurley Building, 2nd Floor
Government Center
Boston, MA 02114
617-727-6718

Michigan

Deputy Director, Financial and
   Management Services
Michigan Employment Security
   Commission
7310 Woodward Avenue
Detroit, MI 48202
313-876-5904

Executive Coordinator
Michigan Occupational Information
   Coordinating Committee
Victor Office Center, 3rd Floor
201 N. Washington Square
Box 30015
Lansing, MI 48909
517-373-0363

Minnesota

Director, Research and Statistics
   Office
Minnesota Department of Jobs and
   Training
390 N. Robert Street
St. Paul, MN 55101
612-296-6546

Director
Minnesota Occupational Information
   Coordinating Committee
Department of Jobs and Training
390 N. Robert Street
St. Paul, MN 55101
612-296-2072

Mississippi

Chief, Labor Market Information
   Division
Mississippi Employment Security
   Commission
P.O. Box 1699
Jackson, MS 39215-1699
601-961-7424

Director
Mississippi Occupational Information
   Coordinating Committee
301 W. Pearl Street
Jackson, MS 39203-3089
601-949-2240

Missouri

Chief, Research and Analysis
Missouri Division of Employment
  Security
P.O. Box 59
Jefferson City, MO 65104-0059
314-751-3591

Director
Missouri Occupational Information
  Coordinating Committee
400 Dix Road
Jefferson City, MO 65109
314-751-3800

Montana

Chief, Research and Analysis
Department of Labor and Industry
P.O. Box 1728
Helena, MT 59624-1728
406-444-2430

Program Manager
Montana Occupational Information
  Coordinating Committee
P.O. Box 1728
1327 Lockey Street, 2nd Floor
Helena, MT 59624
406-444-2741

Nebraska

Director, Labor Market Information
Nebraska Department of Labor
P.O. Box 94600, State House Station
Lincoln, NE 68509-4600
402-471-9964

Administrator
Nebraska Occupational Information
  Coordinating Committee
P.O. Box 94600, State House Station
Lincoln, NE 68509-4600
402-471-4845

Nevada

Chief, Employment Security Research
Nevada Employment Security
  Department
500 E. Third Street
Carson City, NV 89713
702-687-4550

Director
Nevada Occupational Information
  Coordinating Committee
1923 N. Carson Street, Suite 211
Carson City, NV 89710
702-687-4577

New Hampshire

Director, Economic Analysis and
  Reports
New Hampshire Department of
  Employment Security
32 S. Main Street
Concord, NH 03301-4587
603-228-4123

Director
New Hampshire State Occupational
  Information Coordinating
  Committee
64B Old Suncook Road
Concord, NH 03301
603-228-3349

New Jersey

Assistant Commissioner, Policy and
  Planning
New Jersey Department of Labor
Labor and Industry Building
P.O. Box CN056
Trenton, NJ 08625-0056
609-292-2643

Staff Director
New Jersey Occupational Information
  Coordinating Committee
Labor and Industry Building
P.O. Box CN056
Trenton, NJ 08625-0056
609-292-2682

New Mexico

Chief, Economic Research and
  Analysis Bureau
Employment Security Department
P.O. Box 1928
Albuquerque, NM 87103
505-841-8645

Director
New Mexico Occupational
  Information Coordinating
  Committee
401 Broadway NE
Tiwa Building
P.O. Box 1928
Albuquerque, NM 87103
505-841-8455

New York

Director, Division of Research and
  Statistics
New York State Department of Labor
State Campus, Building 12, Room 400
Albany, NY 12240-0020
518-457-6181

Executive Director
New York Occupational Information
  Coordinating Committee
Department of Labor Research and
  Statistics Division
State Campus, Building 12, Room 400
Albany, NY 12240
518-457-6182

North Carolina

Director, Labor Market Information
  Division
Employment Security Commission of
  North Carolina
P.O. Box 25903
Raleigh, NC 27611-5903
919-733-2936

Executive Director
North Carolina Occupational
  Information Coordinating
  Committee
P.O. Box 27625
Raleigh, NC 27611
919-733-6700

North Dakota

Director, Research and Statistics
Job Service of North Dakota
P.O. Box 1537
Bismarck, ND 58502-1537
701-224-2868

Coordinator
North Dakota State Occupational
  Information Coordinating
  Committee
1720 Burnt Boat Drive
P.O. Box 1537
Bismarck, ND 58502-1537
701-224-2733

Northern Mariana Islands

Executive Director
Northern Mariana Islands
  Occupational Information
  Coordinating Committee
P.O. Box 149
Room N-1, Building N
Northern Mariana College
Saipan, CM 96950
670-234-1457

Ohio

Director, Labor Market Information
  Division
Ohio Bureau of Employment Services
P.O. Box 1618
Columbus, OH 43215
614-752-9494

Director
Ohio Occupational Information
  Coordinating Committee
Division of Labor Market Information
Ohio Bureau of Employment Services
1160 Dublin Road, Building A
Columbus, OH 43215
614-752-6863

Oklahoma

Director, Research and Planning
  Division
Oklahoma Employment Security
  Commission
2401 N. Lincoln, Room 310
Oklahoma City, OK 73105
405-557-7116

Executive Director
Oklahoma Occupational Information
  Coordinating Committee
Department of Voc/Tech Education
1500 W. Seventh Avenue
Stillwater, OK 74074
405-743-5198

Oregon

Assistant Administrator
Research and Statistics, Employment
  Division
Oregon Department of Human
  Resources
875 Union Street NE, Room 207
Salem, OR 97311-9986
503-378-3220

Acting Director
Oregon Occupational Information
  Coordinating Committee
875 Union Street NE
Salem, OR 97311
503-378-5490

Pennsylvania

Director, Research and Statistics
  Division
Department of Labor and Industry

1213 Labor and Industry Building
Harrisburg, PA 17121
717-787-6466

Director
Pennsylvania Occupational
  Information Coordinating
  Committee
Department of Labor and Industry
1224 Labor and Industry Building
Harrisburg, PA 17121
717-787-8646

Puerto Rico

Director, Bureau of Labor Statistics
Department of Labor and Human
  Resources
Research and Analysis Division
505 Munoz Rivera Avenue, 17th Floor
Hato Rey, PR 00918
809-754-5332

Director
Puerto Rico Occupational Information
  Coordinating Committee
202 Del Cristo Street
P.O. Box 366212
San Juan, PR 00936-6212
809-723-7110

Rhode Island

Supervisor, Labor Market Information
  and Management Services
Rhode Island Department of
  Employment
107 Friendship Street
Providence, RI 02903
401-277-3704

Director
Rhode Island Occupational Information
  Coordinating Committee
22 Hayes Street, Room 133
Providence, RI 02908
401-272-0830

South Carolina

Director, Labor Market Information
  Division
South Carolina Employment Security
  Commission
P.O. Box 995
Columbia, SC 29202-0995
803-737-2660

Director
South Carolina Occupational
  Information Coordinating
  Committee
1550 Gadsden Street
P.O. Box 995
Columbia, SC 29202
803-737-2733

South Dakota

Director, Labor Market Information
  Division
South Dakota Department of Labor
P.O. Box 4730
Aberdeen, SD 57402-4730
605-622-2314

Director
South Dakota Occupational
  Information Coordinating
  Committee
South Dakota Department of Labor
420 S. Roosevelt Street
P.O. Box 4730
Aberdeen, SD 57402-4730
605-622-2314

Tennessee

Director, Research and Statistics
  Division
Tennessee Department of
  Employment Security
500 James Robertson Parkway, 11th
  Floor
Nashville, TN 37219
615-741-2284

Executive Director
Tennessee Occupational Information
  Coordinating Committee
500 James Robertson Parkway, 11th
  Floor
Nashville, TN 37219
(615) 741-6451

Texas

Chief, Economic Research and
  Analysis
Texas Employment Commission
1117 Trinity Street, Room 208-T
Austin, TX 78778
512-463-2616

Director
Texas Occupational Information
  Coordinating Committee
Texas Employment Commission
  Building
3520 Executive Center Drive, Suite
  205
Austin, TX 78731
512-502-3750

Utah

Director, Labor Market Information
Utah Department of Employment
  Security
P.O. Box 11249
Salt Lake City, UT 84147-1249
801-536-7425

Executive Director
Utah Occupational Information
  Coordinating Committee
c/o Utah Department of Employment
  Security
P.O. Box 11249
140 East 300 South
Salt Lake City, UT 84147
801-536-7806

Vermont

Chief, Policy and Public Information
Vermont Department of Employment
and Training
P.O. Box 488
Montpelier, VT 05602
802-229-0311

Director
Vermont Occupational Information
Coordinating Committee
5 Green Mountain Drive
P.O. Box 488
Montpelier, VT 05602
802-229-0311

Virginia

Director, Economic Information Service
Virginia Employment Commission
P.O. Box 1358
Richmond, VA 23211
804-786-7496

Executive Director
Virginia Occupational Information
Coordinating Committee
Virginia Employment Commission
703 East Main Street
P.O. Box 1358
Richmond, VA 23211
804-786-7496

Virgin Islands

Director, Virgin Islands Department
of Labor
Bureau of Labor Statistics
Labor/Research and Analysis Division
P.O. Box 3359
St. Thomas, U.S. Virgin Islands 00801-
3359
809-776-3700

Coordinator
Virgin Islands Occupational Information
Coordinating Committee
P.O. Box 3359
St. Thomas, U.S. Virgin Islands 00801
809-776-3700

Washington

Director, Labor Market and Economic
Analysis
Washington Employment Security
Department
605 Woodview Drive, SE
Lacey, WA 98503
206-438-4800

Acting Executive Director
Washington Occupational Information
Coordinating Committee
c/o Employment Security Department
P.O. Box 9046
Olympia, WA 98507-9046
206-438-4803

West Virginia

Director, Labor and Economic
Research Section
West Virginia Bureau of Employment
Security
112 California Avenue
Charleston, WV 25305-0112
304-348-2660

Executive Director
West Virginia Occupational
Information Coordinating
Committee
One Dunbar Plaza, Suite E
Dunbar, WV 25064
304-293-5314

Wisconsin

Director
Bureau of Workforce Policy and
 Information
Department of Industry, Labor, and
 Human Relations
P.O. Box 7944
Madison, WI 53707-7944
608-266-5843

Administrative Director
Wisconsin Occupational Information
 Coordinating Council
Division of Employment and Training
 Policy
201 E. Washington Avenue
P.O. Box 7972
Madison, WI 53707
608-266-8012

Wyoming

Manager, Research and Planning
Employment Security Commission
P.O. Box 2760
Casper, WY 82602-2760
307-265-6715

Executive Director
Wyoming Occupational Information
 Coordinating Council
Post Office Box 2760
100 West Midwest
Casper, WY 82602
307-265-7017

INDEX

Fraser, Walter Frederick, Sr., 37, 45
Frasernet, 131–132, 145, 151
fraternities, 171
Frazier, Walt, 238
Freaknik celebration, 8
FreedomFest Coalition, 8
Freeman, Claire E., 184–185
Friday, 200–201
Frito-Lay, 112
Fuchs, Michael, 36
Fudge, Ann, 6, 9
Fugees, 37
Fuller Products, 69
Fuqua School of Business Consulting
  Program, 115

gaffers, 203
Galloway, Sandra, 23
Galloway Braintrust Groups, 23
Gallup polls, 39, 41
Games Channel, 142
gangsta rap, 36–37
Gans, Naomi, 71
Gardner, Ava, 195
Garvey, Marcus, 36
Gaston, A. G., 23, 103, 106
Gates, Bill, 143
gay and lesbian Blacks, 11
GED (General Educational
  Development) Examination
  and programs, 69
GEDs (General Equivalency
  Diplomas), 5
Gellineau, Carole, 104–105
General Accounting Office, U.S.,
  231
General Motors, 278
Genesis, 285
Georgia, University of, 14
Geric Home Health Care, 127–128
Get on the Bus, 195, 283
Gibson, Althea, 223
Giles, Michael, 17
Gillette, 121
giving and sharing, 21, 25–27
glass ceilings, 95

global commerce, 17, 55, 261–279,
  284
  basic information sources in, 264–
    267
  emerging markets in, 269–272
  global funds for, 272–273
  new frontiers for Black investment
    in, 267–272
  resource guide for, 343–346
  working and, 273–274
  see also Caribbean; Latin America,
    Black Investment in; South
    Africa, Republic of
God, giving credit to, 23–24
gofers, 195
Goldberg, Whoopi, 194
Golden Neo-life Diamite, 122
golf, 223, 224
Golf, 239
Gooding, Cuba, Jr., 23–24, 162
Gossett, Hattie, 202
Government Trade Information
  Center, U.S., 265
GPAs, 41
Grammys, 216
Graves, Earl "Butch," 25–26, 170–171
Gray, F. Gary, 200–201
Gray, William, 82
Green, Kim, 199
Griffith, Mark Winston, 97
Growth Association, 25
Gumbel, Bryant, 237
Gumbel, Greg, 237, 238
gypsy cabs, 178

Hadary, Sharon, 110
Hageman, Hans, 72–73
Haiti, 186
Haki Mahabuti, 176
Haley, Alex, 25
Hallmark Management, 176–177
"halo effect," 145
Hamilton Securities Group, 15
Hampton Institute of Virginia, 62
Hanks, Tom, 194
Hanson, Inge, 183, 243–244
Hardaway, Penny, 233

ABOUT THE AUTHOR

George C. Fraser is the founder and chairman of the board of SuccessSource. The company's *mission* is to produce products and services that teach and promote effective networking.

Its *vision* is to lead a networking movement that brings together diverse human resources worldwide to increase opportunities for all people of color.

Mr. Fraser's *goals* are:

- To increase public awareness of Black excellence and quality in business, the professions, and community leadership.
- To promote interdependence and the building of multicultural business relationships.
- To encourage and promote racial pride, self-help, and self-development.
- To facilitate role-modeling and mentoring for Black youth.
- To model high standards and help to establish criteria and accountability for entrepreneurial and professional excellence and competitiveness in the marketplace.
- To promote racial healing and understanding.

Mr. Fraser has served on numerous boards and has received many awards and citations for his community service, including the United Negro College Fund's National Volunteer of the Year Award. He has been appointed to state and city commissions by both the governor and the mayor of his home city and state of Cleveland, Ohio.

Mr. Fraser spent seventeen years in management with Procter &

Gamble, United Way, and Ford. Today, as a popular speaker and author, Mr. Fraser has appeared on more than 150 television and radio talk shows.

His views are solicited by media as diverse as CNN and *The Wall Street Journal*. He speaks more than 150 times a year all around the world. His inspiring talks on success principles, effective networking, wealth creation, ethics, and valuing diversity are as popular among corporate professionals as they are among college students. His words and ideas have been, taped, televised, and reprinted by such prestigious publications as *Vital Speeches of the Day*.

Upscale magazine named him one of the top fifty power brokers in Black America. *Black Enterprise Magazine* called him Black America's #1 networker and featured him on its cover. Personal growth "guru" Stephen Covey called Mr. Fraser a "masterful teacher." TV host and journalist Tony Brown called him a "visionary with the rare combination of leadership and management skills." Many have called him a new voice for African Americans. He is considered to be one of the foremost authorities on networking and building effective relationships. Mr. Fraser attended New York University and received his executive training at the Amos Tuck School of Business at Dartmouth College.

The SuccessSource products and services include:

SuccessGuide: The Networking Guide to Black Resources
Available as of the 1995 printing in Atlanta, Chicago, Cleveland, Cincinnati/Dayton, Detroit, New Orleans, New York City, and Washington, DC

•

Keynote Speeches and Workshops
•

Race for Success: The Ten Best Business Opportunities for Blacks in America, Hardcover and Paperback

•

Success Runs in Our Race: The Complete Guide to Effective Networking in the African American Community, Hardcover and Paperback
Success Runs in Our Race: Audiocassette
Success Runs in Our Race: T-Shirt and Cap

•

Mentoring and Role-Modeling Seminars

•

Custom On-Site Corporate Lectures

SuccessSource
2940 Noble Road, #103
Cleveland Heights, Ohio 44121
(Bus) 216-691-6686
(Fax) 216-691-6685
gfraser@frasernet.com
http://www.frasernet.com

Join SuccessNet
SAVE 50%

Let's get together to get ahead. Learn George Fraser's secrets of becoming an effective networker. Network with thousands of professionals and entrepreneurs worldwide. Find job opportunities, find new customers, vendors, and important community contacts. Using the "Fraser Principles" for effective networking you will develop a strong support system for your success at work, at home, and in the community.

Fill out or copy this order form and get a **50% discount** on this **SuccessNet** package of products and services. Membership includes:

- **For Your Success: Ten Guiding Principles to Power Networking by George Fraser.** How powerful are your networking skills? Do you have the political and social expertise necessary to parlay your contacts into powerful business and personal relationships? With these **six audio cassettes and a 24-page workbook** you will learn everything you need to know about building a caring and sharing, industrial-strength network of powerful contacts for your success . . . Value, $99.00

- **Free Web Site Listing** for one year on FraserNet.com; access thousands of contacts through the Web . . . Value, $39.00

- **SuccessNotes: A Quarterly Newsletter** of valuable information, useful resources, and important contacts. Free one-year subscription . . . Value, $49.00

- **Gold-Plated Lapel Pin: EOROTO,** *Each One, Reach One, Teach One* is our motto; wear this with pride and spread the word. A great conversation starter . . . Value, $10.00

- **Free Membership Card,** which entitles you to a 10% discount on future products and services offered through SuccessNet.

Join the Network. Fill out or copy this order form now and get a 50% discount (a $197 value) on the entire SuccessNet package . . . **all for $99.00 plus $6.50 for shipping and handling charges.** (Please allow 3 to 4 weeks for delivery.)

Name_____

Position/Title_____

Business/Company Name_____

Mailing Address_____

City_____ State_____ Zip_____

Phone__(____)_____ Fax__(____)_____

❑ I would like to be included in your network, and I agree to assist those who contact me through your network.

❑ Enclosed is my check or money order.   Please charge to my: ❑ Visa   ❑ MasterCard
(U.S. dollars only)

Acct. No. _____ Exp. Date. _____

Signature _____

TOTAL ___$_____ Fax your order: (216) 691-6685 (credit cards only)

For shipment outside U.S.A.: Call corporate headquarters for shipping rates and pay in U.S. funds.
$99.00 plus $6.50 + Shipping & Handling (Ohio residents, please add 7% Sales Tax)

Make payable and mail to: **SuccessPromotions**
2940 Noble Road, Suite 103
Cleveland Heights, Ohio 44121

(216) 691-6686 • Fax (216) 691-6685

Success Through Networking